SOUTHERN INVINCIBILITY

Also by Wiley Sword

Mountains Touched with Fire, Chattanooga Besieged, 1863

*Embrace an Angry Wind, The Confederacy's Last Hurrah, Spring Hill,
Franklin, and Nashville* (reprinted in paperback as
The Confederacy's Last Hurrah)

*Sharpshooter, Hiram Berdan, His Famous Sharpshooter, and
their Sharps Rifles*

*Firepower from Abroad, The Confederate Enfield and
Le Mat Revolver, 1861–1863*

*President Washington's Indian War, the Struggle for the
Old Northwest, 1790–1795*

Shiloh: Bloody April

SOUTHERN INVINCIBILITY

A History

of the

Confederate Heart

Wiley Sword

St. Martin's Press ❧ New York

Book Design by Patrice Sheridan

Production Editor: David Stanford Burr

Library of Congress Cataloging-in-Publication Data

Sword, Wiley.
    Southern invincibility : a history of the Confederate heart /
Wiley Sword. — 1st ed.
        p. cm.
    Includes bibliographical references and index.
    ISBN 0-312-20366-7
    1. United States—History—Civil War, 1861–1865—Psychological
aspects. 2. Confederate States of America—Social conditions.
3. United States—History—Civil War, 1861–1865—Personal
narratives, Confederate. 4. Soldiers—Confederate States of
America—Psychology. 5. National characteristics, American.
6. Character—Hisotry—19th century. I. Title.
E468.9.S97   1999
973.7'13'019—DC21   99-15932
                                    CIP

First Edition: October 1999

10 9 8 7 6 5 4 3 2 1

Contents

Acknowledgments

Without the help of others, this would have been a barren and nearly impossible project. The consideration of individuals, and also knowledgeable research staffs at various institutions, was important, and they deserve a special thanks for making available and pointing out relevant material. Their spirit of aid and assistance not only makes the task easier, but represents a contribution to better understanding our history. Without the use of many obscure and often privately held letters, diaries, and photographs, this work would be far less substantive.

For the generous help of the following individuals I am particularly appreciative:

Richard A. Baumgartner, Huntington, W.V.
George M. Brooke, Jr., Lexington, Va.
Kathleen Schaller Herty Brown, N.Y.
Rick F. Carlisle, Dayton, Ohio
Ward DeWitt, Jr., Nashville, Tenn.
Jack Donahue, Bayside, N.Y.
James J. Holmberg, Louisville, Ky.
Dr. Richard McMurry, Americus, Ga.
Tony Marion, Blountsville, Tenn.
Mary Genevieve T. Murphy, Lexington, Ky.
Rev. James K. Orr, Connersville, Ind.

Herb Peck, Jr., Nashville, Tenn.
Lewis L. Poates, Knoxville, Tenn.
Joan Rapp, Louisville, Ky.
Dr. Richard M. Sommers, Carlisle Barracks, Pa.
Ken Tilley, Montgomery, Ala.
John White, Chapel Hill, N.C.
Zack Waters, Rome, Ga.
Bob Younger, Dayton, Ohio
Dave and Todd Zullo, Gaithersburg, Md.

The following institutions and firms provided research materials and I gratefully thank them for their help.

Alabama Dept. of Archives & History, Montgomery, Ala.
Bloomfield Township Library, Bloomfield Hills, Mich.
Bowdoin College Library, Brunswick, Maine
Chickamauga and Chattanooga National Military Park Library, Fort Oglethorpe, Ga.
Duke University, William L. Perkins Library, Durham, N.C.
Emory University Library, Atlanta, Ga.
The Filson Club Historical Society Library, Louisville, Ky.
Florida State Archives Library, Tallahassee, Fla.
Fredricksburg & Spotsylvania National Military Park Library, Fredricksburg, Va.
Georgia Dept. of Archives & Hist., Atlanta, Ga.
The Horse Soldier, Gettysburg, Pa.
Henry E. Huntington Library, San Marino, Calif.
Louisiana State Univ. Library, Baton Rouge, La.
Library of Congress, Washington, D.C.
Miami University Library, Oxford, Ohio
The University of Michigan, Bentley Historical Library, Ann Arbor, Mich.
Mississippi Dept. of Archives and Hist., Jackson, Miss.
Missouri Historical Society, St. Louis, Mo.
The Museum of the Confederacy, Richmond, Va.
National Archives, Washington, D.C.
University of North Carolina, Wilson Library, Chapel Hill, N.C.
Olde Soldier Books, Gaithersburg, Md.
Shiloh National Military Park Library, Shiloh, Tenn.

Stones River National Battlefield Park Library, Murfreesboro, Tenn.

University of the South, duPont Library, Sewanee, Tenn.

Tennessee State Library & Archives, Nashville, Tenn.

University of South Carolina, South Caroliniana Library, Columbia, S.C.

United States Army Military History Institute, Carlisle Barracks, Pa.

University Press of Virginia, Charlottesville, Va.

Virginia Historical Society, Richmond, Va.

Virginia State Library, Richmond, Va.

Western Reserve Historical Society Library, Cleveland, Ohio

West Tennessee Historical Society, Memphis, Tenn.

Special thanks are due to my editor at St. Martin's Press, George Witte, and his staff, particularly Carrie McGinnis. Dr. Albert Castel, Hillsdale, Mich., read the manuscript and offered many valuable suggestions. Don Troiani provided his superb painting, *Forward the Colors,* for use on the dust jacket.

Last but not the least, my wife Marianne deserves full credit for the sacrifices she made in time and companionship, watching TV and "keeping busy" while I worked on the manuscript. Akin to the spirit of southern women who displayed their valor and tenacity during "the war years," her love and commitment is truly profound!

—WILEY SWORD

SOUTHERN INVINCIBILITY

Introduction

The Civil War yet looms as the greatest defining moment in Southern history. As an attempt to establish a separate North American nation based upon a unique slaveholding culture, it was a statement to the world that Southerners were different. Yet, if you had asked many of the gray soldiers who fought for four agonizing years what they were fighting for, the answer most likely would have been a conventional one: "to defend our homes and our freedom."

It was a matter of conditioned perspective: what they saw and read, what they knew and perceived, how they were raised and taught. To "live and die in Dixie" meant a commitment of the soul and spirit. The poorest yeoman farmer and the aristocratic planter could claim a common ideological heritage—that of Southern efficacy. Many Southerners of the 1860s were independent-minded, "can do" people. They believed in their ability to accomplish, persevere, and shape their existence. Above all else they were confident of their ability to fight a war of independence and win. Essentially, it was a superior attitude held in common, based upon the long-standing and proven self-reliance of a people who had overcome much adversity to establish a flourishing civilization of immense pride, prosperity, and success. That Southern culture ran counter to emerging trends of industrialization and social equality seemed to matter but little to many. That culture was perceived to be self-determined, and a bold and resourceful Southern spirit had always served the South well in periods of change.

Secession itself involved larger questions of mental excellence; of attitudes, and the will to win based upon a thriving and superior personal military capacity derived from a largely outdoors-based, self-reliant lifestyle. In simplest terms, the South was better—if not in the physical means to wage war (materiel and manpower), then at least in what many Southerners perceived as the more important arenas of willpower and personal fighting capacity. This is why even to this day many Southerners are raised in the shadow of a defiant spirit, and in the tradition that "the South shall rise again." The vestiges of Southern pride are prevalent today in the South's lingering flag and heritage controversies, Civil War reenactment groups, and still-persistent sense of regional identity. Thus the mental side of the Civil War era holds an enormous fascination and latent importance, more than 130 years after the physical events.

Despite the title *Southern Invincibility*, this is a book more concerned with "why" than with analyzing a culture. Why the Southern soldiers fought so long and well. Why they thought they could win. Why the enormous effort, even in the face of imminent defeat. Why, long after total defeat, much of the pride and passion aroused by the war still remained deeply rooted in the South. These are themes of profound interest and meaning so long as the South is regarded as possessing a distinct culture in America.

The attitudes of Southerners caught up in a vicious war of enormous personal anguish and profound impact reveal much about the American experience as a whole. Moreover, the collective thoughts of both its soldiers and civilians were the binding influence that ultimately controlled the South's war effort.

If an analysis of the thinking of many people involved in the cataclysmic crisis of civil war is necessarily imperfect in its belated and fragmentary interpretation, it is nonetheless relevant to a better understanding of the critical human behavior that shapes our destiny. This book is predicated upon common sense more than upon any pet scholarly theory, and is written on a framework of logic.

Whatever the root elements or impetus of the conflict, it is certain that the Civil War evoked strong emotions. Moreover, these emotions played a crucial part in many personal actions. In a broader sphere, the soldiers' feelings produced consensus attitudes that changed the war itself.

How each man coped with the elation of common success and the depression of repeated failure mattered much in the waging of the war. It made a difference in performance, and ultimately in the relative hope of success—often a defining criterion for the out-manned and underequipped South as it continued to fight.

That attitudes constantly changed, on sometimes a daily, hourly, or even more minute basis, presents a difficulty in assessing a generalized chronological portrayal of the Confederate soldiers' thinking. Yet various trends or common attitude shifts are easily discernible from the hundreds of letters, diaries, journals, and published contemporary accounts. The way Southern soldiers thought as expressed by their own contemporaneously recorded words not only provides insight but sketches the mental dilemmas common to mankind in severe crisis.

Nearly everyone can cope with success; it generally provides reassurance, self-satisfaction, and further incentive. Yet to voluntarily endure repeated defeat is not only a test of one's mettle, but a crisis in endeavor—it cuts at the very basis of a soldier's continued discipline and good performance.

The Southerner's status as a significant entity, viewed either as mid-nineteenth-century-America's societal norm or as an exception, may be argued endlessly pro and con. Yet, aside from considerations that agriculture or the industrial revolution was tipping the nation's scales in 1861, once the war began, what counted the most were each Southerner's own perceptions.

If the average Southern fighting man initially felt superior to his enemy, how did these feelings measure up in the face of actual battlefield experiences? Indeed, what did the soldiers and others believe and later say, as the harsh and bitter specter of defeat drew near?

Here then is my humble attempt to better explain what they were thinking, and why, and also to touch your emotions. This book is thus dedicated to you, that you may better perceive the essence of what it truly was and is all about: the strong feelings within us that compel our most significant actions.

—WILEY SWORD,
Bloomfield Hills, Michigan,
1999

Chapter One

An Ominous Circumstance

Alexander Frederick Fleet—"Fred" to his family and friends—was a precocious youth of seventeen and a student at the University of Virginia in the fall of 1860. Like many others, he regarded the election of Abraham Lincoln as a harbinger of terrible difficulties. Uppermost on everyone's mind was the burning question of the hour—should the Southern states secede? "Upon due recollection, I reckon [so]," lamented Fred in a letter home on November 10, 1860—"although I am not so certain. . . . The South had better secede now, while she can [since moderate James Buchanan is still president] and not wait until she cannot." As he wrote, he ominously noted that there were about 150 rowdy Virginia students roaming about the campus wearing blue cockades in their hats, "after the South Carolina fashion."[1]

A few months later, in February 1861, Fred Fleet had caught the flame. Military companies were drilling on the school lawn every evening, proud and natty in their red flannel jackets, black pants, and glazed military caps. Fred admired their polished muskets, privately purchased by the students, which sparkled in the fading sunlight. Daily, he eagerly devoured the local newspapers. "It will be the worst thing . . . if Virginia doesn't secede and go along with the South," Fred warned his family. "A good many of the Southern students [from the lower South] say they will hold a meeting and all go home, and they, you know, constitute about half of the whole [student body]."[2]

Fred Fleet continued to be enthralled with the disunion fuss. A relative in Washington, D.C., described to him Lincoln's appearance in the city during early March 1861:

Old Abe . . . is now our master (think of that!). . . . Yesterday . . . about 12:30 [P.M.] he started from Willard's [Hotel] down the [Pennsylvania] Avenue to the Capitol, riding in a carriage with Mr. Buchanan and two other men. The procession was led by the marshals, etc. Next [came] the military (D.C., not regulars), next the open carriage with Abe . . . in it, completely surrounded with soldiers—so fearful was the infernal scoundrel of assassination. Next came a concern drawn by six white horses, each of which had a white cloth over him on which was inscribed UNION. On the side of the car . . . another white cloth was hung having the word CONSTITUTION written in letters about a foot long—which broke as it was going up the avenue, an ominous circumstance. . . . [3]

Fred Fleet had heard and seen enough, and he was soon among the ranks of Southern soldiers. He enlisted on June 13, 1861 as first sergeant in the "Jackson Grays," which would become Company I, 26th Virginia Volunteer Infantry. Despite his mother's admonition that "neither Pa nor I [are] willing for you to go to war until there is greater necessity for it than . . . at present," Fred had acted on emotion. His younger brother, Benny, who had supported Virginia's remaining in the Union, was chided by Fred for his "ignorance of the state of affairs."[4]

Fred Fleet's enthusiasm was boundless. Less than sixty days later the new sergeant boasted of his good health, and wrote how pleased he was with a soldier's life: "I have nothing like as hard a time as I expected." When he witnessed a grand review by the celebrity general John Bankhead Magruder, Fleet admired "Prince John's" "splendid uniform, with a wide gold band across his body, and crimson velvet interwoven in a beautiful way." Magruder seemed to be "a most graceful rider, and shows off finely," observed Fred. When further inspired by the "bands playing lively airs," Fleet "imagined how splendidly [Winfield] Scott's 'Grand Army' must have looked [during the Mexican War]."[5]

The hardships of war seemed but an indistinct shadow in the distance. Fred Fleet fervently wrote, "Last week was full of exciting interest. . . . It was reported by official authority that we would certainly have an attack here [at Glouchester Point, Virginia]." When an enemy man-of-war came within a few miles, there was a flurry of activity; yet the ship soon disappeared, "and the excitement in some degree cooled down."[6]

Only when Major General George B. McClellan's Union army invaded the Virginia peninsula in the early spring of 1862 did Fleet witness battle's stern array and hear the sobering crash of heavy guns. On April 12 the Yankees were reported "as being on the next road and advancing rapidly." "You may imagine that we felt a little queer when the ball [was] opened by the enemy's artillery, . . . [and we] expected to see a heavy column of infantry advance right upon us . . . You may say what you please about not being scared and all that, but until you become somewhat accustomed to it, I don't believe there is any man who is not a little agitated when he first hears the roar of cannon."[7]

Sergeant Fleet was beginning to comprehend the true essence of war. If you look deeply into his eyes in a photograph taken about this time, a subtle air of glib uncertainty is evident—a look of pride and yet also of ill-at-ease distraction. His expression is a reflection of the Southern dilemma. Like the Southern Confederacy, Sergeant Fleet's face exuded youthful hope and energy, yet he was heavily burdened with the imminent ordeal of facing an enormous challenge. Though Fleet lacked maturity, his genes and heritage determined that he would take on the task with a Virginian's pride and confidence. Words can't precisely convey Fred Fleet's inner turmoil, but the eye catches the essence of this problem. If his placid facade partially obscures his inexperience, it fails to mask the real threat: would his inner self be able to cope with the dire personal challenges ahead?

"I felt right much excited," admitted Sergeant Fleet in telling of his initial exposure to enemy fire, "but as the firing proceeded, I became more composed." This first fight had been brief—only a skirmish—and the true test of a bloody battle lay ahead. The enemy was said to outnumber them considerably, Fred acknowledged; yet he was not discouraged. "We know that the race is not to the swift, nor [the] battle to the strong, [and] feeling a confidence in the justice of our cause, and remembering we are fighting for our homes and all we hold dear on earth, I trust God may give us the victory,'' he wrote. . . . ''Do not be uneasy about me, for I will try to do my duty.''[8]

For Fred Fleet and a myriad of other Southerners, the consequences of boldly stepping into the great chasm of war involved not only a plunge into the vast unknown but a simple yet profound question: would the perception of warfare become the reality?

Chapter Two

Holding Fast to the Familiar

W̲e are a peculiar people, sir!'' announced Texas senator Louis Wigfall in explaining the sharply conflicting American civilizations North and South. "We are an agricultural people . . . We have no cities—we don't want them. . . . We want no manufactures; we desire no trading, no mechanical or manufacturing classes. . . . As long as we have our rice, our sugar, our tobacco and our cotton, we can command wealth to purchase all we want."[1]

Wigfall's comments on behalf of the South underscores a debate that has continued for more than a century. Were antebellum Southerners truly different? Was their cultural antagonism to Northern society based upon real or merely superficial differences? Several eminent American historians have suggested that many of the differences can be attributed to the South's "folk culture," which was predicated on strong tradition, a rural lifestyle, and a hierarchical social pattern that embraced masculine codes of honor and chivalry.[2]

In fact, beyond many variances North and South in climate, morals, and perceptions, it is apparent that intrinsic fundamental differences did exist in the antebellum years. For example, in contrast to the cultural diversity of the Northern states, where there were many immigrants from a variety of European nations, the South was relatively monolithic. Immigration had been far heavier in the North over the past century due to the cheap slave-labor base in the South. The net result was an even-stronger basis for Southern cultural homogeneity, in which customs and lifestyles remained much the same. While the "togetherness" of the region's people provided a sense of common identity, it also tended to accentuate the South's reliance upon tradition and resistance to change. Consensus attitudes were all the more significant in the South, especially as a widening moral discrepancy with the North had served to exacerbate the many intensifying sectional antagonisms.[3]

Understanding the Southern way of thinking in a societal sense involved key considerations about the region's hardships as well as the South's then-prosperous economic circumstances. For the majority of residents in the Old South, life was difficult. Indeed, problem solving shaped many commonly held attitudes, since adversity seemed such an integral part of life in "Dixie." From blight to pestilence, the often-overwhelming burden of coping with a mid-nineteenth-century Southern existence required a resilient mental outlook. Considering the rather unsatisfactory practical solutions to many of life's ill fortunes, questions were constantly being raised not only about what to do, but why so much suffering was prevalent.[4]

The workings of Divine Providence provided an answer, many Southerners concluded when they sought explanation for so much adversity. It seemed a matter of cause and effect. What had once been attributed to random fate, now, in a more enlightened age, was regarded as Divine will. This change of attitude was significant since appeals to the Almighty might have their intended effect. "The prayers of the righteous availeth much," reflected a Tennesseean troubled by the specter of a Yankee invasion in 1862.[5]

In a society in which refined attributes such as honor, loyalty, charity, and graciousness were revered, many nineteenth-century Southerners tended to consider the inconsistencies and inequities of life in religious terms. While much was obviously beyond human understanding and control, there appeared to exist a covenant with God— of righteousness, justice, and a greater good. He would provide ultimate equity for each person, and also favor their just causes, reasoned many.[6]

This rationale was ironic, for the determination of what was right or wrong was inevitably based upon the consensus perspectives of mankind, as defined and modified by ever-changing concepts. In coping with life's realities, there often were practical versus conceptual discrepancies.

In the South, money seemed both the root of evil and a necessity—

"the chief end of existence," reflected a Texan. The economic prosperity generated by the South's labor-intensive agricultural system
had enabled the wealthy planter class to generally impose specific
values on Southern society at large. Burdened by a high illiteracy rate
(about 45 percent of white Southerners in 1860), the South was dominated by a strong aristocratic hierarchy. The relatively few learned
and elite often determined for the many the course of public affairs.
For example, a focused use of abundant wealth wielded enormous
influence in the South's recommitment of dollars to agriculture and
labor as opposed to the North's increasing investment in manufacturing.[7]

Rather than thriving on diversity, the South in 1861 committed
itself to homogeneity and the status quo. Urbanization and industrialization were depicted as threats to traditional values and the rural
lifestyle enjoyed by much of the South. Since prosperity was a benefit
of the existing agricultural system, it was held that fundamental
change imperiled all Southerners.[8]

In this context, the South's "peculiar institution"—slavery—was a
specific aspect of Southern society that, although troublesome, had
proved to be highly profitable. Accordingly, it was justified as beneficial in the practical views of the Old South. "[Slaves] received in
return [for their labor] more than any other people in bondage have
ever received—as a usual thing, good wholesome food, homes . . . and
tender treatment in sickness," proclaimed an Alabama-reared
woman. Blacks, she asserted, were a race of people sold into bondage
by their own kinfolk, and as a "menial race . . . needed the fostering
care as well as the strong arm of slavery to kindle the latent spark of
intellectual fire."[9]

Rather than merely expressing 1860s Southern self-indulgence,
such attitudes generally reflected the framework of centuries-old practical world history. Traditional Old World perspectives were shaped
on the basis of society's best interest, and hence promoted an ultimate practicality. Slaves were the integral working-class residents of
the Old South. Their contribution was defined in a collective, rather
than personal, sense. Thus, the absence of freedom for blacks was
perceived to be in the best interest of the existing society.[10]

While many Southerners of the antebellum era were religious, and
conservatives in their thinking, they tended to subordinate the moral
issues of slavery to more-practical concepts. Being resistant to change,
Southerners placed their reliance on traditional values when con-

fronted, as in 1861, by instability and pending reform. Indeed, for generations Southerners had emphasized practical resolutions when confronting life's multiple private and public burdens.

Southerners typically had been beset with severe hardships from the time of the region's earliest settlements. Centuries of disasters, both natural and man-made, encouraged continued perseverance, while at the same time instilling a sense of resignation toward so much ill fortune. Life in the South was a sobering experience of ever-changing circumstances—sometimes good, but often bad. The prevalence of disease, floods, war, drought, and storms had heightened Southerners awareness of their vulnerability. This fragile existence insured an individual's resignation to the inevitability of bad fortune to a greater or lesser degree.[11]

Life expectancy was but one troublesome aspect. Sadly, there was always the prospect of being "here today, and gone tomorrow." This was especially true considering the relative ignorance in prevention and treatment of such rampant diseases as malaria, yellow fever, smallpox, and dysentery—many of which were rife only in a warm climate. Crop unpredictability involved another ever-lurking potential Southern disaster. Since agricultural difficulties were accentuated in the more-temperate South—Northern frosts often killed lethal viruses and parasites—there was a greater danger of economic devastation.[12]

The result for the typical Southerner was a culture steeped in the necessity of repeatedly dealing with difficulty and hardened to the unpredictability of life. This awareness of potential helplessness compelled Southerners to cope effectively with uncertainty. The well-being of an individual often rested in his or her ability to function adequately both mentally and physically amid commonly encountered adversities.[13]

It was the same with society. Southern culture demanded of its people a certain faithfulness to societal values. It gave structure to life, and was a natural form of resistance to adversity and anarchy. Rather than a separation of public from private interests, the basic principles guiding a community were those of the family. A threat to the community was a threat to the home. The welfare of each was central to that of the other, and to stand apart from the consensus was generally unacceptable to society.[14]

This traditionalism provided for many anomalies within the cultural matrix; for example, the coexistence of dueling—tragic violence—and "Southern hospitality"—congenial human warmth. So long as the events didn't violate such strongly favored values as honor and bravery, there was acceptance of what was otherwise imprecise logic. Also, appearances—showing manliness, courage, and personal dignity—often counted for more than common sense. Again, there were inherent implications about the mental hardships of a Southern existence. Controlling one's fears by revering values specifically useful in addressing the difficulties of Southern living provided the best chance for survival.[15]

Perhaps this system of principles was a throwback to practical conservatism in the struggle for basic survival, as there was strength in a commonality of interests and solutions. Whereas a certain sense of desperation may have impelled various Southerners in their response to a life of repeated hardships, most were not particularly cynical. Instead, their perspectives were predicted on orthodox values of honor, pride, and ethics—which provided the hope of practical relief and mental solace. Accordingly, conforming to this standard meant gaining acceptance and becoming a pillar of an otherwise-vulnerable Southern society. This was of importance to the security of the community, the person, his family, and their collective well-being. It was also a means of social control.[16]

Ironically, the insecurities of life in the South had also served to promulgate a warped sense of individual freedom. Freedom was ostensibly at the root of all that made life meaningful in Dixie. "To be free from all interference by the peculiar outside world" was an essential part of Southern liberty, noted the Southern historian William Garrott Brown.[17]

This concept rested on the belief that independence was a basic right of both the individual and community. The freedom to choose one's occupation, residence, and spouse, and even to hold divergent political views, was generally unrestricted. In fact, the Southern interpretation of living in America's "land of the free" meant ostensibly the opportunity for any person—excepting slaves—to be all that they might accomplish.[18]

Yet the right to basic personal freedoms was subject to the rigid interpretation of one's own family, friends, and neighbors as to what was proper conduct—and hence the standard to which individuals were expected to conform. The community's collective opinion not only provided a basis of assessing self-worth and defining personal identity, it also did much to undermine many personal freedoms. What could be said and the actions taken, were largely predicated on a common standard as defined by the community. As such, the internal, rigid code of conformity in the Old South directly impinged upon personal freedoms, providing social standards of conduct and dictating one's compliance with the conventions of life. It was more than a matter of social grace: to be ostracized was to be unaccepted; to be unaccepted was to be isolated. To be isolated seemed to many a fate worse than death.[19]

The socially prescribed role for women was but one example of the rigid restraint on personal freedoms evident in Southern society. Women were expected to conform to the traditional roles of wives, childbearers, and homemakers. Theirs was not a life of opportunity in anything but a very confined realm.[20]

Otherwise, because honor was such an important part of Southern culture, it was expected that male honor would be upheld at all costs. Hence the frequent resort to dueling and personal violence. This notion of honor on the other hand, impinged upon one's personal right to a peaceful life without unwarranted danger. Also, in the matter of military service, personal freedoms rapidly gave way to a larger societal need with the advent of the Civil War. In 1861, the individual's basic loyalties were oriented toward a particular community and people, not to abstract conceptions of democracy. Nonetheless, certain freedoms to act independently were soon modified or deleted. The ability of a young man to avoid military duty on the basis of his disaffection with the Southern cause was very limited. The conscription of all able-bodied white males of certain ages was mandatory in the Confederacy after mid-1862. Once he was in the army, a Southerner's personal freedoms were again severely thwarted. The contradictions of life in the Old South were many.[21]

Despite Southern society's prevailing conservatism, within a Southerner's psyche there was frequently an aggressiveness in attacking life's problems. If life was insecure in the South, then the way to best cope with adversity was to overcome it much as if one were involved in a sporting contest—to strive mightily to win. To commit oneself to winning usually entailed taking strong, positive action. As such, applying power either to humble or destroy an opponent was inherent in an aggressive stance. Hence the resort to a bold visage in problem solving. If but another contradiction in Old South ways, it was a characteristic that would profoundly impact upon the waging of civil war.

Prevailing logic suggested that in a crisis proper thinking translated into proactive measures. Thereby, ill fortune and stress were counterbalanced by aggressive risk taking, as necessary, in order to cope best. To do and die was better than not to do and die. It was a spirit derived from frequent encounters with adversity. Underlying this, however, remained an ironic reliance upon the commonly accepted tenet for practical survival—to aggressively resist uncertainty and change.[22]

Ultimately, providing for one's security to the greatest extent possible was the essence of existence in the South. A noted historian has recorded that since insecurity was the lot of mankind, especially in the South, "holding fast to the familiar was the best means of salvation."[23]

Such adherence to tradition explains why many Southerners were so devastated by the change in political control of the nation that followed the 1860 election. And it further reveals much about why the South ultimately went to war.

Chapter Three

A Curse to Any Land

G od forgive us, but ours is a monstrous system and wrong and iniquity. Perhaps the rest of the world is as bad—[but] this only I see." Richmond socialite Mary Chesnut's bitter tirade in her diary against the "hated institution" of slavery reflected the private opinions of various Southerners. Yet such internal distress only accentuated the moral versus practical dilemma of the South with regard to its "peculiar institution."[1]

As an insider, familiar with both the petty abuses and major wrongs that masters inflicted on slaves, Mary Chesnut witnessed firsthand the South's orthodox perception of blacks as inferior people. The Declaration of Independence might have decreed that all men were created equal, but the reality was far different from the Declaration's ideal even in the North. A black man was often regarded as inferior, bestial in nature, and adapted for hard labor or menial tasks. Many Caucasians scorned the Negroid appearance, from allegedly exaggerated facial features to frequently ragged apparel. Blacks seemed to speak with lazy, awkward phrases, and tended to act simplistically—like children. Moreover, according to some "refined" whites many blacks reeked with a pungent body odor.[2]

These "differences" were prejudicial to many observers, and the denial to nearly all blacks of formal education only compounded them, presenting the profile of an ignorant, subservient entity—little better than an animal of the field. Attitudes and actions were influenced accordingly, especially in the deep South.[3]

Here the dehumanization of blacks was particularly evident in their treatment: "Men and women [slaves] are punished when their masters and mistresses are brutes and not when they do wrong," wrote the aggrieved Mary Chesnut in her diary. Mary was particularly offended by black sexual exploitation:

"We live surrounded by [slave] prostitutes." An abandoned woman is sent out of any decent house elsewhere, [but] who thinks any worse of a Negro or mulatto woman for being a thing we can't name? . . . Like the patriarchs of old, our men live all in one house with their wives and their concubines, and the mulattos one sees in every family exactly resemble the white children—and every lady tells you who is the father of all the mulatto children in everybody's household, but those in her own she seems to think drop from the clouds, or pretends so to think.[4]

Mary Chesnut's views were tantamount to heresy in the Old South. The South had grown to maturity with slavery as the basis of cheap labor, which was a viable arrangement in a labor-intensive agricultural society. Like an old, comfortable shoe reluctantly discarded, the institution of slavery was too expansive and too integral a part of the culture to be painlessly effaced, although many Southerners despised or otherwise disapproved of slavery or many of its aspects. Despite a severe moral dilemma rising out of the advent of the modern family there was little impetus to action. Much of the South's white population (two-thirds were not slave owners) simply tolerated it as part of the long-established order.

In keeping with the Old South's rigidly maintained cultural values, slavery endured as one facet of the region's resistance to fundamental change. Individuals seeking to modify this well-established institution were judged critically for upending the traditional best interests of Southern society. Since the South's well-being was endangered there was enormous resistance to major changes affecting slavery.[5]

It didn't matter that moral critics in the North decried the breakup of slave families, in which sons and daughters were sometimes sold elsewhere in a community. Slavery's defenders claimed that even the occasional splitting apart of black husbands and wives was generally a practical arrangement, in which the welfare of each was best maintained by the new master as a productive part of society. After all, each slave represented a valuable investment in money, time, and effort. It was the responsibility of the master to provide for the well-being of his slaves—if only as an investment.[6]

Thus, the emotional fervor of critical indictments such as Harriet Beecher Stowe's *Uncle Tom's Cabin* was decried as fundamentally un-justified. Moreover, when it came to morality, Yankees had little cre-dence with many Southerners. By exploiting "wage slaves"—poor immigrants who had to work long hours at the mercy of capitalist shop owners for minimal pay—New Englanders appeared to be hyp-ocrites of the first rank. Instead of a slave's permanent job and home for life on the plantation, the Yankee wage slave might be fired on a whim and thus lose his alleged independence. So the argument went. It was merely a matter of personal perspective, with self-interest in mind. "Whose ox was getting gored" was a basic question that im-pacted the nation and its slavery dilemma. Those with much to lose were the loudest critics of any anticipated change. In 1861, the po-tential big losers were the South's largest planters, and hence, so those planters said, the whole Southern population—which was largely supported by a limited, crop-product economy.[7]

Economics had long been a major factor in the total concept of the South's reliance on slavery, and from it stemmed a great reluc-tance to alter the status quo of human bondage.

Slaves made cheap and usually reliable laborers. Good, inexpensive labor provided a more competitive and profitable product in the mar-ketplace. Since growth of the South's most important product—cot-ton—was viable only in a temperate climate, and since the market was worldwide, the economics of the South's agricultural system were of vital importance to many.

Beyond the elimination of foreign slave trade in America in 1807, the South's black population had internally expanded multifold to about 47 percent of the future Confederate states' population by 1860. Since the percentage of blacks in the Northern states remained at only about 2 percent in 1860, the threat of so many slaves being forcibly removed from the South's labor force, or else having to be paid by real wages, was an enormous economic shock in the wake of the "Black Republican" national election victory of 1860.[8]

Southern prosperity had been rife throughout the past few de-cades, largely as a result of "King Cotton." That this prosperity was suddenly put at risk sent a shiver down the spines of Southerners.

The South's yield of raw cotton had doubled each decade after 1800 to the point of providing three-fourths of the world's supply in 1860. This virtually tied the South to an export-import economy, whereby her produce was exported, and the products she depended upon were imported due to the lack of a large manufacturing base. Southern exports had grown to the point of accounting for three-fifths of all United States exports, providing an enormous financial inflow to fuel economic growth and westward expansion. Instead of growing crops primarily for home consumption, the impetus was to produce them for the market, thereby gaining access to greater prosperity through the external dollars received. That the marketing of raw cotton involved Yankee-controlled commerce, including shipping, processing, and much textile manufacturing, presented a further economic threat.[9]

Because the South simply had to maintain control of its economic destiny, a national election shifting power to a "radical" element occasioned great turmoil. The threat to the Southern economic infrastructure was perceived as real, and each white Southerner seemed confronted with the prospect of dire changes in his personal well-being.

Throughout history, the threat of losing wealth or the promise of gaining it are among the most powerful factors that incite people to take action. Even the modern quip, "It's the economy, stupid" has become a truism of proven political value.

Differences of opinion existed between the upper and lower South on the practicality of seceding from the Union, based largely upon the disparity in percentage of slave population of the two areas, according to one leading historian. Yet, the relative number of slaves within the population may have been somewhat of a tangential factor in the impetus to leave the Union. The critical circumstance involving an eventual unified secession may have applied more extensively to the financial and political domination of large lower-South cotton planters due to the South's virtual one-product economy. The upper region's population consisted primarily of small, yeoman farmers, and its less-temperate climate was not as well suited to cotton production. Thus, within the total economic realm, the upper South's status was subordinate to that of the lower states.[10]

The impact of economics, relative to the oft-cited moral question of slavery, was a significant impetus to go to war. Certainly, the divisive question of slavery's expansion into the territories vitally affected the eventual promulgation or demise of slavery. Yet, perhaps the common focus was not so much on the great prewar controversy that provided the South with an emotional justification for secession. Rather, Southerners seemed more concerned with the perceived impending dire consequences, particularly diminished prosperity within their economy. The financial interests of the South were threatened, not potentially by the prevention of slavery's expansion in the West, but immediately and vitally in the Southern heartland by the Southerners' loss of political control following the 1860 national election.

Self-interest is an enormously powerful factor in any situation involving major conflict. It naturally emerged as perhaps the most critical factor in the South's view of slavery as an economic necessity in 1861.

That the true or "net" value of slavery to the South was exaggerated was not considered at the time. More troubling to the region was the anticipated upheaval of Southern society which would surely come as a result of constraints that might be imposed upon the South after the Republican victory. The prospect of an adversarial, "Abolitionist" government controlling the nation's destiny frightened first the lower and later the upper South. Instead of being a caretaker of traditional values, the new "Black" Republican administration in the eyes of Southerners, would certainly foster turmoil—perhaps a revolution. Indeed, the very election and installation of Abraham Lincoln as president were regarded in the South as a major threat to the favorable status quo.[11]

Since the "incendiary and malicious" views of the new Republican administration were well publicized in the South, the negative consequences of its election seemed both real and immediate in the light of the popular rhetoric of the time. Continually resorting to bombast and innuendo, Southern newspapers rapidly inflamed the minds and riled the emotions of the people.

Both nationally and locally, the South had always been able to control public affairs to a reasonable extent. Now the loss of that control was apparent. If only the South's political control was threatened in these early stages, the loss of practical control was imminent. As the nation's minority, the South faced a humiliating decline in status. Staring Southerners in the face was the dire unknown—possibly the specter of a collapsing society. Was slave insurrection possible? What about mandated race equality, and the competition for jobs? Would economic sanctions be imposed? Were financial hardship and economic turmoil forthcoming? Who could resist the awful changes that seemed to be looming?[12]

Questions of slavery, economics, and personal welfare in the South had by 1861 reached a crisis-charged point that required resolution. It was as if a bitter dose of poison had been swallowed by the prosperous South, administered by a vindictive North. Only secession seemed to offer an antidote.

Truly, it had become a tangled mess of emotional and practical upheaval—all in the minds of men.

Chapter Four

Secession Rather Than Dishonor

In 1860 secession was a controversial and divisive issue among Southerners. In fact, the majority seemed to oppose secession and the South needed to reach a common understanding of the policy that would best serve it during the crises of that fall. Without a popular consensus, the region faced a prospect of indecision and inaction. Ardent advocates of secession—the "fire-eaters"—took advantage of the tumult and quickly seized their opportunity to act decisively.

Based on the unfavorable 1860 election, which shifted the nation's political control to "radical" Northerners, it was apparent to Southerners that already-heated emotions would soon reach a boiling point. Nonetheless, to bring the South's general populace to active support for secession required a particularly aggressive approach. The fire-eaters' resorting to overt action, particularly in passing South Carolina's provocative ordinance of secession in December 1860, proved incendiary. Also, their appeal to a familiar popular theme, "Southern rights and honor," was crucial in winning the minds and hearts of the Southern people. Appropriately, secession advocates largely sought to focus public attention upon key emotional issues. For that purpose, the popular rhetoric of 1861 was well calculated.[1]

Propaganda became a significant factor in the abrupt rise of the Southern Confederacy. However, because the means whereby secession advocates manipulated the public were such well-established institutions, few recognized at the time the covert dangers and insidious realities.

The primary basis of current mass communications in the early 1860s was the local newspaper, which held a substantial monopoly on news distribution. While books and periodicals frequently provided a variety of information and helped shape popular views, they lacked immediacy. Letters, of course, were the source of current personal news, which was often passed along by word of mouth. But this news had very limited circulation. Telegrams presaged the modern era of instant communication, yet they, too, lacked an expansive readership forum, and had limited accessibility.

Today's news was of great importance to the crisis-charged South in 1861. Delays in communication of weeks and months would have been crippling in the inexorable rush toward a confrontation with the Northern states. The newspaper, which provided timely and detailed information to the largely rural Southern community, was pre-eminent.[2]

As a readily available and cheap source of information, Southern newspapers were widely read and used to understand the events shaping the outside world and local community. Whereas the 1860 circulation of newspapers in the eleven eventual Confederate states numbered only 103,041,436—versus 824,910,112 for the rest of the nation—greater literacy rates, an increased population base, and cheaper costs had quickly established the newspaper as the most important public source of news. Because the newspapers read in the South were primarily of Southern origin, accurate views of the Northern community's beliefs and positions generally went unreported, or else the information given was highly slanted.[3]

Furthermore, considering the inherently political nature of most newspapers of the time, commentary on critical issues was often susceptible to outside influence. Newspaper funding that was tied to political parties, or related to local officials who controlled printing contracts, or even major advertisers, held heavy editorial sway. Also, politicians enjoyed significant power and frequently were the cause of distortion or misinformation in period editorials. Indeed, abuses in editorial practices ranged from what would later be termed "yellow journalism" to character assassination.

Because there was often minimal local competition and the source of news was tightly controlled, there were few practical forums for voicing opposing opinions, or broadcasting evidence that countered published data. If an item appeared in print, a certain credence was given to it, based on the public's very limited access to other news sources.[4]

The dominant communications role of local newspapers in 1861 thus worked to conspire against a reasoned solution to the disunion crisis. Lacking objectivity, many Southern newspaper editors endorsed secession as the only means of upholding personal and community independence from a hostile Northern government. By directly playing upon their readers' emotions, many Old South newspapers intensified a swelling sense of injustice, and heightened fears of Southern society's subversion.

Various editorals portrayed the threat of economic and social ruin as the root of the crisis. Control of the national government by Northern radicals, it was said, would lead to the eventual breakdown of white supremacy in the South. Blacks might be enfranchised and placed in office to control the Southern people and destroy their economy. This scenario would lead to enforced social equality, and thereafter black domination, perhaps even intermarriage and the amalgamation of the races. Newspapers timed their doctrine of fear and misperception to current events. In so doing, they effected a major turnabout from the dispassionate rhetoric of the previous decade.[5]

Ironically, prior to 1860 Southern newspaper editorials were heavily weighted against disunion so long as "Southern rights" were protected. The Little Rock *Arkansas State Gazette* of February 25, 1860, had proclaimed, "The American Union stands on a firmer foundation than ever before. The Union of these states is cemented by a community of interest which will forever operate as a natural check to secession or dissolution. We may assure ourselves that the Union is not in danger." Other Southern papers had endorsed similar viewpoints, and only later, following the events of 1860, did public opinion begin to shift amid a current of highly charged newspaper editorials.[6]

In practical terms, there were several reasons for the drastic change in Southern editorial policy from a pro-Union stance to support of secession. Of great importance in this trend was an altered perception of dangers due to a dark litany of "threatening" events. John Brown's trial and execution following his raid on Harper's Ferry in 1859 had elevated him to the status of a martyr in the North, reflected in poems, songs, speeches, and a variety of potent publicity. This

aggravating influence caused many Southerners to fear what they perceived to be the increasing abolitionist motives of Northerners.

There were other "provocations." Fanned by allegations of
Northern radical–inspired slave conspiracies, like the mysterious
Texas fires of July 1860, complaints about Yankee meddling in Southern affairs intensified. Existing tensions between North and South
were aggravated by strained relationships in the United States Congress, where on several occasions verbal assault led to physical violence. Sectional animosity was so prevalent that many congressmen
carried sidearms on the floor of Congress. Adding further to the
atmosphere of crisis was a devastating drought that withered Southern crops and created an economic downturn that summer.

By the time of the 1860 election, the political climate was excep-
tionally ugly. Already-frayed nerves had nearly unraveled when the
Democratic party divided into rival pro-Southern and pro-Northern
factions. Talk of secession was rife, and became even more widespread
as the Republican party inched closer to its fall election victory. In anticipation of an "irrepressible conflict," militias assumed a new importance in the South, and states like Mississippi and Alabama
committed funds in excess of $100,000 to arm and equip their troops.[7]

When Abraham Lincoln ultimately won the presidency in November 1860, his election occasioned more than yet further escalating
tensions. It incited the South to act on fears and emotions that had
long been held in tenuous check. Since political control of several
key deep-South states rested in the hands of ardent secessionists, the
provocative actions of what once had been a Southern minority initiated the rush toward a final confrontation within the entire region.
South Carolina's formal act of secession in December 1860 demonstrated overt resistance to the authority of the federal government.
Henceforth, the great controversy was no longer simply a subject of
debate—it had become a reality.

Together with the failure of political efforts at compromise, South
Carolina's action sparked an intense emotionalism in other Southern
states, which was fanned by newspaper editorials written in the hope
of inducing a final rush to secession. Popular sentiment began to turn
on the basis of a new reality: the existing break in relations with the
North that would mandate the use of armed force by both sides.

Although some newspapers urged their readers to wait and observe
the practical effect of the Lincoln administration after the March 4,
1861, inauguration, the majority of Southern editors endorsed seces-

sion. Swelling anger and exasperation were evident in many editorials. Citizens were inflamed by rhetoric such as that in the *Richmond [Virginia] Semi Weekly Examiner* of December 18: "The one intelligible, practical policy [of the Northern radicals is] to make this government an agent to repress and extinguish African slavery."[8]

With the secession of seven lower-South cotton states just prior to Lincoln taking office, and the formation of the Southern Confederacy at Montgomery, Alabama, in early February 1861, separation and disunion were an incontrovertible fact. Even before the inauguration of the much-maligned "Black Republican" president on March 4, matters had spiraled out of control. Choices were limited; each individual had to side either with or against the Southern Confederacy. There was no middle ground. As the *New Orleans Bee* reported after Lincoln's election, "Now is the time for all patriotic men to choose positions, for soon they must be found on one side or the other—for the Union or against it."[9]

Incendiary appeals, like that found in the *New Orleans Daily Crescent* of December 20, 1860, left little debate about which choice a true Southerner should make: "The issue is whether to stay in the Union and become abject submissionists to northern domination, and kissers of the rod that smites us, or to resume the rights granted to the federal government for good purposes, but perverted by that government to purposes most unholy and infamous." An editor for the *Daily Missouri Republican* (April 19, 1861) echoed that opinion, writing, "The States are the true guardians of our freedom and our rights, and when their power is gone, the master at the federal capital is the ruler over subject millions—an emperor, elected or self-appointed, as the times determine."[10]

Coercion must be resisted by "the arguments of the sword," argued another aroused Southern editor from *The Daily Herald* of Wilmington, North Carolina (January 3, 1861). Attempts to blockade the seaports of the seceding Southern states and garrison Southern forts should be defeated, he urged. "We have little regard for any man who is fickle in his opinions, or cowardly in giving utterance to them; but we have less for him who stupidly adheres to a blind and unyielding prejudice, or violently advocates a useless and impracticable theory [pacifism]."[11]

Even moderates seemed to draw the line, and on January 3, 1861, a writer for *The Daily Herald* of Wilmington, North Carolina, argued, "Coercion means civil war, and, though we have been educated in

the federal school of politics and do not believe in the right of secession, we would never, as southern[ers], suffer a Southern State to
be driven into subjection by armed force, as long as we could stagger
under a musket. We have argued and protested against secession, but
we should . . . dishonor the blood that flows in our veins . . . if we hes-
itated to beat back the armed aggressor. . . ."[12]

Ironically, the first aggressive moves were committed by Southerners. Several Federal arsenals and forts within the seceding states were
seized by local authorities prior to Lincoln's inauguration, generally
without conflict. Described as "a precautionary measure" by the New
Orleans *Daily Picayune* of January 17, 1861, these seizures were nonetheless acknowledged by the paper as giving rise to "an amount of
northern indignation wholly disproportioned to the gravity of the
offense." The "immediacy of hostile collision" due to "fanaticism
and [Northern] sectional excesses" dictated the necessity for this action, asserted *The Daily Picayune.* Since the Continental colonies seized
Great Britain's forts and arsenals in 1776, the seceders maintained
that they were behaving comparably to the Yankees' own forefathers.
This was revolution—a right of all peoples—based on grievances "just
in the sight of earth and Heaven," asserted the *Daily Nashville Patriot*
(September 19, 1860), and therefore resorting to military seizure was
fully justified.[13]

The entire issue was thus simplified: would it be submission or
resistance? asked *The Kentucky Statesman* on December 28. "We have
written RESISTANCE on our flag," heralded the paper. "We trust
there will not be a submissionist found in Kentucky."[14]

Here was not merely a call to revolution, but a call to arms. As the
Louisville *Daily Courier* trumpeted in an editorial on February 13,
1861, "War may be expected soon after March 4."[15]

On April 12, 1861, when a fiery arc of Confederate shells streaked
high over Charleston Harbor, South Carolina, and burst above Fort
Sumter, the last restraints of newspaper rhetoric were shredded.
"Cowardly duplicity and treachery," shrieked *The [New Orleans] Daily
Delta* of April 18. Abraham Lincoln's "war policies" involved "low
cunning and dishonorable artifice." It was "faithlessness" and "vile
treachery," the newspaper asserted. The "baseness of this pitiable
creature [Lincoln]" was apparent for all to see, announced the paper. "We accept war as a fact," proclaimed *The [Charlotte, Virginia]
Review* on April 19. "From wickedness, or from some strange hallu-
cination, the President has summoned the country to arms—to fight

among themselves. . . . What object but revenge can have stimulated the immense military preparations in progress . . . we cannot discover." The *New Orleans Bee* (May 1, 1861) charged that the North was not waging war merely for maintenance of the Union. "The subjection of the South . . . to the supremacy of sectional foes is the real object of the war," claimed the *Bee*'s outraged editor.[16]

"The time for argument and mere declamation has passed," urged the April 20 *Nashville Union and American*. "Let military companies be formed everywhere and drilled daily, using such arms as they can find. . . . An hour is not to be lost. We may be called on to defend our homes and our firesides sooner than many of us expect . . . Let our people . . . meet the invader at the border with Tennessee's 'bravest and best,' and throw themselves on the very 'crest of the battle,' to chastise the insolent and tyrannical foe . . . Tennesseans! arouse yourselves to action, arm and organize!" "The War feeling is swelling and surging like the waves of the sea. Who can resist a whole people, thoroughly aroused, brave to rashness, fighting for their existence?" asked *The Review* of Charlotte, Virginia, on April 19.[17]

Fervor for war spread across the South like an unchecked epidemic, often fed by newspaper rhetoric. But there were occasional words of caution. Insisting that it was wise to guard against "a common error—that of depreciating an adversary," the *New Orleans Bee* of May 1, 1861, warned. [It would be]:

rank folly to deny the courage of the people of the North. They belong to the revolutionary stock, and had displayed their valor in many a battlefield. They are as brave as the men of the South, and were their cause a just one; were they, as we are, defending their homes and firesides, their freedom and independence against ruthless invaders, they would be, as we trust we shall prove, invincible. Yet they are as numerous as the swarms of barbarians which the frozen North sent from her loins to overrun the Roman Empire, and this is their great advantage. But against this we place our devotion, our unanimity, our strong defensive attitude, our easily protected territory. Let them come in their courage and their numbers, and the South will resist the shock as steadily and successfully as she resisted the veterans of the British army on the plains of Chalmette.[18]

This theory was popular, and many in the South believed that in the final analysis the war would become a question of mind over matter. The will to win would prevail, and the merit of the Southern cause and the mental fortitude of her people in their righteous endeavor for independence would be the inspiration for an inevitable victory.

Unfortunately for the soldiers, the war would not be waged by newspaper rhetoric. It would involve the extreme physical agony of Southerners in proving or disproving what journalists had urged as a matter of emotionalized perception.

Chapter Five

Virginia and the Spirit of the Times

The cry, to arms, to arms! is heard from every lip. Every man is willing to shoulder his musket and suffer death rather than submit to the present occupant of the White House," asserted an excited southern volunteer in late April 1861. Like hundreds of other recruits for the Confederate army, he was anxious to wind up his civilian affairs and join the local rifle company. Even when the initial fighting resulted in casualties, as widely reported by local newspapers, recruits who had missed out on the early combat remained animated. "We are all anxious for a battle," wrote a newly enlisted Virginia-based infantryman. "We want to distinguish ourselves."[1]

A spirit of eagerness and fervor was contagious among young Southern men, many of whom thought of the war as a grand adventure. A surgeon writing home in July 1861 boasted that the soldiers of the 11th Alabama Infantry had endured several forced marches with characteristic Southern fortitude. "[Those] who had never been used to labor or to walk, stood it without a murmur and refused to be so unsoldierlike as to accept a ride in a baggage wagon," he reported. "[An old adage asserts,] 'Tis the mind that makes the man," continued the surgeon. But "with more force than I can say, 'tis the spirit."[2]

The Confederacy's morale seemed to reach new heights during the sweltering summer of 1861. A host of volunteers and state militia were gathering to defend "Southern rights" from the Northern invaders.

"The great strength and power of the Southern army lies[sic] in the individual resolution of the men," urged an early Richmond observer. "Every private feels a determination, not only to carry his regiment through the fight, but to see his country through the war."[3]

Much of the enthusiasm for a rapid Southern victory was rooted in several vague but broadly held nineteenth-century perceptions. Of particular importance was the "Virginia mystique" which seemed to be a means to intimidate the South's opponents. This psyche arose from the popular belief that the Virginian was bred of a superior, "cavalier" heritage. In many Old South novels Virginians had long been stereotyped as planter descendants of the Norman aristocrats who had ruled England for centuries. Such breeding, it was alleged, perpetuated manly virtues: refined manners, aristocratic behavior, and a strong sense of honor. Above all else, Virginia cavaliers were characterized by gentlemanly martial skills like riding, shooting, and outdoorsmanship. In the minds of many Southerners a Virginian was a reincarnation of one of King Arthur's Knights of the Round Table. His display of chivalrous virtues epitomized refined manliness, and, it was said, ideally suited the Virginian to military duty.[4]

Of equal significance was a corollary theory, the popular Old South belief that European "Yankee" immigrants who had settled in New England were burdened by an inferior Saxon ancestry. These individuals reportedly came from the lower socioeconomic classes that had long been dominated by their Norman rivals. Since Northerners descended from less-powerful ancestors, according to the theory, they must therefore suffer feelings of inferiority and lack the confidence to successfully confront the superior Virginians.[5]

The myth was not only romanticized, but misleading of the Virginians who would do most of the actual fighting—the youthful Old Dominion "dirt farmers." Nevertheless, the Virginia mystique played a significant role at the war's inception, if for no other reason than that it gave the Virginia soldier greater self-confidence and a prideful attitude. Moreover, most in the South knew that Virginia led the region in manufacturing and industry, and that the state's potent combination of military prowess and economic well-being would assure her of a leading role in the new Confederacy. In fact, Virginia was expected to be the great pillar of Southern independence. Her ranks of soldiers in gray were enthusiastic and confident, and appeared capable of bearing the brunt of the initial fighting.

Yet, in many respects, Virginians had become an enigma to the deep South. They were far more conservative than the South Carolina radicals who had initiated the calls for secession. If Virginia harbored the South's most valuable assets, its importance was recognized only after the prolonged controversy and political infighting that marked the state's early attempts to avoid separation from the Union.[6]

Virginians were not ardent secessionists at heart. Reflecting a then-popular view of the secession debate, a prominent King and Queen County, Virginia, doctor wrote in November 1860, "Even though Lincoln's election is a fixed fact, the Union need not of necessity be dissolved. My confidence is that an over-ruling Providence will save us from the horrors of dissolution."[7]

This and similar conservative sentiments were rooted in the more practical ideology prevalent in the upper South (Virginia, Arkansas, North Carolina, and Tennessee). In fact, this region's thinking often directly opposed the more inflamed and ardent secession proclivities of the cotton-rich lower South (South Carolina, Mississippi, Florida, Alabama, Georgia, Louisiana, and Texas). The emotional rhetoric of lower-South leaders boasted of Southern-white-male superiority in personal terms, touting that the manly virtues of genteel and working-class farmers of the South were superior to those of the North's servile class of dirty mechanics, ignorant immigrant laborers, and petty out-lot farmers. Virginians remained generally more circumspect. Older and wiser heads had long attempted to mediate in the regional controversy over slavery and secession, and Virginians were among the most prominent of would-be peacemakers. As late as February 1861 the Virginia legislature had called a peace convention (later dubbed the "Old Gentlemen's Convention," led by seventy-one-year-old ex-president John Tyler) that brought forth an ambitious if futile compromise resolution.[8]

Notwithstanding the state's conservatism, ultimately the passions of youth exerted far stronger influence in Virginia's destiny. Since definitive choices and commitments had to be made following the breakup of the Union, the state needed to decide if it would fight for or against her Southern neighbors. In the end, Virginia was more Southern than Northern, both morally and practically.

Following the Virginia convention's vote on secession on April 17, 1861, the en-masse rush to arms by the state's soldier-age population reflected the emotional fervor of her people. By a margin of 96,750 votes (128,884 to 32,134, or 80 percent), Virginians had approved secession in a referendum on May 23, 1861. Her citizens had committed themselves to war and the Southern cause despite Virginia's earlier attempts to avoid civil strife and its lingering ties to Northern commerce.[9]

What remained to be sorted out for individual Virginians, however, were their own motives for giving allegiance to the entire nation or else community. Controversy over Virginians serving in the United States Army stirred up profound emotions. "You will be aides and abettors of the sworn foes—and active foes—of your country (I mean the South, for that is your country) and your own kindred," wrote Virginia novelist John Esten Cooke in urging Lieutenant J. E. B. Stuart's resignation from the United States Army. "If [war comes] then you are sworn to put us to the bayonet at the orders of [Winfield] Scott and Lincoln. . . . Virginia is certain for secession as anything in the future can be. She will join the Confederate States. We are in a revolution, and events rush on too wildly for ceremony," announced the impassioned Cooke.[10]

Cooke's observations were important. Beyond any state's commitment, the war ultimately had to be defined in personal terms. What had once been abstract ideology and patriotic sentiment was now a matter of individual commitment.

Amid the endless personal and financial conflicts the nation was being torn apart by sections. Family ties and Virginia's links to the deep South exerted immense pressure on statesmen in Federal service and those with strong connections to the national government. Robert E. Lee and George H. Thomas, both veteran United States Army officers, wrestled with the issues of ideology and family and made their own decisions—Lee choosing to serve the Confederacy, and Thomas siding with the Union.

Even though he finally joined the Southern cause, Lee was at first reluctant. "Now we are in a state of war which will yield to nothing," he confided to his sister on April 20. "The whole South is in a state of revolution, into which Virginia, after a long struggle, has been drawn. . . . I recognize no necessity for this state of things, . . . yet in my own person I had to raise the question whether I should take part against my native state. With all my devotion to the Union, and the feeling of loyalty and duty of an American citizen, I have not been able to make up my mind to raise my hand against my relatives, my children, my home. I have, therefore, resigned my commission in the Army. . . ."[11]

George H. Thomas had been honored by the citizens of Southampton County, Virginia, for "military skill, bravery, and noble deportment" during the Mexican War. Although the native Virginian had married a New York girl, his ties to the South had remained intact. In 1855, Jefferson Davis, then secretary of war, had appointed Thomas major of the 2d United States Cavalry—Robert E. Lee's own regiment. As one of two or three foremost younger officers in the army, Thomas had been a natural choice for assuming a large responsibility in Virginia's army. Yet he chose to remain loyal to the Union and refused to resign his commission—an act of great moral courage. His decision to fight against Virginia and the South was tantamount to political and social suicide. He was soon denounced in Virginia as a traitor. His family destroyed his old letters and turned his picture to the wall. His name was not mentioned in polite society. His sisters, Julia and Fanny, bitterly proposed to use on him his fine, 1848-dated Virginia presentation sword, which now remained hidden behind the door. They even suggested that he change his name.

Virtually disowned by his family and politically renounced, George Thomas pondered his unpromising future in the spring of 1861. He had risked everything to stand by his principles and soon suffered the consequences. Yet his commitment to the United States remained firm, and he maintained his strong sense of honor. A Southerner by birth and upbringing, he would remain so in spirit, even if he opposed the cause of the Southern Confederacy.[12]

For most, however, the adage that "blood is thicker than water" prevailed, and Virginians overwhelmingly aligned themselves with the Confederacy. Bolstered by legions of Virginia "cavaliers," the Confederate army became one of the most powerful and impressive military forces ever to exist in North America.

In 1861, Southern military leadership consisted of some of the most prominent and widely recognized officers of the Old Army, many of whom were Virginians. Robert E. Lee, Joseph E. Johnston, and Samuel Cooper were among the Confederacy's senior commanders who had strong ties to the Old Dominion State and had left the United States Army in 1861. Of the 1,132 regular officers on duty with the United States Army in early 1861, 304 were from the eleven Southern states that eventually joined the Confederacy. Of these, 137 were Virginians, by far the largest contingent.[13]

Particularly valuable to the Confederacy, especially in the East where such units were widespread, were the state militia regiments which had existed before the war. Though for the most part merely ceremonial and social, they served as a means of rapidly mobilizing Southern military forces. They also provided the means for training troops and building a military organization. The militia thus became a primary source of leaders. Former militiamen with even a little military experience were often promoted to officers or ranking noncommissioned officers within volunteer units as the war progressed. This ready source of relatively disciplined and partially trained personnel gave portions of the South an advantage in organizing and preparing masses of volunteer soldiers. Of the Southern militias, Virginia's was by far the largest, with a total strength of 143,155 officers and men listed on the rolls in late 1860.[14]

Another practical advantage for Virginia and the South's eastern forces was the prevalence of military college graduates. Academies like the Virginia Military Institute and the South Carolina Military Academy (the Citadel) provided a substantial pool of leaders for the Confederate army. A tradition of military training was widespread in populous and well-to-do regions of the South, and such schooling had become an integral part of a gentleman's education.[15]

In all, there was a substantial basis in fact for Southerners' high expectations of the Confederate armies formed in 1861. A popular belief throughout the South was that the Confederacy had the military talent, expertise, and above all else, determination and willpower to achieve its independence by force of arms.

South Carolinian Henry Ravenel voiced this perception in April 1861: "I fear the northern people have an impression that we are unable to cope with them, from inferiority in numbers, want of necessary means, and that our slave population is an element of weakness. It may be necessary therefore that they should be disabused of such impression. If we must pass through this terrible ordeal of war to teach them this lesson, so be it. It may be best in the end. We put our trust in the God of battles . . ."[16]

The God of war seemed poised on the points of Southern bayonets, particularly in the active Virginia theater during the summer of 1861. A familiar faith—that Southern willpower and the spirit of the South's soldiers would surmount any difficulties that lay ahead—pitted Southern dash and know-how against the Yankee minions' horn of plenty. In considering the ultimate consequences, many thought Virginia's martial prowess would prove decisive.

In contrast to the confidence Virginia inspired, there lurked a great uncertainty concerning the other main arena of military operations, the South's middle west, which presented potentially major problems.

The emphasis on Virginia and the East may have misled many about the South's prospects for independence, for the supposedly monolithic Southern culture harbored a militarily diverse population. In the vast western regions beyond the Appalachian Mountains, the citizenry was generally less educated and more backwoods rural than the "planters' sons" of the eastern seaboard, who made up the South's highly lauded military resources.

In 1860, much of what is known today as the middle South was regarded as the West. Beyond the socioeconomic differences between the cotton-dominant lower South and the more industrialized and urbane upper South, the eastern Confederate states (Virginia, North Carolina, South Carolina, Georgia, and Florida) contrasted sharply with the geographic western Confederacy (Alabama, Tennessee, Louisiana, Mississippi, Texas, and Arkansas). Divided from the eastern seaboard by the rugged Appalachian Mountains the sparsely populated western Confederate regions suffered from economic and practical disadvantages.[17]

Nearly half of those eligible to serve in the Confederate army resided in the eastern states, an area that contained only one-third of the Confederacy's territory. Population density per square mile averaged 22.1 in Virginia and the Carolinas, but only 8.3 in most western states. In addition to its dispropartionately small population, the western region's resources were limited. The eastern states had nearly two-thirds of the South's railroad mileage, and they produced two-thirds of all manufactured goods. The western states' scarcity of industry, populace, and transportation would have a profound impact on the waging of the war.[18]

Strategically, the western Confederacy represented a territory too vast and vacant to be easily defended. Yet it was that here the South grew most of its crops. The so-called heartland western Confederate states, as large producers of food supplies, were to be relied on as a partial supply source for the eastern armies.[19]

Of further bearing on the Confederate military were the comparative quality and attitudes of the West's fighting men. The predominant number of troops fighting in each geographic area were local soldiers. It made little sense to transfer large numbers of western troops to fight in the east, and vice versa, due to extensive transportation difficulties. Thus, common sense, acclimation, familiarity with the terrain, and local home-front support dictated that the Confederacy's armies would be composed mostly of troops serving in regions close to their homes. Accordingly, the South's newly formed primary forces in both the East and the West were largely "local" armies.[20]

Of obvious influence in the performance of these Southern armies were the education, training, equipment, and particularly the confidence and self-esteem of the soldiers. Westerners were generally less literate and less likely to be part of an established, trained "militia," and were often less affluent than their eastern counterparts. Nonetheless, they were perhaps more pioneering or adventuresome in spirit as a result of the hardy lifestyle common in the less-urbanized West.[21]

The qualities that enabled western Confederates to cope with greater natural hardships and do without many civilities made them rugged, independent soldiers—and perhaps less amenable to military discipline than their eastern counterparts. As evident in letters from Southern soldiers used to an unfettered civilian existence, being told what to do, when to do it, and how to do it—often by someone just as inexperienced as they—required great patience and a self-sacrificing attitude.

Relinquishing control of one's life was at the heart of creating an effective army in the field. It required trust on the part of the soldiers—trust in their officers, their generals, and the success of their cause. Yet many soldiers had a difficult time coping when military service required them to surrender most of their independence.

Moreover, the validity of a military life was couched in a common purpose, with what were perceived as readily obtainable goals. To the extent that an army's efforts met with success or failure, morale and self-confidence, would rise or fall proportionally. This, of course, was but a further reflection of dealing with an alien military lifestyle.

In the beginning, the effect of morale and esprit de corps within each army was not obvious. Enthusiasm abounded in both major armies, which would become in time the Army of Northern Virginia in the East, and The Army of Tennessee in the West. Beyond the emotion of the moment, however, lurked uncertainties. How would the western soldiers fare in combat with fewer resources, less numerical strength, and perhaps less military heritage?[22]

From Virginia to Kentucky and beyond, the imminence in mid-1861 of an expansive armed conflict warned that an answer would soon be forthcoming.

Chapter Six

THE PENDING CONFRONTATION WITH THE SELF

On March 19, 1861, a startled observer glanced out of a window in Mulberry, South Carolina, and gasped. There was snow on the ground a foot deep! After months of warm, springlike weather, winter had arrived with a vengeance. "Even the climate, like everything else, [is] upside down," wrote a shocked Mary Boykin Chesnut.[1]

It was an ominous prophecy for Southern society. Within a month, the guns at Charleston Harbor, South Carolina, had, in fact, turned the entire nation upside down.* No longer would the whims of a wealthy lifestyle prevail in civil society. "Posing we are in grand tenure," noted Mary Chestnut in June 1861. "There is no imagination here to forestall woe, and only the excitement and wild awakening from everyday stagnant life are felt."[2]

This excitement, often described by the participants in terms of their "enthusiasm" for Southern rights, in many respects fostered an awakening of the Southern soul. If an often-humdrum existence in a rural community was the norm, then anticipation of the war intoxicated many of the South's spirited young men.

The natural inclination of all youth—and it was essentially a young man's war to fight—is for adventure and personal accomplishment. More than a chance to establish a place in the world, here was an

---

*The firing on Fort Sumter, in Charleston Harbor occurred on April 12, 1861. This attack began the war's hostilities.

opportunity to see and do, and escape from the tedium and boredom of commonplace civilian life. For a youth to put himself in danger on behalf of the Southern community seemed both "worthy" and adventurous. A young soldier benefitted from public recognition, a heightened sense of importance, and an earned sense of pride for taking on such a manly endeavor. Being a part of the army was truly exhilarating.

Most of the South was rural, and its young men were often inspired to volunteer for service by their awe of the army. The showy military uniforms with their brass buttons and tailored designs, the thrilling band music and martial airs, and an awareness that one's friends and neighbors were enlisting to "get in" on such a grand adventure all tended to persuade even the most conservative youths to join up. Enrolling seemed to offer a grand but fleeting chance at personal glory and worldliness.[3]

Beyond all of these emotions, military service made practical sense to Southern men who saw a big difference between the personal accomplishments of actively fighting for states' rights and those of tilling the soil. Also, the opportunity to significantly alter the course of history was being offered for a limited time, and only to certain select individuals—the brave and the physically fit. Here then was a chance to share with friends the experiences of a lifetime. The potential for fun, for a change in life's focus, and for doing something important was immediately beguiling. Then, too, there was strength and comfort in the massive resort to arms, for often the whole community was caught up in the effort.[4]

Although there were dire personal consequences to be considered, these were hidden and private. The prospects of advancement, glory, and enhancing one's special skills seemed paramount, and far outweighed any risks.

All of this made soldiering the opportunity of a lifetime—fascinating to many, and almost a compulsion to some. Everyone that was anyone wanted to be a part of this great experiment, the making of soldiers from innocent youths. These new troops would accomplish major changes in the nation's existence by forcibly obtaining the Old South's independence.

"I don't know what you will have to do," wrote a Virginia mother in May 1861 to her anxious son, then a university student, "for of course you cannot sit idly by when our country expects every one of her sons to be up and doing." The impetus to join the ranks was immediate, because of both the natural inclination of youth and society's strictures. Southern boys by the thousands flocked to the standards in 1861. With unbounded enthusiasm they anticipated a great adventure and a change in their personal lives. At the same time, however, many seemed to realize they were moving toward a great unknown—an arena of physical and psychological confrontation.[5]

In the beginning, the physical demands of the army were perhaps the easiest to deal with. Essentially, the agility of youth and the public's blind faith in the ability of young men to endure a rigorous lifestyle provided an initial advantage. Learning to endure sickness and danger was merely part of life in the rural South. The largest hurdle appeared to be psychological.

At first, fear of combat was a remote factor in coping with army experience. Drastically altered lifestyles, constraints on personal freedom in the form of martial discipline, and acting as a tightly controlled military team rather than on the basis of self-initiative were foremost in a new volunteer's regimen. The effects of these changes on a soldier's psyche were pronounced. Most white Southerners were used to an independent existence and enjoyed vast personal freedoms. Yet, obeying orders without question and enduring illogical or unwise commands were essential to the military system that they had agreed to be a part of. Their leaders were generally as inexperienced as they, and placing their lives in the hands of officers who were just learning the art of war troubled many. Yet, the ultimate question many enlistees pondered was how they would measure up as soldiers when they faced the unfamiliar experience of combat.

Much of the problem stemmed from a lack of well-known role models to follow. The Mexican War, fought in a foreign land, had ended more than thirteen years earlier, and so few had participated in that conflict that its lessons and realities were all but unknown to most of the Southern populace. The American Revolution had occurred in such a bygone era that there were few alive who even existed at that time, much less remembered the war and its devastation. Only in books, which often glorified or misrepresented war's agony, was there a hint of what was to come.

The innocence of the Southern volunteer was pronounced; he most often perceived war as an adventure-filled chance for glory. Since self-control was mandatory, and young soldiers were required to stand up to the full test of manly virtues demanded of any Southern white male, they often regarded the prospect of combat with mixed emotions. Society with its honor-based value system expected individuals to exhibit moral and physical courage. Yet an awareness of mortal danger and the instinct for survival were equally compelling.[6]

The decision to go to war thus involved some of the most profound psychological turmoil these men had yet faced. Like most combatants throughout history, a Civil War soldier had to consider many factors that affected his well-being and chances of survival.

For example, as in contemplating any great unknown, there were both positive and negative outcomes to be considered. In looking ahead, it is usually easier, especially for youths, to focus on the positive. It is more comfortable for them to contemplate the potentially beneficial effects of their choices. Conversely, suffering defies measurement. How does a soldier assess likely personal grief, or feelings of entrapment, or the possible mutilation of his young, healthy body? It is far easier for a youth to think in hopeful terms. Even when the unforeseen occurs, youthful soldiers tend to believe in their own ability to adapt as necessary.

Human nature appears to have remained constant throughout the civilized ages. Cynicism is often a by-product of aging. We learn of worldly realities generally through our own experiences, rather than from those of others.

For the Southern volunteer in 1861 there was no holding back. The invincibility of youth, an admitted lack of experience in worldly ways, and the vision of a brighter tomorrow impacted upon each soldier. If obtaining autonomy at first seemed as simple as declaring independence from the Federal government and acting out the part, then later, when the prospect of physical violence became a certainty, optimism about the future continued to prevail. Trust and inner faith impelled and sustained the Confederate army's effort. Because the physical means of obtaining independence were not as prevalent as the desire, the practical side of the war would become the obvious area of emphasis—particularly in the procurement of sufficient war materiel. Strong willpower and high morale were taken for granted.

It was an inexact perspective. Beneath the surface lay a great vulnerability of the Southern rebellion—its profound but nebulous reliance on hope.

Chapter Seven

NATHANIEL H. R. DAWSON/ELODIE TODD

"Am I Not Fighting for You?"

Am I not fighting for you, am I not your knight and soldier?" With these chivalrous words Captain Nathaniel H. R. Dawson bade farewell to his fiancée of exactly one week and departed on the boat from Selma, Alabama, for service in the great war. Nat Dawson well looked the part of a knightly officer, appearing dapper in his ostrich-plumed campaign hat, neatly tailored uniform with shoulder straps, gauntleted gloves, and polished sword with leather equipments.[1]

"I have your sweet likeness and lock of hair in a locket, [and] if the fate of war decides it, they will be on my person when I fall," he promised his fiancée. If sentimental and patriotic, Nat Dawson was typical of many Southern volunteers seeking to play a major part in the historic events unfolding in the spring of 1861. Yet, Nat was leaving behind a haunting past—a legacy of heartbreak and despair that had emotionally scarred him throughout much of his adult life. Although a prosperous lawyer and well-respected Alabamian, Dawson had been unfortunate in his love affairs. His first bride, Anne Matthews Dawson, had died in 1854, and his second wife, Mary Tarver Dawson, had passed away in 1860, only three years after their marriage. Two small daughters survived from the first marriage, both living with their maternal grandparents during Nat's absence.[2]

Once again, in 1861, the ardor of a blossoming romance had fired Nat's passions with hope and desire. A lilting brown-eyed girl with a coquettish smile had smitten him. Yet Nat, at age thirty-two, was nearly twice as old as the pretty brunette he was courting. The young woman was quite a formidable conquest, being nearly a generation younger than Nat and a person of notoriety.

Known as "Dedee" within the family, sixteen-year-old Elodie Todd had been visiting an older sister in Montgomery when she met Nat Dawson, who was attending the February 1861 convention for organizing the Confederate States of America. Even then, Dedee was a quasi-celebrity in the South thanks to her family's prominence. Indeed, it was through her half sister—Mary Todd Lincoln—that most people knew Elodie Todd.[3]

The Todd family of Lexington, Kentucky, was perhaps a microcosm of the divisions that had torn the nation apart. Elodie's father, Robert Smith Todd, was a descendant of some of Kentucky's most prominent pioneer families. The erstwhile soldier, lawyer, and merchant had sired eight children by his wife Eliza before she died at age thirty-one in 1825, from a blood infection following childbirth. Among the surviving children was six-year-old Mary Todd, who was too young to understand why her mother was suddenly gone forever.[4]

After his wife's death, Robert carried on, courting and winning the hand of a new bride, Elizabeth "Betsey" Humphries, an austere woman in her late twenties who refused to publicly reveal her age. With Betsey, Robert Smith Todd produced a second family of nine children, the eighth of whom was Elodie, born in April 1844.[5]

Raised with pride in her Southern heritage and having just turned seventeen, Elodie was an ardent advocate of her Kentucky homeland during the secession crisis of 1861. Although her father had died of cholera in 1849, Elodie was emotionally tied to the South through her mother Betsey, and supported Kentucky's separation from the Union.[6]

The Todd family, although Southerners by tradition, were divided by the crisis of 1861. Of fourteen living Robert Smith Todd's children, eight supported the South and six the North. Three of Elodie's brothers would serve in the Confederate army, and one of her half brothers became a Rebel surgeon. Of course, Mary's marriage to Abraham Lincoln in 1842, had widened the chasm between divided family loyalties.[7]

Marriage and geography had conspired to split apart the Todd family, and much of Kentucky. Although slavery was legal in Kentucky, the state did not rush to follow other slave states in seceding from the Union. The debate in Kentucky intensified following the April 1861 firing on Fort Sumter. Extremists on both sides sought to control the state's destiny, and throughout the burgeoning crisis the Todd family's conflicting attitudes reflected Kentucky's turmoil.

The Todds seemed ambivalent about slavery, and although the institution was not morally condoned within the family, they benefitted from its practice nonetheless. Robert Smith Todd had often appropriated the slaves of his first mother-in-law, and he personally owned at least ten slaves during the 1830s. The intense national controversy over slavery's justification reflected vast differences in perspectives, but among the Todds these differences were exacerbated by a large generation gap.[8]

Between Elodie and her half sister Mary were twenty-six years; they barely knew one another and were linked only by tenuous family ties. Mary, having often been shamed and humiliated by her stepmother, Betsey, was virtually estranged from her step-family. Yet Mary had always expressed a deep affection for Elodie's older full sister, Emilie, who had been born in 1836. In 1857, Mary wrote to Emilie that she hoped Dedee and the youngest Todd offspring, Kittie, would come for a lengthy visit to the Lincoln home in Springfield, Illinois.[9]

That Elodie reveled in the notoriety of being Mary Todd Lincoln's sister was fully apparent in her correspondence. Not being close to Mary, she relied upon Emilie or her younger sister, Kittie, to write to Mary when warranted. As the wife of the president of the United States—even if Abraham Lincoln was vilified across the South—Mary held a certain prestige and even power that Elodie and her Southern-aligned sisters were mindful of. Indeed, the time was not far distant when Elodie would feel it necessary to have Kittie write to Mary for a special favor.[10]

Accordingly, Elodie's privately expressed disapproval of Mary, and especially of Abraham Lincoln, was qualified. It was nothing personal, only political, she claimed. Therefore, in the name of family, but not conviction, it seemed reasonable to Elodie that certain favors might be granted by her half sister or Mary's husband. Elodie's expectations were simply part of the discreet attempts of a seventeen-year-old to establish herself in society and win a man's love.[11]

Nat Dawson had admitted from the beginning that he was "love-sick." Stationed in late May 1861 at Harper's Ferry as part of the

Virginia-based Army of the Shenandoah, Dawson was most insistent in his affection for Elodie. His letters to her were already pressing for an early marriage. Perhaps Elodie would come to Virginia and live the part of an army wife? When she rejected these overtures, Nat began campaigning for a brief furlough so he could claim Elodie's hand as "her protector." She was reluctant to discard their earlier plan to wait for the war's end, since it was supposed to be only a short war. Then, only a few weeks after Nat's departure, new trouble threatened their romance. Following his engagement, Nat had written to Elodie's mother, Betsey, and formally asked for her daughter's hand. This shocking news sent Betsey, then at home in Lexington, Kentucky, hastening to Selma, Alabama, two days after she received Nat Dawson's letter. Betsey was decidedly against the match. She thought Elodie was too young and vulnerable for marriage to Nat.[12]

Elodie's spirited rejoinder prophesied a war of wills. "I have been looked upon and called the 'old maid' of the family," announced Elodie, "and mother seems to think I was to be depended upon to take care of her when all the rest of her handsomer daughters left her." Instead, Elodie declared, "This is the age of secession, freedom, and [when] rights are asserted. I am claiming mine, and do not doubt but I shall succeed in obtaining them."[13]

Nat Dawson looked askance at his plight. At the beginning of his army adventure there had been excitement and enthusiasm everywhere his company, the Selma, Alabama, "Magnolia Cadets," had traveled. In Atlanta, en route to Virginia, they had been feted and entertained. "At every station we have been cheered and bouquets of flowers and the smiles of fair maids and matrons have bid us Godspeed," he quipped. At Newnan, Georgia, a large group of citizens "called vociferously for myself and others. I made a speech, which . . . was loudly cheered," wrote Nat. Following their arrival in the Shenandoah Valley, and having become a part of the 4th Alabama Infantry, Nat's company remained "in fine spirits." Despite a lack of tents, and "suffering many privations," all difficulties were borne cheerfully by his men, asserted Nat. They were "anxious to reach the scene of danger [Harper's Ferry]," he noted, since "most of the regiment wish for a fight." As for facing danger in combat, "I have your prayers and love for my safety," he reassured Elodie, "and I think I will bear a charmed life through the perils of war."[14]

A few weeks later, war did not seem to promise the same grand adventure that Nat Dawson had earlier envisioned. For the thirty-two-year-old captain, the march north through the Shenandoah Valley to Harper's Ferry had been an eye-opening ordeal. "I wished to share with my company all of their hardships," he had announced. Nat thus had walked the entire way from Strasbourg in heavy rain, wind, and hail. "My feet were so blistered and swollen, and I was so much fatigued, that I got a room at a hotel," he confided. When later quartered with other officers in a large government building, and with a single blanket on the floor serving as his bed, he could barely endure the discomfort. Moreover, his soldiers, once subjected to the daily rigors of military life, had become troublesome. Their routine seemed boring and irksome; reveille at 4 A.M., officers' or company drill from 4:30 A.M. to 7 A.M., general inspection, and three hours of company drill prior to lunch. Then there were three hours of regimental drill in the afternoon, a dress parade, supper, and finally tattoo at 9:30 P.M. Day-to-day existence was difficult enough for officers, but for the privates, soldiering seemed an ignominious misery. As independent-minded Southerners, some men in Nat's company were "too nice to do many of the duties required of them," Nat complained on May 14. "Some demur [even] to carrying their knapsacks." "Yesterday . . . I came out of my tent with a knapsack on, with all of my accouterments, rifle, sword, and pistol, and large overcoat. I am obliged to do many of these things for the sake of [setting] an example."[15]

When one of Elodie's younger brothers talked of enlisting, Nat told her to tell him to enroll as an officer: "The duties [of a private] are very tedious [and] he would not like them. A gentleman must feel the position [of an enlisted soldier] irksome."[16]

To add to these rigors, almost nightly alarms kept everybody on edge and generally sleepless. Rumors of a pending attack by the Yankees just across the Potomac River circulated daily. "The whole camp was roused about one a.m. by the alarm that the enemy were approaching, and most of the troops were under arms all night," Nat wearily wrote on May 19. "These false alarms are unpleasant as they try our nerves unnecessarily."[17]

Unfortunately, the wild rumors, false alarms, and nightly calls to arms continued. Moreover, many men were ill with camp fevers and contagious diseases; on May 30 there were fifty-three men sick in the company. Deaths were so frequent that the entire camp seemed depressed.[18]

Nat's "savage" appearance—from a lack of bathing, sunburned

skin, a bedraggled uniform, and a wildly straggling beard—caused him to warn Elodie, "If you were to see me now you would hardly recognize me. . . . The comforts of home seem to be reactions of a diseased imagination," he admitted. "Oh, for an hour in my cozy library."[19]

Beyond the rude awakening provided by army life, some personal dilemmas remained for Nat to settle. Elodie had written about attending dances and benefit fund-raisers for Nat's former militia company, the Selma Blues, which was captained by a man bent on impressing Elodie. "I am afraid that some military rival may contest my claim to your heart," he sheepishly confessed. Even worse, Elodie's mother was now present at Selma, admittedly having gone there to stall the pending marriage. Betsey Todd loomed as a formidable and menacing matriarch, especially when the object of her ire, Nat, was distant hundreds of miles and unable to respond. Perhaps he would lose Elodie, and—considering the danger lurking across the Potomac River—possibly his life as well.[20]

What had he done? Was his old streak of bad luck still haunting him? Had Nat Dawson made a serious mistake by going off to war? "I am entirely sick of it [soldiering], and wish I could put off all of these troubles and lay myself at your feet [as] your willing and faithful spouse," he wrote to Elodie in mid-June. "I will hope and pray for peace."[21]

Nat knew that his ardent emotions were of no use in tempering the consequences of a civil war that now ensnared thousands of people in both the North and the South. Like the other soldiers, he would just have to wait—and take his chances.

"My Mind Is Prepared for the Worst"

Captain Nat Dawson of the 4th Alabama Infantry had thought long and hard about facing the Yankees on a field of battle. During his nearly three months in the army at Harper's Ferry, Virginia, he had waxed hot and cold on the issue. In May 1861, he wrote that he was suitably armed with a "sword, Adams five-shooter [revolver], and a Sharps rifle . . . taken from John Brown['s raiders]." "We will kill all [of the enemy] we can lay our hands on," he assured Elodie. "I am really indifferent to the dangers of battle. . . . I have a great confidence in the justice of our cause, and have an abiding faith that few of our men will be killed."[22]

Having asserted that he "desire[d] to share all of the hardships and dangers of [his] men," Nat went into town to have his sword sharpened in preparation for battle. The swirl of events elsewhere had convinced him that his unit would soon be caught up in the fighting. Colonel Elmer Ellsworth of the New York Zouaves had been shot and fatally wounded during the Yankee army's occupation of Alexandria, Virginia. Captain Dawson responded pensively, "I now fear that we will have much hard fighting to do. [Yet] we are in the right, and this nerves me for the contest. When I think of my loved Elodie, I am stronger and braver," he wrote reassuringly. This "invasion" of Virginia by the enemy "has stirred my blood," Nat continued, "and I think it will be a pleasure to meet our enemies in mortal combat. We will now have a bloody war, and we intend to make it as destructive as possible."[23]

Throughout June, the increasing frequency of alarms and reports of General Robert Patterson's Yankee army advancing upon Harper's Ferry had everyone on edge. "We are now threatened by the enemy," wrote the anxious Alabama captain. "Ammunition is distributed to the different commands. I cannot go to sleep under such circumstances. . . . When this letter reaches you, my dearest Elodie, the writer . . . may have fallen. If so, remember me as one who loved you more than all the world."[24]

All of these alarms had proved false, however, so by the second week in June Nat Dawson again found "the routine of camp life . . . very irksome and monotonous." Moreover, the regiment being "ignorant of the thoughts of our leaders," he claimed they could "form no idea of our future movements."[25]

Only a few days later, while he was at evening drill, a sudden order came from army headquarters to return to camp and prepare for action. "Our regiment returned at the double quick," wrote the anxious Dawson, "and in a very few moments our knapsacks were packed, and I gave the order to strike tents, which was executed promptly."[26]

According to camp gossip, the enemy had "appeared in front and on our flank, and we were to remove farther out, about a mile, on the range of hills . . . which will be our line of battle." The 4th Alabama's wagons were "hardly loaded when a very hard rain commenced to pour down in torrents," grumbled Captain Dawson. Soon word arrived that the order to move was countermanded—it had been only another false alarm. Captain Dawson's shelterless men were forced to endure the full misery of the raging storm, and, noted an embarrassed Nat, they ultimately had to seek shelter in the vacant tents of a nearby Virginia regiment.[27]

These maddening emotional ups and downs had greatly affected the regiment. Moreover, controversy existed about their colonel, Egbert Jones, who, Nat thought, was "utterly incompetent." Some five hundred members of the 4th Alabama had signed a petition "requesting him to resign." The political overtones of Jones's command were disruptive, complained Dawson, and when Jones refused to resign, Nat said, "I shall have nothing to do with him farther than duty compels."[28]

A few days later, Nat predicted the active warfare that he had long anticipated in a letter to Elodie. He told her, "The columns of Lincoln are coming down on us." General Robert Patterson's Yankee army was at last crossing into Virginia, and the evacuation of Harper's Ferry was imminent. With the prospect of fighting looming, Nat suddenly wasn't so sure how much he was willing to risk. Nervously, he decided to play his trump card. He wrote to Elodie, "You are known widely and favorably as the sister of Mrs. Lincoln. . . . Can't you use your influence, or get your sister Miss Kittie to use hers? I hope her influence with Mr. Lincoln will save me the trouble of being hanged should I fall into his power." Again, he implored in a successive letter, "How singular that I should be engaged to the sister of Mrs. Lincoln. I wish you would write her to that effect, so that in case of being taken prisoner, I will not be too severely dealt with."[29]

Within a few days came confirmation from Elodie that Kittie had indeed written to Mary Todd Lincoln, telling her according to Elodie, "Should you [Nat] fall into the hands of [the enemy, we] hope you will be kindly received, [and] presented with a passport to leave King Abe's Kingdom and returned to me with care." Considering the death of Colonel Ellsworth, however, Elodie was "fearful . . . that the southerners will fare badly if they get within their [Yankee] clutches, and [I] hope you will keep as far as possible from them."[30]

Keeping a distance from the larger Yankee army was just what Confederate general Joe Johnston had attempted to do during the tumultuous month of June 1861. His evacuation of Harper's Ferry on June 14 plunged the Army of the Shenandoah into an endless series of marches, countermarches, and camp relocations.

"General Johnston seems determined to keep us on the alert, and moving all the time," Nat grumbled in a letter to Elodie. "The walking is very fatiguing to me, and if we are to have so much of it I will have to get a discharge." Instead of the "many little niceties, as eggs, butter, and chickens as [were available] at Harper's Ferry," they now dined on a meager fare. Accordingly, Nat was so distressed that he confided, "Our baggage has been reduced to a mere change of clothing, our tents have been now discarded and sent away, our meals are badly cooked, and we are suffering the privations of a soldier's life." Less than a week later Nat wearily confirmed his total displeasure with his new circumstances. "I have dined twice at the hotel here [Winchester, Virginia]," he wrote, "and it has made me completely averse to camp life—as the luxury of a clean cloth and knives and forks has something extremely fascinating to me."[31]

Since he had nearly ten months remaining in his term of service, Nat now hoped "that Congress [would] make peace in some way or shape." Also, to keep up Elodie's spirits, he informed her, "I do not think we will have a long war. The idea of subjugating us must be preposterous. . . . I think a battle will take place at Manassas Junction, or at Norfolk, before we have one. I think we will beat them in either event, and their defeat at one place will defeat their general plan of operations."[32]

Tired of soldiering, fatigued by the many hardships, fed up with the stifling military bureaucracy, and emotionally distraught by not doing much as he saw fit, Captain Nat Dawson began to exhibit increasing doubts. On July 11, as he was writing to Elodie, the order to strike tents and prepare for battle was given, creating another "moment of excitement." Yet Dawson remained unruffled. "I am skeptical upon the subject, as we have so frequently been disappointed," he lamented. Nat thus went about his duties with little enthusiasm or concern. Indeed, as with many previous calls to arms, there was no real basis for this latest alarm, and Nat reluctantly went back to his "tiresome" daily routine.[33]

On July 14 Nat Dawson confided how he was becoming "exceedingly lazy" about his army career. "My spare time is spent in studying tactics, and in reading [news] papers." Only the purchase of natty new uniforms for the company—gray pants with a black stripe, close-fitting gray-flannel jackets with a black collar and wristbands, and gray caps with linen havelocks—seemed to briefly replenish the unit's sagging espirit de corps.[34]

Nat Dawson was now merely biding his time in the army; he complained to Elodie about "how much this horrible war has broken in upon our happiness," and reflected on July 16 that during another general alarm on the 15th he remained indifferent. "I have become now quite used to alarms, and can sleep without regarding them," he wrote reassuringly. Then, almost as an afterthought, he added, "If we ever have a battle, I will telegraph the result to Selma if it can be done [to relieve your anxiety]."[35]

A few days later, on July 18, Nat Dawson was suddenly a changed man. He had recently learned that Elodie's mother, Betsey, was now resigned to her daughter's impending marriage and had withdrawn her objections. "Seeing [as] you are determined and there is no chance of persuading you from it," Betsey Todd had told Elodie, she would acquiesce. "He has filled your head with ideas that I have been all my life trying to keep you from possessing," Betsey warned her love-stricken daughter. Elodie, however, had remained defiant and triumphant. "I am much obliged to you, Captain [Dawson], for suggesting the[se] thoughts," Elodie puffed.[36]

In the midst of the lovers' victory, there suddenly was a fresh cause for concern. Something big was happening in the war. There was no mistaking it. The entire camp at Winchester was preparing to march, and the men had baggage packed and knapsacks in place. Although there was a lot of speculation about whether an advance or retreat was in the offing, Nat seemed to know danger was at hand. "Wherever I go and whatever fate [awaits] me . . . , may God in his mercy protect and guard us both," he implored in a hasty letter to Elodie on July 18. ". . . I am quite well, and hope for the best. So far God has been kind. I have done better than I could have expected. . . . I will . . . endeavor to do my duty as a 'brave Southern soldier,' inspired by the love of a 'heroic maiden.' "[37]

Due to the hurried activity in camp, he had time only for a short note. "I think we will abandon Winchester and go to Manassas Junction," he scribbled. It was sort of a last-minute, random presentiment.[38]

Three days later in Selma, Alabama, there was a sudden flurry of news dispatches. The early telegraph reports indicated a major battle occurring at Manassas Junction in Virginia. Elodie Todd wasn't much concerned at first; there had been false rumors of terrible fighting before. Besides, Nat's last letter was from Winchester, Virginia. Elodie, although a little anxious about the battle news, was calmed by Nat's earlier advice about braving the dangers of war: "You must meet these exigencies bravely as a Spartan bride would send her husband to the [battle]field. And we must trust to Providence for protection and safety. . . . If it be my fate to fall, I know you will mourn me, almost as much as if we were married. . . . But I have great faith in returning to claim your hand."[39]

That very day Elodie had been out with Kittie and a neighbor learning to shoot a pistol, and sprightly wrote to Nat, "I can fire without flinching."[40]

On July 22 Elodie received Nat's ominous letter of the 18th, telling her he suspected they were en route to Manassas Junction. That evening the reports of intense fighting at Manassas Junction were confirmed. Within hours the newspapers were filled with wild rumors and exaggerated accounts of the battle. It was reported that the 4th Alabama was severely engaged and had suffered heavy losses.[41]

For the first time, the possibility of losing her fiancé seemed real to Elodie. Only a few weeks earlier she had naively written to Nat, "I do not fear or think for a moment of anything for the South but victory, but dread what that victory may cost me. . . . You must not be killed!" she pleaded. But she had written those words before the personal implications of mortal combat had sunk in, and the news that thousands had been slaughtered at Manassas. What had happened to her Nat? Perhaps she would never see him again! Was he still alive? Maybe her fiancé was lying helpless and severely wounded on the battlefield, or else bleeding and uncared for in some sweltering hospital tent. Then too, he now might be a helpless captive in the hands of the hated Yankees. The suspense of waiting was unbearable. Elodie had a good cry.[42]

On the morning of the 23d, word finally arrived. Elodie had sent a servant to town "with orders not to return until he brought me news from the battle." Now, he had returned, bringing Elodie a telegram from Virginia, which he somberly placed into her hands. She was nervous and anticipated terrible news. Her hands "trembled so violently" that for several moments she was incapable of opening it. Finally, "with a desperate effort," she tore open the telegram, "my mind prepared [for] the worst."[43]

"I Am Really Indifferent to the Dangers"

In early July 1861, Captain Nat Dawson of the 4th Alabama Infantry had predicted with disappointment that although a great battle would "be fought in front of Washington city, . . . we will hardly share in its dangers or its glories." At the time, Dawson was with Joe Johnston's army at Winchester, Virginia.[44]

A week later, with active campaigning underway to counter Union general Robert Patterson's advance on Harper's Ferry, Nat Dawson was infused with an intense martial ardor. He wrote with excitement to his fiancée about the grand military maneuvers he had just witnessed. During a recent night march, he had marveled at the pageantry and beauty of the surrounding scene. "On our right the moon shed its soft rays upon the column of armed men, while upon our left a magnificent comet, with its long nebulous tail, beckoned us onward." High in the cloudless sky glowed the Southern Cross, and the soldiers enlivened the scene by singing "Dixie." Although he hadn't taken his clothes off for a week, and often slept with his head upon a rock, the privations seemed worthwhile. The spirits of the men were high. "The suspense of [possibly] being in a fight is great," he noted; "[yet] I have learned to look upon it with indifference. We become accustomed to [the] dangers."[45]

Such were his feelings before the march to Manassas Junction.

On July 21, 1861, Nat Dawson finally "saw the elephant."* The battle at Manassas and his own exposure to combat had come as unwelcome surprises. Nat Dawson and the 4th Alabama Infantry, after marching across the Blue Ridge Mountains to Piedmont, had been rushed to Manassas Junction by railroad on July 20. On the morning of the 21st—a hot, sultry day—they, along with their brigade, under Brigadier General Bernard Bee, were ordered to march toward the sound of distant cannon fire that came from the vicinity of the Stone Bridge over Bull Run Creek. Following a sweltering, dust-choked march of nearly seven miles, the exhausted 4th Alabama arrived midmorning near Matthews Hill. Here the main column of Yankees was battling a thin line of Confederates under the command of Colonel Nathan "Shanks" Evans.[46]

At the command "Up, Alabamians!" the 4th Alabama was sum-

---

*This was a common term for one's first exposure in battle.

moned into battle by General Bee. It was a "terrible" experience, noted Nat. "The air resounded with whistling balls and hissing shells" that felled men and cut down "trees as large as my body." The 4th Alabama lay down along the crown of Matthews Hill and began blazing away at the advancing Yankee line a hundred yards distant in a cornfield. Amid the 4th's ranks was "Jim Jeff" (James Jefferson), the slave servant of Doctor Samuel Vaughn, who shouldered a musket and fought alongside his master. Despite seeing several men shot by his side, Nat Dawson moved among his company, encouraging them to be cool and shoot accurately.[47]

For more than an hour and a half the 4th Alabama and several supporting regiments kept the Yankees at bay. Yet the enemy was working their way around the 4th's left flank, and a steady stream of wounded men in gray had stumbled to the rear, seriously reducing the number of Alabamians remaining in the fight.[48]

Suddenly, almost spontaneously, their entire line began giving way, and the men retreated in scattered clusters. Captain Nat Dawson was among the last to leave the line, just behind the chaplain and Colonel Egbert Jones. He was crossing a split rail fence when a cannonball struck the rail just below his foot. Nat was thrown ten feet into the air and landed awkwardly on his left ankle, severely spraining it. Simultaneously, Colonel Jones went down with a rifle ball through both thighs, and their lieutenant colonel was later found severely wounded.[49]

Dazed, Nat looked around; he seemed uninjured except for his ankle. Everywhere he saw chaos; the regiment was fleeing in disorder, and he scrambled to his feet and hobbled off into the smoke.

"The Yankees were following us," noted Nat with a shudder, and he soon came upon a milling, bewildered portion of his regiment that their major was attempting to rally. Nat stumbled over to a cluster of men from his company, the Magnolia Cadets, and called upon them to stand by their flag. Amid the terrifying confusion someone shouted that the Yankees were on both flanks—just as a "murderous fire of musketry and artillery" swept through the 4th's ranks. The entire segment then bolted, retiring "in much confusion," according to Nat. "The disorder was indescribable," he gasped. "[We] had to run for our lives." The regiment's major went down in front of Nat, but he continued on, "being anxious to get out of range of the enemy's fire."[50]

When a wounded soldier in his company called out to him for

help, Dawson shouted that he "was unable to do so, from fatigue and lameness." Instead, he would get another soldier to carry the man away, which he later did.[51]

Dawson then ambled onward to the rear amid cries from passing Alabamians that their regiment was "cut to pieces." Locating a make-shift field hospital near a house, Nat Dawson, still in shock, roamed about the yard, occasionally helping with the wounded. Soon, how-ever, he was so prostrated by the sweltering heat that he "got into the shade and remained there until the firing ceased [on the battle-field]."[52]

Nat Dawson had survived, but he was an awed and sickened soldier. His regiment had been scattered and was in disarray, having lost all of their field officers. He grimaced when he saw the mortally wounded General Bernard Bee being carried from the field. Later he learned that out of the 50 men engaged in his company, 23 were casualties. In fact, the 4th Alabama had suffered one of the largest losses of the battle with 210 killed or wounded in a regiment of 700 officers and men.[53]

At about 5 P.M. he started for Manassas Junction with another of-ficer separated from the 4th Alabama. It seemed like a journey through hell. "The scenes were awful," he said. Dead Yankees were scattered everywhere, including about a hundred New York Zouaves with their baggy blue pants and red shirts. "God seems especially to have marked them for vengeance," he grimly noted, but he added, "They are fierce looking fellows [who] fought well." In one spot, "where [General] Sherman's battery was taken," he found "near one hundred dead Yankees," and thirty-seven dead horses." Already the foul smell of death and the gruesome sight of bloated bodies made crossing the battlefield almost unbearable.[54]

Nat Dawson staggered onward, thinking only of his beloved Elodie. From Beauregard's headquarters at Manassas Junction that night he sent the telegram that Elodie received on the 23d, telling her that he was alive and unhurt. "[My safety] I attribute much to your prayers," he wrote in a letter to her that night. Overshadowing the "glorious victory" won that day was his desire to return to Elodie. "I almost regret that I was not wounded, that I might have an excuse for going home," he lamented.[55]

During the following few days, when he had a chance to wander over the Manassas battlefield, Nat Dawson was more convinced than ever that he made a "miraculous escape. . . . It seems a miracle that

I was not killed as several of my men were shot down at my side," he marveled. "I attribute all to the providence of God."[56]

Amid the effluvia of rancid, decaying flesh, and the bloody, torn, and distorted bodies, Nat decided he had seen enough of war's horrors. "The dead presented an awful appearance—and I thought perchance that the fortunes of war might place me in a similar position," he shuddered. When reports that he had been killed surfaced from visitors arriving from Alabama, Nat was so deeply distressed that he sent a telegram to a Selma reporter and explained that he was safe.[57]

Thereafter, he could only step back and consider the whole experience with amazement. "I feel like one who has accomplished a great work and was resting from his labors," he wrote. "We are encamped on the battlefield, surrounded by all the evidences of the sanguinary contest; broken gun carriages, dead men, dead horses, and the graves of the dead. Every home in the neighborhood is a hospital for the wounded of the army." Making matters worse, their regiment remained in a "state of disorganization," reported Nat, who was now acting commander after the loss of the 4th Alabama's field officers.[58]

"I feel much depressed since our battle last Sunday," he confessed to Elodie a week later, "and would give anything for peace and home." Citing that he had "never before been placed in a situation where I had no volition," Nat all but condemned his own decision to join the army. "I am a soldier until next May," he acknowledged, and he would do his duty until then. The "sad task" of writing letters to the families of the dead and wounded in his company had "cast a deep gloom" over him, but he did feel thankful and "appreciate the mercy of God" in sparing him "from the great dangers I have escaped."[59]

To add to the disappointments of his first significant battle, Nat learned from Northern newspapers that the Yankees "will likely prepare another grand army and invade us again in September or October." Thereafter, the discussions around camp centered on a continuance of this increasingly bloody struggle. As Nat noted, the Confederates were suddenly stripped of their earlier belief that a single major victory would win the South's independence. "The opinion prevails that the defeat of Mr. Lincoln's army will have no effect in making peace, but will only stimulate [them] to renewed exertions," he confided. Nat Dawson could only hope that his army's victory at

Manassas might at least have the effect of disheartening the Yankees and opening their eyes to the utter impossibility of subjugating us . . . We may [now] pass the remainder of the season without another great battle" he cautiously added.[60]

His attitude seemed strange to Elodie, who although "truly thankful you escaped so well while others were falling about you," was electrified by the exciting news on everybody's lips—the great victory at Manassas. Nat's seventeen-year-old fiancée was so enthralled by "the glory and exaltation of the moment" that she wondered, "How can men stay at home at such a time? I could never travel fast enough to get to the scene of battle . . . I am so proud of you," she gushed, "and think you are such a great man."[61]

Elodie Todd's exuberance reflected her ardent patriotism and her own quest for success. "We must conquer no matter what it costs, and we must have brave men in the field to do it," she believed. "And one [civilian] does not suffer much more than another, for we all have to make sacrifices, though I am selfish and candid enough to say I would much prefer others to do it than myself."[62]

Nat Dawson was not exactly gratified by Elodie's joy over what for him had been a devastating and sobering experience. "It is honor enough to have been in the battle and to have done our duty," he somberly proclaimed. As for being knocked down by the cannonball that struck the fence he was crossing, it wasn't the "funny sight" that his fiancée had surmised. "I assure you if you had been as badly lamed . . . you would think it a serious matter," he protested. Moreover, the experience of battle was far different than the contemplation of it. "It has had a most demoralizing effect upon the soldiers and seems to have made them careless and negligent," he confided. "It has certainly made me feel indolent and lazy."[63]

Although he speculated that perhaps this malaise was merely "one of the effects of a victory," Nat Dawson perceived a hidden truth about combat—it was more of a mechanical, impersonal ordeal than a chance to win individual glory. Fighting the enemy from a static line of battle was not at all like closing with an opponent for the kind of dramatic hand-to-hand grapple that many soldiers had anticipated. The fearsome-looking bowie knives that many of the men had carried into the fight had proved useless. Also, Nat wore a revolver during the battle that he surmised that "will kill at 200 yards." Yet "[I] did not use it," he admitted. "An officer has really no opportunity to use [side] arms as the Yankees never will allow us to close with them.

They are afraid of the cold steel, and can't stand the bayonet," he asserted. "They ran whenever they were charged."[64]

In the final analysis, Nat Dawson found battle to be a depressing test of body and soul, unlike the grandiose and fanciful accounts of warfare portrayed in dime novels. "How deplorable is this fratricidal war," reflected Nat, who discovered when visiting a hospital "two brothers [who] had met on the battlefield, on opposite sides, and were now . . . both wounded." As such, the emotions one felt in combat were hard to convey to anyone who hadn't experienced them himself.[65]

After Manassas, the 4th Alabama's chaplain, who had been exposed in the fighting, delivered a prayer over their fallen comrades. Nat had joined in the "large assembly of bronzed and bearded soldiers . . . where almost every eye and cheek was moist with big tears. . . . It is singular how much attached we become when thrown together as we are in military life, without knowing it," he remarked. Nat's emotions had been rubbed raw, and he sadly informed Elodie:

When I stood alone at the grave of our four killed men [of the Magnolia Cadets] I cannot express the feelings of my heart. It was akin to the feelings when I have stood at night and knelt at the tomb of one in whose existence my life had been wrapped [a former wife]. I prayed for the presence of the dead, and desired to sink into the same grave. But hope beckons [us] onward, and will induce us to find happiness where we had experienced sorrow and gloom. I have been miserable. I am now happy; [feeling] miserable only in being separated from you.[66]

Beyond the unsettling experience of battle, Nat and his men were soon facing additional hardships and despair. The 4th Alabama was once more without tents or proper equipment. Many soldiers were getting sick, and the men were constantly hungry. "We are not furnished with rations . . . We had no supper nor breakfast this morning. This is quite alarming to one who has a good appetite," complained Nat on July 30.[67]

In addition to his mounting burdens, Nat learned in late August of a rumor circulating around Selma, Alabama, that he had run away in fear on the battlefield.

Elodie was shocked and defiant, and Nat was outraged. While admitting that his "regiment was guilty of a fault common to many other divisions of the army on that day [scattering in confusion after being overwhelmed by the enemy]," he nevertheless huffed, "[We] cannot alone be blamed." Depicting his personal actions on the battlefield in a long letter to Elodie, he lamented:

Why I have been made a victim I cannot understand. If I could find out the author of these reports, I will hold him to a strict account. . . . I am much annoyed. I will take steps to correct the reports. I fear many opportunities will be afforded me to vindicate my courage on the battlefield, and I am brave enough to admit that I am not over anxious to get into battle [again], for I know and appreciate the dangers. [Yet] I would do nothing to forfeit your love, . . . [and] am not willing that your name should be associated with one that was disgraced. . . . I will prefer to die on the battlefield than to live with a tarnished name. I am conscious of having done my duty.

In another letter Nat asserted, "I hope we will have a place in the next battle that we may redeem whatever blame may attach to us for . . . scattering [at Manassas]."[68]

The personal toll of battle and of its aftermath was great, even in a victory such as Manassas. By late August Nat Dawson was ill both mentally and physically, and he went to a Charlottesville hotel to recover. He suffered from chills and fever, and continued to write to Elodie with distressing news from the regiment. Colonel Jones was certain to die, and throughout Charlottesville the horribly wounded lay in misery "without arms and legs, others slowly wasting away," he reported. Dawson had to deal intimately with several "sad" cases, including that of Billy Harrison, who came to him after having lost a limb in the late battle. Nat wrote that Billy was "unwilling to return home"; "[He] wants revenge upon our enemies. Poor fellow, he feels sorely the loss of his arm, [but] wants to join Montgomery's artillery."[69]

The desperateness of these post-battle circumstances pushed Nat to vow to Elodie, "I will [when they were married] owe higher duties to you than to my country. I am not a Roman to give [up] my wife for my country, though I am willing to give my own [life], and all I have, except you."[70]

These agonizing letters from Nat depressed Elodie. First digesting news of the battle and then coping with the emotional aftermath were extremely taxing. Elodie soon confessed a lingering weakness. "I am trying to bear up cheerfully, but sometimes I make a great failure," she admitted. Since Nat continued to convey his expectations of a long war—"I do not think we will have a speedy peace," he wearily predicted shortly after Manassas—Elodie began to evaluate the cause and her commitment to it."[71]

"I have never for a moment doubted that anything but success would attend us," Elodie wrote in somber assessment. "But I have thought of the many who ... must die to purchase it. ... We who are left will find in freedom poor and sad enjoyment when those that are dear to us must die for it."[72]

Also, Nat's spirits were obviously sagging. "I almost wish I had never seen a camp," he wrote a month after Manassas. "It is very certain that I will never remain in one longer than my duty requires, and at the end of my enlistment, I mean to keep my promise to you [to go home]. . . ."[73]

Elodie was seriously burdened by stress. "This dreadful war" was ruining everything; "I think myself the most unfortunate creature on Earth," she fretted. Worried about Nat's attitude and commitment, she realized that if he failed to regain his sense of duty, it would mean a personal and social disaster to them both.[74]

To inspire him to perform greater deeds and endure the burden of another ten months' service, she urged him:

You must not get discouraged. Next May will roll around, and then you will return so much better pleased that for a year you have been doing your duty fighting like a brave soldier for his country— and I will be better pleased too. I could not love you if you had stayed at home content to remain inactive at such a moment. . . . All I ask is that you continue to bear your hardships and trials as bravely and cheerfully as you have done so far. . . . I am confident before the year is out you will distinguish yourself by your bravery.[75]

As if these strictures weren't sufficient, Elodie's personal enticements were equally calculating: "I shall not object to your petting me 'when you have the right' as I like it, and when one is as affectionate in their disposition as myself, they must have affection in return. To be loved is as essential to my life and happiness as the air I breathe."[76]

Nat Dawson got the message. A "love sick swain," he understood the implications of her pointed comments. "I am in the performance of a duty to my country, which, when performed, will greatly add to my own satisfaction,'' he reassured her. ''The chances of my safe return are greatly in my favor. One fourth of the term has passed without [my injury in] a battle, and in a battle . . . a very large majority escape uninjured. To have one-tenth of an army killed and wounded would be a very large loss. More men usually die from sickness than from battle, and I will always endeavor to take care of myself for your sake.''[77]

If a well-intentioned prophecy, it seemed more like a grope at reason and hope in the face of the vicious and bloody warfare only then beginning.

Both Nat Dawson and Elodie Todd were already victims, but the ultimate price they would pay was still unclear.

Chapter Eight

"DON'T MIND MY TEARS,
THEY DON'T MEAN ANYTHING"

[I] would feel it the dearest privilege to be by your side to share every privation and hardship. Without a murmur would I gladly undergo anything to see you once more. . . . The days and hours we have spent together are the brightest spots on the desert waste of memory, and if you are only spared to come back . . . no other joy on earth can exceed it." So pined the apprehensive wife of a Georgia surgeon who had been gone from home for only three weeks in 1861. Another Confederate woman wrote in her diary about a Virginia unit's send-off in June 1861. "I saw some plain country people there telling their sons and husbands goodbye. I did not hear the first word of repining or grief, only encouragement to do their best and be of good service. One woman, after taking leave of her husband, said to two youths. . . . 'Don't mind my tears, boys, they don't mean anything.' "[1]

Though they met the existing conflict with a spirited outpouring of support for their men, Southern women faced the beginning of their own trauma—the absence of husbands, fathers, brothers, and lovers, all absorbed into the civil war. Although they expected the men to be gone only for a short while, the excitement that prevailed in April 1861 quickly faded. Describing women's naïveté at the time, a Georgia girl wrote, "We had an idea that when our soldiers got upon the ground and showed, unmistakably, that they were really ready and willing to fight . . . by some sort of hocus-pocus, we didn't know what, the whole trouble would be declared at an end." Their optimism, like their first perceptions of the conflict, soon changed.[2]

Many Southern women ardently advocated secession and states' rights, but they were quickly confronted with the reality of their convictions—war brought hardship. It was a man's war in a man's world. With the men off fighting, there were few left behind to attend to the daily rigors of family life and farming except women, children, perhaps a few slaves, and the aged and infirm.

Although an introspective matron might aver that "brutal men with unlimited power are the same all over the world," the secession issue had gone beyond questions of masculinity, cultural and economic self-interest, or political disagreement. America was caught up in what would be a prolonged and self-destructive conflict, and Southern women would bear enormous suffering as a result.[3]

"Thank God for my countrywomen," announced a burdened Mary Chesnut in 1861. They had endured generations of patriarchy in Old South society. Southern culture was steeped in male privileges, both subtle and overtly sexist. Now Southern women were being asked to risk their well-being, their security, and the lives of their partners for the sake of a war that would maintain the status quo of male dominance in the South. While the demands of such a war were psychologically devastating to women, the tradition of sexual discrimination in the South left them with little alternative than to acquiesce.[4]

Even if unseemly for a lady, it was at least gratifying for a woman to vent her emotions and express her beliefs, and Mary Chesnut was adept at both. In her diary she spewed venom over the fate she shared with other Southern wives. "My disgust sometimes is boiling over," she ranted. "My country-women are as pure as angels, though surrounded by another race [men] who are the social evil!"[5]

Among the most blatant of male sins were the long-standing sexual privileges that men enjoyed within some circles of upper-crust Southern society. "So it is—flocks and herds and slaves—and wife does not suffice [to satiate male egos]," wrote Mary, perhaps in reference to her wealthy father-in-law. "Rachel must be added, if not married. And all the time they seem to think themselves as patterns—models of husbands and fathers."*[6]

---

*Mary Chesnut believed that her father-in-law, Colonel James Chesnut, had sired children by a slave she calls "Rachel." See Genesis 29–30: Jacob, dissatisfied with

Male dominance and female subordination, were tacit facts of life in the Old South. When put into the context of a puritanical code of conduct imposed on women, coupled with the male initiatives of power, life's unfairness, and random cruelties, it was a burden beyond the ordinary. This was the fate women were expected to endure, supposedly without doing anything untoward. In disgust, Mary Chesnut wrote:

So we whimper and whine, do we? . . . Always we speak in a deprecating voice, do we? And sigh gently at the end of every sentence—why? Plain enough. Does a man ever speak to his wife and children except to find fault? Does a woman ever address any remark to her husband that does not begin with an excuse? When a man does wrong, does not his wife have to excuse herself if he finds out she knows it? Now, if a man drinks too much and his wife shows that she sees it, what a storm she brings about her ears. She is disrespectful, unwifelike . . . So unwomanly—so unlike his mother. So different from the women of his family, the women he was accustomed to at home. Do you wonder that we are afraid to raise our voices above a mendicant's moan? And yet, they say our voices are the softest, sweetest in the world. No wonder. The base submission of our tone must be music in our masters' ears.[7]

The Southern culture's emphasis on total masculinity and its complement, total femininity, was a major basis of female submission. Psychologically, women were raised as inferiors, constantly being reminded of their dependence on fathers and husbands, who were their providers. In fact, the practical lot of a female in Southern life was restricted to marriage. Only through matrimony, the basis of security for any lady, was there any prospect of Southern society's approbation. There was little alternative. In contrast to the North, where textile mills and other manufacturing tasks were open to women, business opportunities in "Dixie" were nil; a woman's duty was to provide comfort rather than income. Thus, women were expected to exhibit restraint, servility, and even contentment in the face of male expressions of passion and honor. Moreover, the physical and mental mistreatment of women was widespread and usually exacerbated by

---

his wife, Leah, also marries her sister, Rachel, and sires children by both, then subsequently by their handmaidens.

masculine attempts to "prove their manhood," often through the abuse of alcohol. Common law permitted a man to flail his wife with a stick less than a thumb's width; hence the expression "rule of thumb." Wife beating was but one form of intimidation that was far too prevalent in the Old South.[8]

"There is no slave like a wife," declared Mary Chesnut. "All married women, all children and girls who live in their fathers' houses are slaves," and it was no wonder that "women of the planters' wives caste . . . [often] took to patent medicine and hypochondria."[9]

Though perhaps Chesnut exaggerated, she was venting her extreme ire over the dominant bluster of men and the general subordination of women in most of the decision-making processes of Old South society. Politically, the treatment of women as inferiors was rooted in the tradition of a woman's subordinate role. As a part of the family unit, her primary task was the rearing of children and the establishment of a comfortable domicile. Male decision making about life's fundamentals, as well as a man's tacit privileges and female submission to a man's will, were as much a part of the Old South as the avowed placing of a woman on the highest pedestal of admiration. Such glib flattery did not alter the fact that women were expected to be both subservient and complaisant. Strength of body was only one manifestation of male superiority; men were generally more educated, decisive, action oriented, and financially sophisticated, and they were the keepers of a proud tradition of "defending the weaker sex."[10]

Yet, in 1861, many women of the South were suddenly asked to administrate or accomplish practical, male-oriented economic tasks. With the mass exodus of men into the army, their women were thrust into the front line of the family's battle for survival. As providers of the family's daily well-being and maintenance, women were now key decision makers in a comprehensive sense. The result, beyond an increase in womens' burdens, was a growing emancipation from the psychological opression of a male-dictated lifestyle. By being freed from only the usual household tasks, many women were able to realize a self-confidence and self-sufficiency that altered society's perception of their aptitudes and capabilities.

Even while contributing as a crucial part of an increasingly demanding war effort, women began taking measure of their altered status. Not only were females relied upon for rearing, teaching, and all the other mundane familial tasks, but their support of the war effort resulted in the production of thousands of homemade or community-manufactured supplies. Because the South lacked a large manufacturing base, the Confederate army depended on women to supply a variety of war materiel, from flags to clothing. Women all over the South were busy knitting socks for the soldiers, providing emotional support through the ladies' aid societies, and nursing the sick and wounded.

The importance of women to the war effort carried over into their domestic lives as well. While acting as the heads of household in their husbands' absence, most wives daily confronted many of life's most difficult and demanding situations. Women were required to make financial, domestic, and other kinds of practical decisions and for the first time enjoyed positions of authority in Southern society. There followed a very noticeable rise in public awareness of women's ability to go beyond society's traditional female roles.

Yet a fundamental, if unarticulated, question remained. Once the war was over, would the women of the South willingly return to the status quo ante, or might they claim greater power in society as a whole?

Inherently, there was an age-old fallacy rife in the Old South patriarchal suppression of women. In fact, it was salient to mankind, a common ground with most civilizations throughout the ages. Equity is a matter of imprecise endeavor; those most worthy are not always the most recognized or rewarded. Not only in the Old South were the burdens of women extraordinary, but in a real sense they have been so throughout history. Only in the late twentieth century has society come to see the true relevance of this disparity.

Chapter Nine

SARAH MORGAN

"Wonderfully Changed in My Sentiments"

Sarah Morgan, a petite and demure twenty-year-old Baton Rouge, Louisiana, belle, had recorded in her diary that "the commencement of [1861] promised much pleasure for the rest of the year." The Louisiana militia officers who had taken possession of the United States Arsenal were "agreeable addition[s]" to the fun-filled parties, and everything was bustle and newsworthy, including the interesting strangers who visited the town. "Our parties, rides, and walks grew gayer and more frequent," merrily wrote Sarah. Life was exciting and teeming with eager anticipation of even-greater adventures.[1]

"We danced that night and never thought of bloodshed," Sarah reflected after the war era had begun in Louisiana with the seizure of the Federal arsenal. "We did not think for a moment that trouble would grow out of it." Yet in May 1862, Baton Rouge was visited by Union warships, and the frowning, black-mouthed cannon from Flag Officer David G. Farragut's vessels menaced the city as the Yankees came ashore. "Oh if I was only a man!" seethed Sarah. "Then I could don the breeches, and slay them with a will! If some few Southern women were in the ranks, they could set the men an example they would not blush to follow. Pshaw! there are no women here! We are all men!"[2]

Word had come of Yankee general Benjamin F. ("the Beast") Butler's iron-fisted suppression of the display of signs and flags of the Confederacy in occupied New Orleans. Sarah, in defiance, thus donned a small homemade Confederate flag. With the "bonnie blue flag" pinned to her shoulder and conspicuously draped over her dress, Sarah walked downtown, "creating great excitement among the women and children." Concealed in the folds of her dress was a pistol and a sharp knife. "The man who says take it off will have to pull it off for himself; the man who does attempt it—well! a pistol in my pocket will fill the gap. I am capable too." One older black man spied the colors and loudly exclaimed, "My, young misses has got her flag a flying anyhow!"[3]

Later, in full view of fifteen or twenty Federal officers standing on the terrace of Baton Rouge's State House, Sarah suddenly felt "humiliated [and] conspicuous." A curious crowd had gathered to stare at the Yankees "like wild beasts." But Sarah "felt a painful conviction" that she was "unnecessarily attracting attention by an unladylike display of defiance." "But what was I to do?" lamented Sarah. ". . . Strike my colors in the face of an enemy? Never!" She stalked off from the crowd while chafing at her "folly." "[I] hated myself for being there, and everyone for seeing me! I hope it will be a lesson to me always to remember a lady can gain nothing by such displays."[4]

Once at home, Sarah reflected upon her attitude and the unsettling experience. "I was not ashamed of the flag of my country—I proved that by never attempting to remove it despite my mortification—but I was ashamed of my position," wrote the repentant Sarah. The Yankees were "gentlemen" of a "fine, noble looking motion . . . which one cannot help but admire." "They set us an example worthy of our imitation," she continued. "They come as victors, without either pretensions to superiority, or the insolence of conquerors; they walk quietly their way, offering no annoyance to the citizens, though they themselves are stared at most unmercifully. . . . I admire their conduct."[5]

The following day Sarah noticed about a dozen Yankee officers in church. "They answered with us. . . . drew out their prayerbooks, found the places, knelt and stood at the right time, so I was satisfied they were brought up in that religion."[6]

"With a conviction that I had allowed myself to be influenced by bigoted, narrow minded people in believing [the Yankees] to be unworthy of respect or regard, I came home wonderfully changed in all my newly acquired sentiments, [and] resolved never more to wound their feelings; [they] who were so careful of ours, by such unnecessary display." Sarah hung her flag on the parlor mantle, there "to wave . . . in the shades of private life—but to make a show, make me conspicuous and ill at ease, as I was yesterday, never again!"[7]

Only a few weeks later, Sarah Morgan once again had to cope with the unexpected. On the morning of May 28, the heretofore-silent guns of Farragut's warships were unleashed against the city of Baton Rouge. Guerrillas on horseback within the town had fired at a boat coming ashore from the U.S.S. *Hartford,* wounding several men. Quickly the ships' cannon began to roar. Sarah and her family were in shock. The family had been preparing for a trip to Greenwell, seventeen miles toward the Louisiana interior, but then the Yankee shells began crashing through houses and exploding in the streets. With her mother screaming in fright, Sarah and her sisters clutched the baby and hastened with the family through the back streets to reach the dusty road to Greenwell. The corkscrew, piercing whine of heavy Parrott-rifle shells arced through the air, and Sarah later remembered "women running by . . . crying and moaning" amid all the chaos. "But I could not join in," she numbly said.[8]

With no food and scant clothes and belongings, they had abandoned their stylish Baton Rouge home to wander like fugitives in the wilderness. "We had saved nothing," Sarah moaned. They had only the dresses on their bodies and little else. So unprepared were the Morgan girls that Sarah determined to return to Baton Rouge several days later, along with her brother-in-law, who had been absent at the time of the shelling. They found the abandoned Morgan home ransacked—"armoires spread open, with clothes tumbled in every direction, inside and out, ribbons, laces on floors, chairs overturned, my desk wide open. . . ."[9]

Even greater despair soon followed in the wake of their forced exodus. The refugees hadn't been able to cope with the want of food and nightmarish living conditions in the interior. "I could not quite reconcile myself to the idea of sleeping in a room with seventeen people, nine of whom were Negroes (. . . . a few who are not endurable in the open air, even)," complained Sarah. "Our condition is perfectly desperate." The choice they faced seemed starvation at Greenwell or yellow fever and enemy bullets at Baton Rouge. "Let us stay and die [at Baton Rouge]," implored Sarah. "We can only die

once; [but] we can suffer a thousand deaths with suspense and uncertainty . . . [at Greenwell]."[10]

Indeed, within weeks the destitute Morgan family was so miserable
that they chanced returning to Baton Rouge, to live under Yankee
rule.

War's harsh reality was now omnipresent; there was no false sense
of security. Having "replaced piles of books, crockery, [and] china"
in their damaged home, Sarah Morgan discovered that she "could
empty a dirty hearth, dust, move heavy weights, make myself generally
useful and dirty, and all this thanks to the Yankees."[11]

Sarah raged in her journal that the Yankees had managed to kill
one woman and wound three when they shelled the crowded streets
on the 28th. More than twenty houses had been riddled with shells.
Two little children had been drowned during the flight, old women
had to arise from their sickbeds and were compelled to flee, and a
baby had been born in the woods. "Hurrah for the illustrious Farragut, the Woman Killer!!!" Sarah protested. "What will happen
next?"[12]

Sarah's once-liberal perspective had been duly influenced by the
siege. She no longer considered these Yankees an honorable enemy.
"It is glorious to shell a town full of women," wrote an indignant
Sarah, and "they do not belong to the retail business, these 'Women
Exterminators.' "[13]

Moreover, when her agony was compounded by new occupation-
imposed restrictions—the confiscation of private vehicles, the need for
official permission to leave town, and the prohibition against moving
furniture and possessions—it was a mandate for hatred. "Their reason for keeping people in town is that they hope they will not be
attacked so long as our own friends remain," ranted Sarah. Virtually
being held hostage was thus an outrage. "They acknowledge we are
not brute enough to kill women and children, as they did not hesitate
to do," she sneered. As for the need to get official permission to
move about—it was tantamount to slavery. "I saw the 'pass,' [it is]
just as we give our Negroes, signed by a Wisconsin colonel. Think of
being obliged to ask permission from some low ploughman to go in
and out of our own homes!"[14]

Sarah Morgan had experienced a mere sampling of the inequity
and insanity of war; and it was only the beginning. "I get nervous
and unhappy in thinking of the sad condition of the country and of

the misery all prophesy has in store for us," she somberly reflected. Notwithstanding these difficulties, with true Southern spirit Sarah seemed confident of coping with the many unforeseen hardships. "Just before I reach the lowest ebb, I seize my pen, dash off half a dozen lines, sing 'Better days are coming,' and presto! Richard [the king in Shakespeare] is himself again!" she penned in her journal.[15]

If the emotional reaction to the roller-coaster experience of war was intense, hope helped make the enormous personal trauma bearable. By looking to the future rather than dwelling on past misfortune, Sarah focused on what she hoped would happen. "The best is yet to come" became a familiar adage. Based on the prevailing belief that the war's resolution would be favorable to the South, there were honor and pride in enduring interim misfortunes.

Yet, as in Southern society in general, Sarah Morgan's attempt to cope with the new realities involved a sense of growing urgency. The oppressive breath of war was now immediate across much of the South, for the conflict had already progressed beyond ideological and emotional boundaries. War was a matter of harsh practical reality, and the consequences were physical. Virtually everyone's life seemed to be affected negatively, and many victims were in extremis. Moreover, the war's lengthening tenure significantly increased the stakes.

Like Sarah, much of the South had overlooked many of the conflict's repercussions in the beginning. The mounting investment in blood, sweat, and tears required a final, decisive resolution of the great question of Southern independence. And the pervasive pain in the South was just one symptom of the entire nation's deepening crisis. Already there were those among the war's many victims who plaintively asked, Was the cure worth the cost?

But there was no turning back now. The Confederacy's commitment only deepened as Southern society trudged farther ahead into the morass of war. The Civil War was beyond the control of individual citizens; it was a larger-than-life reality. That many would fail to survive was now evident as the ordeal continued. Yet what could any one person do? Once committed, be it man, woman, or nation, to retreat down the path of the past was unacceptable, no matter how imposing the task ahead.

Perhaps the greatest tragedy of these circumstances lay in the lack of initial awareness by the Southern populace of where the war might lead. Moreover, as circumstances became more complicated, there was increasing uncertainty about how to resolve the issues.

What had seemed minor errors of public expectation assumed the stature of crucial oversights as the war continued. Each new development that furthered the commitment to war obscured the optimistic view of an impotent enemy without will. Instead of a series of favorable events and developments, there loomed only the North's greater resistance to Southern independence. Southerners now had uneasy tolerance for the progression of minor to major difficulties that they encountered on a day-to-day basis. What remained over the horizon was a yet-larger dilemma. If the hardships were bearable in the beginning, as the war progressed and its burdens intensified, would they become the potential basis for a societal counter-revolution?

Sarah Morgan, like many others, knew the grim visage of war and rued the day of her naïveté. As an individual, she had become a bit player in an unfolding tragedy, while reaping the bitter fruits of an out-of-control and unsavory civil war.

"I am tired of life. I am weary of everything. I wish I could find some 'lodge in [the] vast wilderness' where I . . . would never hear of war, or rumors of war . . . ," wrote Sarah in the bitter aftermath of the enemy's lengthy occupation of Baton Rouge. She knew that her wish was unrealistic. "What paradise that would be, if such a place is to be found on earth! I am afraid it is not."[16]

The extent of her distress would later become fully evident in the price paid by her own family. Sarah Morgan was just one suffering but enduring Southern girl whose fate as a victim and/or heroine was as yet undetermined.

"We Have Lost All Things, Honor Included"

"Honestly, I believe the women of the South are as brave as the men who are fighting . . . ," wrote Sarah Morgan, once again a refugee in the sweltering summer of 1862. When an older woman friend attempted to return to her house and retrieve some prized belongings in the wake of the Battle of Baton Rouge in August 1862, she was confronted by an irate Yankee colonel. He "put a pistol to her head, called her an old she devil, and told her he would blow her brains out if she moved a step," reported Sarah with indignation. "None but [you] damned women had put the men up to fighting, and [you] were the ones who were to blame for [this] fuss," ranted the colonel.[17]

Such women, who persevered in the face of death, deserved to be saints, thought Sarah Morgan. Even Margaret, a Morgan family slave, had acted with bravery to save a cherished painting of Sarah's father when the house was being ransacked by Federal troops prior to their brief evacuation of Baton Rouge later that August. "One jumped on the sofa to cut the picture down when Margaret cried, 'For God's sake, gentlemen, let it be! I'll help you to anything [else] here. He's dead, and the young ladies would rather see the house burn than lose it!' " Angrily, the soldier jumped to the floor, grabbed his revolver, and pointed it at the black woman's face. "I'll blow your damned brains out," he uttered with a loud epithet. Fortunately, another soldier pushed the pistol away, "and the picture was abandoned for finer sport, wrote Sarah."[18]

This vivid scene reflected what Southerners had been taught since childhood—that one must always strive to overcome fear and shame. To a Southern citizen, bravery was the essence of character, for honor was exalted by the highest traditional standards. Yet, in the harsh light of a difficult war, it was increasingly apparent that not all could conform to this demanding code of conduct. The sight of many men from Baton Rouge cowering in the city's asylum at the time of a rumored attack on the town by Confederate forces caused Sarah to regard them "with extreme disgust." "How I longed to give them my hoops, corsets, and pretty blue organdic in exchange for their boots and breeches!" she protested. "All who could go with any propriety, and all who were worthy of fighting among those who believed in the South, are off at the seat of war." There were those in the "Home Guard" and those of military age who "for private reasons" had managed to avoid the dangers of the active army, lamented Sarah. These able-bodied malingerers were often termed "druthers"—because they'd-ruther stay at home, sneered another socialite. Scoffed at by Sarah Morgan as so much "trash," such men, she believed, deserved all the ostracism they received. Indeed, it defied her sense of Southern honor to treat these individuals with civility and respect. "Let us step over them," she harshly commented in her diary.[19]

In a more subtle sense, Sarah herself was subject to critical scrutiny by the community. At one point she became entrapped between the need to conform to the honor-bound Southern standard and her compassion for human suffering.

In June 1862, Sarah Morgan had fixed her gaze at the new theater in Baton Rouge, not a city block away, and thought of the more-than-a-hundred sick Union soldiers lodged there. There were few male nurses to administer to them, and they seemed to be dying like flies. Many Southern women were overheard slandering them, one saying, "I hope God will send down plague, yellow fever, famine, on these vile Yankees, and that not one will escape death." Yet the spirit of Christianity had welled up in Sarah, and she recoiled in horror. "I think of the many mothers, wives and sisters who wait as anxiously, pray as fervently in their far away lonesome homes for their dear ones, as we do here; I fancy them waiting day after day for footsteps that will never come, growing more sad, lonely, and heartbroken as the days wear on."[20]

"What woman has stretched out her hand to save them, to give them a cup of cold water? Where is the charity that should ignore nations and creeds, and administer help to the Indian or heathen indifferently? Gone! all gone in Union versus Secession! That is what the American war has brought us."[21]

Yet Sarah was helpless:

If [only] I could help these dying men! Yet it is as impossible as though I was a chained bear. I can't put out my hand. I am threatened with Coventry [ostracism] because I sent a custard to a sick man who is in the [Yankee] army, and with the anathema of society because I said if I could possibly do anything for [him I would]. . . . [A prominent friend] thinks we have acted shockingly, . . . and that we will suffer for it when the Federals leave. . . . Die poor men, without a woman's hand to close your eyes! We women are too patriotic to help you! I look eagerly on, [and] cry in my soul. . . . Behold the woman who dares not risk private ties for God's glory and her professed religion! Coward. Helpless woman that I am![22]

For Sarah, this anguish had become a burdensome by-product of the pride and honor expected of nearly all in Southern society. From petty gossip and tacit ostracism to outright social banishment, the penalties for expressing undue empathy toward the enemy were significant, even in a war-ravaged locale. The strictures of compliance with cultural codes were demanding, and enormous pressures to do what was "honorable" determined most Southerners' behavior. To lose honor invited personal catastrophe so long as the rigid structure of Southern society remained intact.[23]

Like many other Southern women, Sara Morgan was torn between feeling helpless to aid suffering fellow human beings, and the passions aroused by the brutal acts of war these very same people committed. The contradiction between compassion and society's strictures only became more pronounced as the conflict progressed. War had compelled a reappraisal of that which was morally taught versus that which physically existed, and the results weren't always predictable.

For solace, Sarah's fury was directed at a popular target. In outrage, she recorded that "Picayune [Major General Benjamin] Butler," the notorious Yankee commander at New Orleans, had acted the part of a tyrant by arresting citizens, including the mayor of New Orleans, for alleged threats toward Union sympathizers. It was imperative to resist such despotism to the bitter end, considered Sarah. Her thoughts reflected the emotional metamorphosis that had occurred.

Dearly as I love Louisiana, it can never be my home, under such a sway. I feel that we have lost all things, honor included. We are serfs; we have forfeited the respect of foreign nations by submitting patiently to our yoke of iron; we are bondsmen, no longer free citizens. We are to be governed by men imported from northern states, who are prejudiced and taught to hold us in contempt from their birth; our laws are to be made by them, without suffering us to raise our voice in our own cause; we are required only to submit blindly. Can we so submit? God have mercy on us and deliver us from the hands of our enemies![24]

Sarah's depression as expressed in her diary knew no bounds, and she periodically continued her tirade:

This degradation is worse than the bitterness of death! I see no salvation [on] either side. No glory awaits the Southern Confederacy if it does achieve its independence. It will be a mere speck in the world, with no weight or authority. The North confesses itself lost without us, and has paid an unheard of ransom to regain us. On the other hand, conquered, what hope is there in this world for us? Broken in health and fortune, reviled, condemned, abused by those who claim already to have subdued us, without a prospect of future support for those few of our brothers who return; outcasts without home or honor, would not death or exile be preferable? Oh, let us

abandon our loved home to those implacable enemies, and find
refuge elsewhere! Take from us property, everything, only grant us
liberty![25]

Sarah Morgan's emotional outpouring was rooted in another characteristic revered as an inherent component of proper Southern society—pride.

It was pride that perhaps surfaced most often when a refined
woman like Sarah was faced with unmanageable adversity. The intent
of utilizing pride was to conquer one's personal fears and promote
one's own dignity in the solution of social problems. Yet, as in the
case of the sick Yankees lodged at the Baton Rouge theater, situations
involving the prospect of personal ostracism for "improper" behavior
were inevitable. The clashes of morality, pride, and honor thus sent
anxious paroxysms through the minds of many in polite society, including Sarah.

Sarah's sense of indignation was further compounded by her in-
escapable status as a "mere" woman. "Only ask Heaven why you were
made with a man's heart, and a female form...," she ranted.
"Thank heaven my brothers are the bravest of the brave! I would
despise them if they shrunk back, though Lucifer should dispute the
path with them."[26]

Her limitations as a female had become all too evident in a war-
ravaged, male-dominated society. Thus far, the war had brought only
the cruel realities of displacement and submission to Sarah Morgan
and her woman relatives. Attempting to escape the enemy occupation
of Baton Rouge, Sarah, her sister, and her mother had sought refuge
at Linwood, a plantation twenty miles north of their old residence
and only five miles from Port Hudson, where the Confederates were
fortifying a bluff overlooking the Mississippi River.

There Sarah was severely injured when she was thrown to the
ground in a runaway buggy accident in November 1862.[27]

Unable to walk or move about easily for months due to her back
injury, Sarah worried that as a cripple she was virtually helpless. Her
dairy entries fretted about the consequences:

What if the fight [at Port Hudson] should come off before I can
walk? It takes three people to raise me whenever it is necessary for
me to move. I am worse than helpless. What will become of me?
Port Hudson, I prophesy, will fall. I found my prediction on the

way its defenders talk. I asked a soldier the other day if he thought we could hold it. "Well, if we don't, we know so many by-paths that we can easily slip out," was the answer. I was shocked. That is no way for our soldiers to talk, "slip out"[?] I expected the answer . . . , "We'll conquer or die!" Fancy my disappointment. Defended in that spirit, Port Hudson is lost.[28]

Sarah Morgan's intution later proved correct. Port Hudson fell shortly after the citadel of Vicksburg surrendered, in July 1863. By that time, however, Sarah, her mother, and her sister, Miriam, were in New Orleans. Her half brother, Judge Philip H. Morgan, had remained loyal to the Federal government and continued to reside in the Crescent City as a man of influence and connections. Destitute and fearing the approach of the Federal forces under Nathaniel P. Banks, the three Morgan women journeyed to New Orleans, arriving by schooner in late April 1863.

The greatest trial awaiting Sarah Morgan at New Orleans was not the physical ordeal of her semi-invalid condition, or of living under enemy occupation, but a test of her honor. Upon admission to the city, Sarah and her family were required to take the Oath of Allegiance to the United States. Since she had three brothers fighting for the Confederacy, the family's property was gone, and her heart and soul were invested in the success of the Southern cause, this stricture brought her profound agony. Her mother had at first rebelled against taking the oath, and with a bitter tirade created a tearful scene. Sarah later sat motionless with her hand over her face, praying, as the oath was administered. Soon the pangs of conscience tore at her. "I told the [Federal] officer . . . that I was unwilling to take the oath, and asked if there was no escaping it," she later wrote in self-justification. " 'None whatever,' was his reply. 'You have it to do, and there is no getting out of it [in order to enter New Orleans].' His rude tone frightened me into half crying," remembered Sarah, "but for all that, as he said, I had to do [it]. If perjury it is, which will God punish— me, who was unwilling to commit the crime, or the man who forced me to it? . . . I shall no longer trouble myself as to whether the sin was his or mine, satisfied that the crime would be in keeping such an oath, with my heart on the other side, where as the merit would lay in breaking it."[29]

Honor and pride were at stake, and when a proclamation was issued requiring all families registered as enemies of the United States to leave the city, Sarah ranted, "It seems treason to remain . . . under the protection of this hateful flag, while all our own creed . . . are sent out to starve." Yet, Sarah soon reconsidered. Reasoning that her mother "cannot endure the privations we would have to undergo," Sarah decided ". . . we will have to remain patiently here, and consequently labor under the suspicion of belonging to a side we abhor with all our souls."

Sarah, nonetheless, was moved to reassert, "Oh, if I was only a man! For two years that has been my only cry, and today I fairly rave about it. Blood, fire, desolation, I feel ready to invoke all on these Yankees."[30]

Discretion had imposed its inevitable restrictions. Sarah was older and wiser now, and though still brimming with spirit, she knew the virtues of practicality and the consequences of impropriety.

Although the thought of disgrace had been utmost in Sarah's mind following her oath of allegiance to the United States, the need to survive was now foremost in her actions.

It was a situation with profound implications for many other proud Southerners.

Chapter Ten

Henry King Burgwyn, Jr.

An Ornament of the Confederacy

He was known as Harry, rather than Henry, probably because his father had the same given name, and his appearance wasn't much to ponder in April 1861. A thin, overly serious student of nineteen, Henry King "Harry" Burgwyn, Jr., had a fixed, abstract stare that made him seem somewhat detached.[1]

Describing himself as prudish, Harry told his mother that he wouldn't smoke tobacco although some of the other boys did. "I have firmly resolved not to smoke until I am 25 years old—if I do then, and I hope I shall not," he had proclaimed. Chewing tobacco was so obnoxious that Harry regarded the habit with "disgust." Rounding out his staid image, he reported that in personal grooming he was clean and neat. "As a general thing I take a bath about once a week, he confided."[2]

A privileged North Carolinian by birth, Harry Burgwyn, like so many Southern youths from prosperous families, had been sent away to school at a tender age. His father was determined that his name-sake would have a "proper" education, so Harry departed from home at age fifteen for special tutoring at West Point, New York. A year later, his application for admission to the United States Military Academy was sponsored by his father's friend and political contact, the secretary of the navy. This resort to insider influence brought only disappointment. Harry was denied a presidential appointment when President James Buchanan said his selections had already been made, and promises to others had to be kept. North Carolina congressmen were either unable or unwilling to help the anxious youth; thus in July 1857 he enrolled at the University of North Carolina at Chapel Hill. Two years later, having already earned a bachelor of science degree, the precocious student was admitted to the Virginia Military Institute with advanced standing.[3]

Although his independent existence and varied schooling had given young Burgwyn a maturity well beyond that of many of his contemporaries, he had paid a hefty social price. His father confided in a letter of introduction to the staff at VMI that, although a hard-working student, Harry was a bit reticent. "[He is] not likely to seek companionship unless he is thrown into it," admitted his father. Moreover, his son had "eschewed low and vulgar companions" among college students, and his friends were not numerous.[4]

Since he was only seventeen and therefore much younger than his fellow upper classmates at VMI, it's easy to see why Harry was some-what alone, although he was well mannered and highly intelligent. Not surprisingly, VMI life seemed rather "monotonous," according to Harry. In his senior year, 1861, he felt burdened by his future even though he was a cadet officer who ranked second in his class of sev-enteen. What he would do after graduating was foremost on his mind. "I am so tired of this place," grumbled Harry, and he reiterated his determination to turn down the expected offer of an assistant pro-fessorship at VMI following graduation. "There is no society here," he complained. "The people of this section [of Virginia, being strongly pro-Union,] are an inferior race to that of any other portion of Virginia or the South." There simply weren't enough "attractions" to stay in Lexington, Virginia, and remain a military man.[5]

Yet, becoming an engineer, doctor, or lawyer seemed equally des-picable. "I would never be content with occupying a subordinate po-sition such as a pettifogging country lawyer," he confessed to his father. "The profession of law, however, is the only one by which a man in this country can rise to power. Without speaking constantly, however great be a man's intellectual power, he cannot be much," surmised nineteen-year-old Harry Burgwyn.[6]

Therein lay the secret of Harry's personality and career. He was extraordinarily ambitious and very perceptive. Henry King Burgwyn, Jr.'s, erstwhile goal was to become a planter like his father. Yet his true, burning desire was to be famous and powerful. "I do not wish to loll away the best portion of my life in idleness and become an encumbrance to my friends and a burden to myself," implored Harry. "What shall I do?"[7]

He soon found the answer in the short but clarion speech of his natural philosophy professor at VMI. In February this professor asserted, "The time for war has not yet come, but it will come, and that soon; and when it does come, my advice is to draw the sword and throw away the scabbard." The man's opinion would later count for much, since he was none other than Thomas J. [soon to be "Stonewall"] Jackson. Also, just as Jackson had predicted, the rush to arms was soon underway.[8]

In April 1861, Henry King Burgwyn, Jr., was suddenly caught up in the turmoil. A select VMI detachment with Harry present had served on special duty during the hanging of John Brown in December 1859. Little more than a year later, the senior class received their diplomas early and were ordered to Richmond.[9]

But Harry was unhappy. "Considerable dissatisfaction exists among us that they should expect us to fight as privates through the war; or at all events commence it that way," he protested. "We would thus be the only ones in the whole army who would be denied the opportunity of distinguishing ourselves while having more military knowledge than any of the others." Of his father he implored, "I would like to receive some letters of introduction to persons in Richmond [so as to get a commission]."[10]

While reluctant to fight as a private, Harry Burgwyn was anxious that the South aggressively resist Yankee coercion. "I sincerely hope that [Northern] treachery is prevented by the prompt action of the cotton states in seizing beforehand the forts within their own limits," he urged.[11]

Harry's warlike attitude was supported by his father, who in March 1861 had declared that although he didn't believe in civil war, "when the time of real trial comes, all Southern men will be found bound together, and ready to defend their rights to the last."[12]

Cadet Harry Burgwyn, en route to Richmond on April 22, 1861, was endorsed in his quest for a commission by his friend Major T. J. Jackson, who had penned a note to Confederate secretary of war Leroy P. Walker, recommending him for an artillery officer's commission. "Mr. Burgwyn is not only a high tone Southern gentleman, but . . . possesses qualities well calculated to make him an ornament, not only to artillery, but to any branch of the military service," wrote Jackson, with obvious pride in his former student.[13]

Tom Jackson had measured Harry Burgwyn well. "I am truly impatient on the present position of comparative inaction which I am compelled to assume," Harry had recently told his father. "I know of no power which . . . would prevent me from joining the army of the Southern states in general and my own state in particular . . . I consider my allegiance is emphatically due to North Carolina and [if it] please[s] God I will not fail in it."[14]

Both an ornament and an aristocrat, Harry Burgwyn's future was preordained—and was certain to be fascinating.

An Unsuitable Colonel and an Ambitious Lieutenant Colonel

"I was today elected lieutenant colonel of the 26th Regiment North Carolina Troops. I am now 19 years, 9 months, and 27 days old, and probably the youngest lieutenant colonel in the Confederate or United States service." So boasted the elated Harry Burgwyn in his "journal of events" on August 27, 1861. His persistence and sense of self-esteem had paid off. Aware that he was far more knowledgeable in military affairs than the vast majority of volunteers in the army, VMI graduate Harry Burgwyn was convinced of his abilities and capacity to command. Indeed, though regarded as extremely young, Harry Burgwyn, considered one recruit, was "a youth of authority, beautiful and handsome," where the "flash of his eye and the quickness of his movements betoken his bravery."[15]

Earlier, while in the midst of nearly six dreary weeks of recruiting duty in the mountains of western North Carolina, Harry had become disconsolate and anxious. Isolated "in the wilderness," he seemed all but forgotten while thirsting for action and glory. He chafed in a letter to his mother about his frustrations in arousing the often-lukewarm emotions of the mountaineers. Most of those willing to serve had refused to join the army for longer than twelve months; thus enlisting regulars was all but impossible—few believed the war would be of long duration.[16]

Harry was regarded as a strong disciplinarian while he served as a captain at one of Richmond's camps of instruction in May 1861. Yet the men obviously liked the eager, intense youth. Just before departing for North Carolina, the LaFayette Light Infantry solicited subscription funds for the purchase of a presentation dress sword in his honor. Although the sword was unavailable in Richmond due to heavy demand, it seemed but a temporary delay in recognition and glory. Yet for Harry, it may have been a harbinger of both the successes and disappointments to come.[17]

While stuck in the mountains of North Carolina through the early summer, Harry considered taking a position as an aide on a general's staff, or else joining the artillery. "Anything [would be] in preference to wearing out my time in useless efforts to induce lazy mountaineers to enlist for the war," he harrumphed.[18]

In due time Harry had his wish. By early July 1861 he was a major commanding a camp of instruction near Raleigh, North Carolina. More important, he was now in a position to politick for higher rank. Though disappointed that he could not secure a top position with the 12th North Carolina Infantry, Harry kept trying. Soon he was able to obtain the lieutenant colonelcy of the 26th North Carolina Volunteers, a one-year's-service regiment then being organized at his Raleigh camp. Harry's election as lieutenant colonel—volunteer officers were elected by ballot within their individual units—was admittedly a source of great pride.[19]

That was in August 1861. Before six months passed, however, Harry was once again chafing under the burdens of a subordinate position. The colonel of the 26th turned out to be a lax disciplinarian, and Harry rued the man's inefficiency and lack of expertise. Boldly, he complained to his father in a letter home: "None of our regiments are so efficient as they should be. My own is the best, and if it had a good colonel would be a most capital regiment." Indeed, Harry considered the colonel "a man without any system or regularity whatever, and [he] has so little of an engineering mind as to say that the . . . entrenchments are worthless unless the enemy land and attack us there." Young Burgwyn further warned that the colonel's "abilities appear to be more overrated than those of any other person I know of." Citing the fact that the 26th had been organized for five months, Harry scoffed, "Until today we have not had a color bearer . . . appointed." Many company officers were "exceedingly inefficient in tactics," Harry noted, "Could they only be got rid of, the regiment would be much improved."[20]

Burgwyn's intolerance of carelessness, and his commitment to efficiency, were fully apparent, yet both forewarned of his impatience and an ill-founded arrogance. Further grousing about the 26th's "unsuitable" colonel, Harry informed his father—who was serving as a military aide to the governor of North Carolina—"I am heartily tired of being under his command. As for discipline, not the faintest idea of it has ever entered his head." Officers had been allowed to be absent from reveille without question, and "not a syllable did he say to them," confided Harry Burgwyn with disgust. "If I could get a colonelcy then the objection to leaving this regiment . . . would be justified to all."[21]

The colonel Harry complained about was Zebulon Baird Vance, a skilled politician whose lurking ambition was to become governor of the state. Moreover, at that time, an organized expedition of Federal troops was preparing to attack the coastal defenses of North Carolina. Within days, Harry would be caught up in his first experience under fire. The youthful lieutenant colonel had long anticipated this key confrontation. "Though not desirous of being killed, I am very anxious to be in at least one fight before I go out of service," he claimed, "and my reputation will greatly depend upon my conduct on that occasion."[22]

"My Command Was the Last to Leave"

Harry Burgwyn had suffered from typhoid fever in the fall of 1861, but the physical distress of October, November, and early December rapidly gave way to nervous expectation following his return to duty on Christmas Day 1861. His health was so improved that he attended a New Year's Eve party at Beaufort, where he carefully eyed "all the beauties of the burg." Alas, "out of some 60 or 70 there was not one really pretty," he grumbled with disappointment. He had earlier implored of his mother, "What young ladies will you bring with you? Be certain they are pretty. You know my fondness for beauty."[23]

If Harry's taste in women was discriminating, it mirrored his demand for excellence in soldiering. His relentless regimen of drill and discipline as the lieutenant colonel of the 26th North Carolina Volunteers had well convinced the men of his earnestness. Yet Harry was known to be good-natured underneath his tough facade. He enjoyed joking about the big war news of the day—the ominous appearance of Union Major General Ambrose Burnside's expedition off the North Carolina coast. Although newspapers reported that the Union commander had lost perhaps fifty vessels in a storm at sea, they also assessed that Burnside was determined to press on, having remarked, "I am in the hands of God." Harry thus quipped, "A few more storms, and if he don't mind he will be in the hands of the devil."[24]

A year after entering the army, Harry Burgwyn was rapidly developing into a more personable and dedicated officer, although he remained driven by ambition and a strong sense of responsibility. The supreme test of battle was still to come, however, and although not pessimistic, he was worried most by his own inexperience and the outnumbered coastal force's defensive vulnerability.

Stationed near New Bern, North Carolina, the 26th North Carolina was a part of what Harry Burgwyn regarded as the very weak and scattered defensive network protecting North Carolina's vital seaboard perimeter. "We may expect disaster and defeat . . . just so long as we expose small detachments, unsupported by any convenient troops, to attacks by the enemy," he warned his father. "Whenever New Bern is attacked by the force which Burnside will have it will fall. . . . [Yet] do not understand me as giving up. My spirits, like yours, rise with our disasters. Not a particle of yielding is in me, but I do wish to see better generalship, and that a fair show be given to our men."[25]

Much as Harry Burgwyn had foreseen, Burnside's combined naval and infantry expedition easily seized Roanoke Island on February 8. Four weeks later, the appearance of Burnside's troops along the Neuse River below New Bern, North Carolina, heralded an imminent conflict. Harry Burgwyn's wry humor was gone, replaced by an attitude of seriousness. On the eve of the New Bern battle he wrote to his mother:

The enemy are close at hand and preparing to attack us. . . . The news was received by our men with no cheering, no undue exultation, no efforts to keep their courage up by noisy demonstrations. But every eye brightened, every arm grew nervous, and the most deadly determination is on all. You may rely on a hard fight, but God's Providence is over us all. Through having His omnipotence constantly before me lately, I am much more impressed with it now, and I am sure He will order all for the best. I am in the best spirits imaginable. I used to think the night before a battle I would be anxious for my own fate and that of the day. Now if I had my wish, exclusive of the fact that our defenses may be improved by delay, I would not postpone [the battle] a day.[26]

On March 14, 1862, Burnside's troops attacked the Confederate defenses below New Bern, and for the Confederates there was hell to pay. Their defensive line collapsed when a battalion of militia, posted at a gap in the main fortifications, fled and opened the way for a major Federal penetration. Most of Brigadier General Lawrence O'Bryan Branch's troops retreated in disorder, yet Harry Burgwyn and the 26th North Carolina continued to hold their isolated position on the far right flank. Eventually, they learned of the disaster and hastened to retreat, finally making their way to safety after a difficult crossing of swollen Bryce's Creek.[27]

Fortunately for the morale of the 26th regiment, their part in the defeat had been minimal. Most of the fighting had occurred elsewhere along the line, and because of their limited exposure, they lost only a few men. Harry Burgwyn, however, was angry.

"The battle was lost by bad arrangement of the troops, and the running off of the militia, which exposed our center completely," Burgwyn exploded. Blaming General Branch for the "bad posting of the troops," he asserted that the men had now lost confidence in that general. Harry Burgwyn, somberly assessed his own role in the affair. "My command was the last to leave, and though I say it myself, retreated in better order than any other [regiment]."[28]

Burgwyn's efforts during the combat had been arduous if limited. During the retreat, when it appeared that they would be hard-pressed by the pursuing enemy, Harry admitted "[my] heart sank within me." Impassable Bryce's Creek impeded their progress, and only one small skiff was found, which could carry across just three men at a time. Harry sent search parties up and down the swollen creek, and finally located another boat. Each trip took about ten minutes, yet in little over an hour the entire command was ferried over. Harry Burgwyn stood at the crossing site to keep order, and at one point had to draw his sword to prevent a few panicked soldiers from swamping the boat. Harry and his personal servant, William, were the last to cross, and they calmly swam both of his horses across. During the retreat, Harry became exhausted, and he later confided that if he then had only himself to consider, "he would have laid right down and slept [even] if it had killed me." His responsibility to his men had kept him going.

Having slept only a total of four hours over four successive days, he now was completely worn out. Although he had lost everything except what he was wearing, Harry Burgwyn's spirits remained upbeat. "I am confident we will whip Burnside the next time," he informed his father.[29]

Harry's frustration with this sordid affair quickly mounted as newspaper accounts heaped criticism on the generals and many of their troops. Implications that the 26th North Carolina had avoided fighting evoked an emotional outpouring from the twenty-year-old lieutenant colonel, who was both outraged and embarrassed. He singled out Colonel Vance for lacking expertise as a military commander, and confided in his father, "I wish very much indeed I could be elected colonel of one of the new regiments. I would then have a regiment as . . . a regiment [should be]. Colonel Vance . . . is no sort of a commander. I constructed or laid out almost all of the entrenchments which we occupied, and had a great deal [more] to do with it [the defensive line] than he [did]." Harry further complained to his father, "I am heartily tired of taking all the blame upon myself and getting the last part of the credit, although I had much rather do even that than see a fine regiment ruined for want of discipline."[30]

Discipline was the key to having an effective fighting regiment, Harry determined following his bitter New Bern experience. Lieutenant Colonel Burgwyn thus came away from his first battlefield more convinced than ever that an unbending valor would win on any battlefield. Combat wasn't a test of might, but of courage and control. "[If I ever have] any command, unless prohibited by orders, I intend to charge the enemy with the bayonet as early as possible in the fight and let the relative bravery of the troops be tested. We should go to work now and have the most thorough drills and discipline possible."[31]

As for winning a reputation for bravery in battle, it seemed all too easy. "You will see a great many accounts of the battle [New Bern] but they are all exaggerated," scoffed Harry. "Such expressions as a colonel's rising in his stirrups and saying we can die, but never surrender, are like Wellington's 'La Grade se recule.' It is the easiest thing to get up a reputation on the battlefield; at least [so] it appears to me. . . ." The real essence of battle, he asserted, was terribly distorted by the press. In confirmation, a fellow field officer—a participant in the New Bern action—advised a friend, "Never put any reliance in newspaper reports of a battle."[32]

Ironically, as a result of many newspaper editorials and published letters of endorsement, the commander of the 26th, Colonel Zeb Vance, was soon being touted for governor of North Carolina. With the gubernatorial election approaching in the summer of 1862, Harry Burgwyn became acting commander of the regiment. By late August, with the election of Vance to the governorship, Harry was in line for promotion to full colonel—at the age of twenty.[33]

Chapter Eleven

"We Think Every Southerner Equal to Three Yankees at Least"

Jefferson Davis was in a fine mood. He sat on the plush sofa next to Mary Chesnut and chatted amiably. The whippoorwills were singing sweetly, and a warmth embraced the night air. They were at a private Richmond party in late June 1861, and the first land battle of the war, fought a few weeks earlier at Big Bethel, Virginia, had been won handily by Southerners. This was the favorite gossip of Richmond: how General "Prince John" Magruder had "done something splendid on the Peninsula" by whipping the "damned Yankees" with a handful of soldiers.[1]

Davis talked for nearly an hour. Perhaps the mellow wine had loosened his tongue, and Mary Chesnut sat fascinated by his banter. "He laughed at our faith in our own powers," noted Mary with some surprise. He told me, "we are like the British. We think every Southerner equal to three Yankees at least. We will have to be equivalent to a dozen now."[2]

"After his experience of [seeing] the fighting qualities of Southerners in Mexico, he believes that we will do all that can be done by pluck and muscle, endurance, and dogged courage—dash and red hot patriotism, etc.," Mary Chesnut later confided in her diary. Yet Davis's tone "was not sanguine," she observed. "There was a sad refrain running through it all. For one thing, he thinks it will be a long war."[3]

Mary Chesnut was shocked. She could hardly believe her ears.

"That floored me at once," she admitted. Although others now exuded optimism, Davis seemed almost despairing. "Then [he] said: before the end came, we would have many a bitter experience. He said only fools doubted the courage of the Yankees or their willingness to fight when they saw fit. And now we have stung their pride—we have roused them till they will fight like devils."[4]

Mary Chesnut fidgeted with nervousness. The war, she decided, "has been too long for me already."

The spirit of Southern invincibility had been profound in the camp of the 1st North Carolina Infantry following the Battle of Big Bethel in June 1861. A corporal recorded a general's boast that "we can whip 20,000 Yankees" with their present small force of about 5,000 Confederates, should the enemy advance again. Only a few months later, a new soldier in the same regiment, having just heard about the capture of Hatteras Inlet by the Federals, wrote to his father, "We want to go down there very bad, for it seems they won't give us a chance at them here."[5]

Then nearly a year later, in April 1862, the same soldier wrote home. "A soldier's life is calculated to ruin a young man for business afterward. It is a very lazy life, indeed." Despite nearly a year in military service, he hadn't yet heard the roar of battle or witnessed the thrill of victory. As for the fate of the Yankees, "if [they] don't get sick of fighting us this summer, disease will finish what arms leave," he prophesied.[6]

It came as a stark surprise to many would-be volunteer heroes: the war was to be little of fighting and much of waiting. Soldiering involved an endless routine of drill, camp life, and anticipation. Instead of glory and Southern dash on the field of battle, the average soldier knew mostly boredom, tedium, privation, and exposure to the elements. Worst of all, wild camp rumors, contradictory reports, and false news of the enemy advancing kept everyone on edge. Reliable information was at a premium. No one seemed to know when a decisive movement would be made, although there was always speculation and constant anxiety.

The first year of the war was a psychological letdown. Despite the impressive Confederate victory at Manassas, there was no foreseeable end to the conflict. The Yankees appeared determined to see their cause prevail. The Confederacy's show of force, which many had ex-

pected would induce the North to negotiate peace, instead had resulted only in the enemy recruiting more men to "put down the
rebellion."

The first major premise of the war—that it would be short and
grandly adventuresome—already had been proved wrong. Not surprisingly, there was a corresponding cynicism among many soldiers,
brought on by repeated disappointments. In February 1862, a South
Carolina soldier skeptically wrote home, "I don't hear anything of
peace now, so [I'm] hoping that is a good sign that the war won't
last [much] long[er]." Another infantryman who had found mostly
ordeal and self-sacrifice in the army informed his wife, "God knows
I am very tired of it [the military]. I wish that I could come home to
stay . . . but we are placed under the iron heel of military rule and
are not allowed these privileges during war. What an awful calamity
a civil war is."[7]

More shocking to the sensibilities of these civilian-soldiers was the
true scourge of their army experience—not Yankee bullets, which
were only infrequently encountered, but the constant danger of severe sickness. A South Carolinian expressed his great awakening to
his wife: "We have just done burying P. Wright. He only lived four
days after taking pneumonia. . . . Our regiment has lost more men
than the balance of the brigade. Seven men have died of our company since the first day of January [three months earlier]. It seems
there is more to be feared than battle." Another soldier agreed, and
spoke of his new anxiety: "I do not dread a soldier's life so much if
I can keep well, but when I get sick I am very much depress[ed] in
spirits for fear of a severe attack, and no person to wait on me."[8]

To further worsen the soldiers' plight, many of the basic necessities
of life, normally taken for granted at home, were missing or in short
supply in the army. One Georgia volunteer apologized in May 1862
for writing home with a pencil, ". . . but pens and ink are 'completely
played out' as is almost everything else, ourselves included." Food
was in short supply, grumbled this soldier, thus they were "frequently
without anything" and on half rations the rest of the time. "I came
nearer starving than I ever did before," he complained. "When a
fellow gets so he is glad to get a little parched corn, or will even
steal raw corn from a half famished horse, you may suppose he is
about . . . 'gone up a spout.' "[9]

Long, purposeless marches greatly added to the troops' fatigue, as
did guard and picket duty in inclement weather. Having to march to

Richmond during the early days of the Peninsula Campaign disheartened one 19th Georgia private. The trip was:

the most severe of all time, for it was performed in the night while raining all the time, and so dark you could scarcely see the road. Just imagine a large army; men, wagons, horses, and artillery, passing over a road . . . cut to pieces by thousands of wagons having just passed, and you can form some conception of that night's misery. We stopped about day[light] to rest, but I was wet and muddy from head to foot, and employed the couple of short hours . . . in drying myself. . . . I got a hold of a piece of ash cake and thought I never ate anything half so good.[10]

Food wasn't the only basic commodity missing. With so little time to prepare for a nationwide conflict, the procurement of camp equipage, from kettles to proper shelter, was exceedingly difficult. Their tents were so flimsy one North Carolina rifleman discovered during an evening rainstorm that water "came down by the bucketful" upon him. Everything in his tent was soaked.[11]

Compounding the general sense of discouragement was the absence of modern arms. Many regiments were without adequate weapons and equipment. Some infantry and cavalry units were armed with sporting shotguns, old converted smoothbore muskets, and country hunting rifles. They were hardly the arms to inspire confidence or pride. Even the few companies in regiments armed with rifle muskets were occasionally disrupted by the shifting of weapons necessary for supplying proper ammunition. One company commander protested when he was compelled to turn in his minie rifles for smoothbore muskets, even though "they did it in order that each company should have the same guns."[12]

Meddlesome and overdemanding commanders added to the difficulties many in the ranks faced. Complaining that a would-be captain was "a fake and a drunkard," a North Carolinian wrote home of his disgust with internal politics, and protested that his regiment had "suffered much by not having good officers."

"I have learned that every man in the army looks out for himself," wrote a harassed Georgian; "If I can get out [of the military] upon fair terms I will do so sure," he told his wife.[13]

Beyond the inherent bureaucracy and inefficiencies of the army, there was further cause for discontent. Revolted by the "rough" army life that offended his sensibilities, a soldier complained to his family, "You have no idea of the wickedness that is in [our] camps. . . . There is some . . . men [that] curse, swear, and play cards all night, [even] in a tent where there is a corpse. The death of a man here is nothing more than the death of a hog, or at any rate, not much more."[14]

The most irksome and unappealing realities of war—boredom, inequity, and inefficiency—were fully revealed. One of Stonewall Jackson's troops mirrored the feelings of many when he wrote in January 1862, "There romance of the thing is entirely worn off, not only with myself but with the whole army." Another disillusioned infantryman informed his family, "If I live this twelve months out, I intend to try mighty hard to keep out [of the army], [for] I don't think I could stand it another year."[15]

The war was not going well for the South in the spring of 1862, making the inconveniences of camp life even worse. With the appearance of McClellan's enormous Yankee army on the Virginia peninsula in the spring of 1862, and due to a worsening situation in the West following the loss of Kentucky and much of Tennessee, it appeared that the Confederacy was rapidly losing the war. "It is pretty much given up by all men about here that the Yankees will take Richmond in a few days," wrote a disheartened member of the 34th North Carolina in May 1862. Soon there was more bad news to ponder.[16]

Just when matters seemed to be approaching their worst in that dreary spring of 1862, another hard reality confronted the disillusioned Confederate soldier. Many initial volunteers had enlisted for one year, and their terms were about to expire. But because of the deepening crisis, the Confederate Congress passed in mid-April 1862 legislation requiring all able-bodied men between eighteen and thirty-five years of age to serve in the army. Those who declined to reenlist faced conscription and reassignment other than within their old regiments, many of which were being reorganized for service during the war.[17]

It was a hard blow to men who were sick of the army. Although a substitute might be obtained from those exempt from the draft, indiscriminate noncompliance in some areas and the imposition of martial law heightened the controversy. Skepticism began to pervade the minds of many.

In all, the future was discouraging to the Confederacy and its beleaguered soldiers in the early spring of 1862. A disconsolate lieutenant wrote home in March 1862, telling his father not to volunteer, "Stay at home and take care of the rest as long as you can, for it is uncertain how this war is going to terminate." The soldiers were not the only despairing Southerners, for as this lieutenant noted, wretched times existed even for civilians: "Most of the richest and best farms in this section are deserted by their owners. There is lots of cotton here just lying about, doing nobody no good. Some of the people is hauling their cotton into the woods and hiding it to keep the Yankees from getting it."[18]

Such discouraging news befitted the gloom and misery of most Southerners. Having just "seen thousands upon thousands of dead and wounded" during the fighting around Richmond in June 1862, a Texas Brigade soldier wrote, "If the war lasts [much] longer there will not be many of us left." The war had all but "gone up the spout"—a favorite army expression that appropriately described the crisis marking the one-year anniversary of the Civil War's onset.[19]

Beneath the despair, however, lurked indignation. The men hadn't enlisted to watch the Confederacy waste away from bureaucratic inefficiency and impotent strategic maneuvering. The rancor of the soldiers inspired renewed determination. The manpower pool of the Confederacy remained generally intact, and a growing awareness of latent strength and purpose clarified the thinking of many. Said a North Carolina enlisted man, G. J. Huntley, "I will fight them [Yankees] as long as I can crawl. . . . My intention is to go ahead and fight as near for what is right as I can. If it is my lot to fall and fill a soldier's grave, I shall not be by myself. . . . The prospect is fair for my body to be left in Old Virginia, but I hope if we meet no more on earth that we may meet in a better place where wars shall cease and peace shall reign."[20]

Huntley's grim perseverance embodied the thoughts of thousands of his fellow soldiers. Their resolve "to conquer or die" was apparent, even if many believed that the worst might yet occur.[21]

This renewed spirit of commitment would find its purpose in the remarkable turnabout Confederate offensives during the summer of 1862.

Chapter Twelve

NATHANIEL H. R. DAWSON / ELODIE TODD

"I Attribute All to the War"

With Abraham Lincoln as her brother-in-law, Elodie Todd knew she was under close scrutiny as the war intensified. "Surely there is no other family in the land placed in the exact situation of ours," wrote a melancholy Elodie in September 1861. "And I hope [they] will never be so unfortunate as to be surrounded by trials so numerous."[1]

Elodie Todd's understanding attitude toward her famous brother-in-law, Abraham Lincoln, was generally not shared by her friends and neighbors. During the early summer of 1861 Elodie had written:

There is not one of us [Todds] that cherish an unkind thought or feeling toward him, and for this reason we feel so acutely every remark derogatory to him, except as a president. I never go in public that my feelings are not wounded, nor are we exempt in Matt's [sister-in-law, Mattie] own house, for people constantly wish he may be hung and all such evils may attend his footsteps. We would be devoid of all feeling and sympathy did we not feel for them [the Lincolns], and had we no love for Mary. . . . I wish I were not so sensitive, but it is a decided weakness of the entire family, and to struggle against it seems for naught.[2]

Her fiancé, Captain Nat Dawson, had repeatedly attempted to console her, saying "I have never been able to entertain for him [Lincoln] any unkindness, save as an enemy to my country. I have never believed the slanders upon him as a man, and accord to him the respect that is due a gentleman. It would be strange if you felt otherwise, and did not love your sister [Mary]," he wrote reassuringly.[3]

Nathaniel Dawson's perspective was perhaps typical of the more moderate feelings that existed in the early months of the war, when many hoped for a negotiated separation of North and South. Once widespread effusion of blood occurred, and personal losses intensified the war's agony, expressions of hate became increasingly prevalent. Only a few weeks after the big battle at Manassas, and in the wake of Northern bitterness about the cruel treatment of Union prisoners in the custody of David Todd (their jailer at Richmond), even Elodie's attitude had hardened: "I see from today's paper Mrs. Lincoln is indignant at my brother David's being in the Confederate service, and declares 'that by no word or act of hers should he escape punishment for his treason against her husband's government should he fall into their hands.' I do not believe she ever said it, and if she did and meant it, she is no longer a sister of mine, nor deserves to be called a woman of noble senses and truth . . . ," countered Elodie. "God grant my noble . . . brother will never fall into their hands and have to suffer death twice over. . . . He is fighting for his country."[4]

Likewise, Nat, despondent over the prospect of a long, arduous war, now strongly condemned Abraham Lincoln. "I . . . know well Mr. Lincoln is not man enough to dare to make it [peace]. He is but a tool in the hands of his party, and would not brave their wrath by such a proposition." Yet Nat appealed to Elodie to remain aloof from family quarrels, and told her, "You are in the path of duty . . . and you have reason to be proud of their stand [that is, the stand of the Southern-aligned Todds] . . . [You] should congratulate yourself that [various] brothers-in-law of Mr. Lincoln have taken up arms against him."[5]

In asserting his personal right to condemn wayward members of his own "family," Nat even foresaw Lincoln's death, saying, "It would not surprise me to hear that Mr. Lincoln and his cabinet were assassinated. The north is certainly verging on revolution."[6]

By 1862, many Southerners firmly believed that "Abe" Lincoln was at the root of their intensifying problems. Moreover, as the full scope of the bloody war became apparent, personal resentment toward Lincoln heightened. Nat attempted to steel Elodie for the coming fury over her family association. He cautioned her that many Selma ladies "who are curious of you . . . will conceal their feelings under their bonnets. Mr. Lincoln has become almost the personification of our enemies, and the partisan feeling of the South holds him responsible, but it is only so in a political sense. Good breeding would require persons to speak of him respectfully, or not at all, in your presence."[7]

In fact, Elodie Todd was already feeling the vindictiveness of resentful society ladies. If once hailed prior to the war in the local newspapers as the "toast of Southerners," the temperamental seventeen-year-old Elodie by 1862 had run afoul of Selma's matrons and became a victim of rumors, gossip, and local politics. "Can you stand having a sweetheart who does not belong to the first circle of Selma society?" she queried tongue in cheek. Various "quarreling and fussing" ladies had snubbed her and planned a tableau that "cut [out] the Todds'," she complained. Petty jealousies and rivalry for control and influence had served to fragment the society ladies, so that Elodie commented, "It seems strange to me that so few are together and all helping for the one and same cause that they cannot work together cheerfully and happily, in place of actually working against each other."[8]

This bickering among the elite was not only counterproductive to the war effort, but imperiled positive attitudes, she reflected. The result was inevitable: "I think my patriotism has cooled too much to allow a thought toward your again serving [in the army]," Elodie admitted in a tearful letter to her Alabama captain.[9]

The war was omnipotent, and Elodie's attitudes, like those of many others, were being reshaped in the fiery cauldron of the South's wartime existence. Her own despair was perhaps attributed to her separation from family and fiancé Nat Dawson and "the unfortunate situation of Kentucky," which prevented her from going home. Yet the real difficulty was rooted in her powerlessness to change circumstances that affected her personally.[10]

Since April 1861, the South's focus had been on the war and its outcome. The war's destruction profoundly impacted each individual's existence, despite the collective exercise of freedom and independence, which earlier had been proclaimed as essential. The terrible price to be paid was now beginning to register in the minds of many.

Elodie comprehended as much when in August 1861 she sighed,

"I attribute all to the war, which has made a change in everyone and every place."[11]

It was a remarkable omen, declared the men of the 4th Alabama Infantry. A bald eagle, the symbol of the American nation, had flown over their camp. "As it leisurely passed over the tents of the Legion, a soldier threw a stone and killed it," wrote a duly impressed Captain Nat Dawson. "I hope [the portent] will prove true, and that the United States' armies will soon be dispersed," he cheerfully reflected.[12]

In the immediate aftermath of Manassas, Nat Dawson, like many others, expected the Confederate army to take the offensive. "I think we will advance before Washington [D.C.], and you must not be surprised to hear that Washington has fallen by this time next month," he boldly announced to his fiancée on August 18, 1861.[13]

Nat, however, was again troubled by the risks of pushing forward. "We must have other battles, and you must prepare for the worst, my dear Elodie. My escape in the last [battle] was almost a miracle, as I was in the thickest of the fight, and was alongside of many who were killed and wounded. In the next, I cannot hope to be so fortunate." Was this a premonition? Elodie later wondered.[14]

A month later, Captain Dawson, if more hopeful of his own safety, was already less sanguine about the prospects for the great victory he had anticipated. "I begin to despair of wintering in Washington city," he admitted on September 24. The Confederate troops were building defensive fortifications and masked batteries, but these were hardly signs of a pending offensive campaign.[15]

Also, there were more-personal difficulties to be endured. After a long period of languishing in camp, sickness was widespread and Nat became keenly aware that his fate was tied more to the ravages of disease than to those of the battlefield. In a sentimental letter to Elodie, Nat told her that he frequently heard the volleys of musketry fired over new grave sites filled with men "unhonored and unsung" who had died of disease. "In several regiments near us about three deaths take place daily," he acknowledged. Sickness among the 4th's soldiers was so prevalent that at one point Nat's regiment lost six men in a few days. "Well men do not suffer [in the army], but the sick do," Nat grimly wrote. "They have my sympathies always. Nothing disturbs me more than to walk through the gloomy wards of a regimental hospital." Even Nat was prostrated in October 1861, having "symptoms of the jaundice," which he said was very prevalent among the men.[16]

Adding to Dawson's and his soldiers' growing misery was the familiar army malady of false alarms. "Our regiment was under arms for the third time [in as many days] . . . to meet the Yankees, who were [falsely] reported by a deserter as intending to attack us," complained an indignant Nat Dawson on October 3. Then, a day later, when another alarm aroused their camp at Dumfries, Virginia, Nat was so outraged that he wrote, "I wish General Whiting would be certain of his information before he puts his men to so much fatigue and trouble. It is the fourth time [this week] we have been thus treated. General Whiting, I fear, is an alarmist, who likes these occasions to show his importance. The army has been wearied with such movements too frequently, and the men lose confidence in their commander as a consequence. We are all anxious to be transferred. . . ."[17]

Once again, the monotonous drills and tedium of camp life were taking their toll among the Alabamians. "The regular drills have become very irksome," confided Nat Dawson. "We have learned all that is useful, and the operation, day after day, though essential to keep up the . . . proficiency of the men, is a tedious and disagreeable duty. We now drill two hours in the morning, from nine to eleven o'clock, and three hours in the evening, from two to five. The evening drills are performed by the brigade, and are very fatiguing as we have five regiments and have to march two miles to get a field large enough to drill upon."[18]

In further contrast to the early glory days at Harper's Ferry, Nat and his men now had little contact with encouraging civilians. "We seldom see any ladies now. The country is sparsely inhabited, and most of the good families have deserted their homes as they occupy a [site] that is the common battle ground of the contending armies."[19]

The boredom of army life, added to the effects of severe exposure in combat, foretold a breakdown in morale among these unseasoned citizen-soldiers. "The battle [of Manassas] has produced a visible change in the regiment," Nat observed that fall. "You hear much less hilarity and joyous songs." Due to a scarcity of provisions and the onset of winter the 4th Alabama seemed to be in a state of growing disarray. Captain Nat Dawson noted that while he was relatively comfortable, having "a tent, a trunk, a servant, [and] an abundance of clothing, . . ." many soldiers were exposed to difficulties that never troubled him. "They have been accustomed to the same comforts [at home], . . . and their natures are as sensitive, while their exposure to the petty tyranny of some officers must be galling," he considered.[20]

Nat warned in December 1861 that the attitudes of his men were such that many felt "our volunteer system must be disbanded, and a new one adopted." By March 1862, Nat estimated that most of the men whose twelve months' enlistment would expire in April would not likely reenlist. The 4th Alabama then would be reduced to four or five companies. The basis for the likely defection was a general lack of military experience, thought Dawson. "The privates think they are too good, generally, to endure the rules of discipline," he wrote. Therefore, "the army should be made up of [long-term] men who expect to obey and do their duty or be punished." Nat further observed what made him most anxious. "Our regiment is retrograding sadly under the easy rule of Colonel [Evander McIver] Law, who is too good and mild a man for his post."[21]

The 4th Alabama had been wearied and broken down in health, and was much aged "with gray heads and wrinkles," he told Elodie. "Field service is laborious and you must be prepared to see changes in your acquaintances and friends." In all, it was very sad, considered Captain Dawson on March 28, 1862. "Our regiment is not what it was six months ago. . . . The early expiration of their time seems to have made the men careless in the performance of their duties. I do wish our term was over, as I see that we are of little service. I do not think one hundred men of the regiment will reenlist here."[22]

Nat's own mind was similarly influenced. "I find that the inclination to remain at home is growing upon me," he admitted. Several ugly incidents in camp further persuaded him of his unpromising army future. One evening, an old friend who was a lieutenant in his company became intoxicated and with loud oaths drew his side knife and threatened to kill Nat. "I did not strike him, and he was taken off," wrote the exasperated Dawson.[23]

Although the lieutenant said that he acted out of jealousy and later apologized, Nat wrote, "I can never have for him the same feelings I have [previously] entertained." Infighting was not uncommon, and rumors that the men had planned to shoot an unpopular officer in the midst of battle particularly alarmed Nat. Although he thought such "cowardly" conduct proceeded "from men who were unwilling to shoulder the responsibility of their conduct," it sent a deep psychological shudder through him.[24]

The brutal realities of war as the first year of conflict ended were now evident to Nat Dawson. Being in the army involved far more than just fighting. It was a daily struggle for existence. To be a soldier, even if an officer, was often exasperating, excessively demanding, and generally debilitating. "I long to be free again, that I may do as I please," declared Nat in April 1862. "I hope something will turn up to relieve the sadness that oppresses me."[25]

His camp life, however, was only the half of the dilemma. Beyond difficulties in the field lurked another soul-wrenching prospect—that of deteriorating affairs at home. His inability to administer routine economic and personal family duties was a particular hardship, since the war was devastating the economy. The South's antebellum prosperity had largely rested upon "King Cotton," yet, with shipment to the primary European market generally cut off by the Yankee blockade, there were now few buyers. Thanks to the bountiful cotton crop of 1861–62, wealthy planters and moderately prosperous farmers such as Nat Dawson had plenty to sell, but, alas, nowhere to sell it. "I have made the largest cotton crop I have ever raised," reported the discouraged Nat Dawson in December 1861, "[yet] it avails [me] nothing. I do not know what our planters, who are dependent on their crops, will do." Beset by increased taxation to pay for the war, Nat's former father-in-law registered a typical complaint: "We have no means of getting money unless we can sell cotton."[26]

Rumors that the Confederate government might buy or advance promissory notes on the cotton crop later proved to be unfounded; any such plan would have been impractical. Any contrived exchange of money between destitute parties would provide no real benefit. The South's rotting cotton bales thus only exemplified what was apparent. The decision to go to war had involved many serious miscalculations. Rampant inflation, scarcity of goods, and little inflow of money forced the Southern population into months of self-denial, improvisation, and home production of food just for basic survival. Adding to the stress of having too few resources were various "slackers" among white male residents of the community, who avoided joining the army. Now they "sit in judgment upon our conduct," Nat angrily asserted. Nat's reaction was predictable: "There are plenty [of men at home] to take our place, [thus] we cannot appreciate the reason for remaining." "We will [therefore] return [from the war] to allow others . . . an opportunity of exhibiting their love of liberty and their willingness to give their lives and fortunes in its defense. We care not to monopolize all the glory of winning our independence."[27]

Captain Nat Dawson, gaining more experience in the politics of life, had become increasingly cynical and selfish as a result of serving in the war. When he witnessed others—less deserving in his eyes— receiving favored rank and army positions, he complained, "I shall not continue in the service without position, but will remain at home and stand to my affairs. The people [at home] have little gratitude, and care more for themselves than for the cause in which we are engaged. . . . You are my country, and can be secondary to nothing," he informed Elodie.[28]

Later, Elodie responded emotionally, saying that she too was a victim of war. "I prefer others suffering to myself," she admitted. Having endured "as much as most other persons," Elodie fretted that she acquired "an old and careworn expression." More than ever, she wanted Nat back home.[29]

Nat soothed her concerns, telling her that he would protect and provide for her, even as his central objective of matrimony remained fully in focus. "I am glad that you are willing to marry me immediately upon my return to Selma," he wrote eagerly. "There will be no necessity for delay." This would be the full fruition of their love and lives. "I have determined not to reenlist, but will return home as soon as possible after our term expires, which will be on the 25th instant [April 1862]," he pledged.[30]

Nat Dawson mistakenly anticipated an easy separation from military service. Again, the war reared up suddenly to interfere with his plans. By mid-April, he faced the prospect of combat once more with the 4th Alabama Infantry. Heavy fighting was imminent on the Virginia peninsula, where George B. McClellan's mighty Yankee army was threatening to capture Richmond.

On the eve of being sent to the Virginia peninsula, with just two weeks remaining in the 4th's term of service, Nat wrote about his future. "Such is the soldier's life. . . . I think we will be pushed into a battle to make us work before leaving the service. I have always expected it, and am prepared for any fate. I go into battle with a reliance upon the mercies of God, and a full confidence in the justice of our cause, willing to die for our independence."[31]

Both Nat and Elodie had to reconsider the probability of sharing a life together. Having just endured "a most fatiguing and wearisome march of two days through a storm of wind and rain," Nat had suffered enormously. "I have never before been so much exposed in all my experience as a soldier," he admitted. Then, once at the scene of the conflict, he told Elodie that they were "on the eve of a grand battle which [would] go far to end the war." Ironically, it was the one-year anniversary of their engagement. Although his "mind was made up to leave the service," Nat now had little choice. "Against all my wishes and hopes [I] am compelled to remain here," he observed. Although "not [his] fault," this circumstance was "a great misfortune," which he regretted "exceedingly." If only he survived the coming battle, they would surely find the promised "days of happiness."[32]

Two days later, Nat again wrote hopefully about the pending battle, saying that if he survived it, he would leave soon afterward for Alabama and the realization of his dreams by an "early marriage." By now the firing was constant along the deployed lines and an acquaintance had been killed in a nearby tent, "having his head shot off by a twenty-four pound shell." The last possible obstacle to his returning home—the conscription bill—did not apply to officers of twelve months' volunteers, so everything came down to the pending battle. Nat had recently declined reelection as captain of his company. "Duty to myself, and duty to you, and an unwillingness to remain here in my present position, induce me to do this," he said, sighing. "The regiment will be reorganized in a few days, when I will be released."[33]

Yet the terrible, distant volleys of musketry served as a reminder that Nat was still in the army. A fellow officer predicted, "The battle here will decide the fate of the war." "I do not feel so hopeful," responded the leery Nat Dawson.[34]

At that time, many miles distant in Selma, Alabama, Elodie Todd was unaware of the unfolding events about to impact her life. Indeed, she would soon suffer a great shock following receipt of some terrible war news.

"We Must Change the Tide"

Elodie Todd had once referred to herself as "a stubborn, hardheaded Presbyterian," and declared prior to Manassas in July 1861: "Fighting alone can accomplish our end, and that hard and bloody. We are prepared for reverses, for we yet remember some lost battles in a similar struggle [the American Revolution], and notwithstanding them, success crowned our efforts. And when we lose now we will push forward again with redoubled courage and determination and must and will conquer." Six months later, Elodie's perspectives had evolved into a far more mature understanding: "I never dreamed how horrible war was, and how every day it grows more dreadful to me—how much worse must it be to those who are in the midst of trouble and danger and feel the effects so much more in every way than we, who can hardly realize how changed affairs are."[35]

These abstract misgivings were written before she received unsettling news in April 1862. Early newspaper reports from Corinth, Mississippi had suggested a Confederate victory at the Battle of Shiloh, despite the death of General Albert Sidney Johnston—which "casts a long shadow upon our success," reflected Captain Nat Dawson. Nat then attempted to reassure Elodie about her family, some of whom were present at that battle: "I hope you will soon hear that your brothers and [brother-in-law] Colonel [Ben] Helm escaped unhurt at Shiloh. I feel as if they have not been injured."[36]

Elodie described herself as having felt very uneasy for three days while waiting for word of relatives who had fought there. "These battles and rumored battles keep me miserable all the time, and the changes [in location] so constantly being made, render it utterly impossible to keep posted as to the whereabouts of my brothers," she fretted.[37]

As these burdens added to her worries about Nat's safety, she was increasingly fearful of the future. "I hope I will be able to bear my part of sorrow and trouble caused by so glorious a struggle for liberty with as much firmness as any of my countrywomen," she wrote on April 15, 1862.[38]

That heavy sorrow came to Elodie the very next day. "This morning [April 16] I was awakened by a note from my brother-in-law, Mr. Kellogg," wrote Elodie, "informing me he was . . . on board the *Southern Republic,* and on his way to Montgomery. . . . [He] also informed me of the death of my brother, Sam, killed in the battle at Corinth [Shiloh]." Although she sent a telegraph to New Orleans, hoping to "hear this sad news [was] untrue," her brother's death was soon confirmed. "I little thought another day would bring with it . . . such trials and sorrows," lamented Elodie.[39]

Moreover, with news of a severe battle in progress on the Virginia peninsula and her Nat in mortal danger, there now was the prospect of losing her every future hope, within just days of learning that her brother was killed. Elodie Todd had abruptly acquired a very deep and personal understanding of the war.

With enormous relief, Elodie learned shortly thereafter that the 4th Alabama had avoided heavy exposure in battle prior to Nat's discharge in late April. By the end of the month he was en route home to Selma, and Elodie was much calmed. In fact, she soon discovered she had very good reason to be grateful. Shortly after Nat's departure, the 4th Alabama suffered 210 casualties at Fair Oaks, and during the subsequent Seven Days battles lost 92 of 225 present. It had been a close call. Nat's letters had well described the ordeal and trauma of soldiering, but his battle accounts never seemed to convey the full force of the war's terrible impact. She had taken his survival for granted no matter how graphically he described the action. But her brother's irrevocable death in combat inflicted a brutal personal wound. It brought with it an awareness of the mortality of each person, no matter how greatly loved. The experience created in her a lingering helplessness and sense of personal vulnerability. It was a deep and humbling lesson for her.[40]

As Elodie Todd now understood, the war was beyond any one person's control; it required of civilians a quiet courage—to patiently wait—either for progress or disaster, both public and private. When the news from the war was bad, as it generally was almost from the beginning of the new year 1862, intense trauma confronted the South's white populace. What most had believed would be a short and relatively bloodless war was now shown to be an all-consuming, ever-expanding conflict of unknown duration. It was increasingly apparent that this war would bring to the entire country ordeal and travail as never before envisioned. Moreover, the giddy early promises of glorious victory and Southern battlefield dominance were all but lost in the recent tragedies.

The year 1862 had begun as a time of defeat in the South. There were the terrible losses in Tennessee; Mill Springs and the death of General Zollicoffer in January; and the crippling loss of Forts Henry and Donelson in February. News of the disaster at Pea Ridge, Arkansas, came in March—along with word of the defeat at New Bern, North Carolina. April brought the devastating news of Shiloh—one of the South's greatest failures—and the menace of McClellan's seemingly unstoppable thrust up the Virginia peninsula toward Richmond. The Confederate war was being waged unsatisfactorily, and for the first time there was a gloomy foreboding among some that this protracted struggle might not end in the outright Southern success once generally anticipated.

Although the reaction to these trying events was varied, Nat Dawson had acknowledged in March 1862 that the South's defeats and losses were "unaccountable," and he urged, "We must change the tide." While there seemed to be no easy answer to the recent series of defeats, many held that they were both a necessary lesson in commitment and a mandate to correct previous mistakes. "The whole country seems alive to our dangers, and it is to be hoped that we will shake off the lethargy of the past ... months," wrote Dawson following news of Pea Ridge. It was this "awakening" to the great danger that would inspire more men to enlist, he envisioned, and thus the tide would be turned.[41]

The biggest problem with the war, asserted Elodie Todd as a soldier's bride-to-be, was the terrible mental toll of waiting. There was so much uncertainty about everything. Elodie had long hoped that the Confederacy would take the offensive, force the issue, and thus rapidly end the war. Since this policy had not been implemented by the Davis administration, many impatient Southern citizens were confronted with the prospect of prolonged indecision and further waiting.

Already, with failure prevalent, there was growing criticism of the government and of various military commanders by the public. Nat Dawson's close friend and former father-in-law Joel E. Mathews informed him, "I am rather out with our administration, fearing from the indications so far that a defensive is their policy. If that be so, we are going to have terrible times, I fear. . . . It seems to me that the only way to save our [country] from being ravaged is to carry the war into 'Africa,' or rather to go thundering at the gates of Cincinnati, Philadelphia, or New York . . . We never will conquer a peace until we make the enemy feel on their own soil the horrors of war."[42]

It was terribly frustrating. The people wanted decisive action, an end to the smothering misery of defeat that blanketed the South like a dark cloud. Even Nat Dawson said as much when he hinted of his disillusionment with the South's defensive policy. His exasperation had been evident in November 1861 when he wrote, "We have to wait upon the action of the Yankees."[43]

Despite this early period of disappointment, hope remained intact in the minds of many who were expectantly waiting. Their belief in ultimate victory continued. To console and encourage the masses, Confederate leaders expressed optimism. Recognition of the Confederacy by England or France was reported as likely, especially following the "Trent Affair" of November 1861, in which Confederate commissioners James M. Mason and John Slidell were "illegally" captured on the high seas from a British vessel. Following this event, Nat Dawson considered "war inevitable" between England and the United States. "We may expect an early peace," he wrote.[44]

Although these hopes were soon dashed—diplomats Mason and Slidell were released by the Federal government in early 1862—Nat Dawson continued to believe that foreign intervention eventually would occur. Elodie joined her fiancé in cautious optimism. "I am in hopes" some day to hear of "peace, but so little fighting has been done that [this] day I fear is far in the future," she observed. If only there was "foreign aid in breaking the blockade," lamented Elodie, "we could then do very well [as an independent nation]."[45]

The growing frustration was thus often disguised beneath misguided expectations. A variety of fleeting if whimsical hopes seemed to buoy momentarily the South's sagging spirits and offer encouragement. Rumors were rife that the Yankee government's treasury was depleted, and stories about deaths or resignations among key Union officials were constantly circulating. "We hear, by telegraph, that Mr. Cameron [Secretary of War], [and] Gen. McClellan have resigned, and that England and France acknowledged our independence," wrote a joyous Nat Dawson in January 1862. "Also that Gen. [Humphrey] Marshall has defeated the Federals at Prestonburg, in eastern Kentucky [Middle Creek, Kentucky, January 10, 1862—an insignificant skirmish]. If all be true, an early termination of the war may be expected."[46]

Almost as an afterthought, Nat had then hastily added, "I fear all is not true, but all will come to pass. . . ."

It was a significant remark, for in Nat Dawson's mind, as in the minds of many others, practicality was beginning to take precedent over emotion. Believing only what was observed, not heard, was a natural outcome of military experience.

Perhaps this was the hardest part. If anticipation generated hope, reality usually proved to be something far different from everyone's expectations. Although Captain Dawson prophesied in December

1861 "The end draweth near, and soon the spectacle of a humiliated [Yankee] nation will be presented to the world," the longer this unprofitable war continued, a more pertinent question seemed to be which "nation" might be humiliated.[47]

In the spring of 1862, as the war turned suddenly unfavorable for the South, a righteous reliance on Providence was increasingly invoked as the ultimate means of eventual victory. "Mr. Lincoln and his cabinet are certainly infatuated [with recent victories]," observed Nat Dawson in early 1862. "[Yet] they are [but] instruments in the hands of God to punish a vainglorious and sinful people." If all else failed, "Providence [would] bring the war to a [successful] close," defiantly declared the Alabama captain.[48]

Nat Dawson could afford to resort to abstractions; he was going home. True to his promises to Elodie, he would not rejoin the army, save for maintaining a captain's commission with the Alabama state militia. Rather than return to a difficult and dangerous military life, he became an Alabama legislator, and ultimately ran for governor. Except for a brief period of militia service in 1864, Nat remained at home and in Montgomery, Alabama, supporting the war effort by legal resolution instead of serving in the field.

His marriage to Elodie in 1862 began their much-anticipated life together and resulted in a bond that lasted for nineteen years prior to Elodie's death in 1881. By 1864 a son, Henry, was enlivening their home in Selma, and while on militia duty Nat wrote of visiting a friend whose daughter played "Rock of Ages" on the melodeon. "The music carried me back to my own home and made me feel nearer to my own Elodie and her darling baby boy," he mused.[49]

Music and her bouncing baby boy provided much of life's solace for Elodie Todd Dawson, who continued to suffer innumerable hardships and trauma during the war. Following the loss of her brother Sam at Shiloh in April 1862, another brother, David, was mortally wounded at Vicksburg in 1863, and a third brother, Alexander "Ellick," was killed that fall in a skirmish near Baton Rouge, Louisiana. When her sister Emilie's husband, Brigadier General Benjamin Hardin Helm, died at Chickamauga in September 1863, the Todd family's tragedy was complete—until the Lincoln assassination.

The war had worn terribly on Elodie, and she remained in Selma, devastated, bitter, and afraid when alone—"I cannot bear solitude," she complained in September 1864.[50]

By that time, active combat was only a memory for her lawyer-legislator husband, and Elodie could write to Nat while he briefly served on militia duty, "As long as you are kept from danger I will not quarrel much, and will feel very thankful."[51]

Nathaniel Henry Rhodes Dawson, although still patriotic, continued to keep out of harm's way. He had learned the truth about war and was content to live a life devoid of military glory. "How little we should value public applause," he wrote after his tour of duty was over. "It is [as evaporative] as water, and the longer I live, the less inclined I am to be influenced by it."[52]

Nat Dawson had endured battle and was a survivor. He now knew that what counted in life was far more substantial than military rank or fame.

It had been a hard-learned lesson.

Chapter Thirteen

FRED FLEET

"NOTHING IS NEW WITH WISE'S GARDENERS"

It was all so frustrating! For an energetic Virginia youth like Fred Fleet, who had envisioned glory and honor in military service, the army seemed only an endless litany of drill, marching, and waiting. In their unheralded duty as home guards for Richmond, Fleet's regiment, the 26th Virginia Infantry, was burdened with the tarnished image of their brigade's commander. Fifty-six-year-old brigadier general Henry A. Wise, the former Virginia governor and Democratic politician—who in 1861 was without military experience or training—was a gaunt, embittered old man. He had been in command at Roanoke Island, North Carolina, when that post was surrendered to the Yankees in February 1862, yet Wise was ill at Nag's Head on the day of the battle, and thus had become embroiled in a heated controversy over his role in that disaster. If not disgraced and politically ruined, General Wise was at least regarded as an inept commander.[1]

During the Peninsula Campaign, Wise's troops had remained out of the real combat, and Fred Fleet wrote to his parents about his low spirits. "I suppose you have heard of [Stonewall] Jackson's progress [in the Shenandoah Valley]," he wistfully reported. "What an honor to have belonged to that division it will be when the war is over!"[2]

Although promoted to lieutenant in May 1862, Fred Fleet remained, within his own mind, a warrior in name only. Recently he had gone to Richmond to buy "a good sword that would be of some account to me in a fight...rather than a dress sword which would be of no more account in a fight than a cornstalk." Being enthused that "it was a time for deeds, not words," Fred had informed his father in April 1862 of his "confidence in the justice of our cause," and that he would remember "we are fighting for our homes and all that we hold dear on earth."[3]

Fred thus was extremely embarrassed about not participating in the fighting. Since by mid-1862 the fortunes of war had not included Fred Fleet among those honored or glorified, he became increasingly restless and uncertain about when his regiment might get into combat. "The tug of war has not come [to me] yet," he again complained. "You must not form any opinion as to my great courage until we come to our real conflict—when, there is no telling."[4]

Fanciful reports about martial glory had so colored his mind about combat that fighting turned into an obsession. There were stories about the bayonet attack at Fair Oaks of the 4th Louisiana on a Rhode Island regiment, said to be an elite unit of the Union army. "The Rhode Islanders had come to a [position of] charge bayonets, and were calmly awaiting the approach of our men, who had come within some twenty paces of them," wrote Fred, "when the Louisianians raised the cry of 'Butler, Butler' [in derision of Benjamin Butler—the "Beast" of New Orleans]. . . . At the sound of this name, the vile wretches, knowing they had no quarter to expect, fled incontinently."[5]

Such romanticized myths seemed absurd when Fred Fleet and his comrades finally witnessed the devastation of war while lying in reserve at Malvern Hill on July 1. "I don't know whether you will call it fortunate or not," sighed Fred to his father, "but our regiment has not yet been in action." Nonetheless, the 26th Virginia's exposure to random shelling as they marched forward on July 1 convinced all that war was serious business. "I felt very calm although the shells were bursting all around us," proudly wrote Fred. When several retreating batteries passed by "in great confusion . . . the loose horses rushing by, some wounded and seemingly mad," a caisson overturned in their midst. "If it had exploded, we would all have been killed," the stunned lieutenant realized. Then with a squad of cavalry dashing past "in a perfect stampede" a nearby North Carolina regiment panicked. They "turned around [in the road] and ran," noted the shocked Fleet.[6]

In all, it had been a sobering experience. "The boys [of his regiment] are not the same romping fellows they were at Glouchester Point," noted Fred, "but a seriousness seems to have come over them all. They say they all wanted 'to get into a fight,' but they have had enough of it, until necessity compels them to do it again."[7]

Even Fred Fleet was among those who now pondered the random terror of battle. The day before his nineteenth birthday, Fred wrote, "I have always thought heretofore that I would like very much to be in a battle and run the risk of being shot." But suddenly, he wasn't so sure. Being an officer, and noticing "the great proportion of officers killed and wounded," he began to reconsider his own good fortune in having had only a passive combat role. "I have always thought I would not like for the battles around Richmond to end without having a hand in them, but truthfully, since I have seen the poor mangled fellows and have heard of so many of my acquaintances falling near me, I have come to the conclusion that if I can do my duty, and at the same time keep out of a fight, I shall be satisfied and thankful that my life has been spared."[8]

In noting that Malvern Hill was among the "fiercest and bloodiest" battles of the peninsula fighting, Fred pointed to the influence of God in keeping the regiment safe when it appeared they were about to join in the last, fatal charge. "We would have been compelled to march in [the] face of a raking fire from [the enemy's] batteries, and probably not one in ten would have survived it," he grimly surmised.[9]

Fred admittedly was depressed following his near-battle experiences, and wrote home that if Virginia was evacuated, "one half or probably two thirds of her army [would] refuse to leave the state." For his part, he was "willing to go to Florida rather than give up or be subjugated by the detestable Yankees." Nonetheless, it seemed to him, "if we ever do gain our independence, it will be by the assistance of Providence, [and] in spite of our generals and leaders."[10]

Noting her son's "low spirits," Fred's mother continued to urge him to serve his country well. "I don't want to see you [at home] because of sickness or wounds," she reminded Fred shortly after Malvern Hill, "and I couldn't have you here in health, when our country calls for every man to do his part." Fred's father only encouraged his son to stand at his post and acquit himself "like a man."[11]

Lieutenant Fleet soon reassured his parents of his rebounding spirits, saying, "There has been some talk for the last two . . . days about our going [to join General Jackson]." Only two brigades from Longstreet's division had been left behind, and General Wise was "trying his best" to arrange their reassignment, since the 26th Virginia had never been in a fight, and was "spoiling for one."[12]

Again, Fred Fleet found only disappointment. Once the Peninsula Campaign ended with the transfer of Lee's and McClellan's armies to northern Virginia, Wise's men were once more left behind to guard the approaches to Richmond south of that city. While his men mostly fished, idly chatted about the war, dug entrenchments, and performed routine camp duty, General Wise was content to occasionally shuffle from Richmond to view his brigade, stationed near Chaffin's Farm, Virginia.[13]

To Lieutenant Fred Fleet, this inaction was all the more detestable. Lee's valiant army was then winning glory and victory north of Richmond. "I can assure you I would much rather go up to the Great Army of Northern Virginia than march about or even remain in these parts," Fred forlornly informed his brother Benny. "In fact," continued Fred, "it is a sort of disgrace to belong to General Wise's command, as we are called 'Wise's Gardeners,' 'Fishbone Brigade,' etc."[14]

Ridicule was something Fred Fleet had hardly imagined when he first joined the army. Yet soldiering wasn't at all what he initially thought it would be. What he had presumed would bring glory, honor, and excitement, garnered mostly dreariness, bureaucracy, and tedium. Living in canvas tents, with all the privations of camp routine, weather, and nondescript army food, had taken its toll. When coupled with the absence of the purpose for which he had joined the army— actively fighting for the Southern cause—it was devastating to Fleet.

After one fruitless, night-long, rain-drenched expedition in the direction of Williamsburg during October 1862, Fred admitted, "We returned here [to Chaffin's Farm] . . . having marched through even heavier rain and mud, and having accomplished nothing." Thus, after spending a night in Richmond and staying in a hotel, the thought of "coming from a good, dry, warm hotel to the damp, disagreeable tents" seemed dreadful. Yet Fred wrote, "I had much rather be in active service, and see something of the war, than to be comfortably housed in town."[15]

The whole matter of his regiment's interminable noncombat predicament seemed such a farce that Fred despaired of ever getting into the real war. Even his mother's comment that she couldn't be "thankful enough" that Fred was not in Northern Virginia to suffer in the bloody battles there wouldn't appease him. Fred Fleet rued the day he had enrolled in the army.[16]

Young Fleet's distress was not unique. At times, aspects of the Southern rebellion seemed unreal or absurd. In 1861, women in King and Queen County, Virginia, had eagerly named their babies "Jefferson Davis Beauregard" and "Secessia Beauregard" after the popular heroes of the times. Yet, some months later, men in the same neighborhood were coming to Fred Fleet's father, a local physician, for exemptions from conscription or duty in the militia on such pretexts as of having had their "arm broken when about five years old," or having "one big toe shorter than the other." In disgust, Fred's mother told him that serving as a volunteer private was more honorable than being a militia officer.[17]

The actions of the people reflected their changing attitudes and circumstances. In early 1862, while the war still seemed to progress in the South's favor "Ma" Fleet could write, "Our army has been tolerably well tried and not found wanting. . . . The smiles of an approving Providence seem rather to invite our men to again enlist. . . ."[18]

Only a few weeks later, following the defeats at Roanoke Island and Forts Henry and Donelson, her family's mood had swiftly changed. "Egyptian darkness seems to hover over our land," wrote Fred's father. "If we can only get a change for the better in the War and Navy Departments, . . . may we not hope for a change in the results of the next battles to come off?" Mrs. Fleet then pondered the consequences of this "sad news." In the wake of the defeats, a local youth abruptly accepted a position as deputy postmaster so he could avoid service, and she denounced this perceived cowardice. "If he were a son of mine, I would dress him up in petticoats and set him to knitting and spinning," Mrs. Fleet harrumphed.[19]

Looking on the positive side, these reverses, Ma Fleet hoped, would strengthen the resolve of the army, and she was very thankful something had happened "to arouse us all." "What contempt everyone must feel for anyone who calls himself a man and refuses now to obey his country's call," she somberly added.[20]

The war was changing all people in the way they saw things and the way they reacted, noted Mrs. Fleet. Combat turned out to be no panacea for the South's cause, for it was an all-consuming ordeal that often brought the worst and promised unknown trials to come. That much was now understood. Yet the commitment to the cause of independence, of not being "subjugated," remained intact. So long as the difficulties and pain were not too great, for the Fleet family this determination would mandate bravely carrying on the war effort.

What now complicated matters for citizens of King and Queen County, Virginia, where stood Green Mount, Fred's own home, was the probability of the war coming to their doorstep. Doctor Fleet's fear that the Yankees would winter during 1862–63 in the vicinity and scour the surrounding counties for supplies had him worried. Also, Fred's mother warned, "The war seems coming closer to us than ever before, and I feel weighted down by a sense of coming ill that I can't shake off." Even worse, as the conflict progressed, Fred's father fore-saw the war lasting indefinitely, a prospect that would bring distress-ing political ramifications. "If Black Republicans are elected [in the 1862 fall elections], Lincoln's term will hardly witness its end," he predicted.[21]

Particularly troublesome to Mrs. Fleet was the possibility that her youngest son Benny, now sixteen, would be conscripted into the war within two years. "Oh, son," she complained in a letter to Fred, "there is something horrible to me in this conscription, compelling every youth of 18 to join the army, willing or not. [It is] . . . very despotic to my mind, but I suppose there is no help for it."[22]

The Yankees were far more resolute and capable than many had imagined back in 1861. Southern society now faced losing its sons, fathers, and husbands, in addition to privation and enormous ordeals at home as the war engulfed vast regions of the South. Particularly vulnerable was Virginia, the seat of war in the East. These new cir-cumstances were sobering to the now-apprehensive Fleet family.

Having heard the cannon booming in the direction of Fredericks-burg that winter, Doctor Fleet had all too much evidence that the war had drawn near. But he was yet willing to commit his resources to the conflict—"to give up everything, and begin . . . afresh, to achieve our independence." Meat, bread, soap, socks, and other sun-dries were furnished by the Fleets to a passing unit of J. E. B. Stuart's horse artillery. "I want my children to remember when we are dead . . . that their parents did not make money out of the soldiers, but gave with a free hand," he asserted. Doctor Fleet even obligingly endured the new tax bill, saying that even though he estimated it would cost him perhaps $4,000, "Let it be so, provided everybody pays in the same ratio." He further pledged his entire wealth. "[I will use] the last cent I have on earth . . . freely towards the support of those who are risking life and all that is dear to them for my liberty," Doctor Fleet resolutely wrote.[23]

It was perhaps a concession to conscience. Matters seemed to be going from bad to worse despite the occasional reports of great military success—which mostly proved to be exaggerated or false. The year 1862 had witnessed more than just military disasters. Crops had failed in many regions of the upper South; the corn in one field yielded "the worst crop I have ever seen [from] that land," said the distraught Doctor Fleet. Since Fred was away, he had less help managing the farm's produce. "I must say," he wrote to Fred in despair, "I have seen more real trouble this year than I have before seen in my whole life."[24]

Even worse, the war was revealing inequities between the North's and South's supplies. Because of rampant inflation, there seemed to be no end of shortages in sight. Even good clothing was increasingly scarce. Fred had visited with several Yankee officers on a boat while arranging for a prisoner exchange. They were "dressed as fine as you please," and "seemed to sneer at our men who were without uniform," grumbled the young lieutenant. Fred was particularly taken aback by their dedication: "I talked with some of them, and as a general thing they seemed as much in earnest as we are, and I see no probability of the end of the war." This made him "hate them worse than ever," seethed Fred, especially in view of his unit's distance from any substantial fighting.[25]

In the aftermath of 1862, Doctor Fleet was equally distressed about the war, but for different reasons. The conflict was even then engulfing King and Queen County; in fact, he was now so alarmed that he joined the home guards, despite his infirmity and advanced age of forty-six. News soon reached Fred that their neighborhood and home had been raided by Yankee cavalry that spring, and ten horses and mules were taken from Doctor Fleet—all the working animals the family had. Since most of the able-bodied white men were in the army, only a few boys and aging militia remained to protect the local homesteads. Fred's younger brother, Benny had joined a newly organized home-guard company, but within a few weeks that company suddenly disbanded. "We heard that the Yankees have sworn vengeance against us, the home guard, that they had hung two [men], and said they meant to hang everyone of us," nervously reported Benny in his journal.[26]

The ravages of war were about to come again to Green Mount, and in a more terrible form, Fred and his family realized. Everybody in the neighborhood seemed scared. A boatman at a nearby river ferry became so frightened of a report the Yankees were within two miles that he cut the rope and let the boat drift downriver—only to learn that the report was false. Fred informed his parents of more than a dozen desertions from the 26th Virginia regiment following news of a Yankee raid in the lower country. "We heard they . . . were forcing off all the negroes who would not go voluntarily, and destroying all the property they could lay their hands on," he wrote. The war had engulfed the Virginia countryside, and everyone was at risk. Benny constantly talked about joining Major John Mosby's irregulars, and Fred tried to dissuade him, telling him, "I don't think you ought to be dissatisfied because you can't go into the service, because you would certainly get tired of serving as a private. . . . It is not your fault that you are not old enough, and if all the boys of your age were to neglect their education and join the army, it would be disastrous to the next generation."[27]

To Fred Fleet, the circumstances of his military service had become all the more burdensome. His home was being devastated, and his family and their livelihood were being threatened. Yet he was powerless to do anything about it. Stationed below Richmond with Wise's brigade, the 26th Virginia remained "out of the war." "There is nothing new with 'Wise's Gardeners,' and probably never will be," he disgustedly wrote to his mother. "We have two drills a day, and the rest of the time is spent reading and talking over the events of the day." While others served the cause well, he only observed from afar. "I wish very much that we could have a great outpouring of God's Grace with us, as I see there has been with the noble Army of Northern Virginia," lamented Fred that summer. "How much I do wish I belonged to that noble band of veterans! We are left here as 'home guards' while they . . . are now in Maryland and probably in Pennsylvania, gaining for themselves imperishable renown and glory. . . ."[28]

On the day before his twentieth birthday, Lieutenant Fred Fleet wrote of his predicament. "I am nearly half through life. . . . Now all is dark—not one ray of light breaks out from the war clouds which hover over us. God only knows how long this war will last, and He only can stay it in its course."[29]

Fred Fleet had learned much. The biggest question yet remaining was, had he learned enough?

Chapter Fourteen

A Legacy of Adversity

It was an army of destiny. Although not designated the Army of Tennessee until November 20, 1862, the principal Confederate army of the West eventually would have a great impact on the Civil War's final outcome. Its performance and survival were crucial to maintaining the Confederacy, and it existed as one of the South's two major military forces.

As a hybrid army, the Army of Tennessee was composed of forces originally assigned in 1861–62 to defend the vast western regions beyond the Appalachian Mountains, including the Mississippi Valley.* Under the command of General Albert Sidney Johnston, the forerunner to the Army of Tennessee, the Army of the Mississippi, was the force that had attempted to redeem Southern fortunes in the West at the Battle of Shiloh.

---

*Major General Edmund Kirby Smith's Army of Eastern Tennessee (later called the Army of Kentucky, or Kirby Smith's corps) was one component of the Army of Tennessee. However, its primary forces, as formed in late March 1862, were originally designated the Army of the Mississippi. This "Mississippi" army consisted of two major elements: the Central Army of Kentucky, created in 1861 to operate on the Kentucky frontier under General Albert Sidney Johnston, and the troops assigned to defense of the Mississippi Valley under General P. G. T. Beauregard (these being reinforcements gathered to defend the railroad junction at Corinth, Mississippi including Brigadier General Daniel Ruggles' Louisiana troops, Major General Braxton Bragg's corps from the Gulf region, and the force stationed near Columbus, Kentucky, under Major General Leonidas Polk).

Even prior to Shiloh, this middle-South concentration of troops was burdened by the precedent of defeats at Mill Springs, Kentucky, in January 1862, and the surrender of Forts Henry and Donelson during February. Within the span of a few weeks, the western Confederacy's northern defensive perimeter—along the Bowling Green, Kentucky, line—had been broken and evacuated. Kentucky and most of Tennessee, including Nashville, were lost to the Federal forces.

These failures set a stressful and awkward precedent for the newly created Army of the Mississippi, a force comprised mostly of soldiers who hadn't yet seen combat. The disasters in the West had been at the expense of other troops, many of whom were now Federal prisoners. As such, this conglomeration of troops composing Albert Sidney Johnston's army in early April 1862 remained inspired, if cautious. "[Fort] Donelson, with all its sad results, taught us the necessity of prompt vigorous action," asserted a Mississippi captain. "We needed some lessons that only defeats could teach us."[1]

In the aftermath of defeat, the soldiers' attitudes reflected both the hope propelling the western Confederacy's military efforts and the difficulties that encumbered its progress. One refined Louisiana soldier who hailed from an urbane New Orleans district thought the troops of Sidney Johnston's Kentucky army "unprincipled and very degraded men and officers." Rough-and-tumble in mannerisms, and ragged in dress, they were regarded as yahoos—a poor class of uneducated backwoods ruffians that constantly cussed, drank, and chewed tobacco. Even their officers seemed to be not distinguished upper-class gentlemen, but a tougher sort who dominated by the force of their malevolent nature.[2]

In turn, the backwoods privates of Johnston's command didn't exactly relish the New Orleans dandies. An Alabama soldier confided that the Louisiana troops were "all dutch and irish & frinch [,] the maddest people in the world[.] I think th[ey] [can] stand no [more] than we can tha[t] have bin raised hard [with] not hardly anuf to eate in their lives[.] The most of them are from New Orleans."[3]

While these soldiers' diverse backgrounds may have nagged at the army's spirit of cohesiveness, each regiment acted in camp with much self-sufficiency. They were largely influenced by their confined existence and the military's reliance on small unit accountability. Since each regiment was made up of locally recruited companies—which meant that the soldiers were often neighbors and generally knew one another—the emphasis was on unit performance and loyalties.

Throughout the war, a soldier was constantly mindful of how his actions would be interpreted by his friends and neighbors in the army, and hence by the community at home.[4]

Significantly, the vast majority of soldiers, no matter from what background, were fighting for common objectives. To many, their hopes for Southern independence were focused on the successful defense of their regional homeland. The desire to defend one's community had been an important incentive for going to war. If the Northern troops were intent on compelling compliance with Federal law, Southern soldiers were committed to protecting their rights and property. For many western Rebel soldiers, the urge to preserve both had been their primary reason for enlisting, no matter if they lived in New Orleans or Monterey, Tennessee. Joining the army provided the best means for Southerners to demonstrate both their patriotism and capacity "to defend their homeland."[5]

While most acted according to these values in 1861, by early 1862 there had been widespread shifts in attitudes toward army service. Nearly a year after the beginning of the conflict, frustration with military life affected the Southern soldier, and sometimes led to his outright questioning of the propriety of continuing to serve. The new doubts related to the natural independence of the Southern citizen-soldier, but also to the shared objective of winning, which no longer seemed certain.

The chemistry of successful soldiering involved a mix of components, from adequate food and equipment to good leadership and reasonable hope of victory. By April 1862, the western army's many battlefield innocents were no longer inexperienced soldiers. Most had endured nearly a year of military service characterized by hardship and frustration.

The naïve hopes of mid-1861 by now had become memories among the dark shadows of rigid military discipline and Confederate military failures. It was evident to the soldiers that the sacrifice of their personal freedom was not leading to the victory they had anticipated. Morale inevitably declined.

Just before marching off to fight at Shiloh, Private Joseph B. Lyman of the 1st Louisiana Cavalry acknowledged, "Camp and martial life is in its nature particularly distasteful to a person like myself. . . . The duties of a soldier are so dull and mechanical that I never found anything so little to my taste—especially guard duty—but I go through with these duties faithfully and without flinching." Having had "lovely, warm weather" for the past week, and being amid the songbirds and flowers of spring, Lyman wrote on April 1, 1862, "I can hardly realize this war—can hardly believe that it is anything but a heavy and feverish dream that will pass when we awake." The cursing, drinking, and rowdy troops at Corinth were "disgusting," he continued, "and it is only when I think of the wickedness of our camps that I have some doubt as to what the God of history may design for us." As for the army's chances of future success: "I do hope we have talent enough to penetrate the designs of the enemy," he mused. "As of late they have out generalled us as well as out numbered us. I look for a rather tedious campaign—a great deal of waiting and expecting—[with] hope deferred and expectation dampened." General Beauregard should initiate "a vigorous, forward Napoleonic movement," Lyman concluded. "Our army needs such a policy to prevent the demoralization of our men."[6]

Private Lyman's attitude mirrored that of many of his fellow soldiers. If battle hadn't been their lot, they still were becoming increasingly impatient under their many hardships, from a scarcity of food to petty abuses at the hands of officers. Moreover, they expected success in return for their efforts. In contrast to the Virginia mystique of superiority and military prowess, in the West there often was only the legacy of a meager farm existence in mid-America's backwoods, without the benefit of culture or higher education. Soldiering, an object-driven endeavor that required a discipline most were unused to, could only be justified if they accomplished their common goal, freedom. Western soldiers accepted that they would have to endure hard times. Yet there remained a righteous indignation over the army's inherent inefficiency, undue procrastination, and, above all else, the great waste in lives, time, and effort due to the unanticipated and seemingly inexplicable failures of others.

This subsurface despair, following repeated major defeats in the West, had taken its toll on nearly everyone, from the lowest private to the commanding general. Blamed for the loss of two states and the western Confederacy's entire northern defensive perimeter, General Sidney Johnston was cursed and denounced for his want of leadership. Newspapers added to the furor, reporting that many soldiers were enlisting only on condition that they not be made to serve under Johnston. Nonetheless, the grimly determined Sidney Johnston would not blame others for the failures in his department. Instead, he told

Jefferson Davis, "The test of merit in my profession with the people is success. It is a hard rule, but I think it right."[7]

Aware that a naïve expectation of success usually breeds cynicism and hopelessness when it is not fulfilled, Johnston accepted the pain of watching his men lose faith, but looked to the future for restitution. Sharing Johnston's grief was Lieutenant Colonel Frank Schaller of the 22d Mississippi Infantry. Schaller had noticed the effect of defeat among the women in Tennessee following the shocking loss of Fort Donelson in February 1862. While amid the columns of Confederates evacuating Nashville he saw "the sad, sorrowful countenances of the women standing upon the doorsteps when we passed some quiet town . . . mournfully waving their handkerchiefs as the retreating army passed, with no cheering smile upon their lips, or word of welcome to the tired soldiers." It was difficult reconciling defeat and despair when there had been so much anticipation of success by nearly all, considered Schaller. Thus their reactions had mirrored the uncertainty of what was to come—in the case of Tennessee's citizenry, enemy occupation and control.[8]

For the Confederate soldiers of the Army of the Mississippi, then preparing to attack the unsuspecting camp of Ulysses S. Grant's invading army at Shiloh Church, the imminent fight loomed as the grand battle not only for possession of the Mississippi Valley, but also for Southern redemption. It was believed by many that the contest would decide the fate of their army, and perhaps the war.[9]

Thus stress was both personal and organizational. When the fighting began at Shiloh on a beautiful Sabbath morning, April 6, 1862—in thick woods with cleared plots and meandering ravines that confused tactical dispositions—many soldiers found the experience of combat difficult yet rewarding. At first, the element of complete surprise enabled Johnston's army to overrun the outer Union camps with only scattered resistance. Despite the prevalence of straggling and looting amid the captured Yankee camps, Johnston had his troops poised by midday to complete the victory and push the disorganized foe all the way back to Pittsburg Landing. Since the triangular confluence of several major creeks with the Tennessee River severely restricted enemy maneuvering, the destruction or surrender of Grant's army seemed possible.

Due to an improbable and insidious sequence of events, however, the battlefield situation soon drastically changed. First, because his battle plan committed the Confederate army to overwhelming the Federal army's Lick Creek flank (the Confederate army's right), Sidney Johnston learned about midmorning of the presence of an enemy "division" beyond his extreme right flank. The report came from a captain on staff duty, sent to reconnoiter along the far Lick Creek region. Fearing "that the division in front of me would swing around and take our forces in flank," Captain S. H. Lockett had sent this urgent report to Johnston, suggesting "the importance of having our right flank protected." Since Johnston was then preparing to resume his mostly unhindered advance straight ahead in the direction of Pittsburg Landing, and he didn't have enough troops to both attack frontally and divert to the right, he was faced with a crucial decision. After briefly weighing his options, Johnston chose to halt the advance and send two of his best brigades to the right to confront the enemy. Thereafter, he would wait for the Reserve Corps under Major General John C. Breckinridge to come forward before resuming his advance northward toward Pittsburg Landing.[10]

His choice became a critical error of the battle. Captain S. H. Lockett had been badly mistaken. Instead of a division, the troops he had seen were merely those of an isolated Federal brigade, Brigadier General David Stuart's, posted there weeks earlier to guard a bridge on Lick Creek. Instead of threatening Johnston's right flank, Stuart's troops were confused, frightened, and in a defensive position. The result was a long, roundabout diversion of Johnston's two brigades to reach a point less than a half-mile distant, and the wasting of about two hours before Breckinridge's troops came forward in Johnston's sector to resume the general advance.[11]

The delay proved to have a crucial impact on the battle's outcome. By the time Johnston led Breckinridge's troops forward, a major Federal defensive line had been formed, composed of survivors from the morning's attack and two fresh divisions, Brigadier General W. H. L. Wallace's and Major General Stephen Hurlbut's, both up from the Federal rear echelon. Because the position they occupied was a naturally strong defensive perimeter, later known as the Hornets' Nest, enormous bloodshed and more than three hours were required to break this new Yankee line. Moreover, during the aftermath of a successful charge in the vicinity of the Peach Orchard, in which Sidney Johnston personally participated, a stray rifle ball severely wounded Johnston in the back of his right leg. Before the wound was discovered by others, Johnston had collapsed, and he died soon after from a loss of blood.[12]

The resulting confusion in command was reflected in the repeated piecemeal-style assaults ordered by General Braxton Bragg against the Hornets' Nest. Bragg, schooled in the theories of Mahan and Jomni at West Point, was convinced that the offensive dogma of "throwing masses upon decisive points" was the key to tactical success on the battlefield. "I shall promptly assail him [the enemy] in the open field with my whole available force, if he does not exceed me more than four to one," he had declared a few months before Shiloh. Nearly a dozen disjointed attacks ordered by Bragg were beaten back with frightful slaughter. Further chaos was evidenced in the withdrawal order issued by the new army commander, General P. G. T. Beauregard, following the eventual breakup of the Hornets' Nest. Just as a few Confederate units were approaching Grant's last line at Pittsburg Landing, they were ordered to pull back. More ominously, as darkness fell, the advance elements of Major General Don Carlos Buell's Army of the Ohio were being ferried across the Tennessee River to reinforce Grant's beleaguered troops.[13]

At first light on the following day, April 7, the combined Federal armies assumed the offensive. Buell's reinforcements, together with Lew Wallace's missing division from Grant's army (which had arrived belatedly on the night of the 6th from their post downriver) provided the basis of a hard-fought Union victory. By midafternoon on the 7th the exhausted Rebel survivors were en route back to Corinth, and that night they were slogging through often-knee-deep mire in a demoralizing retreat. More than ten thousand of Beauregard's forty-five-thousand-man army were later listed as casualties. Where so much had been expected, again there was so little profit.[14]

Was it bad luck, or just happenstance? What had started out to be a devastating surprise attack was in the end only another sad, debilitating disappointment. For the gray soldiers it was just one more frustration piled upon many others. The battle seemed to mirror all the agony that they had already endured rather than the glory they had earlier envisioned. Victory, so attainable in the minds of the soldiers, had instead been denied. The effect of another defeat on their morale was pronounced.

"Battle-horror-roaring, and blood," wrote Private Joseph Lyman in an April 11 letter to his wife. Lyman seemed in agony:

The battlefield in an awful place. I am low spirited. Unless we gain a decided victory our cause will wane. There is so much abuse and

mismanagement in the army, . . . It will be a week tonight since I
have eaten anything but a little cracker. . . . A large cannon ball
passed so near my side that it has felt sore ever since and I do not
breathe fully without pain and cannot walk fast. . . . I am worn and
sore and weak and gloomy. But I still live and hope to live through
the next battle [,] which is expected in a week or two. I don't know
of anything but prayer to God Almighty that can help matters at all.
I have no doubt you have recourse there, and no doubt that you
pray for me. . . . I see no prospect of advance[ment in the army]. It
takes money or friends or both. . . . I sleep like a vagrant[,] sometimes on a pile of corn shucks, sometimes on the floor, sometimes
in a shed, and sometimes on the ground. Oh, how I long for
home![15]

Tennessean W. A. Howard of the 33d Regiment wrote to his wife
on April 10 "with a trembling hand and a tearful eye." He wished
"to God" he could tell her all about the terrible fight, "but I can't
do it. I am confused and . . . it is impossible for me to give you all the
particulars," he gasped. Shiloh "terrified" his mind. The "whizzing
of minie balls and rifle shot, and the zing of grape shot, the hum of
cannon balls, and the [bursting] of bomb shells . . . —I have not
words strong enough to describe it," scribbled Howard. "Oh, God,
forever keep me out of such another fight. I was not scared, I was
just in danger." Thanking only God for his preservation, Private Howard added in exasperation, "I long to be at home with you. I would
[forfeit] all that I have in this world if I was loose from this [army]
and were at home, but . . . I do not see any chance of going home."[16]
    To Private Augustus H. Mecklin of the 15th Mississippi Infantry,
Shiloh had been a nightmare. On the night of April 6th, when he
closed his eyes, Mecklin kept hearing "the balls whistle and the musketry roar," and he couldn't sleep. That night, amid a torrential rainstorm, the eerie flashes of lightning revealed the "ground literally
covered with dead heaped and piled upon the other. I shut my eyes
upon the sickening sight." Yet loud moans came to his ears, and
Mecklin heard through the dark "the sound of hogs—they were quarreling over their carnival feast." Too, he was haunted by the pale
faces of the dead, "besmirched with mud and water, [and their] hair
matted with gore." "God grant that I may never be the partaker [of]
such scenes again," he pleaded. "My resolution is set. When released
from this [,] I shall ever be an advocate of peace."[17]

Another somber soldier, Joseph Dimmit Thompson of the 38th Tennessee, found his battle experience sobering. On April 7 their commander was personally told by General Beauregard, "Colonel Looney, I want you to take your regiment and charge those infernal scoundrels, and drive them back!" The Tennesseeans had enthusiastically cried out in response, "We will, We will!" Yet their isolated attack had been smothered by artillery and small-arms fire, and, said Thompson, many of his regiment "could not be rallied." "[The] horror of that blood-stained field no tongue can tell, no pen portray!" he proclaimed. He had seen men greatly confused by the fighting—at one point they had been told to lay down and continue firing, yet one private jumped to his feet and began loading and shooting. "We told him to lay down or he would be shot," remembered Thompson. Yet the man acted foolishly; "God damn the bullets, I don't care [anything] for them," the private had shouted. Just then a minie ball "went crashing through his brains."[18]

Even for the more urbane, the Battle of Shiloh had been god-awful, and it brought an awakening to many. Richard L. Pugh, a New Orleans cannoneer with Hodgson's battery of the Washington Artillery, wrote, "I had no idea of war until then; and would have given anything in the world if I could have been away." During the fighting, Pugh admitted, "I had no time to think." Then, as if to explain away the defeat, Pugh reflected about the lost opportunities at Shiloh: "If we had had [on April 6] only two hours more of daylight we could have driven them into the [Tennessee] river notwithstanding their gunboats." He further informed his wife of the "grand mistake" that led to their defeat:

I heard General Hardee say yesterday in our tent [that] all the generals concurred—the original plan had been to attack the enemy, rout them, and retire after destroying everything which they could not carry away . . . Had this been done, we would have accomplished the most brilliant [victory] on record—but so complete was the rout, and so perfect a success on Sunday, they concluded they could stay and take the whole army. . . . It was a grand idea, and but for the untimely arrival of Buell (whom they thought too far away to come up in time) . . . [it] would have been accomplished.[19]

Conversely, from the Confederate high command came different explanations for the events at Shiloh. To Major General William J.

Hardee, Shiloh had been a revelation, not of what might have been, but of the fundamental capacity of his soldiers. He informed a friend in a letter that he "was not so much impressed . . . [by] the invulnerability of our volunteer [troops] and their determination to be free—they are good for a dash, but fail in tenacity. I don't think we can yet [consider] ourselves as soldiers—our men are not sufficiently impressed with a sense of honor that it is better to die by fire than to run. We fail also in company officers; they want skill and instruction, and lamentably neglected their duty. Entre nous." Echoing the upper echelon's disdain for the rawness of the troops and their lack of discipline, Braxton Bragg informed his wife, "Our failure is due entirely to a want of discipline and a want of officers. Universal suffrage—furloughs and whiskey have ruined us. If we fail it is our own fault."[20]

Amid the ranks, the blame for Shiloh's mistakes was often assessed far differently. Thomas Chinn Robertson of Randall Lee Gibson's 4th Louisiana Infantry witnessed the chaos and confusion of the attack on the Hornets' Nest and reported, "Young Vertner, an aide of General Hardee's, galloped in front of our ranks with the 'stars and stripes' flag around his waist, and a Yankee cap on, both of which he had captured. Some one cried out, 'here's your Yankee,' and immediately a hundred guns were leveled at him, and he and his horse fell riddled with balls. The 4th Tennessee, seeing this, thought that we were the enemy, and opened upon us with terrible effect, killing and wounding 105 of our regiment." Although the battle seemed to have been won on the 6th, continued Robertson, the following morning, as they were "not expecting a battle," many of the men began looting the captured Yankee camps and loaded themselves "with everything we could lay our hands on." Later, when heavy firing began and General Beauregard rode up to the 4th Louisiana with a smile on his face, he took off his hat and spoke eloquently: "Men, the day is ours, you are fighting a whipped army, fire low and be deliberate." With three cheers the Louisianians had rushed into the fray, only to be shot to pieces. "I had to throw away everything [on the retreat] except my canteen and Enfield rifle," wrote Robertson. "The mud was knee deep [along the road], and we were obliged to wade several streams which were waist deep." These were "the longest miles I ever traveled," thought the exhausted Louisiana soldier.[21]

To Surgeon Charles J. Johnson of the 11th Louisiana, much of the blame centered on the lack of individual discipline: "The sight of [plunder] lying about the [captured camps] in such abundance was too much for our men. They loaded themselves with what they most coveted, and before midnight Sunday one half our army was straggling back to Corinth loaded down with belts, sashes, swords, officer's uniforms . . . etc. Thus was our magnificent victory knocked in the head by the superior equipped [enemy] army." "We looked like a pack of fox hounds after a hard chase," admitted a Mississippian once he had returned to Corinth. "We went through enough [at Shiloh] to kill a mule."[22]

The men were both changed and wizened by their Shiloh experiences. One Tennessee private acknowledged, "I have struggled and prayed to God until I am altogether another person . . . Something tells me we will have our happiest days yet after having gone through the refining fires of privations and troubles."

"This war may be all for the best in the end," thought a Louisiana surgeon, since when he returned home he would appreciate his pretty wife all the more. Indeed, "If I ever leave her I'll certainly be crazy," he admitted.[23]

The battle's unsuccessful end—a retreat to Corinth—had worried many of Sidney Johnston's men, and caused much anxiety about the future. "Whether the battle has been of service to us remains to be seen," admitted an officer, who also noted the broken-down condition of the troops. "Oh, for 5,000 fresh men! . . . That our generals will permit the large force here [Corinth] to remain idle I hardly think possible," he continued. "But so far there seems to be but little activity in it."[24]

Reflecting perhaps the postcombat euphoria of survivors, once the initial depression from shock and exhaustion had worn off, many Southern soldiers spoke of having whipped the Yankees in battle. In claiming success, they pointed to the large capture of enemy prisoners on April 6, and boasted about having outfought "three times our numbers" before retiring "unmolested" to Corinth. "The success of the great battle of the 6th and 7th is on our side," concluded a Tennessee captain, who also cited the many captured cannon, prisoners, and small arms.[25]

Such observations may have signified more in terms of restoring psychological equilibrium than in substantive claims of victory. When a doctor who had remained in Corinth during the battle noted the few captured trophies the returning men of his regiment displayed, he asked a soldier what he had taken at Shiloh. This bedraggled Louisiana rifleman quickly replied, "Nothing but hard knocks." It was "quite a characteristic reply," observed the doctor.[26]

Yet the Confederate soldiers had prevailed on the battlefield. Their many tactical-unit victories and hard fighting by large numbers of troops convinced many of the men that they had succeeded. What these soldier-survivors now thought about themselves was important. Their pride in their performance at Shiloh was tempered, however, by the injustice they felt over the battle's outcome. Combat involved factors of random happenstance beyond their control. The individual exertions of any unit's soldiers counted only for so much toward the end result, and there was a natural feeling of disillusionment after the confusion of Shiloh.

The outcome of combat was decided by factors often incomprehensible to the common soldier. Battle ultimately was a terrifying, frightful personal mayhem in the wilderness, where advances and retreats meant little until the senior commanders decided so. At Shiloh, the generals and their maneuverings, the plans and the attacks, had all evolved into a contest between masses of soldiers which turned on factors beyond the simple reckoning of those in the ranks.

Instead of destroying the enemy, the firefights carried out in linear battle lines only wreaked havoc in both armies. Moreover, unforeseen problems like insufficient ammunition, or enemy reinforcements, or uncertainty of proper support, hindered the soldiers' tactical utilization. Even a lack of timely communications, or want of an understanding of what others were doing compromised the fighting. Smaller victories had an uncertain impact on the entire battle, and these minor successes were often only of brief or temporary import. At Shiloh, there had been many small-scale Confederate tactical victories, yet "whipping the Yankees" in a firefight for a hill or ravine hadn't translated into winning.

No matter what the generals said, the men knew now that their unit's physical effort was only one aspect of the larger picture. As such, their inspired fighting would only take them as far as the competency of their commanders. This observation rapidly became the commonsense understanding of many soldiers. And they were correct. While battlefield tactics—not strategy—ultimately meant the most in a physical sense, the whims, obsessions, and mental gyrations of the generals counted much toward the ultimate result of combat. Where and when to send or commit troops, whether to stay and

fight or to withdraw, were crucial decisions, and a commander's reasoning often meant the difference between victory and defeat. These
were hard-learned but profound lessons. Personal valor and courage
counted only for so much.

To those in the ranks, the composite picture of winning or losing
was limited in scope; it extended only as far as their own experiences.
This was why the suspicion of inept commanders often translated into
a focused disdain for the army's leadership. It also provided the basis
for the soldiers' increased confidence in one another at the expense
of lackluster commanders. The soldiers' shared fortune or misfortune
was the glue that tied them together much "as a band of brothers."
They knew what they saw, not what others envisioned. What became
strategic battle defeat often contradicted the troops' tactical perspectives. They trusted their rifles and themselves, and after experiences
like Shiloh they did not return boundless faith in their generals.[27]

If generals thought of defeating the enemy, most soldiers thought
in more practical terms. Simply put, if you advanced after a battle,
you were winning; if you retreated, you were losing. Such became
many enlisted men's and civilians' understanding.

In the West, where Rebel failure was becoming the usual result,
constant retreating and defeat took a heavy toll on Southern morale.
The western soldiers were reduced to relying mostly upon themselves
for strength, which in itself suggested a striking phenomenon. In the
East, where Robert E. Lee and Thomas J. "Stonewall" Jackson had
established victory as a precedent, much of the soldiers' confidence
and willpower emanated down from the higher command. Their senior officers' performance was a source of pride for the troops—not
a liability. In Virginia, there were no Southern retreats to explain;
their retrograde movements were only strategic withdrawals or countermarches, so Lee's men alleged. In justification of their views they
had hard evidence—numerous battlefield victories.

This difference in perception was both pronounced and crucial,
for it determined the mind-set of the soldiers, upon which so much
would depend.

Chapter Fifteen

SANDIE PENDLETON

"I Intend to Do As Well As I Can"

All Sandie Pendleton wanted in life was to find the right girl, get married, raise children, and live the idyllic life of a devoted family man—so he had mused shortly after the beginning of the war. "[The military] is a pleasant enough life," he had confided to his sister, "[but] I would not . . . for any consideration remain in the army after the war. I shall hunt me a wife, get married, and as the proverb has it, 'live in peace all the days of my life.' "[1]

Within months these concepts had dramatically changed. By late 1861, he gloried in his fascination with warfare and the exciting, active life of the army. Later he wrote to his mother, "I sometimes fear I am beginning to love the [military] trade. In addition to the sense of duty which keeps me here, I do find great pleasure in the excitement of the life in every respect, even the battles—and the power, which my position offers with its extended influence, is very gratifying to my ambition."[2]

Alexander Swift Pendleton was as yet a youth, even if mature and worldly, and he reveled in the sense of an important destiny that his upbringing implied. Twenty-one years old when the war began, Pendleton had been a senior at the University of Virginia. Appointed a lieutenant and a staff officer in mid-1861, "Sandie," as he was known to his friends and family, described himself a year later with characteristic lighthearted aplomb: "I am a man twenty-two years old, weight 13 stone [182 lbs.], height six feet, good looks—moderate, brains more plentiful than riches."[3]

Even his philosophy of life reflected his well-tutored ambition to become a pillar of the community: "I intend to do as well as I can, trust in Providence, fight through the war, and get married when it is over, always supposing my God, mother, and sisters [will] find [me] a woman that suits them and will have me—which I think doubtful in such a paragon."[4]

Sandie's privileged status as part of the prominent Lexington, Virginia, Pendleton family had marked him as a favored son of the Old Dominion state and its cavalier heritage. Yet his background had both its difficulties and rewards. Since he was always in the shadow of his celebrity father, William Nelson Pendleton (the Episcopal minister and Confederate brigadier general who became Robert E. Lee's chief of artillery), Sandie's standards for accomplishment were set at high levels. Even his brother-in-law, Edwin G. Lee, had risen to prominence as a Virginia colonel, and was a much-honored soldier. Sandie, from the beginning of the war, had seemed appropriately determined and ambitious, and was enthralled with the adventures that lay ahead.

Much as if he were acting out an excellent script, Sandie's accomplishments during the first year of the war had been impressive. Within months of joining the army, young Pendleton found promotion, success, and even fame through association with an enormous military celebrity, a man with whom he was thoroughly enraptured. As a staff officer, his initial assignment was to assist a general who was both a difficult, eccentric personality and one of the greatest heroes of the Southern Confederacy—none other than Thomas J. "Stonewall" Jackson.

For Sandie it was a great challenge and a wonderful opportunity, which offered excitement. His duties were to carry dispatches in battle, write orders, and even act when necessary as Jackson's representative in interpreting or issuing orders. Sandie Pendleton thus achieved a notoriety of his own. "When I sit down to write home I feel like a little boy again," confided Sandie, "and not like a man in a responsible position, [encompassing] half this great army, with generals saying, 'Captain, I have the honor to be, . . . ' "[5]

Sandie's stature as one of Jackson's key staff officers may have seemed undeserved to some; he was an inexperienced youth with a dramatic part in the war, and had to fulfill heavy responsibilities. Yet, an eager, prideful Virginia spirit inspired Sandie in his duties, and he quickly developed a close bond with the often-demanding and critical Jackson. Moreover, Jackson's singular successes seemed to inspire only a deeper dedication in those who served under him.

Whereas defeat or frustration had bedeviled many of the Confederacy's military efforts beyond the opening few battles in Virginia during the summer of 1861, for Tom Jackson's Army of the Shenandoah, the summer of 1862 brought fame and success. Jackson's 1862 Valley Campaign had created renewed hope throughout the Confederacy at a time when the South's positions elsewhere seemed to be verging on collapse.

Sandie's many letters to his family reflected this great enthusiasm, despite his fatigue. Joyfully, he told of a Federal rout at Winchester, Virginia, that was "worse than [First Manassas]." Then, early in the Valley Campaign, when confronting Federal Major General Nathaniel P. Banks's thirty-eight-thousand-man army, Jackson with less than five thousand troops had repeatedly kept this ponderous enemy force at bay. Even at Kernstown, Virginia, where Jackson was defeated and had to withdraw, Sandie spoke of the obvious superiority of their Valley army:

With not more than 3,500 we engaged about 8,000 [Brigadier General James Shields's division]; held them in check for three hours, . . . and when we drew off the enemy did not attempt to follow. . . . It was a harder fight than Manassas. Our infantry stood up and advanced often within 20 yards of the enemy, and . . . stood the[ir] ground for three hours. With 1,000 more men we could have whipped them, but our troops had marched 30 miles the day before and 20 that day, and expected no fighting. [Our men] never broke, but at the command to fall back, marched off in line. We were driven off by superior numbers, for as one [enemy] regiment would break, another would take its place. Our spy, who was in Winchester [five miles distant,] says their men kept running into the town all afternoon, saying that they were whipped.[6]

Sandie's comments served as a testimonial to the effectiveness of Stonewall's men. They exuded success, even when tactically beaten, and remained confident in their abilities to "whip" the enemy in a fair fight. Since Jackson delighted in repeatedly outmarching and beating the Yankees that summer, Sandie's own enthusiasm soon reached new highs. Although fretting that "Old Jack's" troops were often "too small and too much broken down by constant marching to do much good work," Pendleton wrote confidently about again meeting the enemy's "overwhelming" forces. "Come when they may, they will find us ready for them, [and] trusting in God and our righteous cause," he assured his family.[7]

By the much-practiced concept of high mobility, Jackson's "foot cavalry" had become the scourge of their Federal opponents in the valley. Their continual arduous marches and furious fighting had pinned down thousands of Yankee troops and prevented many reinforcements from reaching McClellan's army on the Virginia peninsula.

Although the name "Stonewall" Jackson was now famous throughout the land, close scrutiny of the man's generalship made his venerable nickname seem somewhat inappropriate. Jackson's military methods were anything but defensive in nature. His aggressive, hard-marching, strike-the-enemy-where-they-least-expect-it style contrasted sharply with the "Stonewall" nickname, which implied conservative fortitude. To the Southern populace, however, it personified combat invincibility in a popular commander—a genius of the battlefield who always won—and they reveled in his image. The overall effect on Confederate fortunes, as Sandie Pendleton found, was wonderful to perceive. In fact, after Jackson joined the Army of Northern Virginia in late June 1862, his notable success had become that of the entire army. Although Jackson's less-than-stellar performance in the Seven Days battles around Richmond resulted in controversy, by mid-July 1862 he and his spirited troops were committed to an important new mission—countering the threat of Major General John Pope in northern Virginia.

At the Battle of Cedar Mountain on August 9, Jackson's three divisions pummeled a larger Union force, and despite a desperate situation in which Old Jack had to rally his former brigade, the Confederates again prevailed. Here, on the battlefield, an awed observer saw "The Light of Battle" radiating on Jackson's face. "His whole person was changed," the man noted. Instead of the indifference and stoicism so frequently associated with their commander when in camp, Jackson now seemed the very "inspiration of heroism." "The men would have followed him into the jaws of death itself; nothing could have stopped them, and nothing did," said a cavalry officer. Grabbing hold of a battle flag and waving it over his head, Jackson had dashed to the front, crying out, "Rally, men! . . . Where's my Stonewall Brigade? Forward men, Forward!"[8]

Jackson's spirit of invincibility had proved highly contagious. "We whipped the Yankees worse this time than they ever was whipped before," wrote a jubilant Mississippi rifleman after Second Manassas. During the same action, a Georgia colonel had joked with his men, "Boys, we have come back to our old stomping ground [First Manassas]. If any of you kill a Yankee, put on his shoes quick, and if you get into a sutler's store, eat all the cheese and crackers you can possibly hold."[9]

The happy-go-lucky, rags-to-riches attitude now prevalent in many regiments of the Army of Northern Virginia was rooted to a large extent in Jackson's bold success. Victorious combatants time and time again, Jackson's soldiers exuded a confidence that permeated the army, and morale continued to soar. Colonel E. P. Alexander observed how the entire army had "acquired that magnificent morale which made them equal to twice their numbers, and which they never lost. . . ." Jackson's bold spirit of triumph led the way, and the molding of the most effective army ever created to that time on the North American continent was the result.[10]

Even when outright victory failed to crown Confederate efforts, a resilience and the immutability of this winning attitude were apparent. In September 1862, while Jackson and his detached troops were capturing the Yankee garrison at Harper's Ferry, Lee's lost operational orders created an enormous opportunity for the Federal commander, George B. McClellan. Lee had to fight off McClellan's entire army on the banks of Antietam Creek at Sharpsburg, Maryland, and suffered heavy casualties in the bloodiest single day of the war. Yet the furious Antietam battle of September 17 seemed only to further enshroud Lee, Jackson, and their army in the mantle of greatness.

Despite the enormous bloodletting, one of Lee's staff officers confirmed their army's high spirits. "We do not claim a victory," he admitted, yet Antietam proved that "[our troops] could contend with and resist three times their own numbers." Confederate newspapers also heralded the campaign, with Richmond's *Southern Illustrated News* of September 20 asserting, "Our brave boys are not to be beaten by any force the Yankees can bring against them." Despite the Antietam setback, the army's attitude of superiority had remained intact, resting on the bedrock of a winning legacy.[11]

Typical of the prideful spirit engendered by past success, Sandie Pendleton wrote soon after Antietam, "I wish we could fight with McClellan's army about Sharpsburg again. The result would be very different from that of the battle of September 17. Our army is 25,000 stronger than then, and in far better condition in every respect."[12]

Although he regarded the Maryland Campaign as not very successful due to the large Confederate losses, Sandie was prompt to consider the positive results from their Maryland foray. As evidence of the bold spirit of accomplishment that characterized the Army of Northern Virginia, after Antietam a large number of stragglers, and some of those formerly disabled, had returned to the army. Also, many of the barefooted men were supplied with captured shoes. Moreover, having returned to Virginia's "land of hallowed memories," Pendleton wrote with renewed pride, "One cannot but feel we are not fighting for gain but for principle."[13]

No matter if he was dealing with victory or a setback, Sandie Pendleton had continued to feed upon the army's spirit of accomplishment. Although on sick leave following Cedar Mountain, Sandie had rejoined the army prior to Antietam. In that battle Sandie had encountered "a storm of balls [he] never conceived it possible for men to live through." While delivering orders, he experienced "shot and shell [that] were shrieking and crashing, canister and bullets whistling and hissing most fiend-like through the air until you could almost see them." I never expected to return alive, the awed Sandie later confided.[14]

His promotion to captain after the Valley Campaign had been earned, and even Stonewall praised him in various reports. Another officer described the young Virginian "as [being] brave as Old Jack; [for] wherever Old Jack goes Sandie is always there."[15]

While acting as Jackson's chief of staff during the prolonged impasse after Antietam, Sandie's attitude continued to be enthusiastic and eager. "We have been idle now for more than three weeks," he wrote rather impatiently on October 8, "and our generals are not given to inaction. Activity and motion have gotten to be necessary for us, as giving some food to the mind."[16]

Sandie's thoughts may well have mirrored his own private predicament. Both emotional and virile, Sandie had found love during the summer of 1862. In fact, he was already engaged. The ardent young man with a burning ambition to marry and raise a family had found his girl. She was the "intelligent and cultivated" Laura Burwell, from a prominent Winchester, Virginia, family. In June 1862, they "privately" announced their engagement to their families.

Little in Sandie's life came easily, however, and soon storm clouds were gathering about the relationship. Sandie's mother, Anzolette Elizabeth Page Pendleton—"Lizzie" to her family—disapproved of the match. According to Lizzie's account, a few months following her son's betrothal, Sandie began to have misgivings that he didn't love Laura "enough." Although Sandie's mother pleaded that he not marry a woman he did not love (and one she didn't like, already having "warned him against [her] last winter"), Sandie felt honor bound to carry out his "obligation."[17]

During October, when he went calling, Sandie was suddenly and inexplicably rebuffed by Laura Burwell. "You may imagine my extreme astonishment at rejection, final, immediate, [and] unequivocal," he wrote with stunned disbelief. Their engagement was broken. "Of the cause of such action, I have not the faintest conception," he informed his mother. Although "not a little chagrined" by the episode, Sandie congratulated himself, and was "most intensely delighted at finding myself thus unexpectedly free again by the unconstrained act of [Laura]."[18]

Perhaps it was destiny. Only a few months after his broken engagement, Sandie seemed anxious to forget the episode and immerse himself in his army duties. He spoke of his quest for more active service, and of renewed glory for the valiant Army of Northern Virginia.

In fact, with the approach of Burnside's Federal army toward Fredericksburg in December 1862, the blood of battle coursed freely through Sandie's veins: "We have been so long without a fight that our army begins to desire another tilt with the Yankees," Sandie asserted. "Despite the cold snap we had, the want of clothing, and scarcity of provisions, our men are in excellent spirits, and can trounce Mr. Lincoln's people well when we get hold of them. The prestige is on our side," he confidently wrote.[19]

A few days later, a "badly bruised" Sandie Pendleton breathlessly wrote to his mother that his life had been remarkably spared during the Battle of Fredericksburg. While he was carrying one of Jackson's orders to Brigadier General William B. Taliaferro, a musket ball had struck him in the abdomen. The bullet penetrated his outer overcoat and his inner uniform coat, but was spent on the fringe of his pants pocket. The clothing had "saved my life," considered the captain, "as the ball would have gone through the groin and fractured the hip joint. I am very stiff and horribly bruised," he noted, yet he had continued to do his duty and even remained on the field until the fighting was over.[20]

This brush with death only hardened Sandie's perspective about the risks of combat. He would take his chances along with the rest, and trust in God for mercy. To Sandie, the importance of Fredericksburg was not that he had survived, but that the Army of Northern Virginia had again demonstrated its vast superiority over its Northern opponents. Sandie's confidence had reached a new high. "We have 80,000 men in as fine condition as ever our army was, fine artillery, and can destroy Mr. Lincoln's hopes as represented by his army, more surely than has been done before," he wrote. Sandie was again eager for combat.[21]

Perhaps he was unprepared for the events that soon occurred. With the coming of 1863, Sandie's priorities were abruptly reshuffled in the rush of emotions after an important new personal encounter.

Once again, Sandie Pendleton had found love. Laura Burwell was but a fading memory now. His new sweetheart suddenly dominated his very being. She was the witty, pretty, and petite Kate Corbin of Moss Neck plantation, Virginia. Sandie, along with Stonewall Jackson's entire staff, had set up winter quarters on the Corbin property beginning in mid-December 1862. Here they remained until the following March, in full view of the bright-eyed Kate and her family. Sandie was an immediate favorite with the Corbins, and spent many pleasant hours with Kate.

Yet the blossoming romance was tinged by tragedy. When five-year-old Jane Corbin, the daughter of Kate Corbin's brother and a personal favorite of Stonewall, died of scarlet fever, Sandie was there to comfort the stricken mother. Sandie wrote with profound sadness:

When I entered the room, she was clinging to Kate Corbin, almost frantic, uttering the most piercing cries I ever heard. I spoke to her and told her she must be calm, when she loosened her hold of Kate and seized me, and began afresh her wild lamentations. I soothed her as best I could, and got her somewhat quieter by repeating . . . such passages as "suffer the little children to come unto me," "the Lord gave and the Lord hath taken away," which seemed the best I could do. She continually would break in, "But why did the Lord take my child?" which questions would stagger me, and unused to such scenes I could answer nothing. . . . Death on the battlefield is not half so fearful as this.[22]

Sandie's calm strength and sensitive kindness had impressed Kate deeply, and within days their engagement was announced among close friends and family. The black-eyed beauty and the rising young adjutant, "Stonewall's man," made a handsome pair, and General Jackson extended his blessings, saying of Sandie, "If he makes as good a husband as he has a soldier, Miss Corbin will do well."[23]

For Sandie Pendleton it was a time of enormous promise and fulfillment. The new year, 1863, witnessed Sandie's elevation to major, a long-coveted advancement. "I am proud of it," proclaimed the twenty-two-year-old Virginian, "and glad that the promotion has come from recognized merit, and accept it as an omen for future success."[24]

Like the valiant army with which he served, the prideful Sandie reviewed the past year and pointed with optimism to the future. His current circumstances were in marked contrast to the beginning of 1862, noted Sandie, and he wrote:

[A year ago] we were preparing for as hard a campaign almost as Napoleon's Russian, with the fate of the country trembling in the balance, and all wanting faith in an unproved cause. Now victory after victory has crowned our efforts, and all feel sure of our success, and that speedily. Though the [new] year be marked with blood, the deepest stream [will be] that poured out by our enemies in their futile effort for our destruction. If the [past] year has closed with a grand victory . . . at Murfreesboro, as a successor and climax to our brilliant achievements here and at Vicksburg, well might one grand "Te Deum" be shouted by the nation in thanksgiving for the past, and in joyful anticipation for the future.[25]

Sandie's comments in many ways echoed the attitude of the entire Southern Confederacy. Adding to the joy prevalent in the Virginia army, word was passed that a daughter had been born to Stonewall Jackson and his wife—their only living child. "All hail to the young Stonewall," wrote one of his staff officers in celebration.[26]

On the last day of 1862 Sandie Pendleton reflected, "It is cheerful to sit by the fireside and feel that the year is going out in [relative] peace . . . I accept it as a good omen. . . ."[27]

About the same time, a former fellow staff officer, Captain Henry

Kyd Douglas, pondered the past and the uncertain future: "I spent Xmas day not without thoughts of those I laughed with one year ago, and of many who laughed with me, who will laugh no more in this world. May this be the last year of the war I would earnestly pray."[28]

"A Glorious Victory, but at What Cost!"

Sandie Pendleton continued to exude confidence. He wrote in buoyant spirits to his mother on April 4, 1863, "We are in fine condition. The army is stronger than I have ever known it, and in an admirable state of organization and discipline. The armament and equipment [are] good also . . ." Only his long experience prompted him to add a word of caution: "Of one thing I am certain, that the struggle has just begun in earnest, and from this time we have to exert all our energies to cope with our foe."[29]

Just how difficult that task had become was soon witnessed by the terrible struggle in Virginia's wilderness, known as the Battle of Chancellorsville. An arrogant new Federal commander, Major General Joseph Hooker, had proclaimed his revamped and reinforced Army of the Potomac "the finest army the sun ever shone on." Beginning his offensive in late April 1863, Joe Hooker had hoped to cross the Rappahannock River upstream, and then envelope the Confederate army near Fredericksburg. Initially put at a disadvantage by Hooker's bold maneuver, Robert E. Lee opted for a dangerous if characteristically audacious plan. He divided his own badly outnumbered army, and planned for an offensive strike against the would-be attackers. As might have been expected, the main instrument of Lee's march around the enemy's exposed western flank would be Stonewall Jackson and his entire corps. When Jackson's secretive sixteen-mile flanking march began on May 2, Sandie Pendleton seemed as animated as Jackson. Later, as he prepared to launch the fateful assault, Jackson emotionally thought about the significance of VMI's contribution to the pending grand attack. "The Institute will be heard from today," Jackson said reassuringly.[30]

Shortly after the assault got underway at about 5:15 P.M. on May 2, it was evident the Yankees had been caught by surprise. Much of the Federal XI Corps was routed, and by nightfall Jackson's troops were within a short distance of cutting off the enemy's vital line of retreat to the United States Ford on the Rappahannock River.

It was then that great misfortune happened. During an evening reconnaissance in front of his advanced lines to discover the Yankees' new position, Stonewall Jackson was mistakenly fired upon by the 18th North Carolina Infantry. Struck by three missiles, Jackson was seriously wounded in the left arm by two balls, one of which fractured the bone just below his shoulder.*

Despite amputation of his left arm, the general remained in good spirits, and he began talking about rejoining the army. Yet within a few days, he caught pneumonia, and on May 10 Stonewall Jackson died, the victim of his own front line aggressiveness.[31]

The void created in the command structure was immediately recognized by all. "[General Jackson's death] is a terrible loss," wrote Robert E. Lee in heartfelt despair. "I do not know how to replace him. Any victory would be dear at such a cost. But God's will be done." Lee was so emotional about Jackson's wounding that he wrote, "Could I have directed events, I should have chosen for the good of the country to have been disabled in your stead."

Most of the South quickly came to grief over the news of Stonewall Jackson's death, and one young girl commented that with his loss the idea first "dawned on us that God would let us be defeated."[32]

Sandie Pendleton was so stunned by the wounding of Stonewall Jackson that when he heard the news he fainted. Later, he told Jackson's widow, "God knows I would have died for him!" On May 3, immediately after Jackson was shot, Sandie lamented to his beloved Kate, "poor Gen. Jackson! It was sad, sad, to see him, his arm amputated." Jackson's subsequent loss far overshadowed the success at Chancellorsville, and Sandie wrote Kate, "We had a glorious victory, but alas! at what cost. . . ."[33]

Once the shock of losing Jackson had run its course, there emerged a sense of renewed dedication toward winning independence. In the wake of the enormous victory at Chancellorsville, Sandie Pendleton predicted the army's march northward into Maryland and Pennsylvania. In an emotional letter to Kate, he exuded optimism:

[Our army is] as a boy in love, anxious to be away, yet unable to break the spell that binds him. Alas! The spell is broken now, the

---

*One ball from a smoothbore musket inflicted a minor but painful injury in the right hand.

order is given, and the command [is to] march! . . . Off! And whither? Off, and for how long? If you could see the gay smile these questions bring up you'd scarcely think our trade one fraught with danger and privation. Nor do I, to tell the truth. I am all boy again tonight, and wide awake with enthusiasm at the thoughts of our trip to Maryland, and the pleasures and excitements, hazards and glories of the coming summer campaign. Oh! For General Jackson! [Yet] be still the vain regret. We have General Ewell, a host too, and the Lord of Hosts is with us.[34]

Perhaps Robert E. Lee said as much about the army's irrepressible spirit when he published General Order No. 61, announcing the death of Stonewall Jackson: "While we mourn his death, we feel that his spirit still lives, and will inspire the whole army with his indomitable courage and unshaken confidence in God as our hope and our strength."[35]

Although the victory at Chancellorsville had been overwhelming, the Federal army had not been destroyed, noted Robert E. Lee. "This army has done hard work," he told Jefferson Davis, but he warned, "There is still harder [duty] before us." In fact, Robert E. Lee wrote only a few days following Chancellorsville that it would be necessary "to reinforce this army in order to oppose the large force which the enemy seems to be concentrating against it."[36]

Believing that Virginia would be "the [main] theater of [the enemy's] action," Lee suggested an advance to relieve the pressure on Confederate troops elsewhere. "If I could get in a position to advance beyond the Rappahannock [River] I should certainly draw their troops from the southern coasts and give some respite in that quarter," he advised Jefferson Davis on May 11.[37]

This aggressiveness was undoubtedly based upon Lee's supreme confidence in his army. "I agree with you in believing that our army would be invincible if it could be properly organized and officered," Lee informed one of his division commanders on May 21. "There never were such men in an army before. They will go anywhere and do anything if properly led." With obvious reference to the loss of Jackson and others, Lee continued, "But there is the difficulty—proper commanders. Where can they be obtained?"[38]

Following the reorganization of the army into three corps (instead of two), and the appointment of one-legged lieutenant general Richard S. Ewell to command Jackson's old 2d Corps, Lee seemed optimistic that this was "the most advantageous arrangement."[39]

By early June 1863, while still ensnared in administration imposed inactivity more than a month after Chancellorsville, Lee had urged meaningful action. "There is always hazard in military movements, but we must decide between the positive loss of inactivity and the risk of action," he informed the secretary of war. Although he was "aware that there is difficulty and hazard in taking the offensive with so large an [enemy] army in front," he believed this would "give us an active force in the field with which we might hope to make some impression on the enemy. . . . Unless this can be done, I see little hope of accomplishing anything of importance."[40]

Ironically, the root of this aggressiveness was despair, rather than confidence. In a remarkable letter to Jefferson Davis on June 10, 1863, Lee outlined his uneasy sense that desolation threatened the Confederacy:

Conceding to our enemies the superiority claimed by them in numbers, resources, and all the means and appliances for carrying on the war, we have no right to look for exemptions from the military consequences . . . excepting by such deliverance as the mercy of Heaven may accord to the courage of our soldiers, the justice of our cause, and the constancy and prayers of our people. While making the most we can of the means of resistance we possess, and gratefully accepting the measure of success with which God has blessed our efforts . . . it is nevertheless the part of wisdom to carefully measure and husband our strength, and not to expect from it more than in the ordinary course of affairs it is capable of accomplishing. We should not therefore conceal from ourselves that our resources are constantly diminishing, and the disproportion in this respect between us and our enemies . . . is steadily augmenting. The decrease of the aggregate of this army as disclosed by the returns affords an illustration of this fact. Its effective strength varies from time to time, but the falling off in its aggregate shows that its ranks are growing weaker and that its losses are not supplied by recruits. Under these circumstances we should neglect no honorable means of dividing and weakening our enemies that they may feel some of the difficulties experienced by ourselves. It seems to me that the most effectual mode of accomplishing this object, now within our reach, is to give all the encouragement we can, consistently with truth, to the rising peace party of the North.[41]

In other words, Lee was concerned not about the fighting ability of his men—of this he was supremely confident—but about the implications of losses in manpower. His experienced officers and soldiers were generally irreplaceable, and the inevitable casualties of active campaigning would tend to destroy the efficacy of his army. His obvious desire was to do something significant with his diminishing assets (the Army of Northern Virginia) that would provide the prospect of peace before it was too late.

To promote the war's end, Lee sought to win a convincing victory on Northern soil. In order to decisively play upon the will of the Northern populace, the military means of discouraging all attempts to conquer the South was essential. Success in an important battle thus seemed to be the key to victory. Then, reasoned Lee, "should the belief that peace will bring back the Union become general, the war will no longer be supported [in the North]." Even though it might be necessary to consider proposals of rejoining the Union, in that sense, "When peace is proposed to us it will be time enough to discuss its terms," estimated the forward-looking Lee on June 10, 1863.[42]

Beneath it all, there was a tacit admission of a growing despair from the South's most successful army commander. To those informed few in the Richmond administration, it should have been significantly ominous.

In contrast to Lee's concerns, Sandie Pendleton wrote while en route north on June 18, 1863:

The war prospers so well that I see more chance of its ending now than for many a day before. The Yankee papers are despondent, the people scared, and our army in fine condition. We will go north for the summer—we and all our corps are off for Pennsylvania. . . . Truly the 2d Corps [of Lee's army] grows to the "Tenth Legion" of the South, and [the boast] "I was of the 2d Corps A.N.V." will be in days to come a prouder record than the famous Civis Sum Romanus of the days of the Republic and early Empire. And I am one of them. Thank God for it. I had rather be here than anywhere else, and I feel that I am doing my duty.[43]

Embracing "Southern chivalry and rigid discipline," Pendleton wrote on June 23 from Greencastle, Pennsylvania, that the Confederate army was currently "dictating to the [local] inhabitants as masters." Indeed, confided Sandie, "I do believe in it [Southern prowess] now more than ever before. There is an innate difference between a Yankee and a Southerner. [This] I have ever believed, but the exalted superiority of one race has never struck me so forcibly as now. . . ."[44]

Sandie's perspective was significant. His comments raised a relevant question. Was the Army of Northern Virginia truly invincible, as Pendleton suggested? Or was Robert E. Lee's estimate of lurking vulnerability more accurate?

Chapter Sixteen

LEE AND JACKSON, AND THEIR INVINCIBLE ARMY

The enemy [again] has been badly, ignominiously whipped, at a time and upon ground of his own choosing, and driven back over the river in disgrace," announced a Virginia major to his wife in May 1863. The Battle of Chancellorsville had been one of the most encouraging in the sequence of major Confederate victories in the East. "I think the Yankees and the rest of mankind must soon come to the conclusion that the South cannot be subjugated," declared Major Thomas Elder. "This last defeat—the greatest sustained by the enemy during the war—must greatly strengthen the hands of the large peace party at the North. . . . [It will also] tend to induce foreign powers to recognize us as an independent nation, inasmuch as it goes towards demonstrating our capacity to defend ourselves."[1]

The reason for this great success and rising hope was quite simple, asserted Major Elder. "Lee continues to grow in the confidence and esteem of our soldiers and people. Our troops idolize him, and . . . I cannot find terms adequate to express my admiration of him. . . . He is, beyond a doubt, much the ablest man engaged on either side in this war." In considering his own role in the quest for Southern independence, Elder then added, "I am glad to know I am serving my country with some degree of usefulness in this her hour of trial. To have served during the war in General Lee's army is indeed . . . a subject of honest pride."[2]

The implications of this and dozens of similar letters were obvious.

Soldiers who enjoyed success on the battlefield were more easily led and exhibited a higher morale. Victory was inspirational. A winning attitude was contagious; an army that knew victory as its common standard could be expected to perform accordingly. Somehow, no matter what the numerical odds, a way to win would usually be found. The soldiers relied upon this faith, and drew strength from their past successes. The commitment to soldiering seemed stronger; the soldiers believed in themselves, and they believed in their commanders. The South's awareness of its own potency counted more than any physical realities. The victory at First Manassas had been so significant in 1861, later reflected the artillerist Edward Porter Alexander, because they had "at least brought off a great morale," to which they "afterward added in almost every fight." To win was to expect future success, and to act accordingly. As such, serving in the Army of Northern Virginia inspired a pride and passion that generally became infused into a common, bold spirit of invincibility.[3]

By mid-1862, the Virginia army's success had already made it a Southern legend. The leaders who produced this result were larger-than-life heroes of the highest order. Repositories of affection and esteem, they reflected the troops' own self-worth and pride as focused on symbols that personified this winning spirit. Both Robert E. Lee and Thomas J. "Stonewall" Jackson had served as such exalted images.

If ever there were two more district personalities who shared the same adoration of their soldiers, it is hard to imagine. Lee was the personification of a dignified and genteel Virginia cavalier. An eyewitness found him in July 1862 "elegantly dressed in full uniform, sword and sash, spotless boots, beautiful spurs. . . . [He] by far [is] the most magnificent man I ever saw." In contrast, Jackson, thought a cavalry officer who came to know him well, was reclusive, eccentric, and characterized in appearance the Roundheads of the Cromwell era. With stooped shoulders, an old kepi pulled down over his left eye, a bushy beard, and plain, unkempt clothes, Jackson looked the part of a commoner—"to be passed by without a second look," remarked an officer.[4]

Yet within the soul of Jackson burned the fiery combativeness that placed him alongside Lee as a commander. A fearless, determined man who believed he was ordained by God for a higher purpose, Jackson embodied a bold spirit of aggressiveness and dedication to duty. Aside from Lee, Jackson had done more than any other general to establish the lofty military reputation of the Confederate army in Virginia. His enormously successful Shenandoah Valley Campaign of 1862 had made his name a household word throughout America. Although he kept his plans and movements secret, and did not often heed the complaints of others, Jackson's sagacity in military maneuvering, speed in marching, and uncanny ability to strike the enemy when and where they least expected had established him as a military mastermind. His skill infused confidence, pride, and a sense of elitism among his troops. His reputation in the army seemed to burgeon with each new battle or skirmish.

Old Jack, as his men called him, seemed ordained by the Almighty to succeed in his every military encounter. Yet Robert E. Lee was equally recognized for his military genius. "Marse Robert," as he was affectionately known, became the leader that the soldiers relied upon most. They believed he wouldn't let them down, and referred to themselves as "Lee's army," a vivid testimonial of their true admiration and trust. Both generals were revered as great leaders, though they contrasted with one another in style, manner, and technique.

There was no set formula for success as a commander. The men might respect a certain leader for his character, personality, and ability, but they loved him for winning. His victory was their victory, and they reveled in the glory of accomplishment. Moreover, the psychology of winning established an acuity among the men that made their suffering more bearable, even when personally devastating. And triumph in combat garnered the expectation that things would get better, not worse.

Unfortunately, a false sense of security lurked beneath such reasoning. No one man is infallible, or possessed of an all-knowing wisdom. Even legendary men make mistakes. Success and winning on the battlefield are complex results that occur out of a combination of factors. The most brilliant strategist or tactician must rely on the performance of others to accomplish his goals. That certain commanders inspired confidence, and hence enhanced performance, was at times more important than their operational concepts. In fact, although the men identified with their success, both Jackson and Lee knew all too well that the ultimate glory rested with the troops. Both generals were well aware of their own limitations as well as of their capabilities. The key was to utilize one's assets wisely; in the Army of

Northern Virginia's situation, those assets included the soldiers' confidence as well as their bodies.

In explanation of the vagaries of popular opinion, Robert E. Lee once wrote, "Truth is mighty, and will eventually prevail." That the truth might later be distorted in his popular image would have perplexed him. Lee's entire life seemed to epitomize a quest for an ultimate truth, even as he was aware of humanity's failings. His patience with imperfection in himself and others was matched by an abiding effort to do his duty as God gave him the ability to see that duty, but to allow for less than perfection. If not an optimist as a military commander, Lee was essentially a hopeful, pragmatic general. His plans were predicated on a discerning assessment of practicalities, and reflected his keen intelligence, ability, long experience, and common sense. Then, too, they reflected his upbringing as a prideful, honor-bound Southerner, and his education as a West Point professional.[5]

Lee was a skillful strategist, a competent tactician, and a brilliant leader of men. But his character shone above all else. As a military leader and as a person, Lee personified the greatest hopes of the South. Considering the enormous responsibility he bore, and the difficulties he encountered, his status as a Southern icon—indeed, an American legend—was appropriate. But Lee as a person was equally remarkable, perhaps a miracle of endeavor and accomplishment despite his inevitable flaws and mistakes.

Robert E. Lee was just the manner of man you would want for a leader. Difficult assignments had been his lot from the beginning of the war. When suddenly and unexpectedly given command of the army defending Richmond, Virginia, on June 1, 1862, Lee had faced a desperate situation. The South was on the verge of losing the war. McClellan's magnificently equipped army was on Richmond's doorstep, and doubt existed everywhere that the capital could be saved. Lee's answer was a bold offensive that played upon his opponent's most vulnerable points—lack of self-confidence and overestimation of Confederate forces, both in numbers and as fighters. Although suffering heavy losses, Lee drove McClellan's army back down the Virginia peninsula, intimidating the Federal commander and averting the certain defeat that would have occurred had the enemy been allowed to execute his own design.

This reflected one of Lee's greatest attributes, an ability to strategize that was well adapted to his own circumstances, but that also exploited the enemy's weaknesses. An opponent's vulnerability, no matter whether physical or mental, was regularly calculated into his operational plans.

During the subsequent 1862–63 campaigns of glory for the Army of Northern Virginia, Lee had typically faced superior enemy numbers. But he acted boldly to concentrate and strike at isolated Yankee segments where possible, and to win by attacking, given the opportunities that such maneuvers created. Even when on the operational defensive, as at Antietam, Lee acted without vacillation, as he was well aware that he faced a timid opponent in McClellan. There was no irresolution in Robert E. Lee. He always seemed self-controlled and well poised, and was willing to take the blame for failures while retaining confidence in his own efforts. There were no scapegoats to Lee.

Conversely, the outcomes of some battles exposed Lee to heavy criticism. Failures as well as victories had occurred under Lee, although the losses were later little remembered in the wake of his successes. In the 1861 Western Virginia Campaign, Lee was ineffective. His troops were confused, ill supplied, and unsuccessful. During the Peninsula fighting his staff work had been abominable, leading to a lack of communication and uncoordinated action. Lee then had no control over much of his army, and this disorganization had led to tactical failures as well as bungled opportunities.[6]

To some of Stonewall Jackson's troops who were used to rapid movements, Lee's actions during the Second Manassas campaign seemed slow and without initiative. Even his much-admired humanity appeared to reflect a corresponding absence of army discipline, and his toughness was questioned. Yet Lee well understood the choice open to a general and he opted to lead rather than coerce. "The volunteer army is more easily disciplined by encouraging a patriotic spirit than by the strict enforcement of the Articles of War," he told a member of his personal staff.[7]

Lee's statement conformed perfectly to his philosophy: win by skill, courage, and finesse rather than by brute force and raw discipline. Lee was always the one to seize the initiative where possible so he could better control critical events. Akin to the prevailing logic of many nineteenth-century Southerners, proactive measures and aggressive risk taking provided the best means of coping with adversity. To do and die was better than to do nothing. Lee's skillful application of that creed had carried him far; his assuredness and success were legendary and had resulted in a growing fear among enemy com-

manders, who often worried about what he was going to do, instead
of what they should do.

Undoubtedly, Lee was the best soldier the South had to lead its
premier army in the quest for independence. His men loved him,
and the South loved him. The remarkable irony of all this was that
Lee's authority never extended beyond the primary eastern theater
until 1865, when he was belatedly appointed commanding general of
the Confederacy's armies, well after any opportunity to win the war
had passed. Lee's quiet competence thus was never exploited to the
fullest.

In contrast, Lee's principal subordinate, Thomas J. Jackson, was in
early 1863 exploited by Lee as an instrument of irresistible dash and
aggressiveness. Eccentric and extremely private—almost reclusive—
Stonewall Jackson exuded a certain mysteriousness that heightened
his formidable image of invincibility. Moreover, a practical-minded,
God-fearing quality radiated from Jackson that many of his ragged
but prideful soldiers could identify with. He was one of them in his
plain appearance and ordinary demeanor, and they admired his intelligence in confronting life's rugged tasks with a sure but subtle
competence. He personified the unsophisticated, "can do" spirit of
the common man.

Captain Blackford, temporarily attached to Jackson's headquarters,
assessed him thus:

There is a certain magnetism in Jackson, but it is not personal. All
admire his genius and great deeds, [but] no one could love the
man for himself. He seems to be cut off from his fellow men and
to commune with his own spirit only . . . Yet the men are almost as
enthusiastic about him as over Lee, and whenever he moves about
on his old sorrel . . . most men shout with enthusiasm. He rides on
rapidly without making any sign of recognition, and no one knows
whether he is pleased or not. It is a saying in the army, if a shout is
heard, "there goes Jackson, or a rabbit." [His] old sorrel is not
more martial in appearance than his master, and the men say it
takes a half dozen bomb shells to wake either of them up to their
full capacity, but when once aroused there is no stopping either of
them until the enemy has retreated.[8]

Blackford's observations explained much about the attitudes prevalent in the original "Stonewall Brigade." If his men were at times

easily distracted and recklessly mischievous, they seemed, like Jackson, unconquerable in spirit. An officer stood amazed in 1862 as some of Jackson's hatless men ransacked Manassas Junction's captured sutler's tents and found "women's hats and tied them on with the long red ribbons and trimmings attached." Though their appearance was "ludicrous," thought the officer, he watched as they "sang songs of merriment and danced around their camp fires at two o'clock that night, eating lobster salad and drinking Rhine wine." Such men, concluded the officer, "could never be whipped upon any fair field . . . no matter what odds were against them. To kill them was the only way to conquer them."[9]

The army of Stonewall Jackson and Robert E. Lee had by mid-1862 become the pride of the Confederacy. Initially composed of some of the finest raw material in any American army to date, it had early established its efficacy on the battlefield. In fact, the major strength of this army lay not only in its capable and exalted senior commanders, but equally in the subordinate officers. The high quality of skilled and trained leadership at a junior level was truly the Army of Northern Virginia's secret of success. As one noted historian has written, effective second-tier talent was one reason why this army outperformed the western Confederacy's "hard luck" Army of Tennessee.[10]

A reservoir of knowledgeable, well-trained company-level leadership both in officers and noncommissioned personnel existed from the beginning of the war in the East. This resulted largely from the prevalence of prewar active state militia units in the region. Not only was the South's population densest east of the Appalachian Mountains, but the area also had a higher concentration of well-organized state military organizations. Men trained in militia units were typically the ones elected to leadership roles in the volunteer regiments, and they had a wealth of military knowledge that they could impart to the thousands of volunteer civilian-soldiers. Many junior and noncommissioned officers serving in the East had been educated at recognized military schools and academies, such as VMI and the Citadel. Their experiences not only provided them with training and practical knowledge, but also allowed them to help sustain the unskilled volunteers during their first months of army life. Most recruits had never been away from home for extended periods of time and had little idea of the realities of soldiering. Indeed, few knew how to properly go about adapting to their new responsibilities.

While many volunteers in both the North and the South shared in their military ignorance, the initial advantage rested with applied rudimentary knowledge. At the earliest test of the respective armies' skill, the Army of Northern Virginia had the advantage of relatively better-trained mid-level soldiers. In comparison to the Confederacy's other major armies, a profusion of Virginia regiments provided the basis of superiority. Training and knowledge had a significant effect both in results and in corresponding attitudes. The early victories at Big Bethel and First Manassas not only confirmed as much, but served to heighten the soldiers' mental and physical acclimation.

Proper training was imperative for infusing new troops with confidence in their military abilities. "You ought to be here to see the boys drill," boasted a North Carolina infantryman. "If the Yankees ever come over on us we could make them think we had been drilling for 500 years, [and] if they ever come we will make a victory, for we will stand while there is a man of us." Drill, drill, and more drill were the order of every day, acknowledged a North Carolina private, who chafed at this endless routine after joining the Virginia army in the fall of 1861. However, when during the summer of 1862, his regiment experienced combat for the first time the private was thankful for their training. His experienced colonel had ordered them to lie down "to escape the bullets then flying by." Although the regiment was severely decimated, the bravery of the officers was an inspiration to the men. Their colonel proudly remarked when he was carried away with a broken leg, "My God! What will become of my regiment? But they have shown themselves to be men."[11]

Though capably trained and well-led soldiers frequently abhorred war, they were better prepared to cope with the realities of military life. However, serving with Jackson's command, or under Lee, did not mean that the trauma of war and the ordeal of army life were any less onerous. Petty camp routine and the sacrifice of personal freedoms wore away at soldiers' morale even in the prestigious Army of Northern Virginia.

Beneath it all, the better-trained, more sophisticated soldier usually kept a resolute perspective when confronted with adversity. "My faith in our course is as strong as ever, and ever [it] will be till the Yankees offer us an honorable [peace]," affirmed a youthful North Carolina lieutenant following early defeats along the eastern coast in 1862. Though "sick and tired of this war and camp fire," the lieutenant's stout defiance was fully evident: "I will fight them [the enemy] as long as I can crawl. . . . They may take every seaport town around the whole Southern Confederacy; they may overrun Virginia, [but] then we are not half whipped. We will fight them as long as there is a man [remaining]. . . . For I had [just as soon] die as [to] become a [Yankee] subject." "We who fight for our wives and children, our homes, and property cannot be whipped," declared another determined Georgia volunteer. "To conquer us is to kill us."[12]

In the Virginia theater, the inevitable emotional and physical distresses of military service were endurable, in part because of the successes of Robert E. Lee's army. A Georgia soldier considered in 1862 that the "tide of war has flowed high and strong over beloved South." Despite reverses in other regions, he boasted that "[Here] there exists nothing but the brightest patriotism." "We are looking for a fight . . . every day," wrote one of Lee's North Carolinians in the aftermath of Fredericksburg, and, notwithstanding the enemy's masses, "if they come . . . they will meet with as great a defeat as they did in December." After Chancellorsville, a Virginia officer proudly reported, "Our men fought splendidly; there was no straggling, and each soldier seemed to feel that he had an important part to act in the grand and bloody drama."[13]

It was a fitting testimonial to both the technical quality and the commitment to service that the Army of North Virginia had long nurtured in its soldiers. The consequences of this heightened morale were evident in the soldiers' reactions to Stonewall Jackson's death at Chancellorsville. "I am very sorry we have lost him," lamented a junior North Carolina officer. "He was a great general [,] though we have others equally as good [,] but they are not so much feared by the Yankees as he was. Let them try it again, and they will find we have other generals besides Jackson."[14]

Serving as perhaps an ultimate tribute to Stonewall Jackson and the excellence of the Virginia army, the comment by a South Carolina infantryman following Chancellorsville reflected what Jackson had most sought. Although the general's death might encourage the enemy, noted this South Carolinian, when they tried Jackson's soldiers again, they would find that it was his men who were the stone wall. "If they come [at us] here we can beat them ten to one," he boasted.[15]

More than contempt or a lack of respect for the enemy, such statement reflect the soldiers' belief in their own potency—in the ultimate effectiveness of Lee's army. This internal confidence could not be shaken by the loss of any one leader. Perhaps it was Robert E. Lee's and Stonewall Jackson's best achievement. Their army, one that believed in itself and and that had victory as a precedent, seemed truly invincible. Drawing on strength from within, it exemplified the power of the human mind.

Despite the army's obvious confidence in their senior leadership, not all boded well for the Army of Northern Virginia. In their spirit of invincibility, many infantrymen did not take into account the severe loss in experienced mid-level officers and soldiers over the past year—a problem that caused Lee to fret about the future. If competence in tactical leadership had been a major strength of Lee's army, was the growing absence of quality second-tier officers now lurking as a fatal vulnerability? And, even more ominous, what about the comparative fighting prowess of the enemy, who could replace their losses and had promoted their experienced veterans to leadership roles?

When the Army of Northern Virginia marched northward in the summer of 1863, there was a strong basis of hope, and even an anticipation that Southern independence would soon be gained. Lee intended that the Confederate offensive into Pennsylvania would effectively deplete the will of Northerners to continue an unprofitable war. Bringing the war to Yankee soil might do much to emphasize the invincibility of Southern arms. Indeed, the ability to influence Northern thinking appeared to rest only upon another, yet decisive, demonstration of what had always been apparent to Robert E. Lee's Army of Northern Virginia—the superiority of their valiant army.[16]

This much-heralded demonstration would certainly occur during what one animated staff officer described as their pending "summer frolic in Pennsylvania." Even as he wrote, the armies had begun marching toward a dusty, little-known town named Gettysburg.[17]

Chapter Seventeen

HENRY KING BURGWYN, JR.

"All Will Turn Out for the Best"

There was good news and bad news, but Harry Burgwyn's ire was roused. The twenty-year-old North Carolina officer had learned in August 1862 that his promotion to colonel was in dispute. While at home on furlough, Harry received a letter from a captain of his regiment warning him that their brigade commander, Brigadier General Robert Ransom, was conspiring against Burgwyn's promotion. "[Ransom] said that he should not recommend you for colonel on account of your age," advised the captain. "He said he did not intend to have any more boys to command regiments in his brigade. I have spoken to several officers and they will not submit to have any one else. They swear they will not stay under an officer appointed over them. . . . The regiment will stick up [for] you without a doubt."[1]

Having experienced too many bureaucratic crises to passively endure such treatment, Harry Burgwyn joined in the fray. From coping with the 26th North Carolina's initial reluctance to reenlist for the war, to bravely leading his regiment through the firestorm at Malvern Hill, Burgwyn had boldly shaped the regiment by his valor and exertion. The men had reelected him lieutenant colonel at their unit's reorganization, and Harry was thus in line for promotion following North Carolina governor-elect Colonel Zeb Vance's resignation.

Although he was up against his own brigade commander, Harry quickly formed a plan of action. A committee from the regiment called upon General Ransom, but they found him adamant; he would not reconsider. Harry then determined to enlist the aid of his father, who wrote a blistering letter to one of Ransom's senior officers. "I shall not submit quietly to it," thundered Harry's father, and he soon took the matter to the secretary of war, demanding that the protocols of army regulations be followed. Harry, as the next in rank, should immediately be promoted, he argued.[2]

General Ransom meanwhile had learned of Henry, Sr.'s, involvement, and went directly to Jefferson Davis. Yet, since the president refused to reinterpret army law, the matter was ultimately decided in Harry Burgwyn's favor. Somewhat as a concession to Ransom, a transfer was arranged whereby the 26th North Carolina went from Ransom's brigade to that of Brigadier General J. Johnson Pettigrew.[3]

On August 24, 1862, Henry King Burgwyn, Jr., became the youngest colonel in the Confederate army. Not yet twenty-one, Harry Burgwyn was elated. He told his mother his objectives had now been achieved.[4]

But not quite. Harry Burgwyn was a young man of action. His regiment remained relatively inactive for months thereafter. As part of a reserve contingent guarding the Richmond area from their camps near Petersburg, the 26th North Carolina saw little combat. Harry repeatedly chafed at watching from a distance while victories by Lee's troops were recorded throughout late 1862 and during the spring of 1863. "As I am doing nothing here but playing second fiddle, I do not care how soon they let me return [to action]," he complained. "Give me the command [to go into a fight] and I'll whip the Yanks and get distinction for myself."[5]

Harry Burgwyn's compulsion, now almost an obsession, to find glory in combat was largely predicated upon his simplified conception of warfare. The twenty-year-old believed that the key to battlefield victory lay in the bold application of superior force. Concentrated strength was the answer to the Confederacy's strategic dilemmas, reasoned Harry. In early 1862, he had urged bringing together the North Carolina coastal defense forces for a concerted action prior to New Bern. His outrage over the disasters at Roanoke Island; Somerset, Kentucky; Forts Henry and Donelson; and over the fall of New Orleans, typified his strong convictions. "Will our generals ever wake up to the fact that we must concentrate or be whipped?'' he had grumbled.[6]

Harry particularly disdained the government's expressed policy of defending every small town or minor population point throughout the Confederacy. The crucial factor, Harry Burgwyn argued, was not the defense of each parcel of territory, but the preservation of the South's principal armies. "Our country may suffer and a great deal of our property [be] lost, but the success of our cause is not even endangered until the immense armies we have in the field are destroyed,'' he proclaimed in May 1862.[7]

For a person so young, Harry Burgwyn's wisdom seemed well beyond his years. Some considered him destined for greatness. A considerable asset in his burgeoning stature among the army's influential was his wry sense of humor. Following the crippling loss of New Orleans, Harry mused, "The Yankees will have to encounter 'Bronze John' or 'Yaller Jack' [popular names for Yellow Fever]. . . . This I believe is the year for a yellow fever feast, and a dainty meal I hope he [Bronze John] will have.''[8]

Although still burdened by ennui from his lackluster assignment, in the spring of 1863 Colonel Harry Burgwyn remained hopeful of finding a way into the shooting war. While at Petersburg he repeatedly touted the efficiency of his heavily recruited and drilled regiment. In Harry Burgwyn's young mind, only the competence of many of the Confederacy's generals was in question, not the abilities of his soldiers. "They [my men] are willing to whip two or three to one, and to fight six or seven to one,'' he claimed. "Whenever we go into battle, [however,] unless we are concentrated, it will be with 'no fear and little hope.' ''[9]

Harry's earlier experience in combat had admittedly shaped his views. Following the defeat at New Bern, young Burgwyn expressed his thoughts about meeting the enemy: "The Yankees . . . are no match for our men if properly led,'' he insisted, adding, "Our troops are not a particle discouraged, but have lost a great deal of confidence in their leader [General Branch], and some time must elapse before they can know their new generals.''[10]

In explaining these early defeats, Harry was typically critical, yet optimistic. The South had only to "gain victories at the decisive points of the theaters of war'' to insure independence, he alleged. Thus, his anger was reserved for "those despondent, chicken hearted men who seem to think that we are ruined simply because we evacuate politically important places."[11]

By mid-1862, with the genius of Robert E. Lee and Stonewall Jackson proved in the East, and competent leaders such as John Hunt Morgan and Nathan Bedford Forest emerging in the West, Burgwyn was outspoken in his anticipation of new victories. There are new "evidences of superior generalship on our part," and these foreshadow, "more successful efforts upon decisive points," he reasoned.[12]

Following news of Second Manassas, Harry became convinced that the path to victory was well defined: "What will prevent us from taking Washington [D.C.] and invading the North now I cannot see. The North has now no disciplined troops; they have all perished either by disease or by the bullet. . . ." To his father he suggested, "The Northern people must see that they are today farther from subjugating the South than they have ever been before. Three hundred thousand men, slain by the sword, or perished by disease, must be a strong peace argument."[13]

All of these statements accentuated his desire to again become a part of the real war. In May 1863, with victory adorning the banners of Lee's post-Chancellorsville army, Harry Burgwyn prophesied an invasion of the North and eagerly anticipated his own role in this campaign. "Our army has not suffered so much as I thought at first," he informed his mother of the Chancellorsville fight, "and our victory is certainly of a very decisive character. Added to the fact that from 30,000 to 40,000 of Hooker's men go out within the next fortnight [discharged due to expired terms of service], I hope this battle will puzzle the Abolitionist government not a little."[14]

In anticipating the reinforcement of Lee's army by his own troops and others then assigned as reserves, Harry prophesied, "Another week may find us lost in the large army now around Fredericksburg."[15]

Much as Harry Burgwyn had anticipated, by early June his regiment and brigade had been assigned to Henry Heth's division of A. P. Hill's corps of the Army of Northern Virginia. Throughout May and into June, Lee's army had received heavy reinforcements. ". . . His whole army is in most excellent condition," noted Harry on June 5. "Something important [in the way of a movement] is expected."[16]

With Lee's army on the verge of going north, Burgwyn wrote his father an intense and significant letter:

General Lee is upon the point of advancing to attack Hooker . . .
That he will do this I have no doubt in the world. When the
achievements of our Army of the Potomac [Army of Northern Vir-
ginia] are written by an impartial historian I believe they will compare favorably with those of the Romans or of Napoleon's Old
Guard. . . . The army that he [Lee] has cannot be whipped by anything in Yankeedom. I do not believe our army in the West fights
with anything like the determination of [the Army of Northern Vir-
ginia].[17]

Believing that Lee would wait before advancing north only until
about June 14 (when the enlistment terms of many of Hooker's men
expired), Harry was ebullient about the prospects of his further advancement. His chance to become a brigadier general was at hand.
Hoping to enlist his father's political support, Harry wrote, "My reputation at home and in the state would be much enhanced by the
fact that at [age] 21 or 22 I was made a brigadier general. It is,
moreover, a cardinal point with me never to lose an opportunity. I
cannot say that I have any expectation of promotion now, or very
soon. But during the summer [campaign] in all probability I will be engaged in some of the great battles which will undoubtedly occur. . . .
After one of these the time would be favorable for pressing the[se]
claims. . . ."[18]

Ambitious, able, and well-connected politically, Harry Burgwyn had
even begun looking beyond his appointment as a general: "In case
of promotion, I shall make every effort to be transferred to North
Carolina, both because an opportunity for distinction is much greater
there than in a large army, and because any success will be much
more appreciated and . . . [contribute] to my future success and perhaps political influence—should the [end of the] war find me in the
land of the living."[19]

Harry Burgwyn's military ambition seemed to be matched only by
his passion for Anne Devereux, a distant relative. Anne was only nineteen in mid-1863, yet this bright-eyed beauty had captured Harry's
heart. She was fond of sending him lemons, so he returned the favor
with captured Yankee sardines and a canteen. They talked of marry-
ing after the war, but Harry was committed to first establishing his
higher path in life, so no specific plans were made. For now, there
would be many pleasant sojourns at her home, Will's Forest, in Raleigh, during furloughs. Amid a correspondence that sparkled with

the sweetness of tender romance, life seemed very good for Harry Burgwyn in the early summer of 1863—almost too good.[20]

On June 15, 1863, Harry Burgwyn completed a long letter to his mother, announcing that Lee was en route north with perhaps one hundred thousand men. "No Yankee army can whip that [number] when handled by Lee. He has completely deceived Hooker thus far," Harry confidently asserted. "Lee is certainly making a very bold movement. . . . I think he will strike a tremendous and successful blow. . . . I have no idea that Gen. Lee expects to stop in Maryland. I think he will essay Pennsylvania. His army is admirably organized and officered and has the most implicit confidence in him. The men are all in good spirits and the whole army expects to go into Pennsylvania."[21]

The war's climactic encounter seemed in the offing. Battlefield distinction, and perhaps a coveted brigadier general's commission, appeared within Harry's grasp.

Only days ahead, along the dusty route north to Pennsylvania, Harry Burgwyn anticipated military glory. His closing comments to his mother thus expressed both a desire and a prophecy. "And now I must bid you goodbye. What will be the result of the movements now on foot God alone can tell. I hope to be able to do my duty to the best of my ability and leave the result to His infinite wisdom and justice. What ever may be my own fate I . . . feel and believe that all will turn out for the best."[22]

"Where Is My Sword?"

Harry Burgwyn had written in July 1862 about the horrors of the battlefield, saying that "war was no pastime." His experience with the 26th North Carolina during the Seven Days battles had sobered his idea of war. While then riding at the head of his regiment, Harry had encountered a shrieking artillery shell that seemed to come "right for [his] head." Harry instinctively had "bowed until [his] hair mingled with his [horse's] mane." The shell then whizzed past three feet above Burgwyn's head and struck the ground only twenty yards distant. Had he been sitting upright, it "would probably [have] stunned me by its proximity," estimated Harry.

Glancing backward toward his men, Burgwyn noted that "about a dozen had dropped down in the same way." It was an instinctive reaction, a telltale groping with the prospect of death, he realized. From that point on, Harry Burgwyn was both a survivor and a believer.[23]

To experience the terror of battle was to know chaos and confusion. Never was there anything like it. When rushing to the attack over fallen foes and friends alike, Burgwyn said he felt a grim determination to participate in the fight, but also to get it over with. Harry tried to compare war's terrible experience with familiar episodes from life. The crash of artillery seemed like "an angry surf beating upon the beach—except that the discharges were much shorter than the [pounding] of the waves." Bullets and "all kinds of missiles" were constantly zipping about, "as the grains of wheat would fly from the threshing machine." Broken muskets, equipment, debris, and dead and wounded lay scattered everywhere. Particularly ghastly were the dead with their glazed eyes staring off into eternity. One soldier he observed had been struck in the shoulder by a 180-pound Parrott rifle shell, which ranged downward through his body—"literally tearing him to pieces."[24]

As for victory or defeat, Harry had presumed "an all just God would lend his aid to the right side"; thus "many a prayer was . . . offered up that our side might be victorious."[25]

Instead of righteousness on the battlefield, Lieutenant Colonel Burgwyn had found only "stupidity." During the fight at Malvern Hill on July 1, 1862, Major General John Bankhead Magruder had ordered an unsupported frontal attack against a concentrated force of Federal artillery and infantry defending the crest of a gently sloping hill. This attack was conducted across a mile of open clover and a cornfield, and Magruder's men had been butchered by the hundreds. Mindful of this "huge blunder," Harry Burgwyn later recalled his experience, providing a vivid impression of the Malvern Hill battle.[26]

While in the midst of their frontal charge, the brigade was halted by their brigadier, Robert Ransom, who wanted the lines dressed and aligned "in close order," Burgwyn remembered. Then, following a brief pause, Ransom simply said, "Go ahead." "Off we went [again]," wrote Harry Burgwyn, "without, as usual, a soul to show us the way." As the road they were following forked, Harry impulsively led his men down the wrong path. By the time he discovered their mistake, they were engulfed by a multitude of panicked, fleeing men. All shouted with terror that they had been "cut to pieces."[27]

Desperate for proper direction, Harry Burgwyn grasped at a wild-eyed fugitive and, drawing his sword, "threatened to kill him unless he led me into the battle." The man was frightened out of his wits, observed Harry. Yet the fugitive decided "it would be better to risk death from the enemy than to get it from his friends," remarked Burgwyn. Led part way forward by the straggler, the 26th North Carolina then sprinted forward through shell fire and volleys of musketry. Huge tree limbs came crashing down about them, adding to the din. The haze of gunsmoke only compounded the gathering darkness, and, said Harry, "We could not distinguish friend from foe." Yet, on they went, until they were within five hundred yards of the blazing line of enemy cannon atop Malvern Hill.[28]

Suddenly someone shouted that "friends were in front," and Burgwyn hastily ordered his men to lie down. Yet one lone, distant company of the 26th failed to hear his order and continued onward. Harry soon saw one man rush to within fifteen yards of the enemy's guns before being shot dead. The fire from the artillery was now so terrific that they were "not able to fire a gun [in reply]," Harry recalled. At one point he counted forty-eight discharges per minute from enemy guns.[29]

As the heavy cannonade continued, the 26th North Carolina remained flat on the ground, awaiting orders, even as the gloom turned to night. "With lips parched with thirst, and bodies cold from the evaporating perspiration," they hunkered down on the battlefield until about 10 P.M., when orders were finally received to withdraw.[30]

In all, it had been a devastating experience. "I can only attribute my escape to an all merciful Providence," Lieutenant Colonel Harry Burgwyn confessed after the action. Most of the brigade's regiments hadn't even been able to fight back; the 24th North Carolina had fired only a single volley. In the following morning's light, it was discovered that the entire brigade was so scattered and "in [such] confusion" as to be incapable of further duty. To add to their misery, a cold front moved in, and a heavy rainstorm pelted the soldiers unmercifully. "I had on a Yankee overcoat and my body coat [uniform], together with an oil cloth coat, [and yet] I was still shivering," admitted the combat-shaken Burgwyn. All about him lay the dead and wounded of both armies. Those still alive were in indescribable agony, particularly the wounded Yankees. "In spite of all the wrongs they had done us, I could but feel sorry for the poor devils who suffered so terribly," wrote Harry.[31]

Having gone for about two weeks without taking off any part of his clothing, Harry Burgwyn reflected that he was truly "an object for curiosity." Powered clay from the dusty roads and "a coating of filth" layered his body, and he was famished beyond belief. "Dry crackers, middling pork, and swamp water" had been his entire fare for the two weeks' campaign. Finally, "cold, wet, and badly used up," Harry Burgwyn admitted, "I only hope I will never be 'pushed to the wall so tightly.' "[32]

For many months thereafter, Harry Burgwyn recalled his battle experience: "I have seen enough of the horrors of war, and I earnestly desire that this Seven Days' battle may pave the way for a permanent and speedy peace."[33]

Of course it did not, and while he had been "low spirited" after his peninsula battle experience, by the summer of 1863 Harry was again eager for the fray—in order to earn his brigadier general's commission.[34]

In July 1863, Harry had the further incentive of knowing that his regiment, the 26th North Carolina Infantry, was among the largest of the Army of Northern Virginia, equalling in strength some brigades'. Having been fully recruited, then subsequently sheltered from major combat exposure during their reserve-duty assignment at Petersburg, Harry Burgwyn's regiment was a source of great pride on May 31, 1863. "I now command nearly as many men as most of our brigadier generals. My regiment numbers 1,090 men and officers present, and very nearly 1,250 all told," Harry wrote. "But few of our brigades are very much larger now than that."[35]

At Gettysburg little more than a month later, the 26th was reduced to 843 present for duty. Their losses reflected the rigors of active campaigning. Yet the 26th consisted of "first rate men, and as well drilled as any in the Confederacy," claimed Harry. "I am proud of my command, . . . and when the occasion offers, shall try to make them proud of me."[36]

That occasion was now. On the morning of July 1, 1863, the 26th North Carolina Infantry, with Major General J. J. Pettigrew's brigade, marched eastward from their position as pickets on the Cashtown Road near Marsh Creek. Moving toward the sound of firing in the direction of Gettysburg, Pettigrew's regiments by midday were at Herr Ridge, fronting Willoughby Run, and just south of the Chambersburg Pike. East of this small stream along distant McPherson's Ridge, the Federal army's First Corps was reportedly in considerable strength. There had been lull in the fighting since before noon, and the advanced infantry contingents of both armies seemed to be awaiting further reinforcements.[37]

It was a swelteringly hot day, and by early afternoon Harry Burgwyn became agitated over the considerable delay. Major General Richard H. Anderson's division was particularly slow in moving up, and Harry fumed that the army was "losing valuable time." Finally, at about 2 P.M., word was passed along the line to prepare. Robert E. Lee had authorized the attack of Heth's division. Posted in the center of Heth's line was Pettigrew's brigade, the extreme left of which consisted of the 26th North Carolina. At the command "Forward March!" the 26th stepped off "as proudly as if they were on a review," reported an observer.[38]

Since the Confederate battle line was formed *en echelon* (a stair-step formation), it appeared to their opponents that they were facing multiple lines of battle. Moving forward across a wheatfield, the 26th North Carolina seemed in advance, although in reality it formed merely a part of Pettigrew's single, *en echelon* battle line.[39]

Harry Burgwyn and his North Carolinians swept down the gentle slopes of the wheatfield and into briar-choked Willoughby Run ravine. Already Federal artillery fire was ripping through their line, killing and wounding a few men. Yet this fire was mostly too high. With aligned ranks, and guided by Harry Burgwyn, who was posted in the center, the 26th North Carolina quickened their pace as they reached Willoughby Run ravine. Here the 26th's line suddenly crowded together in the center, but the men continued to force their way through a tangle of briars, reeds, and underbrush.

Random firing broke out along the 26th's line, in response to a terrible volley of musketry that swept through their ranks from across the creek. Their loss here was "frightful," later recalled a soldier. But the men rushed forward, up the steeply sloping hill in front, many firing at the shadowy forms seen amid the timber ahead.[40]

Unknown to the 26th North Carolina, directly in front were two regiments from perhaps the most famous infantry brigade of the Army of the Potomac—the black hat or "Iron Brigade." Wearing the old-style "Hardee" United States Army black-felt hat with turned-up brim, both the 19th Indiana and the 24th Michigan faced Harry Burgwyn's North Carolinians from their wooded grove (Herbst's Woods) along McPherson's Ridge. With a combined strength of about 804 officers and men, these two units nearly equaled the 843 present in the 26th North Carolina.[41]

Having been trained by their commander for a disciplined, stand-up-and-shoot-it-out manner of fighting, Harry Burgwyn's North Carolinians were about to meet on equal footing two of the elite fighting regiments in the Yankee army. Although Colonel Burgwyn had confidence in his large, disciplined regiment, his pet theory about combat was about to be put to a critical test. "You have no idea how much better it is to have a full regiment," he had earlier written. "[When marching elbow to elbow in line of battle] each [soldier] feels that he is to a considerable extent protected and aided."[42]

Neither of the opposing lines had been intimidated by the initial exchange of firing, and Burgwyn's North Carolinians rapidly closed toward Herbst's grove for the death struggle. Prominently displaying their new arsenal-supplied red St. Andrew's Cross–pattern flag, the 26th North Carolina advanced in closely aligned ranks, shouting the eerie "Rebel yell."[43]

The crash of musketry added to the terrible din. Blinding clouds of gunsmoke billowed from the woods. Within the lines, shrill shrieks of wounded men mixed with guttural shouts of excitement, maniacal yells, and piercing screams. The wild cacophony of combat permeated the air. Madness, confusion, and death reigned. Overlapped by the 11th North Carolina on the 26th's right flank, the 19th Indiana had begun giving way. The 24th Michigan thus had to recoil back up the slope into the middle of the grove to keep from being outflanked on the left. They were pursued step-by-step by Burgwyn's men, now not more than twenty yards distant. Here the stable but rapidly depleting standing lines poured sustained fire into the opposite ranks as fast as the men could load and shoot. "Bullets were as thick as hailstones in a storm," later wrote an eyewitness.[44]

The 26th North Carolina's line shuddered and shook like a blanket in a windstorm. Harry Burgwyn was on foot amid the hail of incoming minie balls. His colors had been shot down nearly a dozen times; in fact, the entire eight-man color guard was dead or wounded. Yet their flag was the symbol of the regiment's pride and defiance. Aligning on the colors and following the flag's movement forward or backward were the essence of the unit's tactical disposition. The big, waving flag was prominent for all to see—and also for an enemy to fire at. The object of downing the enemy's battle flag was to cripple his morale and ruin tactical formations in the noise, confusion, and blinding smoke. Thus, a color bearer was an important target. If dangerous, his was one of the most responsible assignments in a line of battle.[45]

When Harry Burgwyn looked about, his vivid red flag was again down in the midst of that flame-and-smoke-filled grove. Before he could react, Captain W. W. McCreery of Pettigrew's staff rushed up with a message for Burgwyn. "Tell him," shouted McCreery in paraphrasing Pettigrew, "his regiment has covered itself with glory today." Then, acting impulsively, McCreery seized the fallen flag of the 26th and, waving it aloft, started forward toward the enemy. McCreery was soon shot, and he fell on top of the flag with a bullet through his heart. A nearby lieutenant rushed to the fallen captain, pulled the torn, blood-soaked flag from beneath the body, and carried it forward. Yet, a few seconds later he also went down, badly wounded.[46]

The 26th North Carolina's line had stopped advancing. Harry Burgwyn raced forward, reached down, and grasped the fallen Confederate battle flag. Advancing with the colors, he shouted that he wanted those stubborn Yankees run out of the woods. Before moving more than a few paces, he met an officer who, holding up his hand to stop, ordered a private from Company B to carry the flag. Burgwyn handed it over, but the man, Private Frank Honeycutt, went forward only a few steps before he was shot dead.[47]

What went through Harry's mind at this point remains a mystery. Although he knew the risks of battle, Harry Burgwyn had recently dismissed fears about his exposure in combat, saying, "Do not be anxious about me as I have been in more danger since I have been in N.C. than in this summer." Proud and determined, twenty-one-year-old colonel Harry Burgwyn again reached for the fallen battle flag of the 26th North Carolina.[48]

As he grasped and raised the flagstaff, Burgwyn turned sideways to yell for the 26th to close on their colors. Then it happened. The blow was sharp and stunning. A bullet struck him in the lower torso. Ripping through two diary journals in his uniform pocket, the big .58-caliber minie ball burrowed through the bottom of both lungs before exiting his opposite side. Harry Burgwyn collapsed like a rag doll. His lieutenant colonel, John R. Lane, immediately rushed to his side. "My dear colonel, are you severely hurt?" he gasped. Harry Burgwyn's head jerked to the left, and a furtive squeeze of Lane's hand was his only response.[49]

In the next instant, a lieutenant rushed up, grasped the 26th's bullet-riddled colors, and began to carry them forward. Lieutenant Colonel Lane shouted for the man to stop. Lane then promptly seized the flag and rushed ahead, waving the colors and shouting for the 26th North Carolina to follow. Behind him, the 26th North Carolina raised a mighty cheer and rushed ahead, chasing the equally devastated 24th Michigan from Herbst Woods. Lane, however, never saw the result. He was severely wounded, a bullet striking him in the head and emerging through his mouth. Although the Yankees again rallied, forming a third line behind a small ravine, they were ultimately dispersed by the 26th North Carolina's final, desperate assault.[50]

As the fleeing enemy scattered across the sweltering fields back into Gettysburg, the North Carolinians briefly paused to regroup. The scene of their deadly conflict immediately struck all with horror. Their former line of battle at the edge of Herbst Woods was marked by fallen bodies in such a straight line that their division commander later remarked that the 26th's dead lay in a row "[as] at dress parade." In fact, the fighting there had been nearly a massacre. Of the 843 men who began the contest, the 26th lost 86 officers and men killed, 502 wounded, and 120 missing—a total of 708 (84 percent). Their opponents, the 24th Michigan and 19th Indiana, suffered nearly equally, losing 573 of 804 present—a casualty level of 73 percent. Remarkably, this carnage was sustained in only about one-half hour of intense fighting. In all, the grim toll testified to both the viciousness and absurdity of the close-range Herbst Woods firefight.[51]

Although the 26th North Carolina had covered itself with glory, it was a futile glory. Harry Burgwyn's tactical concept of concentrated force utilizing discipline and valor only resulted in a mutual slaughter—not in the triumphant annihilation of the enemy. Moreover, the hard-fought Southern victory of July 1 proved insignificant to the battle's overall outcome.

The aftershock of Gettysburg found the 26th North Carolina physically devastated and emotionally drained. The estimated 216 men remaining after the July 1 fight were again so badly shot up in the Pickett-Pettigrew-Trimble charge of July 3 that thereafter a single captain remained in command of less than a hundred men. The loss of the 26th North Carolina at Gettysburg was later analyzed by a noted historian as the greatest in numbers and percentage of any regiment on either side in any battle of the entire war.[52]

That one of the war's most desperate toe-to-toe contests at nearly point-blank range had occurred between elite units of the Confederate and Union armies on McPherson's Ridge on July 1 soon became but a remarkable if bloody footnote in the history of the Civil War.

*   *   *

Harry Burgwyn was found still alive. Several soldiers had carried him on a blanket to the rear, and another had to chase off at gunpoint a looter who was attempting to remove a watch that hung on a silken cord around the stricken colonel's neck. Harry was suffering terribly, and his wounds burned like fire. He asked that water be poured over the bullet holes. His coat was soon removed, and the water from several canteens splashed about the wounds. Captain J. J. Young, his close friend from the days of the promotion controversy with General Ransom, cradled him in his arms. Burgwyn knew that his wound was mortal, and Young later said that Harry whispered that he was proud of his men and knew that they would never disgrace him.[53]

About two hours had elapsed since the "cruel" rifle ball had ripped through his lungs. Harry Burgwyn's glazing eyes looked up into the azure sky. He was deathly pale, and the blood continued to seep from his wounds. "I know my gallant regiment will do their duty! Where is my sword?" he gasped.[54]

They were his last words. The boy colonel had at last become a Southern legend.

Chapter Eighteen

GETTYSBURG

One of the greatest testimonials to the Army of Northern Virginia's prowess came not from its men, but from an archenemy. Major General Joseph Hooker, the Federal commander who had fought Lee at Chancellorsville prior to leading his battle-scarred blue columns north toward Gettysburg in late June 1863, knew Lee's veterans well. Later, testifying before the Congressional Committee on the Conduct of the War, Hooker asserted, "With a rank and file vastly inferior to our own, intellectually and physically, [Lee's] army has, by discipline alone, acquired a character for steadiness and efficiency unsurpassed, in my judgment, in ancient or modern times. We have not been able to rival it, nor has there been any near approximation of it in the other Rebel armies."[1]*

Hooker's comments expressed not only what was foremost in his mind during that sweltering midsummer 1863 march into Pennsylvania, but also what plagued many among his troops. A captain in the 1st Massachusetts Cavalry considered how superior the Rebel soldiers were to the Army of the Potomac, being "better officered, a better fighting material, . . . and [also] the spirit of this [Lee's] army . . . [being] much better than ours. . . ." To Brigadier General Francis C. Barlow of the Union XI Corps, the Rebels were "more heroic, more

---

*Hooker was replaced as commander of the Army of the Potomac on June 28, 1863, by Major General George G. Meade.

modest, and more in earnest." One alarmed I Army Corps Federal staff officer, writing from Centerville, Virginia, on June 15, 1863, reported that they were then preparing to move northward for an expected battle in Pennsylvania, at which place "discouraged officers and soldiers [believe] we are to have our second annual beating."[2]

Such comments clearly depicted a despondency and apprehension that sharply contrasted with the elation and enthusiasm of the gray-clad soldiers against whom they would soon battle. On June 13, while en route north, a Virginia cavalry officer wrote, "If General Lee can carry out what I believe are his designs he will achieve the greatest victory of the war. At all events this army cannot be routed, and will hold its own against any force which will be brought against it."[3]

Major Sandie Pendleton, fully absorbed in this "summer frolic in Pennsylvania," had listened intently to the loud cheers of the soldiers in Carlisle when the battle flag of the 36th North Carolina Regiment was raised over the town square. It only presaged a great victory that the Army of Northern Virginia would again achieve, predicted Pendleton. Like many in Lee's army, he was generally contemptuous of their opponents, and particularly disparaged the local Pennsylvania militia. Noting that the governor had called out sixty thousand additional men to defend Harrisburg, Pendleton wrote, "They don't go—they prefer staying at home and saving [their] property." "What a race of people!" he scoffed.[4]

Captain William Blackford of the 2d Virginia Cavalry noted that the Army of the Potomac's infantrymen were often stand-ins: "Nine tenths of them are foreigners sent as substitutes for the native-born patriots who thus would bleed vicariously for the Union." Even the native-born were sneered at by Blackford: "Men, women, and children are all afflicted with a Yankee twang that grates against my nerves and ear drums." Likewise, Sandie Pendleton had expressed his contempt for all types of Yankees, but particularly for the women. "Until yesterday when we reached this place I have seen nothing approaching good looks in the women," he confided to his fiancée. "[They are] real specimens of the Dutch Boor. The heavy brutish lips [and] thick drooping eyelids indicate plainly the stupidity of the people. The only way to touch them is to burn their property, and [as] much as I deplore the horror of war, I am ready to begin it."[5]

Pendleton soon had his wish. At the time of his letter the fighting at Gettysburg was only a few days distant.

As Sandie Pendleton and others had witnessed, the Army of

Northern Virginia was in fine condition and high spirits, fully confident of Marse Robert's genius, and eager to win a victory that might
end the war. Yet Lee's concept of risking an offensive to win a crucial
victory on Northern soil had been based upon securing a position of
"decided advantage . . . over the enemy, . . . at points of our selection."[6]

Initially, the prospects of devastating the scattered elements of the
Yankee army, which had lagged behind Lee's columns in the march
northward were good. Lee intended to "throw an overwhelming
force against the enemy's advance," then crush the separate columns
in detail so as to destroy the Yankee army, according to Major General
I. R. Trimble.[7]

Abruptly, this plan and the Confederate army's seeming advantage
were thwarted. Due to the absence of J. E. B. Stuart's cavalry (away
on a "discretionary" raid far to the east of Lee), the two great armies
blindly collided during a chance meeting of advance columns at the
small Pennsylvania town of Gettysburg on July 1, 1863.[8]

Although Lee later claimed, "It had not been intended to deliver
a general battle so far from our base unless attacked," his possible
courses of action were now limited. For the Army of Northern Virginia, "coming unexpectedly upon the whole Federal army," to withdraw or merely await attack would have been "difficult and
dangerous," asserted Lee in his official report. Mindful of the difficulties of gathering food in enemy country with the opposing army
present, Lee reasoned that a battle, "in a measure was unavoidable."
Thus, considering "the success already gained" in the initial action
on July 1, Lee was prompted to continue the chance-meeting engagement, as it "gave hope of a favorable issue."[9]

Thus, already a subtle alteration had occurred in the conduct of
the campaign. Rather than carefully planning a battle, as he had intended, Lee was now required to improvise the contest. At stake was
perhaps the Confederacy's best chance to win a peace under the
circumstances of diminishing resources that so worried Robert E. Lee.

Yet the Confederate commander had supreme confidence in his
men; they had always gone where ordered, and usually won convincing victories. They were, as Lee had earlier stated, as nearly invincible
as any soldiers could be. Despite their bravery, what Lee perhaps most
relied upon was the protection and intervention of Divine Providence. "I trust that our merciful God, our only help and refuge, will
not desert us in this our hour of need, but will deliver us by His

almighty hand, that the whole world may recognize His power and all hearts be lifted up in adoration and praise of His unbounded loving kindness," wrote Lee during the Gettysburg Campaign. "We must, however, submit to His almighty will, whatever that may be," he added ominously.[10]

The intervention of God at the Battle of Gettysburg was not characterized by particularly good fortune for the Confederate army. In fact, there were many unfortunate pivotal aspects of the battle and human failings that later became sources of considerable controversy and criticism.

The trouble began on the first day, July 1, when Lieutenant General A. P. Hill overaggressively initiated the battle without Lee's presence and virtually committed the Army of Northern Virginia to the contest. Then, that afternoon, with three Federal corps beaten and in disarray, 2d Corps commander Richard S. Ewell, Stonewall Jackson's replacement, failed to press an attack on the high ground of Cemetery Hill, where the Yankees desperately were attempting to reform. Ewell's excessive caution caused Sandie Pendleton to later assert, "Oh, for the presence and inspiration of Old Jack just for one hour."[11]

On the following day, July 2, Lieutenant General James Longstreet's turning movement against the Federal left flank was less than inspired, and Longstreet's sullen behavior—allegedly because he was rebuffed by Lee in the conceptual and tactical arrangements for this attack—resulted in the severe criticism of "Old Pete." Longstreet had been instructed to attack along an oblique line north of Little Round Top, since a personal reconnaissance by Captain S. R. Johnston about sunrise had found no Yankees occupying this high ground. Yet Lee had been deceived; Little Round Top was under enemy occupation by the time Longstreet's troops approached late that afternoon. Moreover, Daniel Sickles had spontaneously sent the entire Union III Corps forward to the Emmitsburg Road to occupy high ground there. What Lee had intended to be an oblique attack against Cemetery Ridge became instead a protracted firefight on ground well in advance of the ridge, from the Peach Orchard to Little Round Top.[12]

Prior to the fighting's sputtering out after dark, both Longstreet's and other supporting troops were unable to penetrate to the crest of Cemetery Ridge, with one notable exception. Brigadier General A. R. Wright's lone brigade nearly penetrated the main Yankee line, attacking toward the crest of Cemetery Ridge about 6:30 P.M. Hope was then raised that the enemy-held ridge was quite vulnerable. Wright, in fact, declared that he had gained the key to the Yankees' entire position. Although hurled back by several units of Union Brigadier General Alexander Webb's "Philadelphia Brigade," Wright maintained that he could have penetrated the Yankee line had he been supported.[13]

Wright's assertions raised a key point in the mind of Lee. Throughout that day's fighting, the uncoordination of attacking forces was apparent not only in Longstreet's corps, but also in a portion of A. P. Hill's, which had supported the primary attack.

On July 3, having determined to follow up on the partial successes of the 2d, Lee planned a continuation of the major assault against the Union left concurrently to attacking the enemy's right flank on Culp's Hill with Ewell's troops. Longstreet, however, opposed continuing the original plan of attack, preferring instead a circuitous march south of the Round Tops to reach the Taneytown Road beyond Meade's lines. This course would enable him to attack the enemy in reverse.[14]

When this plan was vetoed by Lee, Longstreet had already given the orders for its execution.*

Longstreet was crestfallen, and after strenuously objecting to Lee's idea of directly assaulting Cemetery Ridge, became depressed and reluctant to obey Lee. [15]

Blame for the Pickett-Pettigrew-Trimble Charge disaster was subsequently laid at the feet of Robert E. Lee. Lee had erred in his strong belief that the valor of his men could overcome command failures. "It's all my fault!" stated Lee repeatedly, as the broken ranks of his men stumbled past him along Seminary Ridge following the attack. Many of the returning officers and men were said to be panic-stricken by the continuing Federal artillery fire, and it was a sad spectacle for Lee to witness—the very men he had regarded as nearly invincible fleeing from the enemy's fire. [16]

Lee assumed responsibility for what was obviously a tactical command failure. Said Lee in his official report, "The conduct of the troops was all that I could desire or expect, and they deserve success so far as it can be deserved by heroic valor and fortitude. More may have been required of them than they were able to perform, but my admira-

*Despite Longstreet's belief that this method would have resulted in a victory, the positioning of the Federal VI Corps, which remained unengaged, would likely have thwarted his turning movement.

tion of their noble qualities and confidence in their ability to cope successfully with the enemy has [sic] suffered no abatement. . . .''[17]

In the sense that Lee's great character forbade him to blame others, even when heavy censure was due, his correspondence and reports served to partly obfuscate others' contributions to the critical Gettysburg defeat. Despite Lee's reluctance to criticize, an analysis of the Confederate commander's thinking throughout the battle provides a fair estimation of what the major points of decision rested upon, and hence where the basis of defeat truly lay.

From the beginning, it was evident that Lee was placing heavy reliance on certain key senior commanders, particularly James Longstreet. Above all else, however, Lee trusted the fighting prowess of his proud and usually victorious army. The attitudes of his men had counted for much in Lee's eyes, and their high enthusiasm became crucial in Lee's plans. A careful examination of his correspondence and reports reveals how aggressively Lee maneuvered in this crucial battle. He had sought a devastating, army-destroying victory, rather than a barren success in which the enemy merely withdrew in frustration or discomfiture. Lee wanted to win a peace by demonstrating the superiority of the Confederate army and thus sapping the North's fighting spirit. With the United States presidential election of 1864 little more than a year away, the political and emotional implications of a decisive Confederate victory would be paramount. [18]

In order to accomplish his goal, Lee made certain mental concessions and took serious risks. On the first day, July 1, although hampered by a lack of intelligence due to J. E. B. Stuart's absence, Lee had regarded the success of the day's operations—an estimated five thousand prisoners and various captured field guns—as evidence that the enemy was partially beaten and their army crippled. Accordingly, Lee's thoughts were not so much on the cost to his own army as on the losses suffered by the Yankees. His objective of inflicting mortal damage on the Union army was apparent when, in his first report on July 4, he emphasized that "the enemy suffered severely" prior to mentioning his own heavy losses.[19]

Because he was unable to obtain a full understanding of the position and strength of the enemy, Lee relied on sketchy reports from prisoners taken on July 1, and random data from scouts, patrols, and skirmishers, to organize a major attack on July 2. His mind was on Meade's defeat, not the potential for his own loss, which he believed the fighting spirit of his army would prevent. [20]

Getting his men into a tactical position from which they could devastate and rout Meade's army required attacking. Again, as his idea was to win decisively rather than to merely win, Lee had rejected Longstreet's suggestion of moving southward to interpose between Meade's army and Washington, D.C.—a plan that had as its major premise the belief that the Union army would attack Lee's forces in a strong defensive position.

On July 2, Lee, as he stated, was encouraged by the results of the first day, and wanted the enemy driven from their position on Cemetery Ridge along the south end of the Union line, and also from Culp's Hill and Cemetery Hill to the north, if possible. The key to accomplishing that objective was obvious in Lee's reports. He intended to utilize the artillery for a penetrating infantry attack. The covering fire from forward, commanding positions would enable the superior Confederate infantry to reach their objectives relatively intact. This rationale was evident throughout the battle, and became a crucial aspect of attempting to "drive" the Yankees from their high ground. [21]

The high ground Lee wanted to occupy on July 2 was the elevation adjacent to the Peach Orchard and the Emmitsburg Road, which was to be the location for Longstreet's artillery. Here the artillery "could be used to advantage in assailing the more elevated ground beyond, and thus enable us to reach the crest of the [Cemetery] ridge," considered Lee. The slaughter that occurred on both sides during the fighting in that sector on July 2 didn't deter Robert E. Lee in his thinking. He regarded as important the fact that Longstreet had "succeeded in getting possession of and holding the desired ground." His position set the stage for a decisive attack on July 3—not in the manner in which it was later conducted, but as a continuation of the original plan.[22]

Lee's fixation with that final objective, gaining the "steep ridge" (Cemetery Ridge), caused him to plan for a renewed assault on July 3 by Longstreet—which would be materially aided by an attack of Ewell's men in the northern sector. The "partial successes" of July 2, as Lee termed them, would thus be used as the foundation for a decisive, full-scale attack the following day.

In support of his belief that the crest of Cemetery Ridge was vulnerable, he had specific evidence. Brigadier General A. R. Wright's brigade had penetrated the crest on July 2. "The trouble is not in going there," Wright later told artillerist E. Porter Alexander. "[It] is to stay there after you get there."[23]

Lee's plans were appropriately calculating. They called for both Ewell's and Longstreet's attacks to occur simultaneously in the early morning of July 3. If want of a proper concert of action and a lack of proper support had been the reason for not winning a decisive victory on the 2d, Lee believed that additional troops and these well-timed attacks would accomplish the task on July 3.[24]

Yet Longstreet hadn't been ready on the morning of July 3, reported Lee. Suddenly his plans had gone awry, and Lee must have been gravely upset, although he continued to keep a calm demeanor.[25]

With Ewell's troops already fighting in the Culp's Hill sector, it was too late to coordinate the two planned attacks. Even though Ewell was eventually beaten back with heavy losses, the emphasis of Lee's plan remained on Longstreet's front, which Lee had earlier regarded as a "most favorable point of attack." When Lee had conferred with Longstreet that morning, a controversy quickly arose between them over the proper course of action. Longstreet wanted to begin a wide swinging movement south beyond the Round Tops. Then, when dissuaded from the plan, he objected to involving his entire command in the pending attack. According to Lee, Longstreet feared the enemy's possession of Little Round Top, "from which his troops could be attacked in reverse as they advanced." Lee's "Old War Horse" was so insistent about the danger that Lee altered his tactical plans accordingly.[26]

In order to defend the exposed flank, Lee allowed Longstreet to keep two of his divisions in place and protect the corps' position against a sortie from Little Round Top. The primary assault would be carried out by the divisions of Pickett (from Longstreet's Corps), Pettigrew, and Trimble (both from A. P. Hill's Corps).[27]

Only the precise objective point of the attack remained undecided. Lee pointed out a mostly bare section of Cemetery Ridge where an umbrella-shaped clump of trees stood as a visible objective point. His reasoning was obvious. Wright's men had successfully approached that portion of the line the day before.* Splitting the enemy lines at this point would both separate their flanks and enable the envelopment of their entire line in either direction. Since nearly fifteen thousand were committed to the attack, Lee reasoned that this force

---

*In his official report Lee made much of Wright's July 2 attack, which, said Lee, "gained the crest of the ridge itself." O.R. 1-27-2-319.

would be sufficiently strong both to dislodge the enemy and sustain any penetration.[28]

Again, the key to taking this enemy-held ridge would be the artillery. Lee had wanted and expected his batteries to bombard the enemy line both prior to, and also during, the grand frontal attack. His entire plan for the past two days was predicated on obtaining favorable high ground from which the artillery could effectively fire in support of the attack against the ridge.[29]

Longstreet did not agree with Lee's plan. He asserted, "There never was a body of 15,000 men who could make that attack successfully." Lee, although undoubtedly burdened by his key subordinate's intense objections, was supremely confident in his men. "There never were such men in an army before. . . . They will go anywhere and do anything if properly led," he had recently written. Lee thus kept the central purpose of his attack in mind, and was further disappointed by Longstreet's inaction that morning. "The enemy is there, and I'm going to strike him!" Lee firmly resolved. [30]

Strike the enemy, indeed! Longstreet's assault that afternoon followed an extensive two-hour bombardment by massed artillery on both sides, and carried to and beyond the very guns posted to defend the stone wall at the deadly angle near the targeted clump of trees. Yet the famous clash there of Armistead's Virginians with Alexander Webb's Philadelphia brigade was mostly anticlimactic. The majority of the attackers never made it to the crest, much less fought hand to hand as did Armistead's men.

One critical reason was that there had been no effective artillery support during the actual assault, as Lee had specifically planned. Most batteries had run out of ammunition before the attack and an ample reserve supply was removed to a considerable distance because of the danger from enemy artillery fire during the long cannonade. "[During the attack] our own [guns] having nearly exhausted their ammunition . . . [they] were unable to reply, or render the necessary support to the attacking party," said Lee in dismay. "Owing to this fact, which was unknown to me when the assault took place, the enemy was enabled to throw a strong force of infantry against our left [and repulse the attack]."[31]*

The Pickett-Pettigrew-Trimble Charge was later regarded as the

---

*For a review of Confederate artillery performance during the assault see Richard Rollins, "Prelude to Pickett's Charge," *Columbiad*, vol. 2 No. 4, pp. 109–129.

high-water mark of the rebellion. Lee implied in his official report that had he known his batteries lacked artillery ammunition just prior to the attack, the assault might never have been made.

Due to the repulse of Lee's grand assault, the battle was finally lost. Although Lee held his ground and awaited an attack on July 4 while his trains and ambulances departed, Meade did not take the offensive. Lee, acknowledging that the enemy's position was "too strong to be carried," lacking sufficient ammunition, and mindful of his "severe loss," reluctantly decided to retreat across the Potomac. The Battle of Gettysburg was over, but the controversy and consequences remained.[32]

What was left for a shocked nation and its army to discover were the effects on morale after the significant defeat of Lee's supposedly unconquerable army. Now that both Lee and the Army of Northern Virginia had been beaten, the myth of their invincibility was gone. What occurred next provided a fascinating view of the Southern social fabric.

To Lee's men, the stigma of having been defeated in the crucial battle of the war by an opponent they regarded as inferior was difficult to cope with. Their reactions to the shame of defeat varied, as did their explanations for the lost battle.

Colonel David Wyatt Aiken of the 7th South Carolina acknowledged, "We have found a great difference between invading the North and defending the South." Aiken knew not what Lee would do next, but he had heard a rumor that Old Marse would "fight them again north of the Potomac." "I . . . hope not," confided Aiken, "for I think a fair calculation will stretch his loss . . . at about 18,000 or 20,000 men. . . . I am sick of Maryland, and never want to come this side of the river again."[33]

Lieutenant B. T. Cotton of the 34th North Carolina had narrowly escaped capture during the campaign, and he wrote, "I would have stopped [retreating] and given up if I had not been afraid the Yankees would have killed me. . . . Our men did very bad in Maryland and Pennsylvania," he continued. "They robbed every house about [the] battlefield, not only of eatables, but of everything they could lay their hands on. . . . I think a good many of our officers were drunk all the time. I have suffered much since being on the march. I do not think I can hold out much longer. Our army is badly whipped." Then, a few weeks later, Cotton further reflected on the lost battle, and wrote home that he soon anticipated another fight. "If we are [again] defeated our cause is lost [unless] some other nation interferes," he warned. The effect of Gettysburg on the army, observed Cotton, was discouraging. "Our soldiers are getting very tired of fighting. The first thing a greater portion thinks about when there is a fight on hand is running. North Carolina troops are deserting daily; 25 or 30 left our brigade a few nights ago, and a great many more say they are going soon. I fear unless there is a change soon it will be a very serious matter."

A few weeks later, Cotton was so depressed that he wondered, "How long will this cruel war last? I am getting very tired of it. I would be willing to make almost any sacrifice to obtain an honorable peace. I want to go home very bad, but can't see any hope for a furlough." The division's soldiers continued to desert in large numbers, he later reported, adding, "They are shooting a good many. Ten are to be shot in our division this week."[34]

Contrasting sharply with Cotton's mood was that of Private Peter Mabry of Company K, 3d Alabama Infantry. Mabry wrote on August 7th:

We fought the Yankees three days and held the battlefield. I consider that we whipped them, but [we were] compelled to fall back to get provisions and ammunition. The Yankees, of course, claim a victory, as they always do. . . . Our army is in good condition, and if the Yankees come we will give them a good whipping. The Yankees think they whipped us at Gettysburg, and that we are very much demoralized, but if they give us battle they will find out very different. I feel very confident that we can always whip them, but unless our Western armies do something, our Confederacy will go up.[35]

To Captain William H. Blackford it was apparent by July 6th that "the campaign [had] failed." Yet, he noted that day, "there is not the least resemblance of a retreat." The army seemed only to be "counter marching," he continued. A day later, he acknowledged that while "the outlook is very far from bright, and this looks like the turning point of the war," he took solace that at Gettysburg "we held our own, slept on the battlefield, and remained there for twenty-four hours without molestation, showing that we had so punished the enemy that they were incapable of an advance."[36]

Sandie Pendleton also remained hopeful and defiant. "Our army is in elegant spirits, and perfectly furious at the thought of having been whipped," he wrote to Kate on July 7. Pickett's division had actually carried the enemy's works on July 3, he asserted, yet "for want of proper support was forced to retire." In another letter on July 16, Sandie admitted, "The sky of the Confederacy seems overcast, but 'tis only the clearing up shower.' " The Army of Northern Virginia remained "confident of victory," said Pendleton, "while the people in the country are wakening to a sense of their danger[s]." That the army will "fight on and forever . . . I have no fear," he concluded.[37]

Among the most poignant commentaries following the battle were the words of Major General George E. Pickett, the man whose name would forever be linked to the fatal charge on July 3. "I was ordered to take a height, which I did, under the most withering fire I have ever known," wrote the grieving Pickett to his wife, Sallie, on July 6. "But, alas, no support came, and my poor fellows who had gotten in were over-powered. My heart is very, very sad!" The memory of those moments before the charge haunted him, and the day after the attack he wrote, "Even now I can hear them cheering as I gave the order, 'Forward!' I can feel their faith and trust in me, and their love for our cause. I can feel the thrill of their joyous voices as they called out all along the line, 'We'll follow you, Marse George. We'll follow you— we'll follow you.' Oh, how faithfully they kept their word—following me on-on-to their death, and I, believing in the promised support, led them on-on-on, Oh, God!"[38]

Pickett now considered "the sacrifice of life on that blood-soaked field . . . too awful for the heralding of victory, even for our victorious foe, who, I think, believe as we do, that it [has] decided the fate of our cause."[39]

Mindful of the tragedy at Gettysburg, where victory had seemed so close, a surgeon with the 13th South Carolina Infantry wrote that the real fault lay in the absence of the martyred Stonewall Jackson. "If 'Old Stonewall' had been alive and there . . . the victory [would have been] completely won," he averred.[40]

Though many Confederates made astute observations about some of the reasons for their defeat, most overlooked the essential cause of their loss. What had turned the tide in favor of the Yankees was not so much Confederate mistakes, but the improved ability of their Union opponents.

The Army of the Potomac fought well at Gettysburg, with much valor and determination. Many of its senior generals had kept their composure, and George Meade, John Reynolds, Winfield Hancock, Gouverneur Warren, George S. Greene, and John Gibbon, among others, had capably carried out their important roles. Young, largely unheralded officers like Joshua Chamberlain and Alexander Webb had made significant contributions with their tactical leadership.

Yet the men in the ranks had made the critical difference. A letter from an unidentified Federal infantryman named Micah, written immediately following the repulse of Pickett's Charge, perhaps tells as much:

> Camp Above the Field
> July 3, 1863
>
> Dear Brother:
>
> I tell you today of the most horrible thing I can. Murder on the worst scale I could ever dream. The Rebels, blessed souls of glory, came at us in a massive line of pomp and glory, only to meet their maker with comrades aplenty to go with them. Our cannon ripped through them like a scythe in a field of dry wheat, and they still kept coming at us. I shot my Springfield [rifle musket] until the barrel could not be touched to charge the powder and ball. I grabbed up a musket from a dead comrade shot through the head and found its barrel gouged by a Rebel bullet.
>
> What men are these we slaughter like cattle, and still they come at us? This place called Gettysburg shall surely be remembered in Hell for all of eternity. I have not known such terror ever, and will not likely ever sleep again. Ten thousand must have been ripped apart by shot or shell, or both. I can tell no more of the sad sight. Be ever grateful you were not here, for surely we [will] all be cursed that stood here.
>
> Love,
> Micah[41]

More than merely a defensive Union victory, Gettysburg was a tactical triumph in which the application of firepower accompanied by endurance and grit on the part of the defenders made the crucial difference. If the veteran Confederate soldiers fought with valor and spirit, their opponents defended themselves with equal intensity. The Yankees' determination boded an adverse future for the heretofore-unvanquished Army of Northern Virginia.

None recognized these dire circumstances more readily than Robert E. Lee. Instead of reporting the defeat of the Union army in detail as he had planned, on July 7 Lee acknowledged "the unsuccessful issue" at Gettysburg.

Of graver concern to Lee after the battle was the loss of irreplaceable manpower. Whereas the enemy could "be easily reinforced," Lee's troops were seriously depleted. The Virginia army was unlikely to pose a major offensive threat again.

Lee characteristically reacted to the Gettysburg disaster by accepting full blame, and having become the subject of implied or direct criticism in some newspapers, he later offered to resign. Lee asserted:

The general remedy for the want of success in a military commander is his [the commander's] removal.

For no matter what may be the ability of the officer, if he loses the confidence of his troops disaster must sooner or later ensue. . . . I have seen and heard of expression of discontent in the public journals as the result of the [Gettysburg] expedition. I do not know how far this feeling extends in the army. My brother officers have been too kind to report it, and so far the troops have been too generous to exhibit it. It is fair, however, to suppose that it does exist, and success is so necessary to us that nothing should be risked to secure it.[42]

Moreover, Lee wrote, "Nothing is wanted but that their [the soldiers'] fortitude should equal their bravery to insure the success of our cause. We must expect reverses, even defeats. They are sent to teach us wisdom and prudence; to call forth greater energies, and to prevent our falling into greater disasters. Our people only have to be true and united, to bear manfully the misfortunes incident to war, and all will come out right in the end."[43]

Lee's ability to cope with disaster, both public and personal, was evident when he learned about the capture of his second-eldest son, William H. "Rooney" Lee, during a Federal raid just prior to Gettysburg. Lee told his wife: "We must bear . . . this affliction with fortitude and resignation and not repine at the will of God. It will eventuate in some good that we know not of now."[44]

The idea of Lee's removal was unthinkable to Jefferson Davis, and in January 1864 a joint resolution of thanks "for illustrious services" was tendered to Lee and his men by the Confederate Congress.[45]

Robert E. Lee, though acknowledging that in battle "the result is in the hands of the Sovereign Ruler of the Universe, and known to him only," would continue to do his duty by attempting "to make every arrangement . . . to meet any emergency that may arise." "I hope [we] will yet be able to damage our adversaries when they meet us, and that all will go right with us," he informed his wife shortly after Gettysburg. "That it should be so, we must implore the forgiveness of God for our sins, and the continuance of His blessings. There is nothing but His almighty power that can sustain us."[46]

Lee might well struggle onward, trusting in the Almighty, and exercise command of his army with hope and courage. But what about his men? In the face of both victory and defeat they paid the price of battle. Now that the Battle of Gettysburg had been lost, would the South's obviously diminishing resources and the improved fighting capabilities of the enemy affect the attitudes of Lee's no-longer-invincible soldiers? Would their efforts be the same?

What was clearly apparent, despite many expressed differences in attitudes, was that the Army of Northern Virginia had been shocked by their experience at Gettysburg. The soldiers no longer regarded victory as certain. A newfound respect for their opponents reflected a change in the Confederate soldiers' perspectives. The men saw the war differently. They no longer had the spirit of invincibility to inspire them in combat. Many even had begun to doubt the outcome of the war.

Lee had been correct. Despite their unswerving respect and love for him, his battle-wise veterans now understood the uncertainty of the war and the mounting difficulties they faced. Under these increasingly dire conditions the extent of their devotion was, for the first time, in question.

Coupled with the devastating defeat in Pennsylvania was word of an equally appalling loss along the Mississippi River, at the key river port of Vicksburg. Even Robert E. Lee was dismayed. His requiem for the Gettysburg Campaign was written with an awareness of the "harder blows and harder work" that lay ahead for the Army of Northern Virginia, and of the South's fate: "The army did all it could. I fear I required of it impossibilities."[47]

Chapter Nineteen

"They Haven't Got Us
Nearly Whipped—Yet"

John Dale of Company B, 24th Mississippi Infantry, found life in the army not only difficult, but far different than what he had imagined: "I haven't seen any satisfaction since I left home," he complained in January 1862. "The water that we have to drink here—it ain't fiten to use. I never was raised on good things, but I had somebody to cook for me, and one that cod [could] cook victal [victuals] that I cod eat. If I live till this war ends they won't get me in another soon and I hope and pray that it will end [soon] so all of us can return to our homes."[1]

Like many other Southerners, once he had experienced military service, Dale was anxious to get out but didn't know how. At first, he determined to wait until his term of enlistment expired, but then, in the spring of 1862, the conscription act required all able-bodied men to remain in the ranks. Desertion was against his concept of honor and pride, and Private Dale remained in the army.

Following Shiloh, which he regarded as a tactical victory, Private Dale became somewhat acclimated to a soldier's life and told his girlfriend:

My life . . . is a hard one, but I will live [as] a soldier the balance of my days before the black Republicans shall rule the South. No, never will we the Southern boys be trampled on by the North. They said last year they would drive us back into the Union; but they were badly out of it. They have been at it twelve months and haven't done it yet. No more will they rule the South. That is a foolish notion. The Southern boys haven't learned the word retreat yet. No, we love our homes too well for a Yankee to whip us. We are looking for a fight here every moment.[2]

Three months later, John Dale remained "in tolerably good spirits about the war." He wrote, "I don't think the North will ever subjugate the South; they have taken over towns, and rivers, and railroads, they have invaded our land, but after all that they haven't whipped us yet. I think peace will be made between this [date] and Christmas, I hope so at least."[3]

Dale's optimism was couched in practical terms. He did not know about the politics of war or the generals' reasons for advancing or retreating. He did know that he had full confidence in the ability of his unit to beat the Yankees, at least those like their regiment had encountered, in a fair fight. It was this small-unit fighting that soldiers like Dale seemed to most regard. Given an equal chance against a reasonable number of enemy soldiers, they would win the fight. That was all they could do; they couldn't win victories, only fights within the battle.

The men had to trust their generals to use them in a proper manner to win the overall victory. Even after severe defeats, like that at Fort Donelson in February 1862, the confidence of many soldiers remained high in terms of unit-level fighting. "If the Yankees will take [to fighting] on land like white men, our Confederates can whip them ten to one," a defiant rifleman reasoned.[4]

It was this belief, a confidence in their own prowess, rather than any reliance on the efforts of others, that had sparked their anticipation "that the war [would] end soon." Like many of his fellow Army of Tennessee volunteers, Private John Dale often fluctuated in his own perspectives. "Some times I think it [the war] will end soon, and again I think it will be a long time," wrote Dale in 1862. "But if [only] wishing for it to end [would help], it would come to a close in a short time," he added.[5]

Ending the war had first been thought of in terms of demonstrating to the North that the South "couldn't be subjugated"—that Southerners would fight till death in defense of their homes and families. By this means, it was reasoned that the North would give up the fray as too costly and totally unfeasible. Then, following significant battles such as Shiloh and the Virginia peninsula fighting, in which the commitment of both sides became evident, some hoped that one major, decisive victory would break the will of the Northern soldiers. They would be convinced that Southern military might couldn't be overcome. "We expect to have an engagement with the enemy in a few hours . . . and the long looked for test will be decided between Northern and Southern arms," wrote Mississippian Hugh L. Honnoll from Corinth, Mississippi, in May 1862. "Believing as I do that our cause is just and that our arms will triumph over the Northern host, I have little fear in going into this, our great struggle for Southern liberty."[6]

When this contest didn't occur, Honnoll could only muse, "It is my candid opinion that the great Corinth battle will never come off, . . . [even so], the spirits of our army are fine, . . . and a more determined set of soldiers never was drawn up in line of battle. . . ."[7]

Thereafter, during 1862, new perspectives began to evolve in Southern minds, particularly in the relatively hard-pressed western regions. In marked contrast to their still-hopeful comrades in the East, many soldiers of the Army of Tennessee and its sister western units began to express doubts about "easily" whipping the Yankees and thus bringing "a speedy termination to this war." Despite the spirited "invasion" of Kentucky during the late summer and early fall of 1862, Bragg's brief campaign ended in a demoralizing retreat back to Tennessee, following several hard-fought but barren tactical battlefield victories at Richmond (Kentucky) and Perryville. A Confederate private, captured during the Kentucky Campaign, tried to remain optimistic, yet expressed a telltale tentativeness and uncertainty while in parole camp: "If they [the Yankees] can be routed from Nashville, I think the chance will be good for peace. If not, the war will last Old Abe's time out, I think. But if we can rout them, peace will be the next move, or that is my guess."[8]

To some, the Perryville battle had demonstrated just what seemed to so plague the men. Dan L. Kelly, an enlisted man who had survived only "by God's Mursey," wrote about that fight:

The regiment [24th Mississippi] suffered badly. . . . Every fourth man was killed or wounded, and to me it does look strange that we was not all killed, for the balls seemingly came as thick as hail. But they [the Yankees] was mostly shooting too high to hit us till we got so close to them that they took to their heels and run like hyenas. . . .

Next morning we started to retreat; this I suppose was done because the Yanks were getting all roused up, and owing to we having
no provisions hardly. . . . Starvation stared [us] in the face during
the whole retreat, [for] we did not get but half rations, three days
[during] which we done on one half pound of flour to the man . . .
During our travels through Tennessee and Kentucky we did not
have any tents at all. If it rained . . . [and] we could not get a tree
[for] shelter, we had to take [to] to an open field. This treatment,
I think, caused more deaths than was killed in the battle. . . .[9]

Dan Kelly's commentary on the campaign was a damning indictment, not of the ordeals that had to be endured, but rather of the
incompetence that abounded in the army. Above all else, it accentuated the unsatisfactory results they continually had to cope with.

After such hard-fought but unsuccessful battles as those around
Corinth, Mississippi, in the fall of 1862, bitter truths began to emerge
for many gray soldiers. Following the Battle of Corinth on October 3
and 4, Orderly Sergeant Richard Walpole of Company D, 15th Mississippi Infantry, wrote, "After two days of hard fighting, we were
forced to retreat in consequence of a larger force getting in our rear.
Our loss was considerable . . . much greater than that of the enemy,
though if they had not cut us off, Corinth would have been ours. Our
Western army place[s] but little confidence in their generals, as they
have all [,] except [Sterling] Price [,] proven themselves unworthy
[of] the respect of such men as compose the army."

Even though he estimated that only twenty-five to thirty-thousand
men were present after this battle, Walpole wondered if their generals
weren't planning another offensive. "I don't think [they are]," reasoned the sergeant, "but there is no telling what our *fool officers* intend
doing."[10]

Again, at the year-end Battle of Stones River (Murfreesboro), Confederate valor on the battlefield was wasted on headlong, piecemeal
frontal attacks ordered by the Army of Tennessee's peevish commander, General Braxton Bragg, and his principal subordinates. The
desperation of some of Frank Cheatham's Tennesseeans in attacking
the Union army's Round Forest citadel was vividly described by a
Yankee cannoneer:

On [our] left was the noted cotton field, through which the Rebel
masses, maddened and half-crazy by [drinking] whiskey and gun-

powder, . . . made charge after charge up to within 30 yards of the
muzzles of our guns. [They came] in solid columns, despite shot,
shell, and canister that tore great gaps in their ranks, but [their
lines] were quickly closed up again, amid a perfect storm of musketry. Never did I see men face the music [so]. When close to our
guns they pulled their hats over their eyes so that they could not
see the flash of our pieces, and moved up as steady as if they were
on the parade ground.[11]

The awful butchery that attended such frontal attacks seemed fruitless, even when the Yankees were pushed back, since usually because
of a want of support or other tactical circumstances, the Confederates
were unable to win a total victory. Although soldiers like Frank Carter
might boast after Stones River that the "Yankees were badly
whipped," what they saw and knew was limited.[12]

The point thus had been driven home repeatedly among the men
of the Army of Tennessee during 1862's barren battles. They still had
faith in themselves and great confidence in their ability to fight, for
they repeatedly waged severe combat and displayed great valor on the
battlefield. Yet they were fighting profitless, losing battles. Their generals' mistakes were causing most of the defeats, not a want of effort
from the men. This disparity in leadership versus performance had
its inevitable result. Many of the western soldiers began looking for
an end to the war, not so much by their winning the kind of tactical
mini-victories on the battlefield that they had once reasoned were the
essence of a decisive Southern victory, but more by any political or
outside means. "I do not believe we can decide it [the war] by fighting," wrote the forlorn Private William B. Honnoll in May 1863. "I
think it will be stopped some other way, and God grant it is soon, for
I believe both parties is tired of the war."[13]

During the summer and fall of 1862 diplomatic recognition of the
Confederacy by the nations of Europe, particularly France and Great
Britain, was regarded as important in obtaining Southern independence. Yet without an important Rebel military success to serve as an
impetus toward peace and as proof of the Confederacy's long-term
viability, there was much indecision and controversy abroad about
recognition of the Southern government. It soon became evident that
France and Great Britain would not aid the South without the Confederacy winning peace on its own.[14]

The uncertainty of foreign intervention frustrated some soldiers.

Private William B. Honnoll of the 24th Mississippi wrote in mid-July 1862 about the rumor of France negotiating a cease-fire, to be followed by an end to the war between the North and South: "It may be that they will bring about peace, but I had rather they would let us alone and let us settle it ourselves, for I am afraid France and England will try to subdue both parties, and keep us in war longer than it would [take] to settle it ourselves. If they will let us alone, it cannot last longer than winter, I . . . think."[15]

To an increasing number of Confederate soldiers, the potential for foreign intervention was only another empty promise of Southern success held out by the Richmond administration to encourage soldiers and civilians alike. Instead, a lurking skepticism began to cloud the minds of many. Talk was cheap, and rampant rumors of a pending victory never seemed to be true. "There is a great deal of talk of peace, but I see no more prospect now than I did when the war first broke out," claimed Lieutenant William D. Kendall of the 5th Tennessee Infantry in March 1863. "It is true it [the war] will be some [what] shorter, but I think it is probable that it will last some five or six years longer." Private William B. Honnoll found that "There [are] so many lies told, I can hardly believe the truth when I hear it, or at least I don't know when it is the truth."[16]

One of Honnoll's companion privates in January 1863 saw ahead only "hardships and privations [that they were] doomed to undergo." Another despairing Southern volunteer acknowledged the soldiers hard life without the prospect of relief. "It is a surprising thing to me that the Southern soldier will fight with so much valor when they are so badly treated," complained Private Edwin Fay. "[Any] Negro on [the] Red River has . . . a happier time compared with that of a Confederate soldier."[17]

What many soldiers of the Army of Tennessee had begun to heavily rely upon was inner strength—their resolute, collective will to continue—simply because, outside of desertion, there really was no alternative. "I can tell you it is hard times in the army, sure," wrote Mississippian Private William B. Holloway in May 1863. "I do not like to complain, but times is getting lean fast, yet we must endure [all] the hardships we can in the war, and will have to fight [it] out the best we can." A few months later, Holloway reflected that although they experienced "hard times . . . we have no right to complain, for it is the best the Confederacy can do, and the longer the war is, [thus] we are bound to fare." One of his fellow Mississippians, Dan Kelly, agreed, writing at the same time that he had "no right to grumble" about the sad state of affairs, "for God doesn't like a murmuring heart." Kelly remained focused and expressed his determination in a letter home: "I feel that this unholy war was forced on me, for I was opposed to it at the start[.] . . . Now I am in favor of prosecuting it to the last extremity. For if we do not gain our independence, I cannot see anything else but [my own] slavery staring me in the face, and . . . I would rather die. . . . I am not willing to be driven back [into the Union] until the last man of us have perished."[18]

Even John Dale, the private who had been so anxious to get out of the army in 1861, was now resolute in his devotion to the Southern cause. He wrote to his family, "I would be better satisfied if they would give me a little better rations, [as] our rations are very short. . . . Still, I will have to bear [it]. You said that you didn't want me to come home unless I came in honor. I never will come [back] unless I come that way. There is but one thing that would make me desert, and that is starvation, and it looks like it is staring us in the face now, but I am hoping for better times." As for the Yankees, "I don't think they have got us nearly whipped yet."[19]

Encouraged by the victories of Lee's army in the East, some of the Army of Tennessee's soldiers began to hope for success in the West with the advent of 1863. Yet, looming on the horizon was the growing effort of the Union forces against the Confederacy's crucial major bastion on the Mississippi River, Vicksburg. With the fall of nearby Arkansas Post on January 11, the crisis along the Mississippi River had intensified. Nearly five thousand Confederate soldiers were surrendered at that site. This development depressed the Vicksburg garrison, which was composed of about twenty thousand troops under Lieutenant General John C. Pemberton, a former Pennsylvanian and a West Point–educated regular army officer with ties to Virginia through his wife.

Among the Vicksburg troops was Sergeant William "Pitt" Chambers of Company B, 46th Mississippi Infantry, an 1862 enlistee in the Covington County "Harvey Desperadoes." Like other rural members of his company, Chambers had eagerly sought adventure and glory in combat. Instead, he found mostly sickness. So many of his regiment had been stricken and had died that first summer that his father suddenly arrived at camp intending to bury him, for he believed that his son was dead. Sergeant Chambers, who was found to be sick and deathly weak, had wept on seeing his father. Later, as his illness continued, Chambers became convinced "that these hills [around Vicksburg] will be my burying place."[20]

Yet, at the end of 1862, Pitt Chambers was healthy enough to finally participate in his first engagement. Although he said his "nerves quivered and [his] heart wildly beat," Chambers's initial combat experience resulted in an astounding surprise. "I did nothing and saw nothing worthy of special note," he wrote in dismay. "A fringe of timber prevented our seeing the assault except through one small opening, but a dense pall of smoke hid everything."

Thereafter, his regiment, like many others, was subjected to regular bombardments by the Union gunboats, and following a change in their unit's commander, many men became disillusioned with the tedium and routine and the stresses of imminent danger. Desertions became so prevalent that a detail under a captain was sent home to round up stragglers and deserters.[21]

What most bothered Sergeant Chambers as the days and weeks wore on during the siege of Vicksburg was his inability to alter the worsening situation. In May his brigade had campaigned hard, marching about 150 miles in less than five days, so that Chambers's feet were covered with blood blisters. His regiment numbered only fifty men following this hard journey. Yet their efforts had been fruitless. Their brigadier, William E. Baldwin, "was too drunk to ride," and other officers had become intoxicated, or disappeared when facing the prospect of combat. Following the critical battle at Champion's Hill (Baker's Creek) on May 16, Pemberton's troops were quickly penned up within the defensive works, and Chambers apprehensively watched the victorious enemy's approach to their outer line of entrenchments. "I dreaded the [coming] battle as never before," admitted Chambers. "It seemed . . . that I should be killed in the fight, and the thought of meeting my God unprepared . . . seemed appalling."[22]

Although his regiment escaped heavy losses on May 17, one of their brigade's units, the 4th Mississippi, had been badly mauled, and many men were captured. It was a prelude to disaster. "The spirit of our troops had undergone a great change," wrote Chambers. "Instead of the high hopes that animated us last week, a feeling of demoralization seemed to permeate the rank and file, and none of us were hopeful as to the result of the campaign." In fact, by this time, noted Chambers, many of the men were suspicious of "the motives as well as doubt[ing] the judgment of General Pemberton."[23]

Rations at that point were down to one-third, and the ordeal of defending the ten-mile perimeter of works arching around the surrounded city of Vicksburg—at a central distance of perhaps three miles from the river—had proved excruciating. Hot, suffocating weather, with little relief from the broiling sun, flies, bugs, and vermin, kept everyone miserable. Sharpshooters made life dangerous for anyone who so much as exposed a portion of his body, and the pungent, offensive odor of decaying corpses lying between the lines nauseated all. The siege was "more like a fearful dream, than an actual experience," thought the war-weary Chambers.[24]

While the soldiers were told repeatedly that Joe Johnston was coming to relieve the garrison, and they only had to hold the lines for a little while longer, the passing days told them otherwise. "The men were so often disappointed that they naturally became skeptical and disappointed," observed Sergeant Chambers.[25]

Within the 46th Mississippi, "a willingness to capitulate" was soon prevalent, said Chambers. The men were starving, and due to a shortage of ammunition they had been ordered not to shoot "unless the enemy came within 200 yards." Moreover, when they attempted to build better breastworks at night, the heavy-bore Yankee siege cannon would demolish all their previous night's work "before the day[light] was an hour old."[26]

The men continued talking; they "had no confidence in the assurances of their officers [that help was coming]," and they saw "nothing before them but death or prison"—all of this after weeks of a "gnawing, debilitating hunger." Their scanty meals were barely one a day as the month of June 1863 continued, and the gaunt, emaciated soldiers could only plead to God for relief.

Despondent and ill-tempered, Sergeant Chambers now felt "condemned in the sight of God." "To turn away His wrath," Chambers began reading the New Testament "a great deal." Yet, "its gracious promises" were not for him, reasoned the depressed sergeant, thus "the condemnation still remained."[27]

Their ceaseless ordeal had produced "a fever of the mind," moaned Chambers, and the despair was much "intensified by the pangs of hunger." There was no escape. Mine explosions, severe Yankee shellings, deadly sharpshooter fire, and men stricken ill from starvation and disease had become routine. As the month of June ended, there was talk of the garrison cutting their way out through the Yankees. "In view of the [depleted] condition of the men, such an attempt would have been madness," acknowledged Sergeant Chambers.

Finally, bread rations ceased altogether. When possible, the men were given daily "about one teacup full of boiled peas, and a small bit—perhaps about two ounces of bacon." After the bacon gave out, about three or four ounces of mule meat were substituted.[28]

Mule meat and peas! The flesh of the mules was coarser, but more tender, than that of an ox, noted the disgusted Chambers, and it had a "decidedly 'horsy' flavor." Yet, to "a starving man," it was entirely palatable. Even dog meat was being consumed in a Louisiana regiment, he grimly noted.[29]

Finally, on July 3, there was a dramatic change. The firing died down and then ceased altogether. Speculation among the men was rife; were there ongoing negotiations for a surrender? Yet, said Chambers, that possibility was hooted at by their officers. Such was so much mindless posturing, concluded Chambers. "The subterfuges resorted to [so as] to keep the men in ignorance" were never wise, he believed.[30]

On the clear and serene morning of July 4, 1863, the Vicksburg garrison slowly marched in front of the works and stacked arms under the watchful eyes of the Yankees. It was both humiliating and painful, considered the numbed Chambers. "Some of us wept, . . . for we realized that this was the end of all our sacrifices. For this ignoble ending we had fought, . . . had hungered, [and] had shed our blood." Bitter, distraught, and angry, the men heaped blame on their Pennsylvania-born commander, Pemberton, who, claimed many, "had been false to the flag under which he fought."[31]

As the Federals marched into Vicksburg, the paroled prisoners marched out. A captain wrapped the shot-torn regimental colors of the 46th Mississippi around his body and hid it under his shirt rather than surrender it. Then the men were ordered to march to Raymond, Mississippi, and thereafter, presumably, to parole camp.[32]

"As soon as we had passed the [Yankee] sentinels, . . . our brigade, disregarding the commands and expostulations of [our] officers, set their faces homeward, and filed to the right. The officers appealed to the Federal guard[s], and were laughed at in reply," reported Chambers. Ultimately, the captured Vicksburg Confederates were granted a forty-day furlough by presidential proclamation.[33]

The initial unauthorized scattering of the bedraggled defenders of Vicksburg was perhaps a fitting end to the soldiers' wretched ordeal.

What had once been heralded in the Southern press as a glorious defense of the Confederacy's "Gibraltar of the West" was now acknowledged as a dismal defeat.

With the fall of Vicksburg coming on the heels of the Gettysburg failure, and with the surrender of Port Hudson, Louisiana, on July 9, disaster had abruptly supplanted the high hopes Southerners had held only a few months earlier. The effect was pronounced throughout the Confederate army, especially in Tennessee, where Bragg's soldiers were forced into a depressing retreat from Middle Tennessee after Bragg was badly outmaneuvered during the Tullahoma Campaign.

Sergeant Richard Walpole of the 15th Mississippi, with the Army of Tennessee, wrote of the pending fight at Vicksburg in January 1863, "It is generally believed that Vicksburg is the strongest point along our lines—every effort will be made on our part to hold that place, and the troops, as well as the country at large, feel certain of victory. I hope they will teach the enemy a lesson in Mississippi. . . . The bloodiest fight of the war will be fought in and around Vicksburg, as we will never surrender while one vestige of hope is left us."[34]

After July 4, 1863, Walpole and his fellow soldiers not only had to explain an astounding defeat, but had to try to maintain a positive outlook. "It is true Vicksburg has fallen at last, but for want of provisions, not courage on the part of the men," wrote Lieutenant William D. Kendall on July 12. "That does not [look] favorable for the commanders, having the garrison so poorly supplied with rations, when the Mississippi Valley is more bountifully supplied than any other portion of the Confederacy, and that point more essential to hold than any other. . . . I am as yet very sanguine of our ultimate success, but I fear that the fall of Vicksburg may protract the war some[what] longer. I was in hopes this year would terminate with peace, but now I see no prospect of it."[35]

To Dan Kelly of the 24th Mississippi, the loss of Vicksburg was sobering, and in the wake of Braxton Bragg's midsummer retreat to Chattanooga he wrote, "It seems we are about to lose all." A companion, W. P. Andrews, even admitted, "I have lost all hopes of peace, for they [the Yankees] are coming in on every side of us and take every place they try to take."[36]

With the Vicksburg garrison unavailable on parole, and Joe Johnston's troops far too few to be of major significance, the last, best remaining hope in the West was for Braxton Bragg and the Army of

Tennessee to reverse the tide of defeat. In the spring of 1862 Albert Sidney Johnston had faced a similar crisis and had acted boldly, only to suffer posthumous defeat at Shiloh.

Yet, unlike the spring of 1862, there was little optimism among the army. Bragg was now in command, and the soldiers' confidence in their ill-tempered commander was badly shaken. Lieutenant William D. Kendall of the 5th Tennessee characterized the mood of the army following the losses of that summer. "[I] have lost all confidence in General Bragg—[but] I never had much. It seems all other parts of the army can do some good but ours."[37]

Reflecting the growing dismay of the soldiers, a Tennessee private, James Hamner, wrote, "There is no use in fighting unless we can accomplish something by it. I think we have one of the best armies in the world, but still if they outnumber us too far, we must not fight them, for when the army we have now is gone, I cannot see where the next one is to come from."[38]

In contrast to Hammer's plain, logical reasoning, General Braxton Bragg, schooled at West Point in the dogma of "throwing masses upon decisive points," had written a year earlier, "I shall promptly assail him [the enemy] in the open field with my whole available force, if he does not exceed me more than four to one." With more troops and massive frontal attacks in mind, Bragg scoffed at the idea of fighting defensively. "Heavy entrenchments demoralize our troops," a staff officer once heard him say.[39]

It was just such thinking that caused one of his disconsolate soldiers to observe in 1863, "Bragg is not fit for a general. If Jeff Davis will just let Bragg alone, I think he will do us more damage than the enemy."[40]

This controversy spoke volumes of the fate of both the Army of Tennessee and the Southern Confederacy. Did the men who executed the orders, or their senior generals who gave them, better understand the nature of war?

Chapter Twenty

Sarah Morgan

"A Peace That Passes Understanding"

Sarah Morgan had found life in occupied New Orleans nearly devastating as the war progressed through 1863. At first refusing to believe newspaper reports of the fall of Vicksburg and then Port Hudson, she had watched from her brother's balcony as

a motley crew of thousands of low people of all colors paraded through the streets with flags, torches, music, and all other accompaniments, shouting, screaming, exulting over the fall of Port Hudson and Vicksburg. . . . We saw crowds of soldiers mixed up with the lowest rabble of the town, working men in dirty clothes, newsboys, ragged children, negroes, and even women, walking in the procession, while swarms of negroes and low white women elbowed each other in a dense mass on the pavement. To see such creatures exulting over our misfortune was enough to make one scream with rage. . . . More than half, much more, were negroes. As they passed here they raised a yell of "Down with the Rebels!" that made us gnash our teeth in silence. The devil possessed me. "Oh Miriam help me pray the dear Lord that their flag may burn!" I whispered as the torches danced around it. And we did pray earnestly . . . , but it must have been a wicked prayer, for it was not answered.[1]

On the heels of this catastrophe came the "dreadful" news about Lee's misfortune at Gettysburg. Sarah tried hard to maintain her spirits. "The skies are dark, but there is a bright side somewhere," she hoped. "Victory and defeat come in waves, now on one side, now on the other. Up to Vicksburg our prospects were glorious; now they are the reverse, but the next flood will land us on the shores of freedom," she wistfully recorded in her diary.[2]

Reduced to sending baskets of food and an occasional note to the Port Hudson Confederate prisoners, now confined in the New Orleans Customs House, Sarah Morgan rued the agony of it all. When her mother despaired over the endless stream of bad news, Sarah rebelled in frustration: "Mother has cried, sobbed, fought all the battles over, knocked the war into a cocked hat, painted the dismal picture of a conquered race. . . ." Thus Sarah "gave her a good lecture." "How I blazed away," she wrote. "When my own faith and belief [were] almost exhausted, I seized the papers that induced her to despair, hunted up stray paragraphs of encouragement, followed up conflicting statements, [and] proved the fallacy of all. . . . [I asserted] the decisive struggle had not come, that Bragg would join Lee and that 'God would have mercy upon us and cause his face to shine upon us.' I am satisfied He will. He will not desert us. He will 'arise and scatter our enemies.' "[3]

Sarah's sentiments to the contrary, the year 1863 ended with as much sorrow as had the previous year. In November, Sarah's favorite brother, Gibbes, a captain with the 7th Louisiana Infantry, was taken prisoner at Rappahannock Station, Virginia, and sent to Johnson's Island Prison. "My dear, lion-hearted brother a prisoner! . . . Oh, this is too hard!" wrote Sarah in shock. "Gibbes! Gibbes! If I was only a man to take your place and fight for you! . . . I hardly know how the war will continue without him; . . . he is so brave and daring! But so are all Southerners. It is nothing unusual—and plenty more left— but Oh, Gibbes!"[4]

Reflecting on the pain and disappointment of 1863, Sarah wrote on New Year's Eve 1863, "It [the old year] is all empty . . . Go, and welcome [1864]! Bring peace and brighter days, oh dawning new year. Die, faster and faster, old one. I count your remaining moments with almost savage glee. . . . When each hour brings us nearer the termination of a bloody strife, who can regret your passing away?"[5]

Sarah's circumstances had placed her in an ever-constricting sphere. The South was struggling; hope for independence was becoming increasingly unrealistic. Her own family was suffering. Confined by the enemy's edicts in occupied New Orleans, Sarah Morgan's resilience was now all the more dependent upon encouraging news—anything to keep her spirits up.

Instead, she received only more bad news. On February 5, 1864, a letter arrived that brought the war into perspective for Sarah Morgan and her family. Gibbes had died of disease at Johnson's Island Prison.[6]

"Dead! Suddenly and without a moment's warning; summoned to God! No! it cannot be!" moaned Sarah. "I am mad! Oh, God, have mercy on us! My poor mother! . . . My brain seems [a] fire. Am I mad? Not yet! God would not take him yet! He will come again! Hush! God is good! Not dead! not dead! Oh, Gibbes, come back to us!"[7]

The news had stricken the family like a thunderbolt. Sarah attempted to hush her mother's anguished cries after she heard of Gibbes's death. "We have brother [Philip], and George [her middle brother], and Jimmy [her youngest brother] left, and Lydia [Gibbes's wife] has lost all!" reasoned Sarah half-heartedly. Yet her sorrow deepened when she learned how he had died. Sick in the hospital for more than a week with a severe headache and sore throat, Gibbes had just seen the doctor, and was talking pleasantly with his fellow patients. Then "he sat up to reach [for] his cup of water on the table. As soon as he drank it he seemed to suffocate. After tossing his arms wildly in the air, and making several fearful efforts to breathe, he died." He had "fought with the bravest of the brave through more than thirty battles," noted Sarah, only "to die a prisoner in a strange land," and never again to see his wife.[8]

When it seemed impossible that times could get any worse, word of another tragedy came on February 11. That morning the Morgan girls were sitting, "talking to mother," trying to cheer her up, when a letter arrived. Sarah's sister Miriam returned shortly with a note from Gibbes's widow, Lydia, and opened it, expecting news of her family.

"Mother! Mother! A horrible voice cried," and Sarah recoiled in disbelief. "[Miriam was] perfectly wild. 'George is dead!' she shrieked, and fell heavily to the ground."

"Oh, my God!" gasped Sarah. "Oh, God, Oh God, have mercy on us! George is dead!" screamed Sarah. Her second-oldest brother, Captain George M. Morgan, had died on January 12 of an illness in the camp of his regiment, the 1st Louisiana Infantry.

Sarah's mother went into shock. She stared blankly into space.

Miriam "lay raving" on the floor. "It is false! Do you hear me, mother? God would not take both! George is not dead!" cried Sarah, who tried "in vain to rouse her [mother] from her horrible state, or bring one ray of reason to her eye." Yet Sarah was unsuccessful. "I spoke to a body alive only to pain; not a sound of my voice seemed to reach her. Only fearful moans showed she was yet alive."[9]

The family was too numb to grieve. "Nothing was real, nothing existed except horrible, speechless pain," wrote Sarah disconsolately. "Life was a fearful dream through which but one thought ran—dead—dead."

Sarah watched as Miriam was taken to her room, "more dead than alive." Her mother soon "lay speechless in hers." The "shock of this second blow" seemed to obliterate recollection of the first—for a time—until her mother's piercing "shriek of horror" that evening, when her torment began anew. Sarah was devastated. "Loss of consciousness would have seemed a blessing," she later wrote, in order to avoid all of the "misery and wretchedness."[10]

"Both [brothers] in a week! . . . Oh, my brothers! What have we lived for except you?" grieved Sarah in her diary. "We who would so gladly have lain down our lives for yours, are left desolate to mourn over all we loved and hoped for, weak and helpless. . . . God knows best. But it is so hard—Oh, so hard!"[11]

Still to come were the horrid details of George's death. He had been misdiagnosed by the army surgeon; instead of appendicitis he had been treated for "something else." On his deathbed he had sent a message: tell his mother "his last thoughts were of her, and he died trusting in the mercy of his Saviour." Sarah reasoned that "if mother or Miriam ever heard of it [the misdiagnosis] it would kill them." She insisted that the details of her brother's death remain undisclosed, and that the burden of that "horrible secret" be hers alone. "I wondered if God would help me bear it," she asked in that night's diary entry.[12]

Her family's naïveté about the war was now painfully evident to Sarah. "If we had any warning or preparation, this would not have been so unspeakably awful," she wrote. "But to shut one's eyes to all dangers and risks, and drown every rising fear with, 'God will send them back; I will not doubt his mercy,' and then suddenly to learn that your faith has been presumption—and God wills that you shall undergo bitter affliction—it is a bitter awakening!"[13]

"How will the world seem to us now?" wondered Sarah with newfound awareness of the realities of war. "What will life be without the boys? When this terrible strife is over, and so many thousands return to their homes, what will peace bring us of all we hoped?"[14]

Sarah, her mother, and her sisters ultimately found solace in worship. God had "reconciled [her] to [a] life which had seemed insupportable before," she proclaimed that April. "A feeling of awe, as though God had talked to my soul," gave Sarah a sense of spiritual rebirth. "Let me believe it was the peace of God," she wrote. "It has left me with a 'peace that passes understanding.' "[15]

Indeed, God had granted her and others who had lost loved ones an enormous insight—the perception of war's cruelty, which only those who had personally suffered could truly understand. Tragedy and grief now ravaged most Southern families. Many were learning that war entailed much more than proclamations of freedom and rhetorical posturing.

Chapter Twenty-one

COPING WITH THE ANIMAL

What was signified by "the animal," a popular expression among Civil War soldiers, was really at the heart of going to war. It was a euphemism for combat—a test of manhood that became the ultimate army experience. The expressions "meeting the animal," and "seeing the elephant," derived from a relatively new phenomenon in North America, the traveling circus, which featured wild African animals. Here one could witness in person the strange, awesome creatures once only known through books and sketches. Since the huge circus elephants epitomized the powerful mystique of the animal kingdom, these beasts were fascinating up close. Yet many elephants seemed mean-spirited and dangerous to the local schoolboys hired to water them. It was scary to approach these towering creatures with their stomping hooves, beady eyes, and menacing trunks. Yet the boys were intrigued by the spirit of adventure these creatures inspired. The usual advice from experienced water boys to those about to "see the elephant" for the first time was "be careful, for you won't like it a damn bit." Combat aroused many of these same conflicting feelings; hence the expressions "seeing the elephant" and "meeting the animal" refered to first-time exposure to battle.[1]

"The animal"—that is, combat—was perplexing to the inexperienced Confederate soldier. Fear of the unknown, or irrepressible worries about safety and performance under the threat of death, induced severe psychological stress among the ranks. For this reason, military leaders traditionally relied on tightly formed battle lines, in which soldiers marched shoulder to shoulder, with elbows touching, to provide feelings of reassurance and support.

Then, too, a significant incentive for performing well under fire came from an awareness of comrades' scrutiny. Beyond a desire to not let their friends and unit down, was a feeling that dishonor was a worse fate than death. Because the basic fighting unit, a single company, was generally composed of local boys recruited from the same region, familiarity with one another extended beyond formal army associations. Fighting was a community endeavor, in which men closely observed each other's behavior. To do well in combat was to earn a comrade's, and thus your neighbor's and the home community's, respect. Conversely, cowardice was stigmatized by an all-pervasive dishonor that was difficult to escape.[2]

Battle thus tested a man's physical and moral courage. The fear that combat would expose any personal weakness caused many Southern soldiers considerable anguish. Those who could overcome that fear had a big advantage in coping with the ordeal of battle.

As suggested by letters and diaries, the majority of Confederate soldiers, both east and west, found that they could bear the stress of combat and still maintain their composure. Yet, contrary to the accepted tenets of that time, the strength of their endurance depended less on the technicalities of battle formations than on faith in Divine Providence. "I never was more calm in my life [than in going into combat], for if it was decreed that I should fall in battle, no power on earth could make it otherwise," wrote Hugh L. Honnoll after Shiloh. "But I hope and trust that I may be permitted to live through this war . . . ," he continued.[3]

Honnoll's expression of faith was common in many soldiers when facing the battlefield's dangers. Trusting God seemed only appropriate, since there was no just or logical explanation for the survival of some men and the deaths of others. Battle was a roll of the dice. Although the majority of men usually passed through combat unharmed, the random dangers of war still frightened many.

Further distorting the novice's conception of warfare was the impersonal nature of combat, which became apparent once he was on the battlefield. Typically, injuries were inflicted from longer range, in an area shrouded in or obscured by trees, where a blow from an unseen bullet or shell came without any warning. Visions many recruits had of grappling hand to hand with an opponent were not realistic.

Of course, some battle experiences were atypical. Particularly horrid combat encounters left scars that even religious solace couldn't totally efface. Soldiers were not so afraid of dying as they were of completely losing personal control in the chaos of the battlefield. To many, the uncertainties of fighting seemed worse than death. For example, being trapped under the enemy's guns with minimal cover and no practical way to escape was terrifying. Under such circumstances some men learned the ultimate horror of combat.[4]

Lieutenant Charles Labruzan of the 42d Alabama Infantry participated in the frontal assaults at Battery Robinett during the Battle of Corinth in October 1862. His graphic account reveals the terror of that experience:

Saturday, October 4th 1862 . . . At fifteen minutes past ten Colonel Rogers came by us only saying, "Alabama forces!" Our regiment with the brigade rose, unmindful of shell or shot, and moved forward . . .

We were now met by a perfect storm of grape, canister, cannon, and minie balls. Oh! God!, I never saw the like! The men fell like grass. . . . I saw men running at full speed stop suddenly and fall on their faces with their brains scattered all around; others with legs or arms cut off. I gave myself to God and got ahead of my company.

The ground was literally strewed with mangled corpses. One ball passed through my pants and cut twigs close by me. It seemed that by holding out my hand I could have caught a dozen bullets. We pushed forward, marching as it were into the mouths of the cannon. I rushed to the ditch of the fort. . . . A man within two feet of me put his head cautiously up to shoot into the fort, but suddenly dropped his musket, and his brains were dashed in a stream over my fine coat. . . . Oh! we were butchered like dogs, for we were not supported.

The men were falling ten at a time. The ditch being full, and finding that we had no chance, we, the survivors, tried to save ourselves as best we could. . . . I and Captain [George] Foster started [running] together, and the air was literally filled with hissing balls. I got about twenty steps as quick as I could, about a dozen being killed in that distance.

I fell down and crawled behind a large stump. Just then I saw poor Foster throw up his hands, and saying, "Oh! My God!" he jumped about two feet off the ground and fell on his face. The top of his head seemed to cave in and the blood spurted straight up several feet. I could see men falling as they attempted to run; some with their heads blown to pieces and others with the blood streaming from their backs. Oh! it was horrible.

. . . I was hardly thirty feet from the mouths of the cannon. Minie balls filled the stump I was behind, and the shells burst within three or four feet from me; one was so near it struck me and burnt my face with powder. The grapeshot knocked large pieces from my stump; it was gradually wearing away.

I endured the horrors of death here for one half hour. . . . I feigned death [since] I was between our own and the enemy's fire. . . . I had no chance whatever. All around me were surrendering. I could do no better than follow suit, but thank God I am unhurt; nothing but a merciful Providence saved me. . . . For the first time in many years, I cried to see our brave men slaughtered so. I have never felt so bad in all my life.[5]

Although the shock of such a butchering was enormous, personal ordeal and sacrifice were acceptable if the results justified the soldiers' efforts. It was victory that the men sought. Indeed, the concept of victory on the battlefield, and hence the key to political victory by military means, lay in the defeat of the enemy.

Yet, as the war continued, the men began to question the definition of defeat. Was it the withdrawal of an opponent from the battlefield? Was the occupation of an enemy fortification or the capture of a defensive position sufficient to insure this result? Or was the complete destruction of the opposing army necessary? Moreover, was the intimidation of each enemy soldier a relevant component of defeat?

An understanding of the fundamental factors of defeat—as an objective in terms of applying maximum pressure on the enemy—was essential to winning the victory and the war. For many Confederate soldiers, it had seemed that one more major victory might break the enemy's spirit and end the war. Yet, the men finally began to ask, was such an end possible when battle after battle occurred, and no matter which side "won," there was always another battle to fight?

Each soldier had to cope with this problem on his own. How he thought, how he fought, and what his attitudes were impacted the tenor of the war. So long as success marked the soldiers' efforts, and conditions remained endurable, there was hope for the future, and a reason for further effort. Yet, when repeated defeat and frustration encroached upon morale, despair often undermined the will to continue.

Diminishing the enemy's and sustaining the Confederate soldier's will to fight thus was an important objective of the Southern army, regardless of whether it was accomplished by offensive or defensive means. Winning possession of a battlefield meant little unless it was accomplished in concert with destroying a portion of the enemy army, or dealing a major blow to the enemy's will.

Many conventionally schooled Civil War commanders simply weighed the risks of physical loss against the potential rewards when they made their operational decisions. It would have been more relevant to consider the psychology of fighting. What would be the attendant effect of any given action upon one's own men—and the enemy's? This line of thinking was crucial, since the factors that generally determined a battle's outcome rested upon the leadership as much as the performance of the soldiers.

Both accomplishing the soldiers' survival and encouraging positive attitudes were key elements in maintaining morale and obtaining the army's optimum performance. So long as the men were given a fair chance to win success on the battlefield, the risk of personal loss was acceptable. Common sense was what the soldiers understood. They cared little for Jomnian Theory or Mahan's tactics, as taught at West Point, but they knew combat. If nothing else, the men knew from personal experience what was possible and impossible tactically, and this knowledge was the key to combat operations.

Standing up and fighting toe to toe with an enemy line scarcely a stone's throw away might be manly in the best tradition of Napoleonic tactics, but as the soldiers quickly learned, it was essentially stupid under Civil War battlefield conditions.

Equally unwise was the resort to direct frontal attacks with linear formed battle lines of massed infantry against well-defended enemy positions. The widespread use of rifle muskets, and later, rapid-firing breech-loading and repeating rifles, obsoleted these tactics.

Instead of facing the weapon commonly used for the past few centuries (the relatively inaccurate and low-powered smoothbore musket), the Civil War soldier usually encountered the far more deadly rifle musket, which fired bullets with improved accuracy and velocity. The old smoothbore musket had several major defects. It allowed gasses to escape past the bullet-to-bore seal, thereby reducing velocity. More important, the musket's accuracy was impaired because the usual spherical ball microscopically "bounced" down the smoothbore upon firing. This effect created a large dispersion of the projectile from the target line at normal battlefield ranges. Beyond fifty yards, it was difficult to hit a man with a smoothbore musket under combat conditions.

In marked contrast, the hollow-base, conical-shaped minie ball, developed in Europe during the 1850s and used commonly with the standard rifle musket by the time of the Civil War, expanded into the rifling grooves. This both spun the projectile for accuracy, and trapped the gasses behind it for greater velocity. The result was an ability to hit consistently a man-sized target at two-hundred-yards' range. Also, due to this increased velocity, there was sufficient power from the standard .58-diameter one-ounce minie ball to shatter bones at extended ranges of five hundred yards or more.[6]

The tactical consequences of this modernized weaponry were enormous. Yankee major Robert P. Findley of the 74th Ohio Infantry perhaps spoke for most "enlightened" Civil War soldiers when he recorded his thoughts on June 2, 1864, during the devastating Atlanta Campaign:

At the outset of the war, a man who would get behind a log or stone was jeered at by his fellows, and the officer who would have stood behind a tree on the skirmish line, [or] cut off his [shoulder] straps to avoid being a target for sharpshooters and not have exposed his person by standing upright and in exposed positions, would have been stigmatized as a coward.

But now, the officer or soldier who won't take these precautions, if killed or wounded, the expressions of [the] soldiers are, "I don't pity him, he had no business exposing himself unnecessarily." Some yet have the idea that it will gain them a reputation for bravery, and expose themselves accordingly. [Yet] it is the duty of an officer to take every precaution to preserve his own life and that of his men, consistent with the performance of duty, and if an officer will expose himself unnecessarily, he cannot consistently require care on the part of his men.[7]

Beyond such acquired practical wisdom was an important factor in combat, later largely overlooked due to the emphasis on what happened rather than why and how it happened—which are the true essence of analyzing battle. In mid-1863 the next significant advancement in small-arms technology occurred with the increased implementation of breech-loading, metallic-cartridge-firing, repeating rifles. They were weapons that would eventually revolutionize warfare. As a wizened Confederate veteran observed after the war, "The difference between a Springfield rifle musket and a Spencer rifle is much more than a matter of sentiment."[8]

The Spencer rifle and carbine, and the Henry rifle, which was the antecedent arm of the famous Winchester lever action rifles, provided a revealing glimpse of twentieth-century warfare fifty years prior to World War I.

Both the Henry and the Spencer utilized the metallic cartridge, a relatively new innovation developed in the decade before the Civil War. The use of a self-contained ammunition unit, consisting of a brass or copper cartridge case; fulminate primer inside the base, which ignited upon being struck with a firing pin blow; plus the powder and ball, provided an effective and reliable cartridge. This new ammunition was impervious to moisture and maintained its durability both in storage and infield handling.

In contrast to the standard Civil War rifle musket's paper cartridge, which was composed of a coated paper envelope attached to the minie bullet into which the powder had been placed, the metallic cartridge provided an obvious advantage. The old musket cartridge was designed to be torn open, with the powder poured down the barrel at the muzzle, then the ball rammed down on top of it—an awkward and time-consuming process. Yet the metallic cartridge had only to be loaded into a magazine containing multiple rounds; then a mechanical action worked to chamber new rounds and extract the old casings after firing.

As the rifle musket had to be capped with a detonating "percussion cap" to ignite the main charge, during combat these loose, separate ammunition components were a constant source of delay and difficulty. Due to the standard length of the rifle musket, which typically had a thirty-two-inch barrel, it was very awkward to load unless the soldier stood upright.[9]

The ability to rapidly load, shoot, and reload with a breech-loading repeating rifle while prone not only reduced the target area exposed to an enemy, but provided an enormous tactical firepower advantage.

About ninety thousand Spencer and nine thousand Henry rifles were available for use by Union troops during the Civil War, generally during the last two years of the conflict. They were enough to make a tremendous impact, and provided a soldier with confidence and an efficacy unmatched by even the best conventionally armed troops.[10]

Typical of the Confederate exposure to these fearsome arms was the startling scene at Gettysburg during the cavalry action on East Cavalry Field, July 3, 1863. A Southern officer from Colonel John R. Chambliss's brigade shouted to his dismounted cavalrymen to sprint for the Yankee line following the first enemy volley from a nearby fence row. "Now, for 'em, boys—before they can reload!" yelled the officer. In an instant, the Rebel yell was drowned out in a second roar of rifles from the fence line. Again and again—always within a few seconds—sharp volleys rang out from the fence row. Within moments, the eerie Rebel yell had given way to the shrieks of the wounded.

When the rapid-fire shooting finally stopped, beneath the acrid-smelling gunsmoke the only gray-clad bodies visible in front of the fence were dead, wounded, or lying stunned upon the ground. Chambliss's survivors were running away "faster than they came."[11]

They had been among the first to experience the new technology. In the hands of their opponents, the 5th Michigan Cavalry under newly commissioned brigadier general George Custer, were new Spencer repeating rifles, the first to be manufactured. Even Custer acknowledged of the Gettysburg fight, "I attributed their [the 5th Michigan Cavalry's] success in a great measure to the fact that this regiment is armed with the Spencer repeating rifle, which in the hands of brave, determined men . . . is, in my estimation, the most effective firearm that our cavalry can adopt."[12]

The amazed Confederate prisoners concurred. In the aftermath of facing those Spencers, one prisoner asked to see the Yankees' mirac-ulous guns, then remarked, "You'ns load in the morning and fire all day." Another captured Rebel told a 5th Michigan private "[I] don't understand how anyone can charge [reload his rifle] so rapidly." "He didn't know we had repeating rifles," said the private. "They are so afraid of the rifles of the 5th Michigan [Cavalry] that they were struck dumb with surprise."[13]

Custer's use of the Spencer rifle at Gettysburg was among the most significant weapons events of the war. Along with the Spencer rifle's debut in Colonel John T. Wilder's "Lightning Brigade" only a few days earlier (June 24) at Hoover's Gap in Tennessee, its appearance at Gettysburg heralded a change that would virtually reshape modern warfare.

As the war continued, Spencer and Henry repeating rifles became synonymous with combat prowess among the Federal units lucky enough to receive them. In May 1864, George A. Custer reported, "Being in command of a brigade of cavalry which is armed throughout with the Spencer carbine and rifle, I take pleasure in testifying to their superiority over all other weapons. I am firmly of the opinion that 1,500 men armed with the Spencer carbine are more than a match for 2,500 armed with any other firearms. I know this to be true from actual experiment."[14]

Further demonstration of the new technology's impact occurred in the western theater, where these new repeating rifles were used in sizeable numbers. George H. Thomas and his subordinate, cavalry commander James H. Wilson, were anxious to arm Wilson's troopers with Spencer carbines during Hood's invasion of Tennessee in 1864. Waiting for Wilson to be resupplied with Spencers kept Thomas inactive at Nashville as Hood approached. The wisdom of this decision soon became apparent when Wilson's dismounted cavalrymen, attacking multiple redoubts defended with artillery, were able to overwhelm the Confederate garrisons with their rapid-firing Spencers.[15]

The other significant Civil War repeating rifle, the Henry, had been available as early as July 1862. A magazine-fed repeater known as the "sixteen-shooter" because of its sixteen-round capacity, the Henry rifle was an expensive arm produced only in limited numbers. Until men in units such as the 66th Illinois—Birge's Western Sharpshooters—and the 7th Illinois Infantry purchased significant quantities with their own money in late 1863 and 1864, the Henry was little noticed. Only when the government armed the 1st D.C. Cavalry with Henry rifles in the spring of 1864 did use of this arm become anything other than token in the eastern theater.[16]

By 1864, however, the prospect of facing better-armed, veteran Yankee soldiers confronted the Confederates. The Yankee soldier armed with a repeating rifle had an advantage in reduced exposure and increased firepower that changed the tactical battlefield. Confederate infantrymen who were compelled to attack rather than defend during the later stages of the war learned this lesson quickly. Since the Confederacy had no means of manufacturing metallic cartridges, capturing these new weapons was largely unproductive. The North had a one-sided advantage, which further diminished the Southern armies' morale.

These formidable new weapons ushered in a more sophisticated modern era of warfare. Many changes in fighting technique had occurred since 1861. By 1864, there were fewer of the stand-up, toe-to-toe slug fests that had so often proved only that both sides could bleed. Also, continual day-to-day probing confrontations replaced scattered one-or-two-day battles.

It was an altogether different war in 1864. The means of fighting had progressed so far beyond the ages-old concept of man-to-man personal combat that no experienced Civil War soldier in 1864 or 1865 would even think of fighting the war in the same manner as he did in 1861.

Those commanders who continued to rely on the old-style, conventional manner of tactical combat became the enemies of their own soldiers, and were generally recognized as such. New, more-effective weaponry and the use of sophisticated defensive methods necessitated new thinking. It was no longer practical to believe that soldiers' valor alone would obtain victory.

Just how devastating weapons such as the Spencer repeater had become to Confederate morale was demonstrated by Rebel prisoners captured by the 4th Michigan Cavalry during the Atlanta Campaign: "Them [Yankees] were the God damnedest fellas they ever see'd," proclaimed one prisoner. As the Michigan cavalrymen dismounted and waded across a river ford, they fired their carbines, then dove beneath the water to reload before again firing. The Michigan cavalrymen had a hearty laugh—their Spencers worked well even if loaded while submersed.[17]

In tragic contrast were the comments of John Bell Hood. On the eve of his 1865 departure from the Army of Tennessee, the beaten, bitter Confederate commander addressed a handful of troops who had gathered outside his headquarters. He told them that he hoped the army might be supplied with more bayonets—because "it was the bayonet which gave a soldier confidence in himself, and enabled him to strike terror [in]to the enemy."[18]

It was no accident that the demise of the western Confederacy occurred prior to the final surrender in the East. Their opponents were courageous and competent soldiers and had by far better weap-

ons than the Army of Tennessee, which, thanks to the outdated concepts of its senior commanders, Braxton Bragg and John Bell Hood,
met with disaster despite the great valor of its soldiers.

Tactical ignorance provided little justification for defeat. The Confederacy's military chain was only as strong as its weakest link—unen-
lightened and unknowing leadership in the face of altered tactical
and technological circumstances.

Instead of submitting to the much-vaunted superiority of the
Southern military mind, it was evident that the Yankees had brazenly
stolen an advantage where none had been anticipated.

Chapter Twenty-two

AN ARMY OF LIONS LED BY AN ASS

They were coming! Longstreet's proud veterans from the Army of Northern Virginia, who knew victory in the spirit of Robert E. Lee's and Stonewall Jackson's legendary leadership, were en route via railroad to Tennessee. As reinforcements for Bragg's hard-pressed Army of Tennessee, James Longstreet's two divisions knew they would soon be compared, in appearance and attitude, to Bragg's beleaguered forces.

When Longstreet's troops arrived near Chattanooga in mid-September 1863, the contrast in clothing and equipment between the Virginia and Tennessee soldiers was striking. A British observer who had visited both armies found that the Virginia soldiers wore gray uniforms and carried good haversacks, canteens, knapsacks, and accoutrements. Conversely, the westerners were motley and ragged in appearance, "without any attempt at uniformity in color or cut [of clothing]." Nearly all "were in gray or brown coats and felt hats . . ." he noted, "as the soldiers preferred wearing the coarse homespun jackets and trousers made by their mothers and sisters at home."[1]

Equipment was haphazardly dispersed among the Tennessee army, especially bayonets. This British visitor observed that only about half of the troops were supplied with them. Many had thrown them away, he learned, since "they assert[ed] that they never met any Yankees who would wait for that weapon."[2]

More ominously, many in the Tennessee army seemed jealous of the troops sent as reinforcements. Well aware of their reputation for unsuccessful battles in contrast to the brilliant victories of the Virginia army, Bragg's men claimed they had to fight a tougher opponent. The western ex-farmhand Yankees, they said, not only were the enemy's best troops, but also seemed to have the North's best generals.[3]

Longstreet's soldiers obviously had a much different perspective. They came west expecting to find the Army of Tennessee's infantrymen demoralized and beaten, and claimed that "they were going to show them the lick it [whipping the Yankees] is done with. Skepticism about Bragg's army was prevalent among Longstreet's veterans. Their doubts seemed painfully apparent to the soldiers of the Army of Tennessee.[4]

The arrival of Longstreet's men thus presented to the Westerners both a blessing and a threat. If only we had General Lee to lead us, one forlorn Tennessee soldier had reasoned in late summer 1863, the war might be won. "[Lee] is the man to do it. I wish we had such a commander. That is the only source I can now look to for success." Instead of Robert E. Lee, however, Lee's "Old Warhorse," Longstreet, had traveled west with six brigades in anticipation of contributing to an important victory in the Confederacy's heartland. One prideful Alabama lieutenant in the Tennessee army "could not bear the idea for him [Longstreet] to come from Virginia and earn all the glory of whipping Rosy [Federal Major General William S. Rosecrans, commander of the opposing Army of the Cumberland]."[5]

What subsequently occurred hardly dimmed the images of Lee's successful, well-led veterans and Bragg's hard-luck, poorly commanded Army of Tennessee.

At the bloody Battle of Chickamauga, Bragg's attempt to smash Rosecrans's army partially succeeded, thanks to a vital but lucky break in an attack by Longstreet. In the aftermath of some irresolute decisions made by the Federal commander, Chickamauga became the greatest Confederate victory of the war in the West. After pounding Rosecrans's army on September 19 in a series of bloody and costly frontal attacks, Bragg determined to continue his offensive on September 20. Although his repeated sledgehammer attacks against Major General George H. Thomas's troops on the north flank were beaten back during the morning of that day, the pressure was so great that Thomas called for additional reinforcements.

Rosecrans, however, in shifting some of his front-line troops to the north, inadvertently created a mile-wide gap in the center of his line.

By mistake, Brigadier General Thomas Wood's division was ordered to close up on a division presumed to be adjacent to his flank, when in fact it was one division farther removed. In one of the more bizarre accidents of the war, at the precise time Wood directed his three brigades to abandon their breastworks and withdraw, James Longstreet ordered his eleven thousand veterans forward to strike that very portion of the Yankee line. Only minutes after Wood's men withdrew, Longstreet's men poured through the huge gap vacated by Wood. Only a single understrength Union brigade opposed their initial movements. The result was the virtual rout of the entire right wing of Rosecrans's army.

The helter-skelter retreat back to Chattanooga by most of Rosecrans's army created an enormous opportunity for the Confederates. Longstreet wanted fresh troops to complete the envelopment of the remaining Yankees under George Thomas in the northern sector. Also, he urged Bragg to pursue the routed enemy rapidly. Yet Braxton Bragg was unconvinced of the stunning victory that had just occurred. Preoccupied with the prior repulse of his right wing, he refused Longstreet permission to use idle troops to follow up his major breakthrough. Instead, Longstreet's subordinates were ordered to hurl their troops at Thomas's entrenched line on Horseshoe Ridge, even as Bragg prodded his stalled right wing under Leonidas Polk to advance against that position again.[6]

The fearful frontal attacks on Thomas's condensed lines resulted only in horrendous casualties and failed assaults. Among the Yankee troops who opposed Longstreet's men were those of John T. Wilder's Lightning Brigade, many of whom were armed with the deadly Spencer repeating rifle. One Confederate prisoner asked of his captor, a corporal of the 72d Indiana Mounted Infantry, "What kind of guns have you got over here? We thought you'd have to reload, but you jus' kept on shootin' and shootin'." After learning he had been captured by "a damn little brigade of cavalry," an officer in Longstreet's army remarked of the Spencer's awesome firepower, "We just thought we had struck about seventeen lines of battle all at once."[7]

Despite the carnage in the Confederate ranks, Thomas withdrew after nightfall from his fortified positions to join Rosecrans's troops in Chattanooga. He was accorded fame as "The Rock of Chickamauga" and the Army of the Cumberland's savior.

Although an enormous bloodbath, Chickamauga represented not only a much-needed victory for the Army of Tennessee, but one of the Confederacy's proudest moments. Newspapers heralded the success, which had occurred in the aftermath of the disasters at Gettysburg and Vicksburg. Many expressed a renewal of the Southern hope that the war would end soon. Moreover, the initiative had once again shifted in the West, in favor of the Confederacy's forces, and even greater success was anticipated. [8]

Among the victorious Confederate soldiers, there was an immediate reaction to their fight in the woodlands along Chickamauga Creek. Although Longstreet joked with one of his officers, "If we had our Virginia army here, we could have whipped them in half the time," many privates and regimental officers of the Tennessee army expressed their unmitigated joy. They had at last beaten the Yankees. "Having been accustomed to defeat and retreat, no one can conceive what a change a victory so brilliant would make . . . unless he could see the joyous countenances of those veterans," wrote a jubilant lieutenant in the Army of Tennessee. "General Bragg's men say that Western Yankees are harder to whip than Eastern Yankees, but this is a mistake," proclaimed a Georgian from the Army of Northern Virginia. "All fight alike. When we give them the bayonet they give way—they can't stand cold steel."[9]

"Our Virginia troops fight like tigers up here in the West," announced another of Longstreet's Georgians, who reappraised Bragg's men after the Chickamauga fight. "I think the Western boys is all right," he commented. "They are not as bad[ly] whipped as we heard they was. They all seem to be in good spirits."[10]

The winning spirit became contagious. A Floridian with the Army of Tennessee wrote after Chickamauga, "Our army never has been in better fighting trim, nor more anxious for a fight."[11]

Yet this brief euphoria was only one of many significant consequences of the Chickamauga fight. Those officers who knew the battle's full circumstances had great contempt for the Army of Tennessee's commander, Bragg, and many of his principal subordinates. On the morning after the battle, September 21, Bragg seemed unaware that the Federals had abandoned the field, and refused to order a pursuit. Nathan Bedford Forrest, who rode with the cavalry along the LaFayette Road toward Chattanooga that morning, encountered the vast floodtide of a Yankee rout. Federal stragglers were gathered in by the dozens, and abandoned ambulances, wagons, and small arms were strewn everywhere. From a spur of Missionary Ridge south of Rossville, Forrest peered through field glasses at Chattanooga. The enemy appeared to be both fortifying and preparing to evacuate the city. Forrest promptly dispatched several messages to Bragg's headquarters urging an immediate advance. Since the enemy was fortifying the city, "every hour [is] worth a thousand men," asserted Forrest.[12]

As the morning dragged on without a reply, Forrest angrily galloped back to army headquarters to confront Bragg. He found the army's commander reluctant to pursue the Yankee army, and also unconvinced of the need for urgency. Engaged in administrative details and making arrangements for scouring the battlefield for small arms and equipment, Bragg scoffed at Forrest's plea to advance. The army was too disorganized, and a lack of supplies prevented an immediate pursuit, he argued. "General Bragg, we can get all the supplies our army needs in Chattanooga," chided Forrest. When Bragg glared at him, Forrest left in disgust. "What does he fight battles for?" growled the cavalry general.[13]

Longstreet's men were even more outspoken in their derision of Bragg. "The suicidal policy which Bragg has adopted has rendered futile the victory which Longsteet won for him at Chickamauga," wrote the embittered Captain William Blackford of Longstreet's staff. "If Lee had been in his place with such an army we would now be chasing the shattered Yankee fragments out of Tennessee. This [Army of Tennessee] is a fine body of men, and with the confidence they would have in Lee they would be irresistible. Bragg is so much afraid of doing something which would look like taking advantage of the enemy that he does nothing. . . . Our great victory has turned to ashes."[14]

In another letter, Blackford again revealed the essence of the psychological difference between the two armies: "[If] Lee was at the helm [it] would be worth untold reinforcements. The belief that most men have in his infallibility of judgment makes them invincible."[15]

What has puzzled many in the wake of such comments are the views some Tennessee army soldiers expressed in letters home, supporting inept commanders like Braxton Bragg. Yet these soldiers' endorsement of their inept commander may have resulted from uncertainty, and their inclination to cling to existing leadership rather than cope with an unknown. Within the ranks, the men knew only the physical side of the war. Advances or retreats, difficulty of duty, and the availability of food, clothing, shelter, and equipment

were the soldiers' basic concerns. They provided evidence of one's
well-being or despair. Since many enlisted men focused on the practical aspects of military life, some tended to overlook or even remain
ignorant of the culpability of senior officers.

Bragg's soldiers were aware of complaints about their commander's incompetence. Yet they were in no position to know much
about the nuances of higher-command decisions regarding battle.
They knew only what they saw and did. While they expressed strong
opinions about how the war should be fought and won, they had only
a distorted picture of command-level performance.

In practical terms, winning a fight within a battle was evidence that
matters weren't so desperate. Even in defeat there was a reluctance
to condemn one's leader to the point of deserting. So long as matters
were bearable, and there was reasonable hope for future success,
many viewed their existence with tolerance or even tacit acceptance.

While the consensus might be that a particular general was flawed,
opinions varied enough that a substantial number of men periodically
expressed support for a general such as Braxton Bragg. Perhaps because of their limited education and common social status, some were
inclined to be passively reactive, relying on hope rather than actively
criticizing their superiors.

To those more observant and less trusting of authority, the small
tactical successes within a battle did not obscure the lack of general
success or of military expertise. Men who payed closer attention to
the larger picture most often condemned generals such as Bragg, and
they were aware that reckless offensive warfare was rapidly diminishing the limited manpower of the South.

Chickamauga cost the Confederacy nearly twenty thousand casualties in an army of about sixty-eight thousand men. As Sergeant
Washington M. Ives of the 4th Florida Infantry noted:

The boys don't talk much about peace now, for . . . they've seen
comrades dwindle away until it almost looks like not one able bod-
ied man will be spared to tell the tale if this war continues one year
longer, and there is no hope of it ending before that time. [Our]
heroic band that has stood the brunt so often is dwindling away
fast, while the enemy can replenish by the millions. . . . If something
miraculous is not done this winter, and next spring, there is no telling what will go [on] with our army, and with our country.[16]

The way the war was waged continued to evolve in such a way that the extent of the soldiers' survival and ability to maintain their morale took on greater and greater significance. The question thus facing many of the Army of Tennessee's most dedicated soldiers remained: would they continue to endure, relying mostly on blind faith, and believing only in themselves?

On September 23 the Confederate army finally advanced to the summit of Missionary Ridge overlooking Chattanooga—only to find Rosecrans's army fully entrenched about the city. Although Braxton Bragg had anticipated the Yankees' retreat across the Tennessee River, it was now apparent that they were defiantly rebuilding the old Confederate line of fortifications. Attacking this formidable line of rifle pits and earthworks would result in an enormous loss of life. Some soldiers who speculated about the prospect of charging their old works swore that they simply would refuse to do so. As even the lowest private among Bragg's army now understood, their costly victory at Chickamauga was of little significance unless the Yankees were compelled to evacuate Chattanooga.[17]

Bragg's strategic response was to besiege and starve the nearly surrounded enemy at Chattanooga while conducting cavalry raids against the enemy's tenuous supply line. Meanwhile, Bragg maintained his army's position on the high mountain ridges overlooking the city. Even though he knew that heavy enemy reinforcements were en route to Chattanooga from the Army of the Potomac, and that William Tecumseh Sherman was marching there with Grant's victorious Vicksburg army, Bragg seemed unconcerned. He held his position on the high ground, occasionally shelled Chattanooga, and kept a loosely organized river blockade.

The psychological consequences of Bragg's inactivity were soon apparent. There had been enthusiasm and optimism among the ranks in the days following Chickamauga, but as the weeks idly dragged by, restlessness permeated Bragg's army. The attempt to shell Chattanooga from Lookout Mountain had amounted to "just nothing," considered an exasperated Confederate artillery officer. After firing forty-four rounds at a range of four thousand yards with several rifled guns, Lieutenant Jackson Neal wrote, "[The Yankees are] too well posted to be shelled out [of Chattanooga], and this business is all foolishness."[18]

Unfortunately for the Confederacy, immediately after Chickamauga, Braxton Bragg was more intent on purging his army of dissident generals than on removing the Yankees from Chattanooga. The bickering among senior generals included Longstreet, who had come west expecting to succeed Bragg as army commander. So intense was the animosity toward Bragg that a formal petition was circulated among the ranking generals for his removal. Bragg answered by launching charges against several senior generals and conspiring against his severest critics, particularly James Longstreet. The infighting among the generals became so intense that Jefferson Davis personally visited the army to straighten out matters. Prideful and stubborn in his decisions, Davis sustained Bragg at the very time Lincoln replaced Rosecrans with Thomas and sent Ulysses S. Grant to take department command (Military Division at the Mississippi) in an all-out effort to mend the situation at Chattanooga.[19]

The difference in the two president's actions thus highlighted one of the war's critical aspects—top-echelon decision making. The South had elected for its president an old-guard aristocrat. Davis found it difficult to keep pride and partiality from influencing his decisions. In contrast, the Northern government was led by a practical-minded man whose actions were largely common sense oriented. The contrasts in their thinking and decision making became more evident as the course of the war turned on pivotal presidential decisions.

By mid-October, Longstreet's Easterners had come to despise Bragg. "I am sorry to inform you that I am not in as good spirits [as] I would like to be," wrote a Georgia sharpshooter. "I assure you I am tired of Gen. Bragg, and am very anxious to be again in old Virginia under my favorite General [Robert E. Lee] the best man of the age." Captain William Blackford reported:

[This] army is badly generalled and the result is there is much demoralization and a want of confidence. Bragg ought to be relieved, or disaster is sure to result. The men have no faith. The difference between this army and Lee's is very striking; when the men move in the Army of Northern Virginia they think they are doing the proper thing, whether it be backward or forward, and if all the success anticipated is not secured, at all events it is not Lee's fault. Down here the men seem to feel the wrong thing is being done whatever it be, and when success is secured they attribute it to anybody else than Bragg. Thus they give the whole credit of Chickamauga to Longstreet, though he commanded only a part of the line, and his troops did not fight any better than the others.[20]

Unfortunately for his soldiers, the ordeal of Bragg's leadership wasn't limited to mental agony. As the crisp autumn weather turned to days of freezing cold and icy rain, the suffering of Bragg's troops became intense. Food was scarce due to a breakdown in the army's logistical operations, and desertions intensified.

As the siege of Chattanooga stretched into November, the enemy's logistics improved as the so-called cracker line was supplemented by the opening of the Tennessee River to supply transports. In sharp contrast, Bragg's supply situation only worsened. Private Robert Watson of the 7th Florida Infantry provided a damning indictment of the Army of Tennessee's supply system:

Sept. 28th [I] drew one day's ration of corn bread and beef for to-morrow, but as everyone is very hungry they eat it all for supper. So we will have to fast tomorrow. Sept. 29th [I] drew one day's ration of corn bread and bacon; just enough for one meal, and we eat it up immediately, although it is for tomorrow. Sept. 30th Nothing to eat but we are all supplied with lice. Many of the regiment [are] sick from drinking bad water and [eating] poorly cooked food. Oct. 1st All hands [are] as hungry as wolves and nothing to eat. Oct. 4th I am very unwell having been up half the night with diarrhea. Oct. 8th I am quite sick, and . . . all of the company are in the same fix from eating bad beef and drinking bad water. Oct. 16th I have a violent cold and pain in the breast. Nothing to eat, for the roads are so bad that the wagons can't get along. All hands are as hungry as wolves. I went to bed but was so hungry that I couldn't sleep. When I would doze off, I would dream that I was at my mother's table, eating all sorts of nice things, then wake up and find it [was] all a dream. Oct. 19th [I] drew two day's rations of meal and beef, which was as lean as carrion. At 1 P.M. the regiment came back [to camp] as hungry as sharks.[21]

Another soldier, one of Longstreet's Georgians, pleaded on October 24, "I am almost crazy for something to eat." Some of the more desperate men broke into a boxcar looking for food, and a guard had to be posted in the camp of the 5th Tennessee Infantry to keep the men from ransacking their commissary's reserve stores. "Not having drawn a pound of meat in five days," a disconsolate soldier grumbled, "In cold weather like this a man wants beef if he has been raised to eat it." Having only a skimpy meal of peas—"with three bugs to each pea''—he complained, "We would not have known how to have lived three or four years ago on what [little food] we draw now.''[22]

Having endured cold, stormy weather on windswept high ground without adequate equipment, provisions, or shelter, Bragg's army was overcome with misery by mid-November. "Our army is lying idle in the ditches watching the enemy," complained Sergeant Lewis L. Poates of the 63d Tennessee Infantry. "We have all been disappointed in not making a move during the [recent] fine dry weather. . . .'' One Arkansas soldier who had been barefoot for two months complained that the heavy frosts were hurting his feet. With the onset of heavy rains in October, units like the 7th Florida had to endure this unrelenting weather without shelter. There were no tents, and on several nights the men had to stand ankle deep in mud during a pouring rain, without "a wink of sleep," according to a soldier.[23]

Sicknesses like respiratory ailments, fevers, and diarrhea, were so prevalent that few regiments could provide more than a smattering of men for duty. "A person at home has no idea of the suffering and hardships endured by the soldiers . . . It seems as if enough [suffering] has been endured to end any war," wrote Sergeant Washington Ives of the 4th Florida. "I don't think there are enough feelings left to stir up another war in my lifetime.''[24]

Dismay such as Sergeant Lewis L. Poates of the 63d Tennessee expressed to his wife was commonly felt by Bragg's soldiers. Poates's spirits sank to a new low on November 15 after he learned that his regiment would receive only one day's ration of beef for six days: "I was hungrier day before yesterday than ever I have been in my life, and I paid four dollars for a little piece of bread which I divided with the boys of [our] mess. . . . Annis, you never was hungry with nothing to eat, and nowhere to get anything, so you don't know how it makes a person feel; but I know . . . Great God! How earnestly I pray that this war may cease. I am tired of it, tired, tired, tired! I want to be at home . . . with my family that I love.''[25]

Remarkably, despite these hardships, many soldiers continued to withstand all. "Our soldiers are willing to live as long as possible on bread and water rather than be conquered and our homes overrun by our enemies," claimed Sergeant Washington Ives. "Our brigade has not drawn but one day's ration of beef in eight days, so that there is not a particle of meat in any of the regiments," he reported in mid-November. "Yet the brigade commanders, aides, etc.

have as much bacon as they desire. . . . Still you hardly hear a murmur."[26]

Ives thus clarified a critical point. Despite their continuing ordeal, the essential glue that held the army together was the commitment of fighting for family, home, and comrades in arms. It was the essence of the soldiers' spirit that prevailed. Even Sergeant Poates, the man who so desperately wanted to go home, continued to express his determined spirit. "I mean to stay at my post as long as I can get a pound of bread a week, and I mean to do all I can to get others to do the same," he informed his wife.[27]

Despite all such expressions, there was a limit to what any man could endure. The prospect of future success was at the root of the soldiers' ongoing commitment, sustaining them when times were the toughest. But, as Texas Private Isaiah Harlan observed, his fellow soldiers were so hungry that they had begun pillaging the surrounding country, taking "everything they can get hold of—cows, hogs, sheep, poultry—nothing escapes them." Although Harlan had resolved "to live upon what ever I draw as long as I can do it," he confessed, "when starvation stares me in the face . . . then I will take whatever I can find."[28]

This admission was a concession to reality. If the soldiers' situation became too unbearable, then personal needs would prevail. It was perhaps ironic that on the very day Private Harlan penned his "starvation" letter, November 15, Braxton Bragg published general orders further reducing the army's daily meat rations. In partial justification, Bragg blamed the ongoing food shortages on the Federal authorities for refusing to exchange Yankee prisoners. This required the Confederacy to feed them with subsistence "which should [otherwise] go to the support of our gallant men and families," reported Bragg. [29]

To many starved, poorly clothed, and sickened gray soldiers this insult was the last straw; they had endured enough. Desertions had increased with the onset of stormy, raw weather, and now they became catastrophic. Thirty-two men from Deas's Alabama brigade deserted in one twenty-four-hour period. Federal units, on the brink of starvation during the early days of the Chattanooga siege, now found their gray-clad enemy deserting by the hundreds for want of something to eat. Even though some Yankees remained on half rations, they were better than the Rebel full rations, considered several deserters from Bragg's army. The large number of Confederate deserters was amazing to a private of the 93d Ohio, who thought, "If they [the Rebel deserters] come in all around the whole line like they do in front of us they will soon lose their army." To a New York soldier posted in the valley below Lookout Mountain, it was routine to gather in starving Confederate deserters. "Some nights 150 come in," he reported. "They say that they cannot stand the cold nights on the mountain without overcoats and not half enough to eat."[30]

Braxton Bragg responded to the mounting number of desertions from his army in his dispatch of November 19 to General Joseph E. Johnston: "Deserters are an encumbrance to me and must be shot or they run off again."[31]

Bragg's mounting problems were not confined to those among his rank and file. The continuing occupation of east Tennessee, including Knoxville, by Federal Major General Ambrose Burnside's troops posed a threat to Bragg's northern flank. Bragg's detachment of two divisions from his army in mid-October to counter a Federal offensive in the Holston River valley (and to otherwise impede Burnside's march to reinforce Chattanooga, which Lincoln had ordered) was turned into a hastily conceived scheme to launch an offensive in east Tennessee. Mindful of Jefferson Davis's expectation that Bragg would go on the offensive following the Chickamauga victory and regain Tennessee, Bragg saw an opportunity both to purge the army of a major detractor, Longstreet, and satisfy the government's expectation. With matters at a stalemate around Chattanooga, on November 5 Bragg ordered Longstreet and his two divisions on an expedition "to expel Burnside" from east Tennessee. That dividing his dwindling army in the face of a gathering enemy might result in disaster at Chattanooga was evidently overlooked by Bragg.[32]

Moreover, now that he had prevailed over his dissident generals, Bragg decided upon a major reorganization of the army. In mid-November, Bragg published orders changing the assignments of various regiments, brigades, and divisions within the Army of Tennessee. Many veteran regiments that had long served in a specific fighting unit were sent to another brigade or division. The ostensible reason for this restructuring was to remove troops enrolled locally from exposure in a common battle unit, and thus prevent undue losses for a given community. Yet Bragg had an obvious political agenda for these changes. The anti-Bragg Tennessee and Kentucky factions were broken up and scattered among units commanded by Bragg's supporters, such as W. H. T. Walker. Opposition generals like Frank Cheatham were largely disenfranchised when Bragg removed all but six of the politically powerful Nashville native's twenty-two Tennessee regiments from his command. Bragg believed that his actions would "keep down the anti-Bragg men."[33]

These events provided a remarkable backdrop for the ultimate decision at Chattanooga, which the entire South eagerly awaited as the follow-up to the Chickamauga victory.

In a coincidence equivalent to the lucky breakthrough of Longstreet's divisions at Chickamauga, nearly the opposite occurred during the decisive conflict at Missionary Ridge on November 25. Following the loss of Lookout Mountain on his left flank on November 24, Bragg was convinced by key subordinates to stay and fight from his main position along Missionary Ridge. Because of the natural strength of this six-hundred-foot-high ridge, which was heavily defended by artillery and infantry, Bragg had long considered mid–Missionary Ridge impregnable. In fact, he only belatedly ordered breastworks constructed along the ridge on November 24, exactly sixty-two days after beginning the siege of Chattanooga.[34]

Bragg worried that Grant's November 23 reconnaissance to Orchard Knob, in front of mid–Missionary Ridge, was a prelude to a major attack, but Bragg had guessed wrong. Grant had no intention of attacking the center of Bragg's line at mid–Missionary Ridge. Instead, the Federal commander planned to utilize William Tecumseh Sherman's troops for the main attack at the north end of the ridge, so as to envelop Bragg's right flank and cut off his retreat via Chickamauga Station.

Yet, on November 25, all went wrong for Grant. Joseph Hooker's eastern troops were ordered to march from Lookout Mountain and attack Bragg's southern flank in the vicinity of Rossville Gap. However, Hooker was delayed by the burning of a bridge over Chattanooga Creek, and by mid-afternoon on the 25th was nowhere to be seen. Even worse, William Tecumseh Sherman, leading the main attack against heavily outnumbered Confederate defenders on the north end of Missionary Ridge, was badly defeated. By 3:00 P.M. Grant was exasperated. Watching through field glasses as Sherman's troops fell back from their abortive assaults on Tunnel Hill, he became desperate.

To help Sherman in his fight on the north end, Grant impulsively ordered Thomas's troops, about 24,500 in all, to make a demonstration against the rifle pits at the base of mid–Missionary Ridge. Grant hoped that this action would cause Bragg to pull troops away from his northern flank to oppose Thomas, and thereby enable Sherman to win that critical fight. Unknown to Grant, Sherman had already called off further attacks against the Confederate positions in his sector, and had pulled back his troops to go into bivouac.

Grant's plan was thus a blueprint for disaster. His decision was not well thought out; by advancing to the rifle pits at the base of Missionary Ridge, Thomas's men would be caught in an untenable tactical situation. They would be trapped under the muzzles of Confederate cannon atop the ridge, and subjected to such a severe fire that it would be impossible for them to stay there.

In one of the most remarkable infantry assaults in American history, Thomas's men not only attacked and carried the lower rifle pits, but realizing that they couldn't remain beneath the Rebels' guns, spontaneously and without orders advanced up the slopes to attack the crest of mid–Missionary Ridge. Grant stood aghast as Thomas's veterans stormed up the slopes. Grant muttered that someone would pay dearly if the unauthorized assault failed.

Fortunately for Thomas, this impromptu assault was helped by faulty Confederate tactics. Many of the defending troops had been split between the top and bottom of the ridge. Although not all received the same orders, most were told to evacuate the lower rifle pits and climb the ridge at the enemy's approach. As many Confederates began fleeing when Thomas's soldiers approached, the natural impulse for the Yankees was to chase the enemy up the ridge.

With so many Confederates scrambling up the steep, rugged slopes, the defenders atop the crest couldn't fire at the Federals for fear of hitting their own men. Then, too, it was found that the muzzles of the cannon along the ridgeline couldn't be sufficiently depressed to accurately fire down the slopes. Furthermore, the recently constructed makeshift breastworks were at the topographical crown of the ridge, and the gray infantrymen couldn't see to shoot down the forward slopes immediately in front of them.

The entire situation was disastrous. When the 32d Indiana and 6th Ohio of Brigadier General August Willich's brigade suddenly broke over the crest, the defenders of Colonel William F. Tucker's Mississippi brigade panicked. Within minutes, Tucker's troops stampeded down the reverse slopes, and chaos spread as other Federals emerged over the crest and captured several Confederate batteries that were attempting to escape. Turning these guns on the confused enemy, Thomas's soldiers created multiple, expanding breaches in the Rebel lines along the ridge. Then, as more of Thomas's troops reached the crest, the crisis for Bragg's soldiers heightened. Within minutes Patton Anderson's entire division, many troops of which had been shuffled about in the recent army reorganization, fled the field. Further intensifying the turmoil, Joe Hooker's Yankee troops suddenly appeared on Bragg's southern flank, quickly routing the defenders there.

The consequences for Bragg's army were terrible; they suffered an unprecedented, shameful disaster. Instead of a brilliant victory, which had seemed assured when Sherman's main attack was beaten back by Patrick Cleburne on the north end of Missionary Ridge, Braxton Bragg endured a stunning defeat. Virtually the entire Confederate army, demoralized by privations during their siege of Chattanooga, streamed from the battlefield in disorder. Only a stout defense by Cleburne's troops along the northern sector preserved a semblance of order and enabled many of Bragg's men to escape.[35]

Having lost more than forty pieces of artillery and having suffered nearly seven thousand casualties (including more than four thousand captured) from a total of about forty-six thousand troops engaged in the battle, the Army of Tennessee was devastated by the debacle at Chattanooga.[36]

Although the soldiers' reactions varied, they all spoke of urgent and immediate needs. Many were so ashamed of what had happened that they even despaired of future efforts. Others resolved to blot out the enormous stain on their valor. Some blamed the defeat on a few troops who failed to fight at a critical time. "The imbecility and cowardice of one brigade involved the whole army in defeat," complained a Georgia artillerist. One of Cleburne's soldiers wrote, "[The Yankees] have driven us from the strongest position that we have got, just because some of our men are so tired of the war that they won't fight at all." A wounded Alabama soldier, now a prisoner, told his captors, "Well, we have received nothing, lived on nothing, been fighting for nothing," and now he would expect nothing from the Yankees.[37]

The effect of these events was evident during the Confederate retreat through Chickamauga Station, which had served as the army's local supply depot. Here immense stores of goods and provisions were piled everywhere—sacked corn, bacon, crackers, molasses, sugar, coffee, rice, potatoes, and hundreds of barrels of flour. Yet in the rush of the retreat toward Dalton, Georgia, the warehouses and provisions were set afire to keep them from falling into enemy hands. Many soldiers were outraged. As one soldier wrote, "All these stores had to be destroyed . . . [and] for months we had been starved for want of these same provisions." It was enough to make "the . . . most patriotic soul . . . think of rebelling against the authorities," he seethed.[38]

To other Confederates, the Missionary Ridge disaster accentuated the need for greater effort. "Everybody, both officers and men, seems to be ashamed of our defeat," observed an Alabama colonel. "I honestly believe that it will have a good effect upon the troops. When they get a chance to meet the enemy again they will pay him back with interest." "This is doubtless our darkest hour," admitted a grim but determined officer. "I fear that you all at home have become beclouded in doubts, fears, and despondency. Shake them off . . . Ere long the star of our independence will arise and shine forth and gladden the hearts of our suffering people." "We have been overpowered in numbers and met with serious reverses," thought a Georgia artillerist. "I hope that out of the disaster some good may yet come. . . . I never want to leave this army till we have punished the Yankees who drove us from Missionary Ridge."[39]

The men were willing; the spirit was still there. Yet the harsh reality was equally apparent. "We want now at the head of this army some general who will act with boldness and follow up every advantage he may gain," wrote a Georgia officer. "This army will fight with all the desperation and valor displayed at Chickamauga, for they are heartily ashamed of their conduct at Missionary Ridge."[40]

As is apparent in the accounts of both officers and men of Bragg's army, many faulted the Confederate infantry for fleeing from an "impregnable" position without reason or justification. Jefferson Davis attributed the defeat to the misconduct of the troops. "If the troops who yielded to the assault had fought with the valor which they had displayed on previous occasions . . . the enemy would have been repulsed with very great slaughter, and our country would have escaped this misfortune," he caustically stated in his message to Congress on December 7.[41]

Yet Davis's comments involved a cruel misperception. The consequences suffered by the Confederate soldiers at Missionary Ridge were rooted not in their alleged cowardice, but in bad command decisions. Strategically, Bragg had planned for a siege, not a frontal assault on his lines. His naturally strong positions on the high ground precluded a direct attack, he had reasoned. As a result, breastworks along the crest, cleared fields of fire, artillery emplacements, and strategic deposits of munitions were all lacking or neglected until the last moment. Bragg's conflict with the army's senior commanders had resulted in disarray and a confusing unit-by-unit reorganization. The gross mismanagement of supplies, and the absence of food, clothing, and basic shelter, had severely affected his troops. These problems in turn, fostered sickness and desertions, and depleted morale. Critical tactical mistakes, such as splitting brigade strengths between the top and bottom of Missionary Ridge and constructing rifle pits along the topographical rather than the military crest, had severely compromised the Confederates' chances of winning. Worst of all, Longstreet's corps, nearly one-third of Bragg's effective strength, had been detached on a whim, and these vital troops were absent during the decisive action.[42]

In perhaps the ultimate indictment of the Army of Tennessee's leadership, one of its long-suffering subordinate generals, Arthur M. Manigault, identified what had become the bane of the Tennessee army: "[A] want of generalship, recklessness, and utter disregard for human life, did more on many occasions to weaken and impair the efficiency of our army then any losses inflicted by the enemy." Echoing the sentiments of a Richmond newspaper editor, who declared it was better to have "an army of asses led by a lion" than "an army of lions led by an ass," a war-wise Tennessee private reflected upon Bragg's dismal role and wrote, "More depends upon a good general than the lives of many privates. The private loses his life, the general his country."[43]

It was significant that the men of the Army of Tennessee, so long confident that victory could be gained solely by their own resolute efforts, had begun to understand that able leadership as well as valor on the battlefield were necessary to win.

Chattanooga provided the coup de grace for Bragg's tenure as army commander. Although he complained that the fault was not his, that the disaster was a result of the troops' "bad conduct," Bragg submitted his resignation four days after the battle. Soon replaced by William J. Hardee, an interim commander, Bragg departed for home as the army retired to Dalton, Georgia, to begin refitting and replenishing.[44]

After Bragg departed, his successors were left to deal with the critical question of declining morale. As the events at Missionary Ridge had demonstrated, any hope of preserving the Army's spirits would depend on the tactical expertise used to fight an ever-stronger foe.

Chapter Twenty-three

"IT'S HARD TO MAINTAIN PATRIOTISM ON

ASHCAKE AND WATER"

On New Year's Eve, 1863, a young Virginian wrote a journal entry: "We have met with more reverses this year than in the two preceding, both together. Oh! that the next [year] may be more promising and may we gain our independence before this time next year."[1]

This soldier's comments reflected the deteriorating prospects of winning the war. At the beginning of 1864, the Confederacy's future was as much a mystery as the past had been a profound disappointment. In the wake of such stunning defeats as Gettysburg, Vicksburg, Port Hudson, and Chattanooga, many were reappraising what the South was fighting for. Southerners were no longer innocent of war. The broken hopes for a quick victory, the enormous amount of effort and ordeal involved, the devastating losses of sons, husbands, fathers, brothers, and friends, and the desolation of the land were at odds with initial conceptions of the War for Southern Independence.

As a result, significant differences in expectations and perspectives were now rife among the Southern populace. An observant officer who had served in both the East and the West perceived a variance in underlying motives, and he expressed his concern. "The people down in these states [Tennessee, Georgia] are not as much enlisted on principle in this war as we in Virginia. They regard it as a war to protect their property in slaves, and when they are lost, take no further interest in it," wrote Captain Charles M. Blackford of Longstreet's staff. "In Virginia we are fighting for the right to govern ourselves in our own way and to perpetuate our own customs and institutions among our own people without outside interference. This feeling being universal, no loss of property or temporary defeat affects our people and they remain true. In east Tennessee, the people are about equally divided and there rages a real civil war, which causes great misery."[2]

Captain Blackford's views were not overly optimistic at the beginning of 1864. Vicksburg's loss had split the Confederacy in two and cut off supplies from Texas. "So great is the disparity in numbers and resources," reasoned Blackford, "that any loss to us is a great loss. . . ." Also, his estimation in January 1864, "There is [now] too little of the terrible earnestness of a revolution," boded ill for the Confederacy's future. "Lee and Jackson are the only men who seem to rise to the height of our occasion," he once considered. Even his own general, Longstreet, he deemed "too phlegmatic to be efficient except when much aroused."[3]

What continued to be the Virginia army's natural reservoir of strength in the early months of 1864 was the mental resolve of Lee's soldiers. Within the ranks of the Army of Northern Virginia, the mounting pressure from defeats and despair elsewhere contrasted with a determination to see the task through. Major defeats in the West did not dampen the confidence and prowess of the men under Robert E. Lee.

Aware that the Yankees' most successful general, Ulysses S. Grant, was coming east to conduct operations in the Virginia theater, a staff officer boasted, "I think that Grant will find us ready for him and won't gain a victory over our army with the ease [with which] he has heretofore triumphed in the West. We are all sanguine of success, and trust we shall be able to serve Lincoln's latest hero [Grant] as we have served his various predecessors . . ." A Georgia captain wrote in early April 1864, "I am of the opinion that Grant intends to . . . go to Richmond, and if he crosses [into Virginia] we will ruin his army. . . . With defeat will go down him and his army of demons, and probably peace will be proposed to us. Yes, to us, the half starved and ragged Rebels of whom they have made so much fun. I am more sanguine of success now than I ever have been."[4]

Many Southern soldiers believed that fighting defensively on Virginia soil would insure not only high spirits and confidence, but victory as well. Throughout 1862 and much of 1863 the validity of that conception had been proved by the brilliant succession of Lee's victories. Yet it wasn't so much the fighting in Virginia that worried the men of Lee's army as the growing despair elsewhere.

Much of the problem with the conduct of the war, concluded Private Peter L. Mabry of the 3d Alabama Infantry, rested with the Tennessee army. "Those fellows down there will not fight," he grumbled. A soldier from Jenkins's brigade fretted about the Army of Tennessee, saying in late 1863, "There is no telling where he [Bragg] is now, [but] it makes little difference, for he won't fight no-how, and he has got the most demoralized army there ever was. He [even] has 10,000 deserters [missing] from his army." Having heard a false report that Charleston, South Carolina, had fallen, this soldier then added, "We are gone for certain if this is true. . . . The Yankees will overrun our whole country before they can be stopped . . . I have never been in so much trouble [in] all my life. I am nearly crazy."[5]

Since there was little the men in the Virginia army could do about matters elsewhere, they focused on their own circumstances. Despite the lack of significant military activity in northern Virginia during the fall of 1863, conditions were not favorable within Lee's army that winter. Desertions increased following Gettysburg, as did executions, reflecting discontent among the ranks. A North Carolina lieutenant watched as a deserter was shot near Orange Court House, Virginia, in October 1863. "The one that was shot today was not killed dead the first fire," he noted. "Consequently he was shot twice. You can not imagine how cruel it looks to see a man shot. Twelve men shot at him at about ten steps. Only one ball hit him in the side. He fell over on his face, was examined by the surgeon, who pronounced him not dead. Two men were then ordered out with loaded muskets who shot him dead. . . . It looks very barbarous to see men shot in that way but it is necessary to maintain the discipline of an army."[6]

Adding to the despair of Lee's men, living conditions were difficult and proper food scarce. An artillerist, Dan Blain, told his fiancée, "Hardly anything will compensate me for what I must endure," but all must "bear up with fortitude becoming Christians." Since things were looking gloomy again, Blain could only hope that God would protect the South.[7]

More and more prevalent in the minds of soldiers everywhere was what was happening at home. Federal control of Southern territory had increased significantly, and the matter of defending one's home was worrisome to many. One soldier, a sergeant with the 29th Virginia

Infantry, promised to do more than just sit idly by if his home in western Virginia was threatened. "My candid opinion [is] that in less than three months the Yankees are going to have all the country west of Christianburg, and when that time arrives you may look for the 29th regiment, for I tell you that we are not going to stay down here and give up our homes. My own opinion is that the Confederacy is going to give up southwest Virginia." When John Martin of the 18th Alabama discovered that only every twelfth man in each company would get a furlough, he reasoned that his chances were so poor that it would be nearly a year before he might be able to see his wife. "[It] seems like I cannot stay [here] that long—I cannot help myself," he wrote in despair.[8]

Growing political troubles in the interior also warned of further difficulty. A rifleman with the 1st North Carolina, W. Hockaday, was cut to the quick when it became apparent that many in North Carolina wanted to rejoin the Union. The state was in an uproar after the Confederate army's losses, and Hockaday offered a soldier's opinion about why Southern fortunes were so distressed: "Our rulers [the Confederate government] have committed an oversight in bringing on so many hot and stubborn battles, and trying to end the war by fighting." John P. Hull of the 4th Virginia Infantry, Stonewall brigade, expressed similar sentiment when he complained in November 1863, "Our independence is mighty hard pressed, but I am not discouraged yet. I do not believe it [the conflict] ever will be settled, that is by fighting."[9]

Both Hockaday's and Hull's comments revealed the soldiers' heightened turmoil. They had expended enormous effort and shed abundant blood, but for what purpose? The war hadn't been won by their superiority as soldiers, as they first anticipated it would be. Many had been led to believe that they were invincible, that determination would prevail over numbers and resources. Yet that theory hadn't proved true. Now the hard reality confronted them. No less capable and determined than they, the enemy was better equipped and far more numerous. Bravery and effort only went so far when soldiers faced repeating rifles, superior long-range rifled cannon, and heavy breastworks. In the backs of the soldiers' minds, troublesome question continued to ferment. Considering the altered circumstances of an increasingly deadly battlefield, supply shortages, and desolated homes, could they win the war?

Characteristic of the indomitable spirit of men who had become toughened by their ordeals, there were many who refused to think of yielding, no matter what the cost. A hardbitten Georgian reasoned in April 1864:

I don't regret the hardships of war if I can gain my independence. I consider it a duty that I owe to my children to battle for their liberty as well as my own. . . . Therefore I endure the hardships of warfare with all of the fortitude of a soldier battling for independence. . . . Should I fall, . . . I indulge in the hope that in the days to come my boys may be enabled to speak of me with pride, and say he helped to secure for us our liberty. . . . And though we never knew him . . . we shall ever refer to the heroic deeds with pride and feel grateful that we had one near and dear to us who secured for us the liberty we now enjoy.[10]

Others resigned themselves reluctantly to the necessity of maintaining the war effort. "There is no real enjoyment in camp," wrote Lieutenant B. T. Cotton of the 34th North Carolina, "situated as we are, liable to be attacked by the enemy at any time . . . and not knowing what moment we may be ushered into eternity; if there is any enjoyment in such a life I frankly say that I have never found it." In February 1864, Cotton was unmoved when his regiment reenlisted after their term of service expired. It made "no difference," he said, "for we are in [the army] for life or the war, thanks to the conscription act recently passed, which extended the ages of military service from seventeen to fifty."

In another letter of the period, Cotton confided that his spirits were low: "It seems there is no chance for peace, and the cry is war, war, war. When we [will] realize the blessings of peace again is unknown, and who will be spared is not revealed, but I hope the ruler of nations will interfere in our behalf and save us from degradation and ruin."[11]

With the coming of spring in 1864, it was apparent that an ordeal was imminent for the Army of Northern Virginia. Captain William Blackford predicted as much on May 3, 1864, just before the ghastly Wilderness fighting began:

Grant is certainly concentrating a large army against ours. If we defeat him the military strength of the enemy will be broken, and we must have peace. Officers and men are confident of success. I am so also. But sometimes I find my fears giving away to the force of numbers. Their army is twice as large as ours. They can replace every-man killed and wounded. We, on the other hand, are using up our reserves. Grant can afford to have four men killed or wounded to kill or disable one of ours. That process will destroy us at last, by using up our material. What a terrible period of anxiety and blood-shed the next ninety days will be! Our very existence may be at stake in a single battle. If we fail, we cannot carry on another cam-paign. Our supplies of men and munitions will not permit it. If we succeed we will have peace in less than twelve months.[12]

Ulysses S. Grant represented a difficult opponent, the likes of whom the Army of Northern Virginia hadn't yet encountered. His tenacious mode of warfare contrasted with the brief campaigns and subsequent withdrawals of the contending armies over the past three years. Beginning May 5, 1864, the warfare in the Virginia thickets that continued from day to day both wizened and saddened Lee's army. "Grant has shown no remarkable generalship," wrote Captain Wil-liam Blackford on May 19, "only a bulldog like tenacity and deter-mination in a fight, regardless of the consequences or the loss. If it required the loss of twenty-five thousand to rob us of six thousand he was doing a wise thing, for we yield our loss from an irreplaceable penury, he from super abundance. Ultimately such bloody policy must win, and it makes little difference to them, as the vast majority of the killed and wounded are foreigners, many of whom cannot speak English."[13]

To Lieutenant B. T. Cotton, the bloody fighting in the Wilderness and at Spotsylvania was terrible even if minimally successful. "I have not any idea he [Grant] can succeed [in the campaign]," he wrote on June 11. "We are very strongly fortified. I do not think all of the Yanks in the North could move us from our position unless they flank us . . ." Yet Cotton was mindful of the realities. "We are seeing very hard times, [and] losing so much sleep makes us feel very bad," he continued. "[I] have not changed clothes but once since the 1st of May . . . We are all very dirty . . . but in tolerably good spirits and con-fident of success whenever Grant sees fit to charge our works. . . ." Within his letter there were signs that Cotton's morale had been af-fected. "I wish the Yankees would go home and let us alone without any more shedding of blood," he remarked. "How long this cruel war will last is unknown to us. Oh, that we could once more have peace and liberty!"[14]

Although Robert E. Lee was able to frustrate the new Federal commander's continual attempts to get beyond the Confederate flank and strike at Richmond, "Grant's War," the relentless pressure of daily combat, was slowly wearing down the Army of Northern Virginia. "Old Grant is a hard customer, very hard to [be] satisfied," admitted a North Carolinian following the intense fighting of May and June 1864. After Spotsylvania, an Alabama private confided:

We have had a hard time of it since the 6th instant [May], not a day without more or less fighting. There is nothing since the war commenced to equal it . . . [We] have killed any amount of Yanks. I have never [seen] anything to equal it. In some places the ground for miles along our breastworks [is] covered with dead Yankees. If Grant will continue to charge us we will kill his whole army . . . Old Grant is a hard fighter, and if he continues for a month longer as he has been going on, he will have all of his men killed . . . I feel certain that we will be able to whip out Grant up here. . . .

To B. B. Hunter of the 41st Virginia Infantry, the Federal general was known as "Butcher Grant," and he and his comrades joked about "Grant's War," which had cost the Yankees, he estimated in July 1864, "over 100,000 men." "They do most of the charging," wrote Hunter, ". . . [since] the enemy seems determined to capture the Rebel capitol [sic] and crush the rebellion. . . ."[15]

As these soldiers described it, Lee's army was largely confined to the defensive, and Confederate soldiers quickly adapted to the new manner of warfare. "Our men delighted in firing from behind breastworks; [but] they have had but little experience in such work," wrote the observant Captain Charles Blackford.[16]

Although an aggressive general and one who usually sought to attack, Robert E. Lee wisely opted to maintain defensive operations consistent with his altered situation. His blocking tactics resulted in tremendous Union losses that depressed the spirits of a war-weary North during midsummer 1864. On May 17, shortly after the deadly Bloody Angle fighting at Spotsylvania, a Virginia cannoneer in Graham's battery wrote, "All of our men seem to be in the best of spirits and they want Old Grant to fight us again so we can slaughter the drunken scoundrels again. There is hundreds and thousands of their dead lying in front of our breastworks yet unburied."[17]

Despite Union casualties, the effect on Confederate morale of Grant's relentless offensive was soon evident. "We are being conquered by the splendor of our own victories," noted a Virginia officer. The Confederate losses numbered at least one-fourth of the Yankee casualties, he admitted, and they could not be adequately replaced. The daily fighting mentally exhausted many Confederates. Moreover, the constant moving from one place to the next confused the men, said a rifleman, and many troops were as badly fatigued as he had ever seen them.[18]

Although morale generally remained high during the actual fighting, too often the euphoria proved to be only brief. The grinding war of attrition was repeated so often, frequently with high Confederate losses, that it weighed heavily on the minds of Lee's veterans. The continual musketry and shell fire was taking a terrible toll in morale. Grant's soldiers kept coming at them, and the Yankees acted as if they were winning by forcing Lee's men to shift rapidly from one position to the next. An officer remarked, "It is hard to get the truth of what happens now, and [even what] happens just in our front." Many of Lee's men were beginning to question what the ultimate results of the campaign might be.[19]

Without appropriate food, clothing, and equipment, and facing daily combat, Lee's haggard infantrymen endured circumstances that bore little prospect of improvement. One war-weary rifleman wondered, "How much more we that are living will have to suffer before this war ends. . . . There is no telling how much trouble and misery may yet be in store for us. . . ."[20]

"Our living is now very poor; nothing but cornbread and poor beef . . . ," a captain informed his wife that August. "I merely eat to live, and live on as little as possible. You would laugh, or cry, when you see me eating my supper—a pone of cornbread and a tin cup of water. . . . It is hard to maintain one's patriotism on ashcake and water."[21]

Adding to their burden, the worries of the men now extended beyond their own plight. The threat of multiple Federal armies advancing across a broad front was particularly menacing to the South's interior. Fearful of what would happen since their homes were in "so much danger," Private John A. Johnson of the 19th Georgia Infantry explained to his wife the despair he felt at being helpless to protect her and their homestead:

I have been exposed to danger alone heretofore, but now danger threatens [you]. Mine is generally under excitement and often times not felt at all. . . . But yours is of that kind—dread of approaching evil—which is hardest of all to bear. Mine is frequent but of short duration. Yours is at all times before you, and it often happens that the reality is much easier borne than the dread or anticipation. Is it not natural that under the above circumstances my anxiety should be greater than when the country was in less danger?[22]

Many Confederates began to focus more and more on what was happening at home and in the West as the sweltering days of midsummer began. Lee's army was bogged down in a stalemate south of Richmond, and his troops were confined to a vast network of fortifications that protected the Richmond-Petersburg region. Hunkered down in their trenches, many men could think only of home and family. One Confederate, who had tried five times to get a furlough, wrote that he "wanted to go there [home] so bad I can't rest." Thoughts of the "peaches, apples, cider brandy and everything of the sort" that he was missing had reduced him to a state of depression. Mindful of the devastation threatening his home, one Georgian in the Virginia army wrote, "We all feel anxious about our homes in Georgia, but can only hope the tide of battle will soon turn in our favor."[23]

With the strategic diversion of Jubal Early's troops into the Shenandoah Valley in June, which was intended to draw off strength from Grant's army, the prospect of further Yankee campaigns near his home caused Captain Charles M. Blackford to despair. "I am in agony of apprehension about you all," he wrote to his wife in mid-June. "To think that my whole family, wife, child, mother, sister, are probably this very morning subjected to the insults and indignities of a band of freebooters makes my blood boil."[24]

Major Willis F. Jones, serving on the staff of Major General Charles W. Field, wrote home from Petersburg on August 29, 1864:

My heart bleeds when I think of my family, which is every moment of the day. I dream of you all at night. I often resolve not to brood [over] our troubles and misery, and if possible discard all thoughts of home and family. [I] strive to be gay, joyous, and happy, and perform my many onerous and responsible duties as becomes a man and a soldier. But often, after my many resolves, I feel that I have had more than my share, and but for my family all would be right with me. But for hope, what would become of us? This state cannot always exist. I am buoyed up with the joys and happiness that certainly must attend us all when we meet.[25]

As was too often the case, the anticipation of securing peace and returning home became unrealistic hopes. Major Jones was killed during the Petersburg fighting shortly after he wrote his letter.

By the fall and winter of 1864, with the onset of raw, cold weather, the suffering of Southerners intensified everywhere. It was soon evident that the situation in Lee's army was becoming increasingly desperate, particularly in terms of morale. In the trenches near the infamous "Crater" at Petersburg, rifleman Luther Mills told his brother that the suffering of November 1864 was "much greater than it should have been." Mills wrote that "many of the men were entirely destitute of blankets and overcoats, and it was really distressing to see them shivering over a little fire made of green pine wood." Private Mills observed that the soldiers "are generally for peace on any terms toward the close of a cold wet night, but after the sun is up and they get warm, they are in their usual spirits. I have never seen an army so completely whipped. . . . We have to carry some men to [the] hospital for frostbite, etc. Some have come in off picket crying from [the] cold like children. In fact, I have seen men in the trenches with no shoes at all. . . . We have been supplied within the last few days with shoes and blankets, and it is hoped that our men will do better."

Noting that "the men do not seem to fear the winter campaign so much as they do the coming of spring [and active fighting]," Mills considered that the prospect of yet more combat might ruin the army. "Some men desert from our brigade nearly every day or two, [and] I believe there will be a great many more next spring," he added.

The answer to these problems, reasoned Mills, was not difficult. "One good decisive victory in the [Shenandoah] Valley or Georgia would do a great deal towards cheering our men up."[26]

Victory was now increasingly elusive to an army that had once known only success and enthusiasm. Robert E. Lee tried everything to insure victory while defending northern Virginia, and had repeatedly pleaded, mostly in vain, for the return of those elements of his army detached elsewhere. Convinced that Grant's vast columns would mount a relentless offensive against Richmond in the early spring of 1864, Lee had sought to seize the initiative and disrupt Grant's plans. Lee wrote in mid-March 1864, "If a good move could be made before they [enemy] are ready to execute their plans, we would confound their schemes and break them up. . . . If not, we shall be obliged to conform to their plans and concentrate wherever they are going to attack us."[27]

Although he had wanted to take the offensive in the spring of 1864 to disrupt the enemy's own offensive in Virginia, his "hands were tied," said Lee. A want of troops, provisions, and forage for the army's animals prevented any major effort. Accurately predicting a two-pronged Federal effort against Richmond, via northern Virginia and up the James River from the southeast, Lee wrote in mid-April 1864, "I cannot even draw to me the cavalry or artillery of the army, and the season has arrived when I may be attacked any day. The scarcity of our supplies gives me the greatest uneasiness."[28]

Particularly frustrating to the Confederate commander was his inability to do more than block Grant's main thrusts despite being able to anticipate the enemy's every move. When Jefferson Davis delayed taking major corrective action, Lee warned the president:

I regret that there is to be any further delay in concentrating our own troops. [Other plans] will not compensate us for a disaster in Virginia or Georgia. Success in resisting the chief armies of the enemy will enable us more easily to recover the country now occupied by him. . . . We are inferior in numbers, and as I have before stated to Your Excellency, the absence of the troops belonging to this army weakens it more than by the mere number of men [that is, it was a negative psychological factor].

Lee's situation was so discouraging that even when Longstreet's troops were restored to the Army of Northern Virginia, Lee was unable to disrupt the enemy's plans by attacking, even though he actively looked for any opportunity to strike at a weak point.[29]

By the beginning of the Petersburg siege, Lee was worried about being pinned down and rendered unable to maneuver. He was particularly weakened by supply shortages due to the vulnerability of the network of railroads leading to the Richmond-Petersburg area. Although still thinking offensively, Lee suffered what he had been so apprehensive of in 1863, when he anticipated losses in the army's irreplaceable reservoir of manpower. Without adequate numbers of men—"where are we to get sufficient troops to oppose Grant?" he asked—disaster seemed imminent. "Unless we can obtain a reasonable approximation to his [Grant's] force, I fear a great calamity will befall us," Lee had confided to President Davis the previous November. "The inequality is too great." Also, he had warned Secretary of War James A. Seddon that the future consequences of a siege were serious: "... We should ... be prepared for unfavorable results, and [not] neglect precautions that may lighten any calamity that may befall us."[30]

Lee was caught in a dilemma in which he was forced to push and prod the Richmond authorities to replenish and provide for his army, while at the same time he needed to encourage his soldiers to bear up under their greater difficulties. All he could offer his men was limited optimism. To bolster their devotion to duty, prior to the 1864 campaign he issued general orders steeling them for the task ahead. "Soldiers! You tread with no unequal step the road by which your fathers marched through suffering, privations, and blood, to independence [in the American Revolution]. Continue to emulate in the future, ... their valor in arms, their patient endurance of hardships, their high resolve to be free ..., and be assured that the just God who crowned their efforts with success will, in his own time, send down His blessings upon you."[31]

By the onset of winter 1864, the psychology of sustaining the war effort had begun to occupy Lee more and more. Realizing that conditions were austere, and knowing their effect on morale, Lee pondered the ultimate result at Petersburg. At one point in the siege, Lee complained to Jefferson Davis about the lack of soap, which was more than just a minor irritant: "The great want of cleanliness which is a necessary consequence of these very limited [soap] issues is now producing sickness among the men in the trenches, and must affect their self-respect and morale."[32]

Believing that Grant would try "to starve us out" rather than assault the heavily fortified Petersburg lines, Lee constantly sought to remedy the dwindling quantity of supplies reaching his army. Yet, many of his efforts were an attempt to sustain troop morale, as well as to provide for the army's physical needs. By mid-December, the supply situation had worsened, and Lee was desperate for food and forage. On January 11, 1865, he telegraphed to Richmond, "There is nothing within reach of this army to be impressed. The country is swept clear. Our only reliance is upon the railroads. We have but two days' supplies."[33]

Since the railroads were constantly being torn up by the enemy's cavalry and raiding columns, and due to the horrendous weather (a "heavy freshet" had destroyed a portion of the Danville Railroad), all supplies were temporarily cut off in mid-January. Lee made an appeal to local farmers for food, and he reported an "alarming frequency of desertions."[34]

In confirmation of Lee's comments, Private Luther Mills wrote on January 31, 1865, "I saw a man catch a large rat and eat it about a week ago. What is it that a dirty soldier won't do?"[35]

Death and squalor had become inherent in an army once characterized by a bold, almost reckless pride and spirit. It permeated the souls of those who had once thought only of being the victors and not the vanquished. The men were dying like flies, if not for want of food or by disease, then by the Yankees' probing attacks, deadly sharpshooters, and heavy shell fire. It was a hell that the soldiers had hardly imagined back in 1861. Yet Lee's patient if dwindling veterans were still there, bleeding, starving, suffering, and dying.

Perhaps Robert E. Lee said it best when he wrote that winter to his daughter Agnes, telling her, "Every day is marked with sorrow and every field has its grief, the death of some brave man!"[36]

Chapter Twenty-four

DOING THE UNTHINKABLE

Major General Patrick R. Cleburne developed a bold new proposal to save the Confederacy's sinking military fortunes. Formally presented during a closed special meeting in January 1864 by the distinguished combat commander, it was, he said, "a concession to common sense."[1]

Cleburne's plan to enlist blacks as fighting men in the Confederacy's armies raised a crucial question. Considering the South's rapidly depleting pool of white males of military age, to what extent was the South prepared to make concessions or sacrifices in order to win its independence?

This controversial strategy would require Southerners to choose between practicality and pride, common sense and tradition. Slavery's future was at stake as fundamental changes altering Southern society would be made in exchange for the greater prospect of independence. The proposal, in fact, went to the heart of Southern perspectives; was the continuance of slavery worth the intensifying risk of defeat?

It was evident from the beginning that the emotional nature of this issue would impinge upon the war's conceptions. Many astute military men knew of the odds facing the Confederacy at the beginning of 1864. Ahead was the wasting war of defense, which would bring further loss of Southern territory, more hardship to civilians, and diminishing resources for all. The South was losing the war slowly, inexorably.

Yet some among the South's senior commanders immediately opposed Cleburne's idea because it involved making a distasteful and horrific concession that would abolish a fundamental institution of the venerable Southern society. Self-esteem, pride, and honor were at stake.

Pat Cleburne proposed the enrollment of slaves in the army in exchange for their freedom. Mindful that the Union enlisted blacks under white officers in a legion of "United States Colored Troops," Cleburne sought not only to counteract this mounting threat but to enroll loyal blacks to defend Southern soil. He astutely foresaw that blacks would enable the Confederate armies to become "numerically superior to the North."[2]

In contrast to the North, where the black population numbered only about 2 to 3 percent, blacks represented about 47 percent of the Confederate States' 1860 population of 9,103,333. There were nearly 4 million blacks within the eleven Confederate states, and in early 1864 the number of black males who were of military age might be estimated at about 1 million. The potential for adding up to perhaps 500,000 black soldiers to the existing Confederate ranks (which had dwindled to about 480,000 men under arms by 1864) was enormously important because the entire Federal army numbered only 861,000 at that time.[3]

The disparity between Northern and Southern troops was obviously a crucial issue, and Cleburne saw an opportunity to "save [the] country" by augmenting the Confederate army with black soldiers. "Every soldier in our army already knows and feels our numerical inferiority," he asserted. A "want of men in the field" had caused great despair. Cleburne's reasoning involved the obvious:

The fruits of our struggles and sacrifices have invariably slipped away from us and left us nothing but long lists of dead and mangled. . . . We are hemmed in today into less than two-thirds [of our territory], and still the enemy menacingly confronts us at every point with superior forces. Our soldiers can see no end to this state of affairs except in our own exhaustion; hence, instead of rising to the occasion, they are sinking into a fatal apathy, growing weary of hardships and slaughters which promise no results. . . . It is easy to

understand why there is a growing belief that some catastrophe
is not far ahead ... unless some extraordinary change is soon
made. . . .

Cleburne also noted that desertion, restlessness, disregard for private rights and property, and even disrespect for officers were some
of the consequences of the current army malaise.[4]

Essentially, the South's population of whites eligible for service was
all but exhausted. "As the necessity for more fighting men is upon
us," the only practical resource was slaves, reasoned Cleburne. Using
slaves as soldiers would "change the current of [Yankee] success and
sweep the invader from our country." The Confederacy might even
"take the offensive, move forward, and forage on the enemy." Beyond these possibilities, the Irish-born general adroitly pointed out,
"Slavery ... has now become, in a military point of view, one of our
chief sources of weakness." Slaves provided the enemy with information, supplied him with men for his armies, caused some owners
to take the United States oath of allegiance so as to save their property, and were so motivated by the prospect of freedom that they
abandoned their plantations upon the enemy's approach, thus rob-
bing the South of labor for the war effort. Furthermore, noted Cleburne, England and France would not recognize the Confederacy
because they did not condone the practice of slavery. Therefore, the
only remedy for the South's current ills was to utilize slaves as productive parts of the quest for independence.[5]

Would liberated slaves fight for the South? Cleburne was certain
they would: "If they can be made to face and fight bravely against
their former masters, how much more probable is it that with the
allurement of a higher reward, and led by those masters, they would
submit to discipline and face dangers?" he asked. By giving a slave
"not only his own freedom, but that of his wife and child" and "securing it to him in his old home ..." the South could enlist his sympathies far more effectively than the North, he concluded.[6]

At stake, warned Cleburne, was the survival of the South as they
knew it. Was it not better to "give up the negro slave, rather than be
a slave [of the conquerer] ... ?" he queried.[7]

His was an extraordinary proposal, and Pat Cleburne was likewise
no ordinary man. He based his ideas on logic and common sense.
Perhaps the most brilliant tactician in the Confederacy in 1864, Cleburne was a master at fighting and perhaps the South's best combat

general. Moreover, he had been able to inspire in his men a devotion that bordered on idolatry. He was a leader who had led soldiers to tactical victories in battles that others had lost.

Yet Pat Cleburne was never given his due. In fact, Cleburne's lost potential was one of the great Southern misfortunes of the war. Although he was one of the best and brightest commanders in the South, he served in a subordinate role with the downtrodden Army of Tennessee. Had Cleburne fought with Robert E. Lee, there seems little doubt that his name would have become as famous as Stonewall Jackson's.

Cleburne was burdened with one disadvantageous characteristic, a "flaw" that condemned him to a tragic end. As a man concerned more with what was right than with what was politically expedient, he was politically vulnerable. Born in Ireland on St. Patrick's eve, 1828, which some believed was an omen of greatness, he immigrated to the United States in 1849. A self-made success, Cleburne was a former enlisted man in the British Army who later rose to prominence in his Helena, Arkansas, community. Cleburne also advanced quickly in the Confederate army following his enrollment in 1861. Within a year of volunteering, he was a highly regarded brigadier general. At Shiloh, Corinth, Richmond (Kentucky), Perryville, Stones River, Chickamauga, and other important battles, he had proved his enormous worth. By the end of 1862, Pat Cleburne had been promoted to major general and was given command of a division.[8]

Unfortunately, there was a dark moon rising in Cleburne's life, and he was too often unable to reach his ultimate potential. Virtues, not vices, kept getting in his way. His even-tempered modesty and easygoing personality failed to attract attention. Unwilling to compromise his principles or dignity for political gain, he had run afoul of army politics. All that mattered to Pat Cleburne was that he acted solely upon what he knew was right. In his mind's eye there was only black or white, with very little gray to compromise one's judgment.

In voicing his proposal for enlisting slaves in the army, Cleburne faced a tremendous ordeal. While maintaining no animosity toward Braxton Bragg, he had twice been called upon by Bragg for a candid opinion of his campaigning. On both occasions, despite the acerbic North Carolinian's expectations, Cleburne had not supported Bragg. Cleburne consequently remained in limbo within the Army of Tennessee's command structure despite his brilliant record.

In January 1864, aware that a vacancy in corps command might bring him a promotion to lieutenant general, Cleburne nonetheless proceeded with his controversial proposal to enlist slaves in the army. He had been warned by his staff officers that because of its radical nature the plan might cost him his chance for promotion. Yet Cleburne replied that in view of the crisis in the South, it was his duty to present the proposal regardless of its effect on his career. Despite his devotion to his division, he was willing to take command of a division of black troops if need be. If the worst happened—facing court-martial and being cashiered—Cleburne said that he would enlist as a private in his old regiment and continue to do his duty. Cleburne's great character again remained foremost.[9]

The Irishman was nonetheless unprepared for the storm of controversy that soon followed the presentation of his proposal. An ardent opponent, Major General W. H. T. Walker, who was aligned with the old Bragg faction, insisted on sending a copy to the Davis administration. Walker wrote that such a plan would result in the South's "ruin and disgrace." Within a month, the reply from Richmond outlined Jefferson Davis's outrage at Cleburne's proposal. Not only was such an idea unacceptable, it was, said Davis, "injurious to the public service that such a subject should be mooted or even known to be entertained by persons possessed of confidence and respect of the people." Davis informed W. H. T. Walker that, accordingly, he had instructed the army's commander, Joe Johnston, "to avoid all publicity" and to express to all concerned "my desire that [the proposal] should be kept private. If it be kept out of the public journals its ill effect will be much lessened."[10]

Upon learning that Davis had expressed his concern through the secretary of war that even discussing the matter would be "productive only of discouragement, distraction, and dissension," Joe Johnston told Cleburne that the proposal was to be "suppressed."[11]

Dutifully, a disappointed Pat Cleburne accepted President Davis's verdict without rancor. He told a friend, "After such an opinion . . . I feel it my duty to suppress the memorial and to cease to advocate the measures mentioned." He then had his staff officers destroy all copies, except the one returned from Richmond. Thereafter, he was careful to make no public mention of the proposal, in full compliance with Jefferson Davis's wishes.[12]

Yet Pat Cleburne soon discovered that this matter would have a profound effect on his military career, for the Davis administration seemed to thoroughly discredit him just after he presented his proposal. The vacancy in corps command that Cleburne had hoped to fill was taken by John Bell Hood, a personal friend of Davis's. It was one of the most fateful decisions ever made by Jefferson Davis, and began a bizarre sequence of events that ultimately led to disaster. A few months after Hood's promotion, Lieutenant General Leonidas Polk was killed, and Cleburne was again denied corps command. A. P. Stewart, Cleburne's junior in rank as a major general but a Bragg supporter, was promoted and given Polk's spot. When another vacancy occurred due to Hood's promotion that summer, his corps went to Stephen D. Lee. Perhaps most distressing of all, when William J. Hardee departed from the army in September 1864, the hard-drinking Benjamin F. Cheatham was assigned by Hood to command of that corps.

Four vacancies in corps command within the Army of Tennessee over the span of eight months, and the best general had been summarily passed over on each occasion. The obstinacy of Bragg, who served as the president's personal military adviser, and of Davis was never more apparent. Cleburne's staff officers had been correct when they predicted that the controversial January 1864 proposal would cost him advancement. Though not court-martialed, Pat Cleburne was effectively blacklisted from further promotion.[13]

The Army of Tennessee was initially committed to campaign on the defensive in 1864, thought its new commander, General Joseph E. Johnston. Reduced numbers and resources necessitated this strategy. Yet Jefferson Davis dissented. He wanted that army to assume the offensive in order to prevent the enemy from seizing the initiative. Particularly worrisome to Davis was the prospect of a major Yankee offensive against the important rail center at Atlanta.

The president thus posted newly promoted Lieutenant General John Bell Hood to the West. Davis hoped to counter the threat to Atlanta by inspiring agressiveness in Joe Johnston's army. Hood was known as a bold fighter, if not a particularly smart one. One observer said that Hood might have a lion's heart, but there was a suspicion that he had "a wooden head." Jefferson Davis, nonetheless, wanted someone well aligned with the administration who would be a major conduit of information, and thus provide a reliable means of monitoring the operations of the western army.[14]

Joe Johnston, although an old Davis nemesis, had been appointed with reluctance by the president on December 16, 1863, to command the Army of Tennessee. Due to the limited selection of available senior generals, Johnston seemed the least objectionable. He had strong support in the Confederate Congress, and many in the army favored his appointment. Yet Davis was well aware of Joe Johnston's conservative style and uncommunicative ways, so by posting Hood with the Army of Tennessee he sought to scrutinize Johnston's compliance with the administration's policies and objectives. Hood, being generally unrecognized as a Davis man, was in a key position to keep his eye on Johnston's management of the army because Johnston was unlikely to suspect Hood of maintaining direct correspondence with Davis, Bragg, and other officials. Serving as the president's watchdog, Hood provided candid private information on Johnston's conduct and methods. As might be expected, given Hood's burning ambition and his awareness of the president's dislike and distrust of Johnston, the information he forwarded was highly distorted and subjective. He portrayed Joe Johnston in unfavorable terms and severly criticized his lack of initiative.[15]

The consequences were enormous. As Johnston idled during the early spring of 1864, protesting that he had neither sufficient transportation nor other means to take the offensive, Davis began using leverage to prod him forward. Together with Braxton Bragg, now his Richmond confidant and adviser, the president admonished Johnston, telling him that few reinforcements would be forthcoming for the Army of Tennessee until it began an offensive. Accordingly, in early April, Longstreet was ordered to return from east Tennessee to Lee's army rather than rejoin Joe Johnston's forces.

Johnston, believing his army badly outnumbered by William Tecumseh Sherman's troops in Chattanooga, remained adamant. He saw "no other mode of taking the offensive here [in Dalton, Georgia] than to beat the enemy when he advances, and then to move forward." In other words, Johnston planned to keep to the defensive, defeat Sherman when he advanced, then strike north to regain Tennessee thereafter.[16]

Since Davis became convinced that Johnston was merely making excuses for not attacking, he decided to allocate more of the Confederacy's limited resources to the Virginia theater, where it appeared the enemy would make their greatest effort. When Johnston countered with evidence that Sherman's army was more than one hundred thousand strong, and that a major enemy effort was in the offing against Atlanta, Bragg contradicted his claims, telling Jefferson Davis that Sherman had only about seventy thousand men by a "liberal" estimate. Davis, believing that the United States government would be unable to conduct large-scale offensives both in the East and West, and convinced that the enemy's Virginia forces were the troops to be reckoned with, subordinated the interests of Johnston's army. On hand to sustain Davis's opinion that Johnston was being deceitful about his situation and was unwilling to carry the war to the Yankees were various private letters from John Bell Hood, including one dated April 13:

[I] am sorry to inform you that I have done all in my power to induce General Johnston to accept the proposition you made to move forward. He will not consent. . . . I regret this exceedingly, as my heart was fixed upon our going to the front and regaining Tennessee and Kentucky. . . . When we are to be in a better condition to drive the enemy from our country I am not able to comprehend. To regain Tennessee would be of more value to us than a half dozen victories in Virginia.[17]

To his men, Joe Johnston seemed a kindly and popular commander, and they took an immediate liking to the small, dapper, fifty-six-year-old ex–United States Regular Army and West Point– educated general. "Old Joe," they termed him, and as the replacement for the despised Bragg, he was looked upon as a savior, a fresh breath of air for the mauled Army of Tennessee. Indeed, under Johnston, rations improved, and new issues of clothing and a regular system of furloughs pleased the soldiers. In place of the old attitude of "whatever should be done will be left undone, and whatever should not be done, Bragg will do," the army now seemed sanguine that under Joe Johnston they would fare well.[18]

Ordnance Sergeant John P. Kendall of the 5th Tennessee Infantry wrote in March 1864, "I have the utmost confidence in our present commander, Gen. Johnston, he is said not to fight unless he is certain of success. . . ." His brother, Lieutenant William D. Kendall of the same regiment, mirrored similar thoughts a month later. He wrote home, "[There is] no lack of confidence on either side [Joe Johnston's or the troops'], [for] we are satisfied that he knows how it is to be done, and I think he is equally satisfied we know how to do it."[19]

Once the active campaigning began, with Sherman's army advancing to outflank Johnston's position on the west at Dalton, Georgia, the Confederate commander was compelled to withdraw nearly halfway to Atlanta within a span of two weeks. A planned counterattack in the vicinity of Cassville, Georgia, failed because Hood belatedly discovered Federal cavalry in his rear, which caused him to hesitate and finally withdraw.[20]

Again retreating to the vicinity of Allatoona, and then Kennesaw Mountain, Joe Johnston was forced back to within twenty miles of Atlanta by mid-June. In what seemed to be a vindication of Johnston's defensive policies, a large-scale Union assault on the fortified lines at Kennesaw Mountain on June 27 failed spectacularly. The Yankees suffered more than two thousand casualties while the Confederates lost fewer than five hundred men.

So far, most of Johnston's men remained in good spirits and were hopeful. In fact, their morale had improved. One historian having located more than forty letters of the period that express an opinion about their commander, concluded that 90 percent of the army supported Johnston's policies in June, whereas only 70 percent expressed confidence in him just one month earlier. "The health and spirits of the troops are excellent," proclaimed Lieutenant William Kendall to his parents on June 24. "All are yet perfectly confident of an easy victory if the Yanks will only attack us. Our having to fall back has not dampened the spirits or ardor of any. We have inflicted heavy loss upon the enemy whenever he has given us a chance, while we have lost comparatively few." "Hell had broken lose in Georgia, sure enough!" said another Confederate soldier after fighting in the sweltering one-hundred-degree heat at Kennesaw Mountain.[21]

Johnston's tactics of fighting on the defensive from behind breastworks, and forcing the enemy to either attack in front or maneuver around the flank, seemed to be working. "We have got the best of every fight we have had with them," boasted rifleman John W. Hill on June 11, who noted that the Yankees' casualties were reported to be at thirty thousand men thus far. In his diary entry for July 3, Captain Mumford H. Dixon, 3rd Confederate Infantry, spoke volumes: "There is one thing we all know, or think so anyway, that is that we will whip the Yankees whenever and wherever we fight. Our confidence in ourselves and General [Johnston] is unshaken notwithstanding we have retreated eighty miles."[22]

Yet, further difficulty was imminent. When Sherman again outflanked Johnston from his lines near Marietta on July 1, the Confederate army soon withdrew to the line of the Chattahoochee River. Then, on the afternoon of July 8, some of Sherman's soldiers established a beachhead across that river east of Johnston's position. By the 9th, using pontoon boats, the Yankees had firmly secured the crossing site. Although on July 1 he claimed to visiting Confederate senator Benjamin Hill of Georgia that he could hold the line of the Chattahoochee River "for a long time," Johnston withdrew his army across the river into the outer network of Atlanta's defenses on July 9.[23]

This retreat came as a surprise to Johnston's troops, and by early July there was increasing concern among the men about their army withdrawing so far without a decisive battle. Writing from within two miles of Atlanta, a private of the 10th Texas Infantry noted in his diary on July 9, "Here we have stopped again, and perhaps [we] will give them a fight before we leave here. It seems we have gone as far as we ought to go unless we intend to give up all of our country and not fight anymore. That is not the idea—it is victory or death."[24]

After watching Johnston's army fall back without checking Sherman's relentless offensive against Atlanta, Private Robert D. Patrick of the 4th Louisiana Infantry wrote on July 15, "Our army is like a lion at bay, now and then turning in desperation on their relentless pursuers. [We] have literally disputed every inch of ground from Dalton, down to our present position. The[se] unexampled, desperate fighting qualities have even won the admiration of the Yankees, and as they say, 'it begets a sad regret that we are not engaged in a holier cause.' "[25]

A few days earlier, on July 10, the same soldier had grimly observed, "I don't believe Johnston can hold Atlanta. I am sorry to admit that, as the Frenchman says, 'I am losing the grand confidence'. . . . If Sherman whips Johnston out of Atlanta, we may bid farewell to this part of the country, for I have yet to hear of our ever retaking any captured territory."[26]

In fact, Joe Johnston had been pushed back as far as he could go without losing Atlanta. Warily watching these alarming events were the Richmond officials, many of whom fretted about Johnston's intentions to defend Atlanta. Since Johnston provided meager explanations about the withdrawals, and was secretive about his forthcoming plans, Davis sent Braxton Bragg to Atlanta on a personal fact-finding mission on July 9.

Bragg arrived on the 13th and met that day with Johnston. He never disclosed the nature of his visit, asked few questions, and offered no advice to Johnston. His presence was a mystery to Johnston's staff; perhaps his appearance was only the unofficial visit of a functionary, they thought.[27]

Bragg's extensive correspondence to Davis revealed just how mistaken they were. His disdainful telegrams and letters reported that Johnston's depleted army had lost ten thousand men since June 10, and that Johnston proposed no offensive operations. Although Johnston later claimed he was then making plans to attack Sherman's troops as they crossed Peachtree Creek, Bragg wrote otherwise, claiming he had no evidence that Johnston "has any more plan for the future than he has in the past." Having met with John Bell Hood and other friends who provided damaging information, Bragg forwarded three telegrams and a lengthy letter by special courier on July 15 condemning Johnston for being weak and for vacillating.[28]

About the time these reports arrived, Senator Benjamin Hill came to Richmond and relayed to Davis Johnston's assertion that he could hold the line of the Chattahoochee for at least a month. Davis only grimaced. He had on hand Johnston's telegram of July 10, reporting that he had withdrawn across the Chattahoochee River to Atlanta's outer defenses!

On July 17 a telegram was sent to Atlanta relieving Joseph E. Johnston from command of the Army of Tennessee.

Taking his place was the man who had been Jefferson Davis's private informant, John Bell Hood.[29]

"God damn Jeff Davis!" came the shouts from the ranks on July 18. "Hurrah for Joe Johnston," they continued. Within minutes of hearing the news, "groups of three, five, seven, ten or fifteen men could be seen all over camp discussing the situation," noted one of Cleburne's stunned line officers, Captain Samuel T. Foster. Foster's ire was roused:

General Johnston has so endeared himself to his soldiers that no man can take his place. We have never made a fight under him that we did not get the best of it. And the whole army had become so attached to him, and put such implicit faith in him, that whenever he said for us to fight at any particular place we went in feeling like Gen. Johnston knew all about it and we were certain to whip. He never deceived us once. . . . He was always looking after our comfort and safety. He would investigate our breastworks in person, make suggestions as to any little addition or improvement that would make them safer or more comfortable. Gen. Johnston could not have issued an order that these men would not have undertaken to accomplish. For the first time, we hear men openly talk about going home, by tens and fifties. They refuse to stand guard, or do any other camp duty, and talk of open rebellion against all military authority. All over camp can be seen this demoralization.[30]

The following day the clamor continued. "The noise and confusion was kept up all night," said Foster. "General Johnston was serenaded, and if Jeff Davis had made his appearance in this army during the excitement he would not have lived an hour."[31]

Johnston's dismissal was a highly emotional matter to the Army of Tennessee, for his ouster "took all by complete surprise and cast a deep shade of sadness upon the army," admitted a Tennessee lieutenant on July 19. Joe Johnston "had their confidence fully," he continued. "All regarded him as the general to command this veteran army . . . and [we] mourn his departure deeply. . . ." Since there was no official explanation for this action, the lack of information not only confused the troops but depressed them and shattered their morale as well. Johnston's removal is "a mystery which no one seems to divine," wrote one officer. "None can see the least cause for it in his management of the army on the present campaign. In fact, all have been struck with admiration by the care, skill, and military tact with which he has conducted the retreat from Dalton. Madame Rumor, for once, is speechless, and attempts no solution of the strange, inexplicable action of the Richmond Military Dept."[32]

Johnston's departure thus was both a shock and a glaring revelation that the Richmond authorities either knew little about the soldiers' opinions and circumstances or didn't care about them. "By this act the army was outraged," fumed Captain Elbert D. Willett of the 40th Alabama on July 18. "An older, experienced and successful commander relieved for one untried at this critical period in so important a campaign—it came like a thunderbolt to the army; so unexpected, so undeserved." "I can bear witness to the spirit of mutiny that filled the minds of the troops, who to a man, were willing to throw down their arms and quit," wrote a Tennessee private in his diary on July 18. "[It is] a fatal blunder, that removal of Johnston. Old Joe was our idol."[33]

While the reaction to Johnston's removal was extensive, sincere, and profound, Hood's appointment inspired uncertainty. As an outsider, and one who was largely unknown to the Army of Tennessee, Hood provoked mixed emotions among the men. Tennessean William D. Kendall informed his parents on July 19, "Of our new general we do not know a great deal . . . [yet] we will follow Gen. Hood with the same spirit and determination that we have cherished during our soldier lives. . . . We are soldiers and must bear our sorrow and do our duty."[34]

Captain Samuel Kelly, a Johnston supporter who did not "object to Hood," hoped the change was for the best. Another soldier observed that while most regretted the loss of Johnston, some were "perfectly satisfied" with Hood.[35]

Amid the pros and cons of Hood's selection as the new Confederate commander were the remarks of one of his former fellow classmates at West Point, who was now a Yankee general in Sherman's army. In a letter to his wife on July 23, Major General Oliver O. Howard minced few words in his remembrance of Hood. "He is a stupid fellow but a hard fighter—does very unexpected things."[36]

Despite the sudden controversy, about one thing nearly all could agree—a big fight was imminent. Hood's mandate from the Davis administration was apparent in Johnston's removal order. Old Joe had been replaced since he had "failed to arrest the advance of the enemy to the vicinity of Atlanta." On July 18 Davis instructed Hood to correct "a [defensive] policy which had proved so disastrous."[37]

Yet, Hood was now on the spot as an outsider—another Virginian who had been sent west to correct matters—and whose appointment greatly aggravated some senior western officers. Worse still, he was no longer in a strategically strong position with Richmond as the administration's favorite son and Johnston critic. Instead, he was expected to demonstrate the success of his theories of offensive warfare and the merit of his bold criticisms of Johnston.

Beyond any anticipated success in the coming battle, of the greatest importance to the men was the prospect of winning the war. Prior to the beginning of the Atlanta Campaign, a Tennessee sergeant had written:

There are a good many flattering themselves with the belief that
peace will be made before there is another battle fought. . . . But I
can see no just ground on which to found such a belief. [I] think it
is done to encourage the timid and to cheer all. Without the inter-
cession of some foreign power, or a division of sentiment in the
North, or a decided victory and almost a total annihilation of a
branch of the Federal army, I can discern nothing verging toward
peace. They have the advantage of us in everything except in valor
and generalship [Joe Johnston was then commanding], [and] have
been driving us back. . . . Can anything like peace be deduced from
these facts, unless it is the Confederacy's yielding—which I know is
not the case.[38]

Yet, another soldier, A. J. Neal of the Marion Light Artillery, had
been so optimistic that he wrote in May, "I hope the Yankees will
assault our lines, for I want a victory here to balance those in Virginia
and out West. I fear the Yankees will fall back and not give us the
opportunity we so much desire. I am of the opinion that such a victory
here as Shiloh, Murfreesboro [Stones River], or Chickamauga, would
end the war speedily."[39]

Neal was not far from making a reasonable interpretation of the
truth as the summer of 1864 wore on. The stalemate in Virginia,
including the devastating losses of Grant's overland campaign, combined with Sherman's heavy losses and frustration at not engaging
Johnston in a decisive battle, had accentuated the war-weariness of
the North. A major Confederate victory might bend the will of the
Northern people. With the presidential election coming in November, this summer's campaigning would serve as a referendum on the
war.[40]

For their leader in accomplishing this crucial task, the Army of
Tennessee now had a man who had ranked at the very bottom of his
West Point class in ethics, and nearly so in tactics. His idea of combat
was couched in his inflexible credo of direct, vigorous attack. There
would be no more fighting the enemy with "picks and shovels," like
his predecessor did, said John Bell Hood. Instead, the army would
use their guns. And their bodies.[41]

Chapter Twenty-five

BEATING THEIR OWN BRAINS OUT

On July 19, 1864, the men of the 5th Tennessee Infantry were issued sixty rounds of cartridges. "This is always evidence that a fight is imminent," wrote a lieutenant who anticipated stopping "the flanking game of Sherman."[1]

The fight for Atlanta was about to take a crucial turn, and the men expected hard combat; some awaited the battle with trepidation over the loss of Joe Johnston as their commander, others with a grim resolve to do their duty under John Bell Hood. Whatever the soldiers' sentiments, the general impression throughout the Army of Tennessee was that they were as ready to fight as ever. No matter what, said an Arkansas private, "we fought for the cause, not the general."[2]

Although things "looked squally enough," mused a Tennessee veteran on July 19th, he hoped that Hood wouldn't let "the 'blue bellies' get all around us." Artillery Captain Thomas J. Key also pondered the situation, and on the same day reported, "The eventful period of a great battle cannot long be postponed. We have retreated as far as policy or safety will admit."[3]

Key was correct. Within seventy-two hours, on July 20, the Army of Tennessee was striking at Sherman's forces at Peachtree Creek. They struck again just east of Atlanta on July 22. Hood's large-scale assaults resulted in the most ferocious fighting of the summer, and affected the spirit of the army for months to come.

Typical of many Confederates' experiences was that of Georgia Colonel James C. Nisbet, whose regiment, the 66th and 26th Georgia Battalion (consolidated), attacked on the morning of July 20 at Peachtree Creek. Notified that the enemy had just crossed the creek that morning, and thus were not fortified, Nisbet and his men rushed on, only to find plenty of Yankees behind "well constructed earthworks" directly in front. Although Nisbet's men and some other troops captured a portion of the line, many fell victim to an enfilade fire and were swept back by enemy reinforcements because they were unsupported. Having lost one-fourth of their officers and men, Nisbet and his regiment were forced to abandon the captured works and run for cover.[4]

The Confederate leaders learned that many enemy troops had crossed Peachtree Creek the previous evening, and, as customary, most had promptly fortified their position. "Hood was acting on misinformation," noted Nisbet, "and the fight was a miserable affair on his part, from start to finish. For the want of concert of action, the army lost many valuable lives and accomplished nothing of benefit."[5]

Two days later, during the Battle of Atlanta (or Bald Hill), Hood's sortie to attack the Federal column advancing east of Atlanta again miscarried when delay, bad luck, and poorly timed charges resulted in a significant and bloody failure. Hood's flanking column under Major General William J. Hardee had difficulty finding their way during a 15-mile night march, was blocked by a flooded mill pond, and after being rerouted, struck the refused flanks of the enemy line, rather than hitting them beyond their defensive perimeter, as intended. When Hood delayed attacking a separate front with Frank Cheatham's corps until Hardee had been beaten back, the uncoordinated assaults resulted in losses of between fifty-five hundred and eight thousand compared to Yankee casualties of half that number.*

"It did seem hard," complained a South Carolina officer who led one of Cheatham's attacks on July 22 against the same entrenchments their brigade had vacated under orders the day before. "We had built these breastworks, given them up to the enemy, retaken them at a very heavy sacrifice, and now we had to give them up again. The whole struggle of the afternoon, the lives lost, the suffering inflicted,

---

*Albert Castel, in *Decision in the West,* p. 412, places the Confederate loss at about 5,500 from perhaps 35,000 present; Thomas L. Livermore, in *Numbers and Losses in the Civil War,* p. 123, estimates the loss at 7,000 killed and wounded and 1,000 missing.

had all been for nothing. And this was but an example of what happened to us of the Western army very often; marches, skirmishes, battles, all seemingly with no good result."[6]

In a third attempt, Hood ordered a desperate assault at Ezra Church, west of Atlanta, on July 28. Here the Yankee defenders again had time to entrench themselves or erect breastworks on high ground. Lieutenant General Stephen D. Lee's unsupported and uncoordinated attacks were shattered at the cost of nearly five thousand Confederate casualties. In little more than a week, Hood had squandered about fifteen thousand men in fruitless attacks that did little to stop Sherman's relentless campaign against Atlanta.[7]

Hood's controversial abilities as a general were now fully in focus. While planning Army of Northern Virginia–style flank attacks, Hood had ignored the evolved 1864 manner of warfare. The tactical defensive now ruled the battlefield. Due to the inevitable presence of at least rude breastworks, his soldiers' found difficulty in routing any hours-in-position enemy force. Furthermore, Hood's absence from the immediate locale of crucial operations served to hinder rapid communications, which were of vital tactical importance in attack coordination.

Hood's offensive strikes at Sherman's forces resulted in a military failure of unprecedented magnitude, and he now had little choice but to withdraw into Atlanta's extensive line of fortifications and endure the misery of siege warfare. Within days, the crumbling walls of Atlanta's shot-riddled houses and buildings symbolized the increasing gloom felt by soldiers and citizens alike.

The survivors among Hood's men mulled over these bloody events in the wake of Joe Johnston's removal, and a sampling of their opinions reveals a growing awareness about a new era in battlefield tactics.

"We got near the works, but our fire done them but little damage as they was protected by splendid earthworks, and was literally mowing our men down," wrote an Arkansas captain of the charge at Ezra Church. "We fell back with fearful loss, the worst we had in any one battle . . . for the number of men engaged in it. The report was that we went into that charge with 2,600 guns, and lost about 1,300 killed and wounded. . . . This battle discouraged our men badly, as they could never understand why they should have been sent in to such a death trap, to be butchered up with no hope of gaining anything. . . . We fell back to our line in a terrible, shattered, and demoralized condition."[8]

Many participants noted the toll the fighting had taken in soldiers' lives only a few days after Hood took command, and their despair was profound. "The fine army of Gen. Johnston was thus decimated in five days without any beneficial results," wrote a Georgia colonel. Another eyewitness, a soldier with the 1st Arkansas, was dismayed by the affair at Bald Hill on July 22 and remarked "The splendid, unconquered army was swept off the earth into the grave. . . . This was Hood's second defeat. In two battles he had lost 10,000 men—more than we had lost in the whole campaign, in seventy-four days' battles and skirmishes. It would not take long with such tactics to wipe out [our] army."[9]*

Even their Federal enemies were appalled at what had happened. A Yankee major who was a staff officer of the XVI Corps wrote to his wife on July 31 that after the Ezra Church fight he rode "over a space about 400 yards long by about 75 yards in width." In that area, he "scanned the faces of 225 dead Rebels, and then had not seen more than one-third of those who lay there." It was a sobering experience and the major expressed his amazement:

I returned feeling very thankful that I was not a Rebel and especially a dead Rebel. The Rebel loss in their several attacks on us since we crossed the river must be full 20,000, while ours has scarcely reached one third that number. I felt satisfied that the Rebels would fight to the bitter end for Atlanta, . . . but did not expect them to manifest such senseless desperation. Why, it was perfect murder. We slaughter them by the thousands, but Hood continues to hurl his broken, bleeding battalions against our immovable lines, with all the fury of a maniac. Reason seems dethroned, and despair alone seems to rule the counsels within the walls of Atlanta. Nothing but defeat and utter destruction stares Hood in the face.[10]

*Some historians have contended that many soldiers saw Hood's sorties around Atlanta as "victories," citing that they claimed in their letters that they had punished the enemy severely, and boasted about capturing prisoners and cannon. Based upon the preponderance of evidence, it appears these were largely expressions of limited tactical victory amid the greater, overall context of the various battles, which were, of course, severe defeats. The few cases of enthusiasm for Hood's bold aggressiveness seem to represent future hopefulness more than the writer's strong conviction. See Larry Daniel, *Soldiering the Army of Tennessee*, 144–49, and Richard McMurry, "Confederate Morale in the Atlanta Campaign," *Georgia Historical Quarterly*, no. 44 (1970): 226–43.

A sergeant with the 127th Illinois Infantry wrote after the Battle of Atlanta:

We buried 2,420 Rebs and sent over under a flag of truce to the Rebs 800 dead, which makes 3,220 dead Rebs that we know of. . . . We kill a great many Rebs in the fights, now more than ever, because they come out from their works and charge our men, which is useless for them. For they do not do any good, only get their men *slaughtered.* Our men [began] the other day in burying the Rebs. They smelled so they got a rope and put [it] around their necks, and four or five [men] get a hold and start with him, drawing them up in line, just as they lay R. R. ties. It looks rough . . . , you know how a piece of fresh meat would look all covered with fly blows.[11]

At the Battle of Ezra Church on July 28, the same soldier described how the Rebels had been caught out in the open and took cover behind a fence. "[They] laid in line of battle behind a chesnut rail fence, dead as stones, our balls passing through the rails as if [they were] nothing more than paper." The Yankee generals believed Hood's tactics would only result in killing his own men. When informed on July 28th that the Rebels were making a determined assault on John Logan's corps at Ezra Church, William Tecumseh Sherman responded, "That's fine, just what I wanted, just what I wanted. Tell Howard [Logan's commander] to invite them to attack. It will save us trouble. . . . They'll only beat their own brains out."[12]

Ironically, prior to the advent of John Bell Hood, many in the Confederate army were convinced that by inflicting large losses on Sherman's columns they would win by exhausting the Yankees' reservoir of men faster than they could be replaced. "If we can keep this up," Captain James I. Hall of the 9th Tennessee had predicted, "we will win." Now the situation was exactly reversed, and many Confederates questioned their own survival. "Our death or permanent disability [seems] . . . merely a question of time," wrote a gloomy Confederate officer.[13]

Perhaps the ultimate indictment of Hood and his methods was written by a quartermaster's clerk following Peachtree Creek. "There seems to be a general dissatisfaction among the men on account of the headlong way in which they were put in yesterday," he confided in his diary. "They think that it 'costs more than it comes to.' They say Hood cares no more for the lives of his men than Grant does."[14]

Hood's army had been both physically and mentally devastated, and although Hood had often sought to outflank the enemy, the tactical reality was far different from the strategic conception. Generals might conceive of bold plans to strike an enemy position in flank, but in the new era of warfare that tactic wasn't easy. Regiments habitually entrenched themselves upon halting for the evening after a march, or when occupying a position near the enemy for any length of time. The ability of veteran troops to prepare rude but effective cover upon short notice was frequently demonstrated during the Atlanta Campaign. Indeed, by 1864, assaults were rarely made without facing some form of prepared barricade, and frontal attacks against such defensive positions were usually devastating to the attackers.

Winning a pitched battle was a far more sophisticated process than merely fighting the enemy on a chosen field or planning an aggressive flanking march. The concept that your opponent, be he Yankee or Rebel, was an incapable or inferior fighter had been disproved early in the war. Therefore, if combat success was expected, factors of time, place, and circumstances had to be taken into account, along with an effective method of fighting. Only the combination of these elements would provide an advantage over an equally determined and capable foe.

Tactical expertise was the key to winning battles. Flexible, innovative concepts, and a logical use of manpower, were of more importance than textbook theory. Commanders adept enough to understand the ever-changing battlefield had the most potential for attaining victory.

Within the Army of Tennessee existed perhaps the finest combat general in the Confederacy, Major General Patrick R. Cleburne. Cleburne's remarkable military talent stemmed from his great common sense. An intelligent and thoughtful man, he nurtured individual soldiers as effective fighting instruments rather than abstract components of massed ranks. Cleburne trained each soldier to use his full capabilities on the battlefield and obtained the best weapons for his men, usually Enfield rifle muskets for the infantry, and costly Whitworth and Kerr rifles for his battalion of sharpshooters.

On the battlefield, Cleburne had learned and crafted combat tactics to such a point that he stood alone in his brilliance. Aware of the futility of piecemeal frontal attacks such as those employed at Shiloh, he tried to avoid when possible the headlong assaults that had so devastated the Confederate ranks.

Cleburne's tactical innovations were perhaps the best evidence of his importance to the army. In mid-1862, he organized a select battalion of sharpshooters to disrupt the enemy at extended ranges. Also, at Perryville, Kentucky, Cleburne repeatedly demonstrated his ability to innovate. Here he placed battle flags in the forward line of skirmishers as they advanced over a hill, leading the enemy to think that they were the main line of battle. His scheme caused the Yankees to empty their rifle muskets at the skirmishers, and they were unable to reload before Cleburne's second, main line attacked. Pat Cleburne's masterful management of the fighting at Tunnel Hill on north Missionary Ridge at Chattanooga was probably never excelled by any commander during the war. By rapidly shifting about his four thousand troops, Cleburne had decisively beaten William Tecumseh Sherman, who had thirty thousand men. Twice during the war he won the formal thanks of the Confederate Congress for his battlefield exploits.[15]

During the Atlanta Campaign, many of the interbattle tactical victories gained by the Confederates were achieved by Patrick Cleburne's troops, even though these successes ultimately resulted only in lost opportunities. Directed to make exposed frontal attacks, Cleburne attempted to overcome the folly of such orders to whatever extent possible with innovative tactical deployments. On July 22, his skirmishers were ordered to approach Federal lines through heavy underbrush without firing a gun, so as not to alert the enemy of the attack in mass. To facilitate speed in the attack, the men were instructed not to stop for spoils or return with any prisoners, but to push rapidly on with their full strength.

The subsequent assaults by Cleburne's Arkansas brigade, commanded by Brigadier General Daniel C. Govan, carried a formidable line of abatis-protected earthworks—regarded as an impossible task by many, including Federal major general Oliver O. Howard. Yet the accomplishments of Cleburne's division were negated by subsequent delays and a lack of support. The battle for Bald Hill on the 22d resulted in the useless sacrifice of many of Cleburne's valiant men, including 492 of Govan's 772 effectives (a 64 percent loss).[16]

The results of the Atlanta fighting seemed only to confirm what was widely known—that Cleburne's soldiers were the Army of Tennessee's shock troops, the men to be relied on in a crisis. Daniel C. Govan candidly asserted, "It really seems as if it were intended that we should do the fighting of the army—as where the severest opposition is to be encountered there we are surely to be placed."[17]

Notwithstanding the lofty combat record of Cleburne's men, most Confederate soldiers displayed a common bond of dedication during the Atlanta fighting. Besides Cleburne's division, there were plenty of other Confederate soldiers within the Tennessee army who were still infused with valor and commitment. A veteran staff officer with the Army of Northern Virginia acknowledged as much, assessing during his tenure with Longstreet's troops in the Army of Tennessee, "The raw material [here] is first class" and was "only badly mangled by Bragg's incompetency."[18]

Despite Hood's gross tactical misuse of the Army of Tennessee, there were many veterans of this proud but ragged army who were yet willing to continue trying until death or total defeat.

Because of this intense commitment, a key question loomed in the minds of many in midsummer 1864: would the troops' determination and valor be enough to keep Sherman from capturing Atlanta that summer? It was a critical matter, for, as an element of timing, even the outcome of the war seemed to totter on events that would be decided during that campaign's fiery ordeal.

As the siege of Atlanta continued throughout August, the Confederates' situation seemed strangely out of sorts. Rather than the Army of Northern Virginia receiving most of the publicity, it was the Army of Tennessee that was in the limelight. The midsummer of 1864 had witnessed a stalemate in the Virginia fighting, and it was increasingly apparent that the pending decision in the West would have enormous impact on the issue of Southern independence. In fact, the necessity of a major battlefield victory at Atlanta seemed to require an all-out effort from both sides. The politics of the war demanded such.

At the beginning of August, the war-weary North teetered on the verge of despair. Grant was bogged down in an unpromising siege south of Richmond, had lost heavily in terms of both men and prestige, and soon became known as "butcher Grant." The situation in the Shenandoah Valley was equally doubtful; the new Federal commander, Phil Sheridan, had advanced, then retreated, and hadn't been able to defeat forces sent from Lee's army under Jubal Early. In Georgia, Sherman was barred from Atlanta by Hood's aggressive attacks, which had resulted in a prolonged siege. Even "that devil

Forrest" was loose in Mississippi and western Tennessee, wreaking havoc among Federal garrisons with his will-o'-the-wisp cavalry raids. There was little good news to be had for the Lincoln administration. Despite Admiral David Farragut's victory in Mobile Bay, that city yet remained in Confederate hands.[19]

Amid these events, the Northern Copperheads, or Peace Democrats, decreed the war "an utter failure," even while they pointed out that the carnage would long continue. "Seventy-five thousand tons of human blood have been spilled in Dixie's soil . . . and the end is not yet," heralded the *Jefferson County [New York] Union*. A negotiated peace to end the war—initiated by an armistice—was the answer, said some. Moreover, the war, which was begun to preserve the Union, now involved the freeing of slaves, thanks to the special interests and views of a fanatical minority, warned the *New York World* on August 18. "Until this ceases to be the case, the stacks of corpses will grow higher, . . . and the government, already on the brink of bankruptcy, will be engulfed in total financial collapse, dragging down everything and everybody with it." The solution to saving the nation, the *World* declared, would come in November with the presidential elections, when Lincoln might be voted from office.[20]

These conflicts represented to the Confederacy a grand opportunity; perhaps they needed only wait two months for the North to self-destruct. The South would surely survive that period, but would the Northern war effort? Should various Union armies be severely defeated or annihilated, the effect was not hard to imagine. If the dismal war news continued to be publicized in the North, then their ongoing draft would perhaps fail, and the veterans of Federal regiments whose time was expiring might go home without reenlisting.

Even without Union military defeat, the war situation seemed promising for the South. Rancorous politicians at the Democratic convention were certain to spread seeds of discord throughout the North. The terrible toll in Northern lives and the devastating cost of fighting would hit home that summer as never before.

As the *Richmond Sentinel* proclaimed on August 20, 1864: "Six weeks hence we are almost sure to be in a much better condition to treat for peace than we are now, and our enemy in a much worse condition. . . . We have little to apprehend and much to hope for within that period. Time is victory to us and death to our enemies."[21]

Victory seemed within the South's reach; all that was necessary to obtain peace was to deny the North a major military triumph. The want of Union military success, and the alleged impracticality of defeating the South while the emancipation of slaves remained a major issue, were factors that would intensify sentiments for peace in the minds of the Northern public.

Over the next two months, the Union intended to rely on the abilities of Ulysses S. Grant, Philip H. Sheridan, and William Tecumseh Sherman. Countering them on the Confederate side were Robert E. Lee, General Jubal A. Early, and John Bell Hood. Editor Edwin Pollard wrote in the August 30 *Richmond Examiner,* "The prospects of the Confederacy were never brighter and better."[22]

Rather than winning by waiting, Hood's men expressed other, more practical thoughts as the siege of Atlanta dragged on throughout August. By that point, they were suffering the consequences of physical and mental hardship. Food had become scarce to the point of affecting morale, and even sleep was difficult to obtain. "There is very little rest here, or sleep either," wrote a haggard Georgia rifleman in late August. "It grows hard with the soldiers, [and] we get very little fruit or vegetables . . . Irish potatoes [are] worth $1 per quart, dry peas . . . from $2 to $3 per dozen, watermelons [cost] from $1 to $15 apiece."[23]

Despite many shortages and his soldiers' ordeal, Hood attempted to keep up the spirits of his army by asserting that Sherman's flanking maneuvers had been stopped. The enemy would soon be forced to assault Atlanta's strong defenses, in which case victory would be certain, he suggested.

Yet Hood had lost the initiative in Georgia and now relied on sending Major General Joseph Wheeler's cavalry against Sherman's long railroad lines of supply, which stretched from Nashville and Chattanooga southward. Believing that by cutting off many of Sherman's supplies he could compel him to storm Atlanta's defenses or retreat, Hood eagerly awaited the results of Wheeler's foray.

Beginning August 10, Joe Wheeler's month-long raid with about four thousand troopers achieved little. After destroying a few miles of track in north Georgia, Wheeler scurried into east Tennessee, then made a roundabout dash through midstate. He belatedly rejoined the Army of Tennessee by taking a circuitous route through Alabama.[24]

Meanwhile, having failed with his own cavalry raids to cut Hood's railroad lines south of Atlanta, William Tecumseh Sherman broke off the siege of Atlanta in late August and suddenly disappeared. Instead of departing north, however, Sherman began shifting nearly his entire army southwest of the city to seize Hood's two remaining railroads.

Believing Wheeler's cavalry raid might have forced Sherman into retreating north, Hood carelessly allowed Sherman's men to gain a lodgment on the vital Macon and Western Railroad near Jonesboro before responding. Then, thinking the Yankee thrust at Jonesboro was only a diversion while the enemy prepared to attack Atlanta from the south, Hood attempted to shuffle troops in different directions as he repeatedly changed his estimation of what Sherman was planning. Hood's faulty strategy caused Hardee's expeditionary force to attack on August 31 the Yankees who had entrenched behind rude breastworks in the vicinity of Jonesboro.[25]

The final result at Atlanta was inevitable. A Confederate survivor of Jonesboro wrote in his journal that night, "They [the enemy] were armed with breechloaders and . . . had built some breastworks of rails, and had position along the edge of a field, across which we had to charge to get to them. They just fairly made it rain bullets. . . ."[26]

The next day, Sherman was able to deploy four corps of infantry on Hardee's front and decisively beat the heavily outnumbered defenders. As Hardee withdrew south to Lovejoy's Station, Hood hastily ordered the evacuation of Atlanta at 5 P.M. on September 1, barely escaping to the southeast with the remnants of his army during an all-night march.

Confederate engineers set on fire twenty-eight railcar loads of Hood's reserve ammunition supply to prevent them from falling into enemy hands. Hood's sullen ranks trudged from the stricken, abandoned city as all of the ammunition exploded at once. On the morning of September 2 the Yankees were in Atlanta, and by that afternoon their bands were heard playing "Hail Columbia" amid loud shouts and cheering from Sherman's troops.

Atlanta had fallen, and with it went the Confederacy's best chance for a negotiated peace.[27]

Unwilling to accept the blame, John Bell Hood placed the onus on Hardee for losing at Peachtree Creek, Atlanta, and Jonesboro. His quartermaster was blamed for abandoning the stores in Atlanta. The army's regimental officers were cited for a "want of discipline," and even the soldiers were impugned for their lack of courage. "There is a tacit if not expressed determination among the men of this army, extending to officers as high in some instances as colonel, that they will not attack breastworks," Hood brazenly complained to Braxton Bragg on September 4. On September 10, Hood sent a telegram to Richmond begging Bragg to "please ask Gen. Lee to send me my old division." Maybe they could show the Army of Tennessee how to fight.[28]

Even worse, Hood seemed to have learned little from the fighting, and continued to adhere to his foolish "headlong attack" concepts. Following the Battle of Atlanta on July 22, he chided his soldiers, "Experience has proved to you that safety . . . in battle consists in getting into close quarters with your enemy. [Captured] guns and colors are the only unerring indications of victory. The valor of the troops is easily estimated . . . by the number of these secured."[29]

By now, the majority of men and officers had come to dread the folly of Hood's "killing times." Major General Samuel G. French, a division commander, was so aggrieved over the widespread "feeling of depression" in the army that on September 14 he personally implored Jefferson Davis to investigate their circumstances. Already, so many soldiers had abandoned the ranks after the Atlanta fighting that Hood beseeched President Davis for emergency funds, citing his "urgent appeals" to pay the troops in order to help keep the men from deserting in crippling numbers.[30]

Beyond having to cope with his tactical ignorance, had his men known of Hood's private correspondence questioning their courage, there likely would have been more actions like those of Private Van Buren Oldham of the 9th Tennessee Infantry. On July 29, Oldham recorded in his diary, "The plan Gen'l Hood has adopted of charging breastworks . . . will soon leave him without an army, if continued as hitherto."

A few weeks later, Private Oldham, a veteran soldier who had fought valiantly in the ranks since April 1862 at Shiloh, decided to go home and swear allegiance to the United States government.[31]

Chapter Twenty-six

SANDIE PENDLETON

"Suffering Somewhat in the Good Cause"

Major Sandie Pendleton had been disillusioned. The devastating defeat at Gettysburg, coming in the aftermath of Stonewall Jackson's death, was both depressing and ominous. Yet, as a proud Virginian devoted to the Southern cause, Sandie quickly made his resilience evident. A young man with supreme confidence in Robert E. Lee and the fighting spirit of the Army of Northern Virginia, Pendleton after Gettysburg possessed a reasoned attitude of persistence, patience, and stout if somewhat forced optimism.

Sandie revealed his faith in an ultimate Southern success to his fiancée, Kate Corbin, by asserting only days after Gettysburg, "The enemy dare not come out of his works to fight." He further claimed that the Army of Northern Virginia remained "in elegant spirits" but was "perfectly furious at the thought of having been whipped." Sandie wrote that Lee's army was "ready for another advance, and confident of victory." "The sky of the Confederacy seems overcast, but 'tis only the clearing up shower," he reflected. Even the loss of Vicksburg and Port Hudson was "of no intrinsic importance," as the prisoners taken by the enemy would soon be exchanged, thus "the loss of materiel and prestige is all we gave up." These events might cause the Southern people to awaken to the danger, and "appreciate more thoroughly that we are battling for existence," Sandie concluded. Finally, the lost battles seemed only to "protract the struggle," and the Confederacy "nil desperandum" could "fight on, and forever."[1]

Later, perhaps mindful of his overly sanguine expressions, Sandie revealed his innermost thoughts to Kate: "Of one thing only I am sure, that to the war shall my powers be devoted until it or I am finished by act of God. And if the latter, which I do not anticipate, I hope to be ready to go."[2]

Were his words a prophecy, or merely an expression of his resolve? These thoughts must have whirled through Kate's mind, and touched the core of their commitment to the Confederacy and to one other.

For the past few months, Kate had immersed herself in plans for their wedding in the fall. After traveling to Richmond in July 1863 to gather her trousseau, Kate Corbin shared a brief few days in August with Sandie at her brother's Moss Neck residence, and they had agreed on a wedding date of October 23. Meanwhile, perhaps ominously, a new bonnet purchased in Richmond for her honeymoon was ruined when a roof leaked during a heavy rainstorm.[3]

Soon the couple was forced to postpone their wedding. On September 13, 1863, Kate's brother Richard Corbin, the owner of Moss Neck and a private in the 9th Virginia Cavalry, was killed in a skirmish near Culpeper, Virginia. Kate immediately went into mourning, and Sandie found himself in the midst of the Bristoe Campaign, after which he hoped to obtain a thirty-day furlough to be married.

While visiting Moss Neck in late October, Sandie was able to arrange for a November 25 wedding ceremony, provided the army's situation then allowed his absence. By family decree, Kate would be married in black, with few attendants, due to the extended period of mourning for her brother.[4]

Yet, in November Sandie participated in the Mine Run Campaign, against a short, ill-advised offensive launched by General Meade. Although the maneuvering was to be relatively brief, General Lee canceled all leaves of absence, and Sandie lamented to Kate, "I was in high feather at the thought of getting my furlough, when, lo, this morning all my dreams vanished to thin air . . . [due to] the order of Gen. Lee." His presence was "important here," he told Kate, and although postponement of the wedding was "a most bitter disappointment," he would "try and bear up."[5]

Sandie was torn between two powerful attractions. His restless martial spirit had manifested itself throughout the late summer and fall of 1863. Following his promotion to lieutenant colonel on General Ewell's staff in August, Sandie expressed to Kate his profound feelings:

The distant sound of heavy cannon at Culpeper comes to my ear like music. It delights me, for it promises action, energy, movement, excitement—something to do in exchange for the lazy, idle existence of the last few weeks. I do not love fighting. Far from it, [for] I get horribly frightened every battle I go into. But I am tired of camp, and being shut up to one place, and would like to be off once more after the Yankees—to hear again the shout of victory go up from a glorious field, and know that the Army of Northern Virginia has struck another blow for the freedom of our land. If the prospect of . . . separation [due to] battle is saddening, we must submit to suffer somewhat in the good cause.[6]

Although a romantic, Sandie was cognizant of wartime realities, and he confided to his mother the pressures he felt regarding his impending marriage. "I begin to get afraid of the responsibility of marriage," he admitted, "and have a sort of feeling that, during the war, a man should not run the risk of entailing misery upon a woman he loves. However, I have no idea of withdrawing now, but I cannot prevent this feeling of shirking."[7]

Kate was equally confused, and had become depressed, her moods shifting from "an agony of suspense" to nervous resignation. In November 1863 she wrote to Sandie about her despondency and suggested breaking off the engagement. During "a flying trip" to Moss Neck in mid-November to save their "ill-starred" romance, Sandie persuaded Kate to have faith and patience, and although the wedding was postponed indefinitely, he hoped to return in December to claim his bride.[8]

On November 25, the second intended date of their wedding, Sandie wrote to Kate that although battle was imminent, he would "go into the next fight . . . with a light heart. I have done what I could to make our life happy here upon earth. I trust to be spared to add to that happiness. . . . [Yet] with all my natural anxiety for the issue, and shrinking from the dangers, I long for a battle that another victory may be gained and our cause thus made to look brighter, and the hopes of our army and our people be raised by a grand success. . . ."[9]

The next day, Sandie confided in a loving letter, "I am, I know,

now a much better man than before I loved you. And oh! I do love you so much."[10]

Clearly, Sandie was in love, but duty was foremost, and his code of honor remained strict. With the defeat of Bragg's army at Chattanooga he reminded Kate, "The war must become a part of all our religion. I trust to make it so myself. Since the defeat of Bragg's [army] all must be fully determined to give everything, even life, for the cause. I believe I am. But I hope it won't come to that, for I do want, oh! so much to live for you and with you, and enjoy the blessings of home in our own free land."[11]

On November 25, at Moss Neck, guests for the wedding arrived without having learned of the postponement. "You would have laughed," wrote Kate to a friend, "to see the wedding party assemble on the 25th and look blank at the absence of the groom." Kate, at first nervous and "confumblicated," managed to keep her composure, and eventually, she said, "we became merry over our woes and disappointments, and had such a good time as time and place permitted."[12]

Kate's spirits again soared a few weeks later when on December 14 Sandie informed her that he had applied for an immediate furlough, and would be at Moss Neck in two days. She should prepare for the wedding. "We all set to work," Kate informed a close friend, "and killed the fatted calf and scoured the house, but no groom arrived."[13]

Sandie had been denied a leave at the last minute, and was en route with the Second Corps to the Shenandoah Valley in Virginia.[14]

It was a cruel joke; the on-again, off-again wedding had been postponed three consecutive times. Christmas was at hand, and there seemed no end to their predicament in sight. Kate Corbin blamed, among others, Robert E. Lee for canceling all furloughs.

Finally, on December 24, Sandie wired his father in Lexington, telling him that he had at last obtained a leave and would hasten to Moss Neck for a wedding on December 29. Kate, not having access to rapid mail delivery or telegrams at Moss Neck, was shocked when Sandie, having traveled through a snowstorm, unexpectedly appeared on December 27 and announced that their wedding would take place two days hence.[15]

"I could have freely choked him—to stay away all this time and then come poking down here," especially when she was so tired and had no heart to do anything but complain, Kate confided to a close friend. Thus, there was "something unreal" about actually getting married, she concluded. While Sandie hastened to Richmond to get his father, who would officiate at the ceremony, and his groomsmen, Kate pondered his return date of the 29th, their fourth planned wedding day.

On the 29th the morning passed without sign of the groom and his party. Yet by late afternoon all had arrived at Moss Neck, and the ceremony was quickly performed. Kate Corbin Pendleton was at last a bride!

The following morning the honeymooners were en route to Lexington, Virginia, via Richmond, and within days Kate could write to her friends about how delightful she found marriage. "Oh, girls, get married," she gushed to a girlfriend and her sister, "the evils are not as bad as you might suppose." Sandie seemed "so thoughtful of [her] slightest wishes," and was "good and true." "My soul [is] so bound up in him," she glowed. By the time they reached Lexington Kate proclaimed that the past few weeks were "the happiest" of her life.[16]

Sandie Pendleton returned to the army in February 1864 a happy and devoted man. "It was quite pleasant returning," he informed Kate. "Everybody was so unaffectedly glad to see me, congratulated me so kindly, and asked so cordially after you. I could have kissed the whole party, almost old Mrs. Ewell [his commander's wife]. I shall drop into harness tomorrow for another steady pull."[17]

In fact, the harness of war was to be Sandie's lot for many months to come, and he often wondered about the uncertain future. "If we can weather the storm this summer with anything like success, I believe we may then see the 'beginning of the end,' " he told Kate. "Our army is in glorious trim now, and when the furloughed men return, [it] will be in strength sufficient to accomplish something, I hope, which shall redound to the good of the cause and the glory of the Army of Northern Virginia."[18]

Beneath the cheerfulness, however, there was a subtle change in Sandie's attitude. What had once been expressions of his unabated confidence in the Confederacy's eventual success were now more-hesitant declarations of hopefulness. The harsh realities of war had become all too apparent to him. The results of recent fighting were less than glorious victories, and his fading pride contrasted sharply with the feeling of accomplishment he had experienced under Stonewall Jackson.

During the past six months Sandie's growing awareness of the army's vulnerability had manifested itself in criticism of his superiors.

Writing of events since the Gettysburg Campaign, he confided to his mother: "Gen. Lee has shown the same power as ever," but in the Third Corps [A. P. Hill] "there has been the most disgraceful and culpable blundering." A. P. Hill was pegged by Sandie as "a fool and a woeful blunderer." Even Richard Ewell, his own commander, was singled out; he "lacks decision and is too irresolute for so large and independent command as he has," thought Sandie. Ewell's "want of promptness and decisive action, which will surely occur again, [will] surely prevent the Second Corps from ever accomplishing in the future such grand achievements as made it glorious in the past under Jackson," he complained. "It has done well merely when it should have done superbly and accomplished great things for the country and cause."[19]

At the root of this bitterness were Sandie's expectations of renewed military glory and redemption from the stigma of reverses that had begun with Gettysburg. "I earnestly hope General Lee will soon attack and let us retrieve our lost reputation," he pleaded following the distressing affair at Rappahannock Station in November 1863. "It is absolutely sickening, and I feel personally disgraced by the issue of the last campaign [Bristoe Station], as does everyone in command. Oh, how each day is proving the inestimable value of General Jackson to us."[20]

Sandie's commitment to victory was never more evident than when he turned down a chance for promotion to brigadier general and command of a brigade because he believed that his service was more valuable at corps headquarters as a senior staff officer.[21]

With the coming of spring campaigning in 1864, Sandie once more seemed optimistic about the war. "If we do get into Pennsylvania again this summer," he told his sister, "I'll try to do better than I did last Gettysburg campaign. . . . I will bring [home] as much plunder as I can get." To another sister he wrote, "We are all sanguine of success and trust we shall be able to serve Lincoln's latest hero [U. S. Grant] as we have served his various predecessors on the road to Richmond."[22]

Sandie's thoughts mirrored those of his close friend Jed Hotchkiss, who wrote to his wife on the eve of the Wilderness Campaign, "We have accepted the issue, 'liberty or death.' There is no retiring now from the contest. We are to fight it out and leave the issue in the hands of the Dispenser of all events."[23]

Having asked Kate to pray for his safety, Sandie was fortunate to survive the Wilderness and Spotsylvania fighting, despite several close calls. Two horses were shot from under him at Spotsylvania, and General Pendleton, Sandie's father, wrote to Kate that it "was almost a miracle" that her husband had escaped unscathed. "Looking up to God" was the only remedy that the general could suggest for the strain and anxiety of knowing her husband was in great danger.[24]

The personal trauma of this vicious fighting became evident to Sandie when his friend Colonel Edward "Ned" Willis, who had once served with him on Stonewall Jackson's staff, was mortally wounded at Bethesda Church on May 30. Finding Willis in the hospital, Sandie attempted to comfort his dying comrade, telling him, "Ned, I trust you have as good cause not to fear death as you had not to fear the enemy." Ned was engaged to Sandie's friend, Moxley Sorrel's sister, and the stricken officer affirmed that he was not afraid to die. "I don't mind it myself, but it will almost break her heart and my poor father's and mother's," grieved Ned. "Tell her not to be distressed. I die in the best cause a man could fall in." With tears in his eyes, Sandie noted that Ned said nothing more, but seemed "a good deal moved." Returning two hours later, Sandie found Ned dead.[25]

To Sandie it was a tragic reminder of the toll of war on nearly everyone. "No man of more promise has been cut off during the progress of this war," commented Sandie to Ned's father in a letter of condolence.[26]

His grief over the loss of Ned and other friends had hardly abated when, in June 1864, events occurred that would change Sandie's own life. In mid-June the Second Corps, Army of Northern Virginia, was transferred to the Shenandoah Valley, and became known as the Valley Army. Soon Sandie was on terrain over which he had campaigned with Stonewall Jackson in 1862. Ironically, Sandie had recently complained to his mother about the hot, dusty weather near Richmond. "[Such] makes us sigh for the mountains again," he had wistfully remarked, and added, "I trust we shall see them before long."[27]

His wishes having come true, with them came good feelings about the progress of the war. Since Grant had thus far failed to take Richmond, "Every day that we withstand Grant lessens his chances of success and strengthens our cause," assessed Sandie that June.[28]

Sandie's good luck continued into July, when the Valley Army, commanded by Jubal Early, having swept up the Shenandoah Valley and cleared it of the enemy, was able to cross the Potomac and briefly threaten Washington, D.C.

Sandie dined on the evening of July 9 in Frederick, Maryland, enjoying ice cream in the company of his friends. A brief foray to the outskirts of Washington, D.C., several days later was filled with excitement, and he complimented Jubal Early for "good management" and his prudence in withdrawing without attacking the "tremendous" enemy fortifications around the city.[29]

By August, Sandie was back in the Shenandoah Valley with Early's army. Here he was greeted with news of the arrival of his wife, Kate, at his father's home in Lexington. He had last seen Kate on June 12, when she was in Richmond. Now, he was given the best news of all. Kate was expecting a baby in November![30]

"It Is God's Will, I Am Satisfied!"

His letter was dated September 16. Sandie Pendleton expressed his appreciation to his family for the tender care given to Kate in her delicate condition. Being separated from her own family, Kate now had a "peculiar need of making friends" and to be treated with love "for her own sake," which was better than "were it for my sake alone," acknowledged Sandie. As for the military situation, "everything here [Bunker Hill] is as quiet as possible," Sandie noted. "The Yankees are seemingly content to be left alone, and we are quite glad to rest."[31]

A new Yankee commander, Philp H. Sheridan, was present in the valley, and he had attempted a brief advance in mid-August, but then promptly withdrew north toward Harper's Ferry. Sheridan's main force was near Berryville, and they didn't show any intention of advancing. Thus, a division of infantry detached from Lee's army was sent back to Richmond on September 14.

With little more than listless maneuvering expected during the remaining good weather, Sandie was optimistic about their comfortable status. Almost as an afterthought, Sandie wrote in his September 16 letter, "I hope we shall soon be ready for whatever may turn up."

What did turn up unexpectedly was Sheridan's army, on Early's close front on September 19. Early had unwisely divided his forces, sending two divisions north to Bunker Hill, Virginia, on the 17th, and he was unprepared for the sudden attack that came at Winchester on the 19th. Outnumbered and forced back by superior numbers, Early retreated to the vicinity of Strasburg that evening, having lost nearly four thousand men from his effective strength of sixteen thousand.[32]

Three days later, Sheridan again assaulted Early's command, stretched out in an attenuated four-mile line that rested on Fisher's Hill, overlooking Strasburg. Taken in flank by a heavy attack on the afternoon of September 22, Early's line crumbled, and they hastily abandoned their strong position on Fisher's Hill. In the aftermath of this stunning defeat, Lieutenant Colonel Sandie Pendleton desperately attempted to restore order.

It was dusk, and the light was barely sufficient to see into the gathering gloom. Sandie was aiding in the placement of a rear-guard brigade across the road near the village of Tom's Brook. As the Confederate troops rushed to a nearby fence row, scattered firing broke out. An instant later, Sandie crumbled to the ground. A minie ball had struck him in the abdomen and ripped crosswise through his body.

Since the enemy's skirmishers were advancing, Sandie pleaded with the men around him to leave him lest they be captured. Yet a small party of men, including his friend Henry Kyd Douglas, hastened to Sandie and carried him back to an ambulance. Driven to the small town of Woodstock, he was taken to the home of a local physician, Doctor Murphy, and his wound was examined by Doctor Hunter McGuire.

Reminiscent of the bedside vigil held over the failing Stonewall Jackson little more than a year earlier, Sandie Pendleton's fate seemed equally tragic. Doctor McGuire examined and dressed the wound, then informed Sandie that it was mortal. Later, burning with fever, Sandie suffered intensely and "constantly craved ice," sometimes talking wildly in his delirium. Although Doctor McGuire stayed with him until after midnight, the approach of the Federal forces mandated that Sandie be left behind.[33]

On September 23 Sandie endured intense pain, and was constantly administered to by Doctor Murphy's wife and daughters, who soothed his brow and attempted to relieve his suffering. Aware by evening that his death was near, he requested one of the daughters to cut off a lock of his hair and send it to his wife. Then, expressing little fear of death, Sandie Pendleton calmly awaited the end, telling the Murphy family, "It is God's will; I am satisfied."

ELODIE TODD DAWSON, ca. 1869: Known as "Dee Dee" to her friends and family, Elodie was a half sister to Mary Todd Lincoln, and became a quasi-celebrity among her contemporaries. Although only eighteen, she conspired to marry a much older Montgomery, Alabama, widower, who had volunteered for war duty to find glory and honor. Their subsequent relationship revealed that both had much to learn about themselves and the meaning of war.

(Courtesy of Mary Genevieve Murphy)

CAPTAIN NATHANIEL H. R. DAWSON, 4th Alabama Infantry: Elodie Todd's dapper fiancé, dressed in his natty army uniform, was about to learn the realities of military duty. His 1861 spirit of pride and intensity is well reflected in this portrait; it was that of a man who would come to realize that there was greater glory elsewhere.

(Courtesy of Alabama Department of Archives and History, Montgomery, Alabama)

PRIVATE JOHN RULLE, Co. K, 2d Tennessee Infantry: Armed to the extreme, Private Rulle in this 1861 photo displays the spirit of Southern invincibility to the fullest. His grim, determined countenance reflects the belief that Confederate soldiers would prove more than a match for their Yankee opponents.
(Courtesy of Herb Peck, Jr.)

COLONEL HENRY KING BURGWYN, JR., 26th North Carolina Infantry: One of the youngest colonels in the Confederate army, "Harry" Burgwyn entered the Gettysburg Campaign determined to win promotion to brigadier general. Instead he paid a heavy price in becoming a Southern legend.
(Courtesy of the Rare Book, Manuscript, and Special Collections Library, Duke University)

LIEUTENANT ALEXANDER FREDER-
ICK FLEET, 26th Virginia
Infantry, ca. 1862: This young
officer's look of both pride
and ill-at-ease distraction
mirrored the Confedera-
cy's youthful hope and
energy, and yet bears
witness to the enormous
challenge ahead. As
"Fred" would discover,
combat was an experience
that shaped one's lifetime
attitudes.

LIEUTENANT HENRY
HOWE COOK, Co. F,
44th Tennessee Infantry,
ca. 1861: This eighteen-
year-old volunteer officer
exemplifies the inno-
cence of the Confeder-
ate soldier in 1861, as
adventure-seeking boys
marched off to war in
hopes of finding glory
and achievement. Most
would find only height-
ened maturity or worse.
(Courtesy of Miller's Photographic
History of the Civil War)

MAJOR ALEXANDER S. "SANDIE" PENDLETON: Wearing a black armband, Sandie Pendleton poses in mid-1863, his grim countenance befitting the grief he felt over the death of his beloved general, Stonewall Jackson. Pendleton's mourning would assume a new meaning following Sandie's future personal ordeal, and also that of his young wife, Kate, and their baby.

(Courtesy of Tony Marion)

KATE CORBIN PENDLETON (BROOKE): Amid the bright promise of a romantic courtship, Kate Corbin had married one of Stonewall Jackson's best staff officers, Sandie Pendleton. Kate's subsequent valiant struggle amid some of the war's most tragic anguish provided a story of ultimate heroism.

(Courtesy of George M. Brooke)

BRIGADIER GENERAL WILLIAM NELSON PENDLETON: Sandie's father played a key role in the failure of the Confederate artillery to win the fight at Gettysburg. An ordained Episcopal minister, he often preached to the troops about faith, but the bitter loss of his son, and later his grandson, inflicted some of the greatest pain of his life.
(Courtesy of Tony Marion)

LIEUTENANT GENERAL THOMAS J. "STONEWALL" JACKSON: "Old Jack" was a favorite of his seemingly invincible men; they reveled in the aggressive but common ways of this eccentric genius of the battlefield. His legendary status was at its height when he attempted to escape the nervous, mistaken firing of the 18th North Carolina Infantry during an evening reconnaissance at Chancellorsville.
(Courtesy of Leib Image Archives, York, Pennsylvania)

Rutledge's Battery, 1st Tennessee Light Artillery, ca. 1861: Their unsoiled if unmatched uniforms, and innocent expressions belie the ordeal they would soon face in battle. Like other Confederates, they would come to know the war in real terms, that of misery and travail among the performance of the duty to the extent of one's capabilities. *(Courtesy of* Miller's Photographic History of the Civil War)

SARAH MORGAN: This beguiling Baton Rouge, Louisiana, belle found the prospect of a Southern rebellion exciting, yet within months after it began, her diary entries revealed that Sarah had come to know the awful misery of war.

(Courtesy of the Rare Book, Manuscript, and Special Collections Library, Duke University)

View of Church Street, Baton Rouge, Louisiana, ca 1863: Sarah Morgan's family home is partially hidden by the foliage, but the front is visible to the left of the trees.

(Courtesy of the United States Military History Institute, Carlisle Barracks, Pennsylvania)

GENERAL ALBERT SIDNEY JOHNSTON: Regarded as the savior of the Confederacy's western heartland, Sidney Johnston brought from the old army a distinguished record and enormous character. His bright promise was unfulfilled when he was mortally wounded by a stray rifle ball at Shiloh. He had boldly cast the "iron dice" of battle, but destiny was against him.

(Courtesy of the National Archives)

Officers of the elite Washington Artillery of New Orleans: Proud and well equipped, these distinguished officers from the South's largest city posed for the camera before the Battle of Shiloh. Their proud record and the terrible losses they suffered in the war endeared the Washington Artillery to Southerners.

(Courtesy of Miller's Photographic History of the Civil War)

Officers of the 9th Mississippi Infantry, ca. 1862: Not long before facing their initial combat, these soldiers posed for the camera while in camp. Their rifles are stacked ready for use, and the men seem studious, intent on learning the art of war. They would soon find a grim reality that no textbook could convey on that bloody April 6th morning at Shiloh. (*Courtesy* Miller's Photographic History of the Civil War)

MAJOR GENERAL PATRICK CLEBURNE: He was one of the Confederacy's best combat generals, a tactical master of the battlefield. Though twice given the formal thanks of the Confederate Congress for his fighting prowess, Cleburne was never fully utilized to the fullest in the Army of Tennessee. The Davis administration's outrage at Cleburne's proposal to enlist slaves in the army seemed to insure his blacklisting from well-deserved promotion.
(Courtesy of Mark M. Hull)

Confederate soldier armed for battle, 1862: This image of an unidentified volunteer provides a glimpse of the war fever prevalent in the early months of the conflict. Wielding a double barreled shotgun and the means for fighting hand to hand with his D-guard Bowie knife, this wild citizen-soldier personifies the spirit of adventure and the fierce determination that characterized many 1861 volunteers.
(Courtesy of Herb Peck, Jr.)

PRIVATE H. REUBEN NATIONS, 12th Louisiana Infantry, ca. 1862: With his musket at the ready, and fully armed with a revolver, Bowie knife, and bayonet, the steely-eyed Private Nations seemed ready to take on the Yankees. His countenance may not have been so assured following the loss of both legs to a Yankee shell at Decatur, Alabama, in October 1864. *(Courtesy of Georgia Department of Archives and History, Atlanta, Georgia)*

Confederate soldiers marching through Frederick, Maryland, on September 10, 1862: In this rare photo of armed Southern soldiers in the field, Lee's lean veterans are depicted en route to Antietam and the bloodiest day of the war. *(Courtesy of Mrs. Benjamin Rosenstock)*

Dead Confederate soldiers at Dunker Church, Antietam battlefield, September 19, 1862: The war's bloodiest day had claimed the lives of thousands of Lee's best soldiers, and this photo, taken two days later, reveals the gruesome reality of war and the terrible toll on Southern manpower—men that Lee would have difficulty replacing.
(Courtesy of the United States Military History Institute, Carlisle Barracks, Pennsylvania)

DANIEL PARKER:
Many older Southern citizens were as anxious to serve as were the youthful volunteers. As most aged Confederate soldiers soon discovered, it was difficult to reconcile one's stamina with martial spirit once the realities of going to war became known.
(Courtesy of Herb Peck, Jr.)

GENERAL JOHN BELL HOOD: Sent from Virginia by Jefferson Davis at first to watch over and then replace Joe Johnston as commander of the Army of Tennessee, Hood's tenure led to disaster. His reckless concepts caused the death or disabling of so many of his men that the army was virtually destroyed.

(Courtesy of the United States Military History Institute, Carlisle Barracks, Pennsylvania)

The grisly carnage at Corinth, Mississippi, in October 1862: His body shattered by the terrible ordeal he and his men had faced, Colonel William P. Rogers lies on the left amid the pile of valiant soldiers who paid the ultimate price of Southern valor in frontally attacking fortified positions such as Battery Robinette at Corinth.

(Courtesy of Alabama State Department of Archives and History, Montgomery, Alabama)

"Sherman's Sentinels:" These two standing chimneys along the road in Virginia graphically depict the desolation of Sherman's concept of total war, which brought the grim realities to the Southern homefront in 1864 and 1865.

(Photo by E & H. T. Anthony & Co., Minnesota Historical Society)

GENERAL BRAXTON BRAGG: As the peevish, disliked commander who repeatedly led the ill-starred Army of Tennessee into defeat, Bragg was noted for purging dissident generals when it appeared they were a threat to him. Bragg's late war role as military advisor to Jefferson Davis led to many disastrous decisions.
(Courtesy of Chickamauga and Chattanooga National Military Park)

Confederate prisoners after Spotsylvania in 1864: Gaunt and yet still defiant, these prisoners await transportation to Northern prisons. Lee's losses during the continuous manner of warfare that began with Grant's arrival in the eastern theater, boded ill for the Confederacy's fortunes. These men were irreplaceable. *(Courtesy of the Western Reserve Historical Society, Cleveland, Ohio)*

Dead Confederate soldier, Spotsylvania, Virginia, May 20, 1864: He was once one of those of whom Robert E. Lee wrote, "they will go anywhere and do anything if properly led." Now there were far too few of them remaining. Lee's remark, "There never were such men in an army before," had assumed a new meaning. By late 1864 they would be spoken of in the past tense. *(Courtesy of the Library of Congress)*

By nightfall Sandie Pendleton was dead; he had died only five days short of his twenty-fourth birthday.[34]

Kate Pendleton was nearing her period of confinement. Although aware that fighting was ongoing in the valley near Winchester, the Pendletons were completely in the dark as to the results and casualties. Newspapers were scarce and badly outdated, and with Sheridan's troops occupying the contested battlefields in the valley, only murky rumors surfaced from distant sources.

On the 25th, three days after the fight at Fisher's Hill, word from a courier arrived in Lexington that Sandie had been wounded and left behind in Woodstock. Despite these ill tidings, Kate and Sandie's mother remained hopeful. "I trust we are not too confident or presuming on the mercy of God to risk some hope of our precious one being restored to us," penned his sister Sue Pendleton Lee to her husband that day.[35]

They were beginning an odyssey of anguish and misinformation. The South was struggling to maintain adequate communications, and evidence of the Confederacy's deteriorating overall situation was never more apparent than in the difficulty of obtaining vital personal news. Extended active campaigning made letters from the field infrequent, and those that were written were often delayed for want of transportation. The breakdown in communications placed enormous burdens on families and soldiers alike, for there was no reliable way to get information, aside from random means amid increasingly unstable circumstances.

Aware of wild rumors, and mindful of false hopes, Kate and Sandie's family attempted to cope with the news of Sandie's wound. They interpreted a secondhand message from Doctor McGuire that Sandie's wound was dangerous to mean that he might recover. A note from Henry Kyd Douglas that arrived on October 31 gave them reason to believe in Sandie's recovery and eventual return home. "The whole family is buoyed up with hope," wrote Sue Pendleton Lee. Nearly two weeks had elapsed since the Fisher's Hill combat, but as of yet the family had no definitive word.[36]

The anguish of not knowing, of anticipating the worst but hoping for the best, finally came to an end on October 4. Doctor McGuire arrived in Lexington on that date and informed Sandie's mother,

Anzolette, who had rushed to his hotel, that Sandie had died on September 23. [37]

The Pendleton family was instantly stricken with "deadly sorrow." Kate had been bewildered by the contradictory accounts, and only "the grace of God has upheld her," noted Sue Pendleton Lee, who had told her the painful news. Since Doctor McGuire didn't have firsthand knowledge of Sandie's death, Sue feared that pending certain news and the full details the agony would continue.[38]

Any lingering suspense finally ended on October 17, when Sandie's family received a letter of condolence from Mrs. Murphy, who had attended Sandie at Woodstock. The area finally had been evacuated by the Yankees, and was reoccupied by Early's troops on October 12.

Expressing her faith that Sandie, her only son, was now in "the Kingdom of Heaven," Anzolette Pendleton told of the brave manner in which Kate and the others were bearing up. Yet she knew the forthcoming funeral and Sandie's reburial would renew their pain. Due to the chaotic conditions, it was unknown when Sandie's body would arrive. [39]

Mercifully, the body reached Lexington on October 24, escorted by a military honor guard, and the funeral was planned for the following day in the Episcopal church where Sandie's father had long preached as rector. Kate, nearing her delivery date, had been kept uninformed of Sandie's arrival until that very day.

Anzolette Pendleton later described how she had gone to Kate's room and tenderly informed her, "We expect him today." Kate asked who. "Our beloved," responded Mrs. Pendleton. Although weeping "more than usual," Kate took the news calmly. She wanted a wreath made for the funeral, and asked "to lay her head on the coffin."

That evening at dusk, Kate was driven to the church to bid farewell to her husband. Too overcome with grief to attend the funeral on the 25th, Kate remained in her room and was constantly attended to by family members. [40]

The following day she was driven to the grave in Lexington Cemetery, and amid the fresh wreaths, Kate stood in tearful silence and viewed the newly tilled plot. Nearby stood the grave of Stonewall Jackson. These two Virginia warriors, one middle-aged and the other young, had come to their final resting place in Lexington.

General Pendleton, who was serving with Lee's army and unable to attend Sandie's funeral, wrote, "If this world were all [there is], . . . what a strange dispensation would be the removal of one like Sandie, every way so superior! But in view of the heavenly world to which he is [ascended], it is no longer perplexing. . . . Sure of this, we can combat the sadness, and find more than comfort in the certainty [of eternal life] for him, and the hope for ourselves." [41]

That day, as the family gathered in Kate's room, they read aloud many of Sandie's letters at her request. Among the words read were passages from a memorable letter to her: "I have been very happy since I first loved you, and you . . . have been able to brighten [my] life amid the sorrows of the times. And now, good-bye; 'tis only God be with you, and has no share of parting in it. Two hearts so joined as ours never part, but if separated . . . they turn to the God and Father of all, the Giver of light and life and love. There they are united again in happiness. God bless you." Then, in a more recent letter, Sandie had written, "Pray for me, my dearest one, and as I derive happiness from your love, help me to gain eternal life." [42]

Sandie's last message to Kate, spoken to Mrs. Murphy on his death-bed, had been sadly appropriate: "Meet me in Heaven." [43]

It was a boy! On November 4, 1864, only ten days after her husband's funeral, Kate Corbin Pendleton gave birth to a healthy baby. The gloom and despair of the past few months were immediately broken. "He is Sandie," wrote the proud and adoring paternal grandmother. "I am thankful for God's great mercy in bringing Kate safely through her trouble, and for giving her a fine, healthy child." [44]

Kate reveled in her baby. Although described as not handsome, he was "very sweet and submits to be kissed as often as I like, and gapes as frequently as I ever did." Grandma Pendleton observed that "the baby grows amazingly, and jumps almost out of your arms." To her father, Kate wrote that her "little man" was "so sweet and such a comfort." The baby bore a likeness to his father, and she proudly informed grandfather Pendleton that "the lovely smile and sweet cooing" caused even the neighbor's children to take notice. "From the amount of study he is bestowing on his fat little fists," mused Kate, he seemed destined to be an expert on "the hand and its uses." "I could write for a week about him," she admitted. [45]

Amid the joy, there always was the lingering memory of little Sandie's father. "[Perhaps] I would have loved him too much [at the baby's expense]," she reflected in February 1865. "Maybe my poor weak heart would have passed its bounds and idolized my husband."

Thus, little Sandie seemed to "bind us closer together." "So great a treasure has been laid up there [in Heaven]," pined a melancholy Kate, that it becomes hard to contemplate. "Oh! our country bleeds at every pore. Truly we are selling all our pearls in the purchase of freedom. . . . And each precious sacrifice makes the cause worth a harder and fiercer struggle. Surely such blood must be redeemed," Kate sighed. [46]

Unfortunately for Kate and the Pendletons, their redemption would be measured only in more grief and blood. To the fate of war soon was added Kate's economic destitution. The trustee appointed to manage her funds inherited from the Corbin estate had invested them in Confederate bonds and commercial stocks, all of which became worthless following the collapse of the Confederacy in April 1865. Moreover, some real-estate property in Richmond that Kate owned was destroyed in the fire following that city's evacuation.

Now a penniless war widow with an infant son, Kate continued to rely on the Pendletons following the general's return from the war in mid-April. Although burdened by their own financial difficulties, the Pendletons survived by planting a garden and by relying on a meager income from the former general's reappointment as rector of the Episcopal church. Having once earned a large regular salary, Reverend Pendleton now received funds amounting to less than $300. In June 1865, Mrs. Pendleton described the plight of the family in a letter to her daughter, Sue. "We have plenty of flour, but not a bit of meat, though we have been a few days with a dinner of herbs. This week we had dried apples, lettuce, and our good Georgia molasses. The next morning . . . Colonel Gilham of VMI sent me a fore-quarter of nice mutton, which made us comfortable for four days. Yesterday and today we dined on herbs. True to my resolution not to open the molasses until your father's return, we have it now in our scantiest times." [47]

Without question, little Sandie remained the greatest joy in the entire household, "a new motive in life" for the entire family. "The baby grows beyond everything else here," reported one of Kate's sisters-in-law that summer. "He is devoted to both his grandparents and it is amusing to see their efforts to entice him to leave the arms of one and go to the other." Usually "sweet tempered" and uncomplaining, the infant at one time fussed over and refused to eat fresh strawberries sprinkled with sugar. The family had a great laugh over the matter—little Sandie had "so little experience of the good things in life" he didn't know the difference, they joked. [48]

Sandie turned nine months old on August 4, 1865.

He never saw ten months. In late July he was stricken with a sore throat and a respiratory infection. He had contracted diphtheria, a frequent killer of infants. Although lingering until September 1, 1865, little Sandie quietly died that morning, a victim of infectious bacteria that had induced an acute heart infection. [49]

The following evening he was buried at the foot of his father's grave in Lexington Cemetery. "Father and son are in spirit, we believe, now in the presence of the Saviour," wrote the grieving Reverend Pendleton the following day.

Kate Corbin Pendleton nearly lost sight of life's meaning. She seemed doomed to a life of sorrow. Her great burden and her Southern mettle were reflected in the emotional letter she composed several days later to her father, who had never seen baby Sandie:

God has called my little lamb to his own green pastures. And I am left utterly alone and desolate. When my husband died there was some comfort to look to in the coming of my little baby. . . . Ever since he was born he was such an unspeakable joy to me that I couldn't believe he was going to die. Though his delicate life hung by a thread for long weeks, and I saw him gradually wasting away . . . still I thought he would be spared to me, and that as soon as he was better I would carry him home and put him in your arms and hear your praises of him.

Oh! Pa, you would have been so proud of him. He was such a noble, lovely boy, and if ever grace dwelt in so young and tender a creature, my child's heart surely was filled with it. I have often heard Ma say . . . [her baby sister who had died shortly after birth] was sanctified from the womb. I have often recalled it in connection with my little Sandie, even before this painful illness came on which he endured so patiently and sweetly.

Dear little precious one, he loved me best of all to the last. The beautiful, unclouded eyes watched and followed me till the dimness of death came over them, and the last faint breath was drawn. Little Angel, he passed away without much struggle, but he had suffered untold torture before death came. Very little change came over him, and when I took my last kiss from the sweet lips and lofty brow, he lay in his little narrow coffin as peacefully as though asleep in his crib. He looked so lovely and natural I could hardly believe him dead. It will always be a grief to me that you and sister never saw him. I so longed to see him with you.

. . . I wonder people's hearts don't break when they have ached and ached as mine has done, till feeling seems to be almost worn out of them. My poor empty arms, with their sweet burden torn away forever. . . . Oh! Pa, unless you lose your only one you don't know how sharp the pain is, and no words of mine can tell the agony of my struggle to give up my baby. I went up this morning early, before the world was fully astir, and sat by the sweet little grave all covered with flowers. He is close by his father's arms in his quiet bed, and oh! how glorious they both must be in the Kingdom together. All my work in life now is to try and live so as to meet them in Heaven. . . . If God loves all he chastens, surely I have good reason to believe he loves me. I trust so, indeed.[50]

Lieutenant Colonel Sandie Pendleton would have been immensely proud of his wife. She was a survivor. She maintained her dignity amid the worst life had to offer. She kept her faith in God. The resilient spirit of humanity was never more evident.

Chapter Twenty-seven

FRED FLEET

"I Know Something about It Now"

Over the dinner table, Doctor Benjamin Fleet, Fred's father, discussed the salvation of the Confederacy with a friend. The reason their side often whipped the Yankees, asserted the friend, "was because we had the best generals." No, countered Doctor Fleet. "Our cause was the right one, and the Lord helped us." On and on the debate continued, without resolution. Later, Mrs. Fleet, who had been listening, commented rather tentatively to Fred in a letter, "Pa was right—don't you think so?"[1]

Lieutenant Fred Fleet admittedly relied on God, being convinced "the Almighty has shown his watchful care over us and has shielded us." But he was equally convinced of being correct in his assessment of the South as having too many lackluster generals. His regiment, the 26th Virginia, was still stuck with Brigadier General Henry A. Wise's "ragged brigade" of "Gardeners," and Fred longed for active service in the real war. "General Wise is under a ban, and will never have the post of honor," he wrote.

Generals like Robert E. Lee, Stonewall Jackson, and Sterling Price were, Fred believed, the great men of the Confederacy, and they were the ones who could make a difference. Therefore, he desperately wanted to be a part of their success.[2]

When 1863 had begun without disaster to any Southern army, Fred Fleet had prophesied, "With the smile of Providence, success will attend our efforts this year." The Confederacy's armies were in "fine spirits, well disciplined and organized, and capable of enduring as much as any veterans of modern times," he had believed. Also, they had "confidence in their generals and the justice of [the Southern] cause." Perhaps 1863 would see the end the war, he had counseled his parents. "Everything looks bright, and with God's assistance, I can but hope this campaign will end the war."[3]

That was before Gettysburg and Vicksburg. Once the extent of this "succession of tragedies" became known, Fred revised his thinking. "I fear this will be a long war," he now predicted. Moreover, the frustrations of his own situation became more bothersome. His determination to get into active combat was spurred by a relative's description of the charge, made in "beautiful style," at Gettysburg on July 3. [4]

Fred's own blood was flowing a little faster after his first taste of combat since he witnessed Malvern Hill from a distance more than a year before. During a minor skirmish with a few Federal gunboats patrolling the James River in early August 1863, Fred heard the whine of three artillery shells as they sailed overhead, and he termed the action "a real fight, however improbable." Yet the 26th Virginia suffered no casualties, and Fred Fleet again began to despair of his "unfortunate position" away from the major action.[5]

His cousin Charlie Fleet, an artillerist with the Army of Northern Virginia, warned Fred about his unchecked emotions. "Anxious as I am to see you and be in the same portion of the army, yet I hope you will not be transferred from your present place to this army," he wrote. "For the infantry service is not only very dangerous, but very hard. . . . [The] dull, monotonous routine of drilling and fighting and living in camp will wear away any man's energies." Even his mother cautioned him about being reckless in his quest for combat duty. While she sympathized with his feelings, she hoped he would "remember [you are at] your post—not of your own choosing, but [that] which has been assigned to you—where the Providence of God has placed you. Read Phil. IV:11 and don't complain."[6]

Fred would not be pacified, however. He was determined to find glory with the Army of Northern Virginia. Hopeful that the arrival at Wise's camp of two brigades from Major General George E. Pickett's

division in September might in turn lead to his brigade's transfer to
Lee's army, Fred learned that a movement of Wise's troops was imminent. "I am inclined to think that we will go to northern Virginia
to take the place of some of Lee's troops," he wrote on September
11. What's more, Fleet was now acting as adjutant of the regiment,
and would have the opportunity to ride on horseback during the
forthcoming campaign.[7]

Once again, Fred was keenly disappointed. Wise's brigade was ordered to Charleston, South Carolina, and although "willing to go,"
Fleet envisioned less-than-exciting service, and even less than milk-
and-honey duty such as they had experienced near Richmond. "We
have been having an easy time long enough, and now we ought to
expect to have a little of the hard times," he reflected.[8]

When many of Wise's troops became upset about their pending
transfer, and five men immediately deserted, a double line of guards
was posted around their camps. One soldier even cut off his foot "to
keep from going," shuddered Fred, but "there being no surgeon
[available] . . . , he bled to death in about four hours."[9]

Once at Charleston, the self-esteem of Wise's troops only worsened,
for again they were involved in dull, lackluster duty. The regiment
spent their time drilling twice a day for two hours, and the brigade
twice a week. "Colonel [P. R.] Page drills the brigade . . . as General
Wise could not do it to save his life," commented Lieutenant Fleet.
When their brigade did attempt an expedition to John's Island, a
fiasco occurred after the supporting artillery failed to damage the
targeted enemy gunboats, and the whole party returned to Charleston, embarrassed by their well-publicized failure. To add to their difficulties, Wise's command was criticized for pilfering the natives of
potatoes and other produce, which caused Fred Fleet to protest, "It
looks hard that we are here defending their property and they will
neither give nor sell anything to us."[10]

Matters in Charleston were not developing the way Fred Fleet had
hoped. Even promotion to captain and duty on the brigade commander's staff did not appease the restless youth. His horse had been
borrowed, and the owner soon asked for its return, causing Fred to
write, "If I cannot get a horse, I cannot remain in my present position
as the other[s] . . . have horses and in case of another expedition . . .
I would have to walk, which. . . . would be very humiliating."[11]

The dull routine and their status in South Carolina weren't altered by the approach of the Christmas season, and Fred Fleet wrote home that even the girls in Charleston seemed uninspiring. "I don't like them as much as I do the Virginia girls," he sighed.[12]

Fred's parents must have shrugged in disbelief at their eldest son's complaints as the year 1864 began. His difficulties seemed minuscule in comparison with the problems they faced at home in King and Queen County, Virginia. The year that had begun with so much optimism was ending in despair. On the Fleet farm, several male slaves had run away, many cattle had died of disease, ten horses had been taken by marauding Yankees, and the gloom of diminished crops and a looming economic crisis had cast a pall over the entire family. Even the youngest son, Benny, now seventeen, would soon be subject to conscription, and he was determined, despite his parents' objections, to join Major Mosby's battalion of scouts and guerrillas.[13]

Wearily, Doctor Benjamin Fleet noted in December 1863 that the war appeared to be "a punishment for national sins." "I must confess," he continued in a melancholy letter to Fred, "that the clouds seem more dark, lowering, and portentous, than they have ever before appeared." Being thankful that "neither you or I had any hand in bringing on this most barbarous war," Doctor Fleet informed his son that he had begun to wonder what further "terrible scourge" the war would entail. To Doctor Fleet, the war seemed omnipotent, and his tolerance for hardship was running thin. Moreover, angered by recent alarming war news, particularly word of the defeat of Bragg's army in Tennessee, Doctor Fleet ranted that Bragg should be "dismissed from the service, and at once." "If the president insists on keeping him in," raged the doctor, "I predict he will be impeached."[14]

Doctor Fleet's outlook affected even his young son, Benny, who wrote in his journal on December 31, 1863, "We have met with more reverses this year than in the two preceding, both together. Oh! that the next may be more promising, and may we gain our independence...." Then, on a more personal note, Benny concluded, "Where will I be this time next year? If I live . . . I certainly will be in the army. I am resolved now to go with Mosby in the summer."[15]

The Fleet family was fully ensnared in the war. There was no turning back, despite all of the misery and travail, and Doctor Fleet continued to hope for victory. His spirit foretold of "fighting it out as long as we can raise 50,000 old men in the Confederacy." Yet these were his sentiments before the stunning events of February 1864.[16]

*   *   *

Benny Fleet had always been his brother's fondest "project." Fred
had advised him against joining the army, suggesting that instead he
attend VMI to be better qualified for any position he might seek. But
Benny saw only the adventure of war, and chafed at his restraints with
the restlessness of youth. To Benny, the army was an irresistible at-
traction. Even the demise of his friend Boone Dew, who had rushed
off to join a cavalry unit and was killed in a skirmish two days later,
failed to deter him. Benny's mother had written, "We have no idea
of letting him go into service till he is eighteen. . . . He is so useful at
home I don't know how we could get along without him." Yet Benny's
plans were carefully laid to join "the gallant Mosby" as soon as the
wheat was threshed that year.[17]

When word came in mid-February 1864 that Congress had lowered
the conscription age to seventeen, Benny began gathering equipment, a uniform, and even a letter of introduction to join Mosby's
command. "I expect to start up and join him next week," Benny
wrote on February 24.[18]

Adding excitement to the forthcoming adventure, his brother Fred
had just returned home on furlough, and the two went riding and
skating, and generally "had a very nice time." Since Fred planned to
return to the army on Wednesday, March 2, Benny said he would go
with him as far as Richmond, then join Mosby. On Monday, February
29, Benny happily recorded that his father bought him that day "a
splendid Canadian horse, 8 years old, very fat, etc., for $1,000." It
was his going-away present.[19]

Two days later Benny was dead.

Continuing the tragic swirl of events that had so bedeviled the
region from time to time, the war's violence came suddenly to King
and Queen County on March 2, 1864. As part of the abortive
Kilpatrick-Dahlgren Raid on Richmond, Yankee Colonel Ulric Dahlgren, having been separated from the main body, attempted to
escape through the county that day with about two hundred men.
Informed only that morning that the Yankees were nearby and were
endeavoring to escape by crossing the Mattapony River near Aylett's
house, Benny and several young companions attempted to scout the
territory in that direction.

Spotting three riders dressed in Confederate uniforms in their
front along the road near Aylett's house, Benny and his friends ap-

proached to within thirty yards of the party, only to suddenly discover Dahlgren's troopers advancing in the road directly behind the group of three horsemen. Jerking their mounts about, Benny and his companions attempted to escape, but shots from the three advance riders rang out. Benny and another friend went down in a heap. Struck in the left arm, Benny ran into the woods to escape. He had no tourniquet to stanch the blood flowing from the severe wound. Benny collapsed in the woods, and soon died from a loss of blood.[20]

The following day, Benny's new Canadian horse was discovered grazing on the lawn at Green Mount, and his dog, "Stuart," led searchers to where the body lay. The grieving Doctor Fleet wrote in the family bible, "Benjamin R. Fleet was murdered by the Yankees on Wednesday, 2d March 1864 in King William County, . . . where he met the advance guard of the enemy dressed in Confederate uniforms, and was killed by them. Aged 17 years, 5 months, and 1 day."[21]

Fred Fleet, devastated by the loss, remained in the county until March 9. On March 2, the day of his brother's death, he had helped pursue Ulric Dahlgren's men, and was present when home-guard units and others ambushed and captured or dispersed the Yankee raiders near Walkerton. Dahlgren was killed in a flurry of bullets, but his death offered little consolation to the Fleet family. Thereafter, Fred Fleet wore black crepe around his arm in memory of his brother, and in late March he remarked that he was constantly reminded of him by little incidents which occurred every day.[22]

Fred Fleet began contemplating his own death. In March 1864 he heard a sermon, "We Glory in Tribulation." The minister preached that hardships required "patience and experience [in coping]." Yet to Fred Fleet the ordeals of war now seemed both endless and debilitating. Periods of depression came over him.[23]

When he returned to Wise's command, Fred found that they had been ordered to Florida, and he hastened to rejoin the brigade near Baldwin. Within days of his arrival there, he reported, "We are all quite tired of Florida," which to Fred seemed swampy, thinly settled, and "uninteresting." In the movement, units of Wise's brigade were sent to different locations and Fred Fleet began again to despair of ever realizing his coveted goal of serving in the Army of Northern Virginia.[24]

Even when Wise's command returned to South Carolina, Fred Fleet remained depressed, since he was once more frustrated in knowing "the vast armies of the enemy [were] concentrating for a final death grapple [in Virginia]. I wish very much we could all be there," he added. When en route back to Charleston, they had not been told of their destination, and many of the men's spirits soared because they believed that they were headed for Virginia.

Yet "when they got off the [railroad] cars . . . instead of going right through Charleston, I never saw more long faces in my life," thought Fleet. "And now it seems we are settled down here 'for the war.' I would give a great deal to get to the Army of Northern Virginia . . . ," he continued, "but they will send all the other troops there before us."[25]

General Wise's reputation was to blame for his troops' inactivity Captain Fleet concluded. Army politics would keep them in Charleston Harbor, "with nothing at all to disturb the monotony of the dull, tiresome sound of the guns from the Morris Island Batteries." On April 27 he wrote home, "You know my position about getting into a fight; that I am not particularly anxious for it. But I must say that I really think that is something we ought to be ashamed of, in being kept in a position comparatively out of danger." Fred hastened to add, much as a prideful native son, "We Virginians naturally turn with restlessness and anxiety to the Old Dominion, and feel desirous to add our quota in the defense of our capital . . ."[26]

The war had left him out; he was an observer from afar, merely a witness to the deeds of others. For more than three years he had been out of the shooting war, away from combat, unable to share the high honors earned on glorious Virginia battlefields. Fred's letter of May 1, 1864, only reiterated his anguish and discomfort. "I want to get to Virginia," he pleaded. Nonetheless, he said he must be "satisfied with whatever our generals think best." Fred also described how the pickets between opposing forces had agreed not to fire on one another, and the subsequent absurdity of breaking up a game of marbles between some Rebel cavalrymen and their Yankee counterparts. It was fitting evidence of his downcast spirits.[27]

Fred Fleet should have known better. Just when all seemed placid, there was hell to pay. That was the nature of this war.

As an aide on the staff of General Wise, Fred bristled with excitement when the brigade was rushed to Virginia in mid-May to help defend Petersburg. Several days of skirmishing resulted in only slight losses to the 26th Virginia Infantry, and with the Confederate forces having "bottled up" Benjamin Butler's troops in their Bermuda Hundred lines, an attack was organized at Ware Bottom Church on May 20.[28]

Captain Fred Fleet was put in command of a line of couriers so that he could communicate orders between the primary attacking unit and Wise's brigade, which would support the assault. Following their successful attack on a portion of the enemy line, the Confederates hastily began throwing up earthworks for protection from the incoming fire of the second Yankee line. Fred Fleet witnessed the intensity of this heavy musketry and artillery fire, and noticed that it rivaled what he had heard at Malvern Hill.[29]

Then, while carrying orders along the captured line, Fred suddenly felt a sharp pain in his left side. A minie ball had ripped through his coat and sliced into his body, inflicting a wound of unknown severity. Since adrenaline was surging through his veins and there seemed to be little blood flowing from the wound, he kept going. A few minutes later, Fred felt a stunning blow on his right leg. A bullet had struck him "in the fleshy part, just above the knee." When he looked down, Fred saw a (minie) ball roll off his foot. He presumed his leg had been hit by a spent bullet, so he again remained on duty. Painfully limping about, Fred Fleet was ordered by his commander to return to the rear to have his wounds examined.[30]

Carried by ambulance to the field hospital, Fred Fleet soon learned the full extent of his injuries. The wound in his leg was nothing severe, merely a superficial injury. But the one in his side gave Fleet cause to be thankful for his good fortune. The bullet had ranged across his side for nearly two inches, inflicting a wound only "a quarter of an inch deep." Yet, had the missile struck "half an inch to the right . . . it would have pierced my left lung and would probably have killed me," noted the stunned captain.[31]

Fred Fleet had been extremely lucky. Exposed to heavy fighting for the first time after more than three years of uneventful service, Captain Fleet had been struck and wounded. His relief was great, and he expressed a "profound gratitude to God that my life had been spared." His close friend in the 26th regiment, Lieutenant Miller, had lost his right arm and would soon die of an "imperfect" amputation. Combat had proved to bring less glory and honor than pain and suffering. The lesson would not be forgotten. God's mercy had inspired Fred to take a new perspective on life.[32]

*   *   *

As Fred Fleet soon learned, the capricious devastation of warfare was not limited to the battlefront. Even as he lay on a hospital cot, at home in King and Queen County, Virginia, his family was suffering multiple indignities and privations due to the sudden appearance of the enemy. Green Mount had been "invaded" on June 4, 1864, by Yankee Major General Philip H. Sheridan's cavalry corps, whereupon Sheridan established his headquarters at the Fleet residence. For the three days prior to Sheridan's columns' departure on the Trevilian Raid, the Fleet family knew personal devastation from a war gone awry. The Yankee troops tore down their fences, drove away all of the slaves except two who moved into the house, ransacked the premises of all valuables and food they could find, and took all of the horses, cattle, sheep, hogs, and chickens. At the time, Fred's mother was home alone with her five children, ages seven to fourteen. Doctor Fleet had earlier ridden into the countryside to visit patients, and now didn't dare return home for fear of imprisonment.[33]

Phil Sheridan soon proved his humor in Mrs. Fleet's presence; when offered a chair to sit on the porch, the bantam major general had chosen the largest, saying, "A little man always likes a big chair." Although three guards were assigned to protect the Fleet household, after the Yankee cavalry's departure stragglers continued to roam the neighborhood. On June 7, four derelict Yankees broke into the house looking for gold and silver. For hours they ransacked the premises and terrorized the family, one even threatening to rape the oldest daughter. Finally, they lay down under an apple tree to play cards. A contingent of home guards captured the Yankees that evening and led them away to an inevitable end. Informed by neighbors that these stragglers were the very same men who had pillaged their house and abused their family, one of the home guards remarked, "They should never annoy [any] woman, and *they never will!*"[34]

Following Sheridan's "visit," the Fleet home remained devoid of many necessities, yet Ma Fleet wouldn't give in to despair. "They left the garden, the house, the farm, and all of us alive," she thankfully considered. "I have been through so much, and suffered so acutely that my strength has well nigh failed, but I never felt so little like giving up in my life."[35]

Mrs. Fleet's attitudes about the war and life had changed. Though she once remarked that she had never turned away a soldier who was sick, wounded, or hungry, and would help even a Yankee soldier in trouble, she now wrote that her heart was hardened: "If I were a man I would never take a prisoner but would consider it my duty to rid the world of such monsters." Hate for the Yankees was now manifest in her. The war was no longer about someone else being injured or agonized. It confronted *her* with broken furniture, stolen silverware, and the fading tintype of her dead son. "There is some consolation for those who have lost friends in defending their homes—death is far preferable to subjugation to the vile Yankees—I know something about it now," she proclaimed.[36]

Beaten down but defiant, Maria Louisa Fleet adopted another new perspective. Her attitude about having Fred at home was changed. If earlier she had said that it was his duty to fight, and that he couldn't stay at home with honor, she now realized the worth of her son's life. Benny's death, Fred's narrow escape, and the devastation of their home all spoke volumes. "You don't know how many hopes and dreams I have about your being able to spend a month or so at home with loving hands to wait on you . . . ," she pined. To these sentiments were added the dire pleas of Fred's father, who somberly wrote, "My troubles are great, as you must know. Nevertheless, I trust [in] the kind hand that has always sustained us. . . . I simply write to ask you to come home as soon as you shall be able. . . ." Saying he needed Fred's army horse, since the family's horses and mules had been carried away by the "vandals," Doctor Fleet fretted, "I trust we shall be able to make bread to eat next year, and having done that, . . . we must be content."[37]

The war had lessened everyone's expectations. Hardship had a new meaning. And Southern rights took on an altered significance. Ahead for Fred Fleet, once his wounds were healed, was duty in the Petersburg trenches with Robert E. Lee's Army of Northern Virginia. Ironically, this fruition of Fred's long-sought quest was full evidence of the Confederacy's despair; the region's last remaining reserves were being fully committed. For Fred and the South, the price yet to be paid could only be imagined.

Chapter Twenty-eight

"Tennessee, a Grave, or a Free Home"

I am still hopeful of success; our cause is in God's hands," wrote Chaplain Marcus B. DeWitt of the 8th Tennessee Infantry in early September 1864. Following the fall of Atlanta, the despair was so profound in the Army of Tennessee that as DeWitt observed, looking to God seemed to be the only answer. "I am confident that our final success is recorded in the mind of Providence, but it is not yet announced" was how the chaplain expressed his unwavering belief. To DeWitt, God's approval of the Southern cause was the reason for continuing on.[1]

Like hundreds of others who had come to embrace divine intervention as the Confederacy's last hope in an increasingly bleak military situation, DeWitt could explain by citing God's power what otherwise might not be logical. If "many of our boys are sad and troubled," noted Chaplain DeWitt, the answer lay in religious faith. "Our army is greatly in need of the scriptures," estimated DeWitt in late September 1864. Since the "workings of a kind Providence [had] saved us at Jonesboro on August 31st and September 1st," the Chaplain now determined it was important to "supply our army with bibles and testaments."[2]

DeWitt's resort to Providence was not without precedent. Revivalism had swept through the Army of Tennessee in the spring of 1863 and had continued throughout the following year, even in the aftermath of the Atlanta Campaign. Although the reasons for this spiritual reawakening were varied, many of the soldiers' strengthened faith appeared related to growing insecurity, both personal and collective. Their defeats had lessened the South's prospects for victory, and the loss of close friends and comrades in the army had heightened everyone's awareness of their own mortality. Being denied furloughs and suffering deprivation due to a want of supplies and adequate food further compounded the stresses burdening the gray soldiers. Yet, perhaps most of all, the fear of death drove many to look to God for support. The uncertainty of surviving enemy missiles and the ravages of disease caused thousands to put their trust in God. So many had died, and so many would die, that faith offered the only logical protection or salvation.

Yet turning to religion had a noticeable practical effect. The consequences of faith seemed to be measured not so much in terms of survival as in terms of morale. Worship and trust in God, and a belief in the hereafter, made life amid the horrors of war bearable. Religious conviction also created an inner harmony among the ranks that served to bind the soldiers in spirit and faith.[3]

This bond was of primary importance, for the Army of Tennessee's spirits were at an all-time low following the fall of Atlanta. The morale of the soldiers, in fact, became the problem that John Bell Hood most regarded in the immediate aftermath of the Atlanta debacle. "The whole country is full of stragglers, and there are thousands of men deserting and going home," wrote an appalled Louisiana clerk caught up in the despair of the Atlanta retreat. "It is a disastrous affair, and I think that this army is so weakened and demoralized that it will never be worth a curse again." Another, more hopeful observer thought, "If the Georgians and Alabamians will quit deserting, we may be able yet to hold the enemy in check."[4]

Defeat had resulted in an inevitable despair, and the psychological pressure on the ranks was enormous. "I feel low spirited because everything is working very badly for the Confederacy," wrote an enlisted youth from Louisiana, "and I am uneasy about the family at home."[5]

Hood realized that both the efficacy of the army and his own job were at stake in the measures taken to restore the Tennessee army's disastrously lost military prowess. To boost morale, in September 1864 Hood issued urgent appeals to pay the soldiers in order to keep them from deserting. Moreover, a ten-day suspension in hostilities allowed civilians to evacuate Atlanta and provided a much-needed respite for

his exhausted and dispirited troops. Hood utilized the time to prepare for another campaign—one that might cripple Sherman's supply lines and force his withdrawal from northern Georgia.[6]

The Confederate army was certainly in no position, politically or
physically, to retreat farther south. "Many think that we cannot find
sufficient subsistence with the limited territory back of us," wrote an
astute observer. Indeed, Hood's own logistics were so poor that he
promised his men in a speech that if they would live on parched corn
and beef, he would give the command "forward," and they might
remove Sherman from Georgia and Tennessee. "The boys were loud
in applause," wrote one in the audience. "The[y] declare they are
ready to go [on] living for days on parched corn if we can rescue
Tennessee."[7]

These circumstances, however, were symptomatic of the plight of
the men. They desired with all their hearts to recover their homes
and hurl the invader back. Yet they knew the improbable odds. Their
army's limitations, from a want of supplies and equipment to their
unsuccessful commanding general, were all too apparent. Yet the desired objective was once again presented as a question of their minds
overcoming physical obstacles—a matter long familiar to the ill-fated
Army of Tennessee. Most men thus resolved to make another valiant
effort.

Notwithstanding their willingness to try again, the soldiers' doubt-
ing, more cynical mood remained. When Jefferson Davis came west
to visit the army in the aftermath of the Atlanta defeat, his reception
by the men reflected their frustration and mounting anger. On September 26, when Davis reviewed the troops in Hood's company, the
president met with a cool reception. A soldier in the ranks of Sears'
brigade watched as Davis and Hood approached. "As the presidential
party passed in front of our brigade, Col. [W. H.] Clarke, who was a
small man with a thin voice, cried out, 'Three cheers for President
Davis and General Hood!' Waving aloft his sword, he, with one or
two others, raised a feeble yell. Instantly, someone in the ranks cried
out, 'Three cheers for General Joe Johnston!' " A deafening cheer
from the ranks was quickly taken up by other units, the soldier observed, and a crescendo of Rebel yells burst on the startled dignitar-
ies' ears. Sternly, "Davis turned and looked back as if to see where
this unseemly demonstration originated." It was all very embarrassing
and humiliating to Hood, for there were many calls from the ranks
for Joe Johnston to be restored to command. After the review, Davis

and Hood seemed unusually glum. "The troops do not like Hood" was how a soldier bluntly summarized matters in his diary.[8]

Hood had good reason to despair. Following the Atlanta disaster, Davis was under heavy pressure to replace the one-legged commander. Yet Davis's pride and his unwillingness to be proven wrong in the selection of Hood as Joe Johnston's successor once again prevailed. When the experienced William J. Hardee refused to serve any longer under Hood, Davis relieved Hardee, as he had requested, and retained Hood.

Although Davis soon appointed P. G. T. Beauregard as theater commander, this was a superficial act, done in the hopes of deflecting some of the criticism of Hood and also to appease the public outcry for corrective action. Later, in a private conversation, Davis told Hood's fiancée, Sally "Buck" Preston, that Hood was a gallant soldier and a noble gentleman. He had only appointed Beauregard over him, said Davis, because of the "Macon [Johnston] clique," which was undermining the presidency and because the public might be more satisfied by a name they knew better.[9]

Disliked or mistrusted by many of his men, Hood was once again in a crucial spot. He knew he must soon do something spectacular, or his career and army would vanish. Anxiously, before the president's departure on September 27, he elaborated his plan for a raid against Sherman's vulnerable line of communications, which ran from Chattanooga to Atlanta.[10]

The prospect of marching north seemed to rekindle many of the troops' spirits, and with the belated issuing of better rations, even a Hood skeptic could report, "I feel like a new man since I got something fit to eat. . . . I didn't know before that a man's diet could create such a change in his feelings." Lauded by encouraging speeches from their unit commanders, such as that of Brigadier General D. H. Reynolds—they had "done well in keeping the enemy out of Atlanta as long as [they] did"—many soldiers seemed to anticipate better results in their impending railroad raid.[11]

During the last few days of September, Hood's columns began marching into northern Georgia, and they were soon astride Sherman's main supply artery, the Western & Atlantic Railroad. In two major forays during October, Hood laid waste to more than fifty miles of track, bending the iron rails over piles of burning logs to fashion what the men jokingly called "Old Mrs. Lincoln's Hair Pins." Small Yankee garrisons at Big Shanty, Acworth, and later Dalton were captured. So successful were these early actions that a new spirit of anticipation was evident among the army. When French's division was sent to capture the fortified town of Allatoona with its large storehouse of a million rations, an officer remarked that taking the place would be easy, a "breakfast task." Yet in a desperate frontal assault on the vastly outnumbered Federal garrison on October 4, the Confederates came up against the 7th Illinois Infantry, largely armed at its own expense with sixteen-shot Henry repeating rifles. The Henrys put out such a volume of fire that one soldier found that they were facing a terrible hailstorm of bullets. After being trapped on the ground within thirty yards of the Yankees' breastworks, this soldier could but marvel at his escape. His rifle had been struck and disabled, he found a bullet partially protruding from the back of his cartridge box, and he had suffered a severe wound in the shoulder, all within a few moments. While crouching behind the body of his close friend, he could "hear and feel the balls as they struck the corpse." After wishfully eyeing several abandoned Henrys lying on the ground nearby, the frightened soldier concluded that matters were hopeless, and he dashed back over a rise of ground to make his escape.

Facing the enemy's deadly repeating rifles was not part of the plan, and remembering his earlier reference to an easy "breakfast task," this soldier grimly wrote, "Anybody was welcome to my share of that breakfast."[12]

The failure at Allatoona cost French's division nine hundred men out of a force of about two thousand, yet Hood was so encouraged by the overall results of these railroad raids that he soon revised and greatly expanded his plans. He now wanted to draw Sherman's forces north into Tennessee, and began planning a raid, across the Tennessee River, that might carry beyond Cincinnati into the northern heartland.

By ordering a difficult transfer of his supply base west to Tuscumbia, Alabama, Hood hoped to gather there food and material for this major northern raid. Yet, already his men were becoming discouraged. They had marched through mud and rain en route to the vicinity of the Tennessee River at Florence, Alabama, and were again suffering from near starvation. A handful of parched corn was the army's staple, but nearly a week had passed for many soldiers without any rations being issued. So desperate were some units that they detailed parties of hunters to shoot squirrels for something to eat. Morale was again at a low, and Chaplain DeWitt wrote, "Our hearts leap forward . . . toward the coveted scenes [in Tennessee], but we realize [only] disappointment from hour to hour." Moreover, the soldiers had begun heavily pillaging the local residents for food.[13]

In mid-November, the army remained idle near Florence, where it had been unhappily camped for more than two weeks. Threatening weather was at hand, and the horses were in such poor condition that many could not easily pull wagons or artillery up a hill. A general state of disarray was evident. "The [supply] trains are all mixed pell-mell. Nobody knows where to find anything or anybody. There are no bread rations," complained a supply clerk. "We now miss the master hand of Gen. Johnston. Nothing worked wrong when he had command."[14]

Many men already anticipated another disaster under Hood's rash leadership and careless planning. "I fear this campaign will prove a failure, though I will continue to hope for the best," thought a Louisiana soldier. To add to their burdens, it was soon learned that Lincoln had been reelected, and the war would go on indefinitely.

The mood of many men may well have been represented by that of Robert Patrick, one of Hood's quartermaster clerks. "Well, I suppose that we are in for four years more [of fighting]. Damn the day, fight it out, I say, as long as there is a man [remaining] to fight with. I am devilish tired of Jeff Davis and his crew, but I am not in favor of stopping the war until we are independent."[15]

When it was learned on November 17 that Sherman had cut loose from Atlanta and was marching south toward the seacoast with his main army, Hood was compelled to make a hasty decision. His plan to draw the enemy after him in pursuit through Tennessee he now knew was defunct. Yet there was little chance to pursue Sherman through Georgia. There were too many miles separating the armies, and Hood's transportation system was so broken down that a rapid march in pursuit of Sherman was virtually impossible. What seemed inevitable was a risky counteroffensive into Tennessee.

Despite having only a short supply of rations, Hood ordered his Tennessee offensive to begin on November 21, an ominous day of freezing cold wind, with blustery snow. Hopeful, yet aware of the difficulties that lay ahead, some of his troops erected at the Tennessee state line a sign that read, "Tennessee, a grave, or a free home" as they crossed the border from Alabama.[16]

By November 28, Hood's troops were gathered at Columbia, Tennessee, on the banks of the Duck River in midstate. Here the opposing enemy force, a column of about twenty-two thousand under Major General John M. Schofield, confronted Hood directly across this imposing river. Major General George H. Thomas, the Federal commander at Nashville, had sent Schofield and his troops to delay Hood's advance and thus provide enough time for a defensive army to be gathered from reinforcements en route to Tennessee. Schofield was under orders not to bring on a fight unless compelled to do so.

Yet, in a manner reminiscent of Sherman's maneuvering during the Atlanta Campaign, Hood determined to outflank the Yankees at Columbia by crossing the river well east of town and making a rapid flanking march to Spring Hill, Tennessee, twelve miles to Schofield's rear. He then planned to steal a march on Nashville, and perhaps capture that city before the enemy could well defend it. By leaving nearly all of his artillery and his largest corps, Stephen D. Lee's, to bombard and threaten Schofield's lines at Columbia, he sought to deceive the Federal commander about his presence there.

Encouragingly, Hood's plan worked to near perfection on November 29—but this occurred prior to the bizarre events of that afternoon and night.

Just when it seemed as though Schofield's Yankee troops were trapped far behind at Columbia, and that many might be captured or their retreating columns broken up, a strange command failure occurred. The enemy was allowed to march through and past Spring Hill during the night, virtually under the muzzles of the Confederates' guns. Hood had left the field in early afternoon and gone to a nearby residence to rest. The subordinate left in charge, Major General Benjamin F. Cheatham, failed to understand the altered objective of Hood's dispositions. He attempted to capture the town rather than cut off the critical turnpike leading north. Then, darkness intervened prior to Cheatham's poorly organized attack. Amazingly, the entire Yankee force managed to escape and reach the neighboring town of Franklin, Tennessee, another twelve miles north along the banks of the Harpeth River.[17]

John Bell Hood was livid the following morning when he discovered what had happened. Blaming Cheatham and his subordinates John Brown and Patrick Cleburne for a lack of aggressiveness, Hood belatedly organized a pursuit, which he at first deemed fruitless. Later he learned that Schofield's forces were still at Franklin with all their wagons and equipment. Hood soon observed from a high hill two miles south of town that the Yankees were hastily attempting to repair two bridges across the Harpeth River so they could continue their retreat to Nashville.

On the early afternoon of November 30, John Bell Hood impulsively ordered a massive frontal attack with his entire force present, which was less than two-thirds of the army since Stephen D. Lee's Corps, the largest, was yet en route from Columbia with the artillery. Despite strong objections from those generals on hand, including Nathan Bedford Forrest, who urged a flanking movement, Hood would make no changes. In fact, he shuffled troop alignments so that Frank Cheatham's corps would bear the brunt of exposure during the massive headlong assault. Cheatham's troops were soon formed in the center, where the enemy's fortifications were strongest and the ground entirely open. Hood's orders were intended to serve as a corrective lesson, if not an outright punishment, for their behavior at Spring Hill. Hood later wrote that the "unwillingness [of his army to fight] unless behind breastworks" was an evil he sought to eradicate.[18]

At 4:00 P.M. on that fateful Indian summer–like afternoon, Hood's deployed ranks, more than twenty thousand men, marched across the open plain toward the enemy's frowning earthworks. These formidable emplacements were defended by nearly as many Federal troops, with tangled hedges of osage orange fashioned as an abatis in front. Massed batteries of Union artillery poured shell and then canister into the gray ranks as they attempted to cross the two miles of cleared ground. With flags flying and bands playing "Dixie," the Confederate assault columns presented one of the most imposing sights of the entire war. It soon became one of the most horrific battles ever endured in North America.

Fired into by serried ranks of defenders covered by log parapets, the Confederate columns were butchered at close range, yet still they kept coming. Entire ranks of Rebel infantry fell in lines so straight that it seemed to some as if a fence had been suddenly toppled over. The ragged butternut and gray lines shook violently under a hailstorm of bullets; their ranks were seen to stagger and reel like a herd of drunken men. Desperately, the survivors dove headlong into the three-foot-deep outer ditches at the earthworks.

Although some of Pat Cleburne's and John C. Brown's men breached the Yankee defenses at the center turnpike, they were soon driven back in ferocious hand-to-hand fighting. Amid combat that survivors later described as the worst ordeal of their army experiences,

Pat Cleburne, the Army of Tennessee's most brilliant general, was shot and killed a few yards from the enemy earthworks. He had asked no men to go where he would not, and died in a heroic effort to accomplish the impossible.

Moreover, the surviving attackers were now trapped, and lay for hours in the blood-soaked ditches a few feet from the muzzles of the enemy's guns. The crowded depressions, filled with writhing gray-clad bodies, were continually fired into from front, side, and rear due to the projecting and irregular line of enemy earthworks. Often hiding under the corpses of their comrades, the survivors could but wait until nightfall to crawl away from those godawful ditches.

John Bell Hood was not satisfied, however. He ordered Stephen D. Lee's newly arrived troops to make a night assault, which failed spectacularly and only added to the already-enormous butchery. Adamantly refusing to give up hope of breaking through the formidable Yankee lines, Hood then ordered another massed frontal assault for the following morning, once the army's artillery was in place.

Fortunately for Hood's remaining troops, the Federal commander, Schofield, decided to withdraw to Nashville during the middle of the night, having by then effected the removal of his wagons and supplies. On the morning of December 1, it was discovered that the Yankees had gone, and only the ghastly, smoke-shrouded battlefield, covered with bloating corpses and the wounded, remained.

Here was one of the most cruel and severe defeats of a major Confederate force during the war. Hood's massive frontal attacks had proved only the extreme valor of his gaunt and suffering veterans. Of the twenty-three thousand infantrymen present for the various assaults, about seven thousand were lost in five hours of fighting. So devastating were these casualties, especially in officers, that many units were now commanded by junior officers or even enlisted men. Thirteen of twenty-eight Confederate generals were killed, wounded, or missing. Sixty-five commanders of divisions, brigades, or regiments were likewise lost.[19]

The Army of Tennessee was a wreck. Survivors looked about them on the morning of December 1 and could hardly put into words their grief. "Many of the dead were shot to shreds," observed a Mississippi rifleman. "And I saw scores of [wounded] men . . . who had put their thumbs into their mouths, and had chewed them to shreds to keep from crying, coward like, as they lay exposed to the merciless fire. . . . Franklin was the only battleground I ever saw where the faces of the majority of the dead expressed supreme fear and terror. . . . Their eyes were wide open and fear staring.'' That terrible ditch was too horrible to long witness, noted the Mississippi rifleman, containing as it did fetid pools of blood, and bullet-riddled corpses piled high to shelter the initial survivors, most of whom had succeeded only in delaying their own deaths.

Thereafter, the ghastly specter of Franklin ''stalked among us,'' noted this Mississippian. The men were distraught and their spirits irreparably broken. The Army of Tennessee was but a hollow shell, intact in form only. ''[We were] led out in a slaughter pen to be shot down like animals'' was the way an angry Confederate officer assessed the entire sordid affair.[20]

Hood's ordering of a frontal attack was tantamount to murder, reflected an embittered officer in his journal. Their commander's deception of his own troops was clearly apparent. ''General Hood has betrayed us,'' wrote Captain Samuel Foster, one of Cleburne's Texans. ''This was not a fight with equal numbers and choice of the ground. . . . The wails and cries of widows and orphans made at Franklin, Tennessee, November 30th, 1864, will heat up the fires of the bottomless pit to burn the soul of General J. B. Hood for murdering their husbands and fathers.'' Hood's actions couldn't be described by any other term than ''murder,'' asserted Captain Foster. ''He sacrificed those men to make the name of Hood famous; when [and] if the history of [Franklin] is ever written it will make him infamous.'' The men had a right to be told the truth, and led wisely. ''Vengeance is mine, sayeth the Lord, and it will surely overtake him.''[21]

The Lord was in for heavy questioning by Confederate soldiers following the Battle of Franklin. One stricken Rebel survivor wrote, ''How could a just God look down . . . and witness this horrible tragedy, and not by some hidden hand stop it?''[22]

John Bell Hood's thought, however, seemed directed elsewhere. The worsening military situation demanded success, and thus the disaster at Franklin was proclaimed as a victory of sorts in his dispatches to the Richmond authorities.

On December 2 advance elements of the Confederate army arrived in front of the Nashville defenses to find a formidable array of forts and entrenchments blocking their way to the city. After settling down into a ''siege'' of George H. Thomas's troops in Nashville, Hood considered that he was heavily outnumbered. He thus sought to force the enemy to take the initiative by attacking the Confederate defensive positions set up along a range of hills south of Nashville over a span of about four miles.[23]

Hood had his wish on December 15, following a week of bitterly cold and snowy weather that had caused extreme suffering among the ranks of his largely, shoeless and semistarving army. George Thomas's troops, reinforced and reequipped, attacked the flanks of Hood's defensive perimeters, routing the defenders of several log redoubts along the Hillsboro Pike. Thomas's dismounted cavalrymen, firing Spencer repeating carbines, had been more than a match for the isolated, small redoubts, defended mostly by several cannon and a few infantrymen. The fruits of that day for the Federal attackers were sixteen captured guns, about one thousand prisoners, and the sweeping back of the Rebel lines more than eight miles.

As Hood's beaten troops staggered rearward that evening to a new line improvised along another range of hills, a critical question remained—what would Hood do next?

A staff officer observed, "The men seemed utterly lethargic and without interest in the battle." Their army had been saved from being cut off only by the early winter darkness, and Thomas's columns were menacingly close for another strong attack the next day. "I never witnessed such a want of enthusiasm," continued the staff officer, "and began to fear for tomorrow, hoping that Gen'l Hood would retreat during the night."[24]

Instead, Hood determined to gamble everything, in the hope that somehow he might win a tactical victory by defending the high ground his troops now occupied. Hood was desperate. To retreat now would sacrifice any prospect of a successful campaign. He could only lose by withdrawing. His career was at stake, and risking complete disaster was preferable to the disgrace certain to follow an ignominious retreat south.[25]

On December 16, a failed attack by brigades of Federal black troops on Overton Hill gave the Confederate commander great hope. Yet, in late afternoon, the Yankees on the opposite flank suddenly stormed Shy's Hill, considered impregnable by the Southern commander due to its imposing height and steep slopes. Hood had earlier detached many troops from this site, sending them to head off a rapidly developing attack beyond the Confederates' western flank. When the Federal division commander confronting Shy's Hill noticed that it was minimally defended, and that the Confederate artillery atop the hill could not be sufficiently depressed to fire into his attackers, he ordered an assault upon his own responsibility.

Brigadier General John McArthur's grim veterans stormed the hill under cover of an artillery barrage and not only broke the Rebel lines, but created a panic that spread like wildfire through Hood's ranks.

Gray regiments and brigades scattered as other Federal units along the line observed what was happening and began advancing in force against the Confederate lines. Within minutes, the entire Confederate army was in headlong retreat. McArthur's division alone captured two brigadier generals, 4,273 prisoners of war, twenty-four cannon, and about forty-five hundred small arms during the Nashville fighting. It was the most complete defeat of any major Confederate army during the war.

Hood and others tried to rally the men. They wouldn't listen. One young staff officer attempted to block the road, pointing back in the direction of the enemy and yelling, "Halt! Where are you going? There is no danger down there." A powder-grimed veteran, covered with mud, angrily spat out as he passed without halting, "You go to hell, I've been there!"[26]

"It's impossible to give you any idea of an army frightened and routed," a staff officer later wrote. This "wide awake nightmare" was only too painful to deny. A stunned brigade commander, Colonel Andrew J. Kellar, later wrote a formal apology for the conduct of his men. "It was not by fighting, nor the force of arms, not even numbers, which drove us from the field," he conceded.[27]

Kellar was correct. Hood's army had given way to fear, but not the fear of fighting. They were afraid of wasting their lives, of again being abused in the field and sacrificed to no sensible purpose. Hood's soldiers had suffered to the point that further suffering just didn't make sense anymore. Since the Battle of Franklin, the army had been a disaster waiting to happen. They were an army running away—from its enemy, from its commanders, and from itself. No longer were the soldiers proud and enduring in spirit. At that time, their thoughts weren't of military duty, but only of individual survival. It was an army pushed beyond the brink.[28]

Barely surviving a bleak and ruinous retreat south to recross the Tennessee River in late December, Hood's army had straggled all the way to Tupelo, Mississippi, by mid-January 1865. What had been an army of about thirty-eight thousand in September 1864 had dwindled to perhaps fifteen thousand including garrison troops picked up from other locations following the evacuation of northern Alabama.[29]

The army was on the verge of collapse. Desertions were so prevalent that two thousand Rebels had been gathered in by the Federal authorities during the last few months alone. "We whip ourselves faster than the enemy could possibly do it," wrote a cavalry officer. So embittered over his depleted command was Nathan Bedford Forrest that he sought permission to visit Richmond. "The Army of Tennessee was badly defeated and is greatly demoralized," wrote the "Wizard of the Saddle," "and to save it during the retreat from Nashville I was compelled almost to sacrifice my command."[30]

Eventually reorganized and sent to the East to fight in the Carolinas under the command of their beloved Joe Johnston, most of the Army of Tennessee's survivors could only look back with despair over the tragic events of the past six months. A veteran Mississippian, returning to the army after a prolonged absence due to a wound, was shocked at the small number of men that remained. "The Army of Tennessee is among the things that were," he observed. Moreover, the soldiers were "utterly despondent, and would hail with joy the prospect of peace on any terms," he concluded. "It seems to be a fact—shameful though it be—that three-fourths of the Army of Tennessee, and perhaps as great a proportion of the citizens of Georgia, Alabama, and Mississippi, are in favor of peace on any terms, no matter how ignominious they may be."[31]

"Hood's army is completely cleaned out and demoralized" was the way another veteran assessed matters. "This campaign has been the most disastrous of the war, and is certainly a severe blow to us [the Confederacy]."[32]

Just how depleted were the gaunt survivors of nearly four years of arduous campaigning was revealed by an orderly sergeant of Sears's brigade in an emotional journal entry:

My regiment, the whole army in fact, [is] in a deplorable condition. Twenty beside myself of Co. B [46th Mississippi Infantry] are here, but there is not a gun in the company. The regiment numbers about 150 men, about half of whom are barefoot. All are ragged, dirty, and covered with vermin, some not having sufficient clothing to hide their bodies. There are perhaps twenty guns but not a single cartridge box in the regiment. The men are jovial enough in regard to their condition . . . , but when it comes to discussing the war, they are entirely despondent, being fully convinced that the Confederacy is gone. . . . I do not think there is a stand of colors in the brigade.[33]

The wretched state of the Army of Tennessee was appalling to those observers who saw the ragged remnant following the Tennessee Campaign. Although endeavoring through his friends to distort the harsh realities, John Bell Hood quickly became the focus of a storm of criticism once the sad story of this campaign was publicly known.*

As was to be expected, Hood received angry censure from those in the army who had so long endured his recklessly aggressive concepts. An officer commented in reflection on the disastrous appointment of Hood as their commander, "[Having] butchered 10,000 [men]" around Atlanta and "as many more in Tennessee," Hood had "betrayed his whole army. . . . He might command a brigade, and even a division, but to command the army, he is not the man. General Joe Johnston has more military sense in one day than Hood ever did or will have. . . . [To] call him a general is a disgrace to those generals . . . who are worthy to be so called."[34]

Although John Bell Hood had attempted to save his career by a familiar tactic—blaming others—he was relieved of command on January 17, 1865, and ordered to Richmond. In the wake of his departure, the remaining Confederate soldiers contemplated the severe changes that had occurred over the last six months. Atlanta and a host of other important Southern cities had fallen, the Army of Tennessee had been virtually destroyed, Sherman's marauding columns were wreaking havoc in Georgia and the Carolinas, and even the civilian populace was suffering despair as never before.

"[In] beholding the ragged, frozen, half-starved survivors of the terrible campaign just ended," wrote a numbed soldier, "[and in] reflecting on what they have suffered, and the less than nothing gained, I ask myself, is there a way to stop this wholesale slaughter?"[35]

A growing, final despair was now evident among the ranks, and the soldiers knew where it was leading. Once again, the only trust seemed to be in a familiar place.

---

*An article written by Gustavus Woodson Smith, Hood's special friend and distant relative, in the Augusta, Georgia, *Daily Constitutionalist* of February 5, 1865, claimed Franklin was "a decisive victory" in which the Army of Tennessee had been restored to "its old fighting spirit."

"It may be that God designs our overthrow," wrote an Army of Tennessee veteran. ". . . If so, may He prepare us for the ordeal that awaits us as a conquered people. There is too much iniquity in the land in high and low places . . . , for us to expect any interposition of Providence in our behalf. May He teach us our duty."[36]

The religious faith among the ranks, which for so long had served to bind them in a unity of martial spirit, seemed to be rapidly tending toward a new interpretation.

Chapter Twenty-nine

SHERMAN'S SENTINELS

His words conveyed an unorthodox perspective. "Until we can repopulate Georgia, it is useless to occupy it," wrote the eccentric if talented general whose name would forever be linked with the events in progress. "The utter destruction of its roads, houses, and people will cripple their military resources . . . I can make the march, and make Georgia howl."[1]*

He was William Tecumseh Sherman, the Yankee general who reasoned that to sooner end the war he would have to make its horror felt by the deep South's civilian populace as well as its soldiers. First expressing his ideas in terms of their practicality, he had queried Ulysses S. Grant in October 1864, "[Why not] march across Georgia to Savannah or Charleston . . . ?" By "breaking roads and doing irreparable damage" Sherman would continue "smashing things" to the sea, then move north through the Carolinas to appear in Robert E. Lee's rear.[2]

Grant's subsequent approval included some rather unique advice: "You will, no doubt, clean the country where you go of railroad

---

*The repopulating of Georgia apparently refers to W. T. Sherman's idea of "re-peopling"; massively infusing Northerners from such states as Iowa and Wisconsin into Georgia to obtain a loyal population base. This concept involved the transfer of houses and property to those willing to remove to Georgia. See Lee Kennett, *Marching Through Georgia,* HarperCollins Publishers, New York, 1995, 98.

tracks, and hoof stock, as well as the negroes. As far as arms can be supplied, . . . I would put them in the hands of negro men. Give them such organization as you can. They will be of some use."[3]

Although Sherman intended no slave insurrection, he had for encouragement in his policy of destruction and deprivation the words of Henry Halleck, the Federal army's chief of staff. "Your mode of conducting war is just the thing we now want," Halleck told Sherman on September 26. "We have tried the kid-glove policy long enough."[4]

Sherman's "March to the Sea," which began on November 15 with the destruction of much of Atlanta, involved the premise that war would be conducted on a total scale, rather than a purely military one. A multiple agenda was clear in Sherman's mind. His concept was to march his army "right through" Jefferson Davis's most productive territory, thereby demonstrating to the world "that we [the Federal military] have a power that Davis cannot resist." Sherman wanted all observers to "reason thus: If the North can march an army right through the South, it is proof positive that the North can prevail in this contest. . . ."[5]

Yet it was Sherman's idea of bringing the physical war home to those who were its abettors that seemed to fire his ardor most. Those with the strongest wills to break, those who dwelled in the Southern heartland and supported Rebel resistance, from newspaper editors to planters to the humblest of farmers, were the enemy. "You cannot qualify war in harsher terms than I will," he had earlier warned the city officials of Atlanta. "War is cruelty and you cannot refute it, and those who brought war into our country deserve all the curses and maledictions a people can pour out. . . . You might as well appeal against the thunderstorm as against these terrible hardships of war. . . . Now that war comes home to you . . . , you depreciate its horrors. . . . I want peace, and believe it can now only be reached through union and war, and I will ever conduct war with a view to perfect an early success."[6]

Sherman soon outlined his new mission to a key subordinate, George H. Thomas: "I propose to demonstrate the vulnerability of the South, and make its inhabitants feel that war and individual ruin are synonymous terms." "We are not only fighting hostile armies," Sherman wrote with further emphasis, "but a hostile people, and must make old and young, rich and poor, feel the hard hand of war."[7]

Sherman most wanted to break the will of all Confederate people to continue waging war. He said the "smashing" of their property, houses, buildings, and even their livelihoods would carry a strong message. Beyond denying the Confederacy's armies food and supplies, it would defeat the populace mentally. "Even without a battle, the result operating upon the minds of sensible men would produce fruits . . . ," grimly wrote Sherman. He would shorten the war by terrorizing Southern civilians, he firmly contended.[8]

Sherman's concept meant in essence that the war, his war, would be waged for domination of Southern minds. Its methods would involve applying extreme stress and bringing trauma to Confederate families, not just to soldiers. Perhaps the best way to damage a soldier's willpower, reasoned Sherman, was to strike at his family's.

Word of Sherman's ravaging columns spread like wildfire throughout Georgia in late November 1864. Beginning with the widespread destruction of small towns and supply depots in northern Georgia, a pall of flame and destruction scourged the countryside. An appalled Georgia girl, then returning to her Decatur residence, wrote, "[we found] a war stricken section of country where stood chimneys only" amid the smoldering ruins. No wonder they were called "Sherman's sentinels," she observed, "as they seemed to be keeping guard over those scenes of desolation."[9]

With sixty-two thousand Yankee soldiers cutting a swath that ranged from twenty-five to sixty miles wide through middle and southeastern Georgia, the sight of rising black smoke and hordes of fleeing refugees became common. For nearly three hundred miles over nearly a month, until Sherman's two primary columns reached the sea at Savannah, Georgia, and captured Fort McAllister on December 13, the destruction and pillaging continued. With Hood's army in northern Alabama, and only "bushwhackers," local militia, and Wheeler's twenty-five hundred cavalrymen contesting the Yankees' progress, Confederate resistance was minimal. Even the ravages of Wheeler's gray riders, who destroyed livestock and provisions while operating on the fringes of Sherman's columns, added to the pillaging and destruction.[10]

The ground Sherman swept through was soon known among residents as "the burnt country"—the vast, desolated Georgia countryside that he rendered a wasteland. A Georgia girl, Eliza Frances Andrews was appalled at what she saw:

There was hardly a fence left standing all the way from Sparta to Gordon. The fields were trampled down and the road was lined with the carcasses of horses, hogs, and cattle that the invaders, unable to consume or carry away with them, had wantonly shot down to starve out the people and prevent them from making their crops. The stench in some places was unbearable . . . The dwellings that were standing all showed signs of pillage, and on every plantation we saw the charred remains of the gin-house and the packing screw, while here and there, lone chimney stacks, 'Sherman's Sentinels,' told of homes laid in ashes. . . . Hay ricks and fodder stands were demolished, corn cribs were empty, and every bale of cotton that could be found was burnt by the savages. . . . I saw no grain of any sort, . . . [and] there was not even a chicken left in the country to eat. . . . [11]

Another distraught victim watched as Sherman's men burned her gin house, the year's crop of cotton, the seed of the prior crop, the carriage house, the wagon shelters, and every carriage, buggy, and wagon. Then they came to ransack the house. "Not a panel of yard fence was left intact," she bemoaned. "In their search for gold and silver and other valuables they did not leave an article of furniture untouched. Bedding was stripped off and thrown on the floor; every lock on doors, closets, or wardrobes was broken and the doors smashed with the butts of guns; every bureau drawer was thrown on the floor, contents strewn in every direction."[12]

Among the Yankee foragers, known as "bummers," hunting for plunder came to be such sport that a youthful Illinois sergeant described in a letter home how the men would take their ramrods from their rifle muskets and poke in the freshly disturbed soil, seeking to find valuables buried by the desperate residents. Sergeant Eugene A. McWayne of the 127th Illinois Volunteers said:

The boys . . . came across some fresh dirt [on a plantation], so they pushed their ramrods down. It struck a board, so they commenced digging. Well, to their surprise, someone beneath the board yells out, 'Hold on, let me *out!* I will surrender!' Well, they dug on till they could get hold of the board, and pulled it out. And there was a *Johnny!* He had dug a hole . . . , placed a board over it with a hole in it, so he could get air. Then [they] covered it over with dirt, but was careful to keep the hole open to get a supply of fresh air. This

was done by the aid of the women folks, I suppose. You may bet he
was a scared Johnny.[13]

Many victims of the dreaded "vandals" felt personally violated. The
loss of valuables and keepsakes of all manner proved the malicious
nature of these Yankees. Although some soldiers were simply having
fun—quest for booty was particularly appealing to some youths—the
outrage would endure for a lifetime in the minds of the sufferers.
Despite Sherman's Special Field Orders Nos. 119 and 120, which prohibited the burning of civilian "mills, houses, cotton gins, etc.," permission was given for the destruction of these structures should "local
hostility" occur. In fact, "a devastation more or less relentless" was
recommended when guerrillas or bushwhackers fired on foraging
parties, or else burned bridges.

In practice, Sherman's orders were often interpreted by the men
as a license to do what their consciences permitted. "We are to forage
as much as we want off the country" was the way one soldier understood the directives. Another believed that the Union army intended
to "not leave enough to subsist a flea on the country through which
we passed." "The impression among officers and men is that we are
to pass through the country burning as we go," remarked a chaplain
in his diary.[14]

While houses were ransacked, and the cattle and farm animals destroyed or carried off, most of the occupied homes were left standing.
After destroying gin houses, crops, and other farm production buildings and equipment, the foraging parties departed, leaving in their
wake not only despair, but economic destitution.[15]

This deprivation tormented the sufferers the most. A displaced
Georgia resident, Mary Gay, found a heartrending scene in Decatur:
"a young mother, beautiful in desolation, with a baby in her arms,
and on either side of her, a little one, piteously crying for something
to eat. 'Oh, mama, I want something to eat, so bad!, Oh, mama, I
am so hungry—give me something to eat!' . . . [They] were begging
for what the mother had not to give. She could only give them
soothing words." To sustain their families, some young girls took to
gathering lead minie balls from the old battlefields around Atlanta
and trading them to Confederate authorities for flour, meal, and
meat.[16]

What for Sherman's troops had become a scavenger hunt—a cornucopia of food, forage, and fun—to the Georgians was needless preying upon civilians and a cause for bitter loathing. "If all the words of hatred in every language were lumped together into one huge epithet of detestation," wrote a Georgia girl, "they could not tell how I hate Yankees."[17]

The March to the Sea had, as Sherman intended, caused Georgians to despair. Sherman claimed five thousand horses, four thousand mules, thirteen thousand head of cattle, 9.5 million pounds of corn, and 10.5 million pounds of fodder. Added to the three hundred miles of wrecked railroad track, and hundreds of burned cotton gins and mills, buildings, homes, and barns, it was a catastrophe for the South. As he had promised, Sherman had brought "individual ruin" to Georgians.[18]

The effect on morale, both at home and in the army, is not hard to imagine. A Georgia officer with Lee's army wrote to his family in Hancock County, Georgia, prior to learning of the havoc Sherman's troops had wrought, "Our homes will soon be in Yankee hands, and at Yankee mercy, so cheerfully as I can, I submit to the necessity. Though I know they will sweep me clean, it is only what a hundred thousand others have suffered."[19]

Once the extent of the devastation became known, however, many became gloomy and frustrated. Another veteran, Samuel Wiley, of the 15th Georgia Infantry, fretted from Richmond, Virginia, that matters were "rapidly going down hill now." He foresaw "the probability of a crowning disaster" at home, envisioning "Sherman's raiders among you [his father] in your house, stealing, plundering, and destroying everything; then burning your house, dear old 'Rocky Hill' and my own home. You all [will] perhaps be despoiled of everything, turned out to seek the charity of a district equally impoverished." Wiley's only thought was of inflicting greater carnage on the enemy; "I feel impelled to rush to the front . . . and [do] what I [can] to avenge your private wrongs and insults."[20]

Despite their swelling anger, Georgians serving in the army had been compelled to watch from afar as detailed accounts of the devastation trickled in, often from captured or exchanged Yankee newspapers. Lamenting, "I have no doubt the hated swarm of Yankees have passed over us, and our loved home has been partly stripped and desolated," a Georgia captain in late November blamed the authorities. "I think the management of affairs in Georgia has been wretched," he bitterly wrote. "Since the removal of [Joe] Johnston, the preponderance of brains has been terribly against us. If our people could have arranged to hang a mammoth bell around Sherman's neck, they might have divined his movements."[21]

Worries about conditions at home and the survival of loved ones preyed upon the minds of Georgians on military duty. The stress was such that many deserted or became "submissionists" in attitude. Combined with the soldiers' anger about recent events was their despair over their inability to protect their families. Their letters home were less concerned with endurance and hope for ultimate success than with placing blame, and in this they expressed an increasing frustration. These letters reflected the spreading decline in morale in Robert E. Lee's Army of Northern Virginia, especially among its extensive number of Georgians.[22]

Although many of the Georgia soldiers' families bravely endured the devastation and managed to survive, the number of refugees and homeless presented a nightmare of suffering. To these people, it was not states' rights that mattered anymore, it was their own survival. They wanted the war to end.

The destruction of Southern property had only begun for residents of the deep South at the end of 1864. Next to feel the wrath of Sherman's ravaging columns was what the Yankees regarded as "the cradle of secession."

"South Carolina cried out the first for war," observed an Iowa soldier who contemplated the fiery campaign ahead, "and she shall have it to her heart's content. She sowed the Wind. She will soon reap the Whirlwind."[23]

The Carolinas Campaign that began February 2, 1865, with Sherman's advance toward Columbia, South Carolina, became even more severe in its destructiveness than the march through Georgia, particularly in the burning of houses. Revengeful Yankee soldiers considered the devastation of South Carolina a special objective; it seemed their tacit duty to teach the state a severe lesson for its fire-eating secessionist role. Thus, there was a conspiracy among the men, reported a New Jersey officer, "to burn everything in the state." Despite orders to the contrary, "houses, in some way, get on fire and nearly all we have passed thus far are, I think, in ashes," he wryly observed. News of Sherman's ravaging of the land spread rapidly, and the burning was often made easier by the flight of white residents before the marauding columns arrived.

Large portions of entire towns or villages were burned and pillaged, including Orangeburg, Lexington, Camden, Winnsboro, and Chesterfield. At Columbia, the state capital, 460 private homes, more than one-third of the city, were consumed in one horrendous wind-driven conflagration on February 17. The blackened ruins would serve as a warning to future generations about the consequences of rebellion, thought one Yankee soldier.[24]

The resultant bitterness and outrage that welled up in the native population were expressed by killing Yankee soldiers caught foraging by the Confederate cavalry and Militiamen. Several hundred Federal soldiers are estimated to have died at the hands of their captors during the Savannah and Carolinas campaigns. The sight of a Yankee corpse hanging from a tree, or alongside the road with its throat slit, was intended as a threat to would-be foragers.

When Sherman's troops retaliated by executing captured bushwhackers or burning local residences near the site of recovered soldiers' bodies, the violence only escalated.[25]

Then, with the destruction and devastation spreading into North Carolina as Sherman's columns passed northward in early March, there was a profound awareness among the citizenry that they had lost control, and that the Southern government no longer had the means or power to protect them.

To the victims the government's weakness could signify but one thing—that the war was lost. Thus, the attitudes of Southerners surviving Sherman's heavy hand of war ranged from embittered defiance to reasoned submission. "Can we ever live in peace with the desecrators of our homes and the murderers of our fathers, brothers, and sons—never—we are bound to rise again," seethed a North Carolina woman. Yet to another Southern lady in Winnsboro, the path to surrender was evident. "The Confederacy seemed suddenly to have changed. A glory had passed from it, and . . . we felt the end was near." Even the refined Mary Chesnut, after fleeing from Columbia, South Carolina, foresaw nothing but despair. "When people are without a cent, how do they live?" she implored. "I am about to enter the noble band of homeless, houseless refugees. Confederate pay does not [even] buy one shoestrings."[26]

The emotions of the people had unmasked the nervousness of their existence.

The Confederacy rested on the effectual maintenance of its armies, but the existence of the armies tottered on the willpower of the people, who provided its soldiers and supporters. The policy of devastation of both soldiers and civilians by total warfare was apparent in the aftermath of the Sherman Savannah and Carolinas campaigns. The Southern revolution was critically stricken in means and mind. "When I see and hear the misery occasioned all over the land, my heart shudders and bleeds," wrote a distraught Georgia wife to her officer husband in February 1865. "What next? Heaven knows."[27]

Implied in her words but left unsaid was what she and many others knew, yet could hardly bear to consider.

Chapter Thirty

To Justify a Reasonable Hope of Success

Their grief seemed to grow with each new day. His army was half-starved and ragged, without shoes and clothing, and the men were too few. Indeed the remaining soldiers had only their intense spirit to steel themselves for the imminent fray.

Robert E. Lee, at the advent of 1865, was beset with obstacles too numerous for him to hope for outright victory for his beloved Army of Northern Virginia. He could only seek to preserve its diminished potency.

Accordingly, if Lee's professional attitude in early 1865 was that the Confederacy's cause was not necessarily lost, he knew it was in grave doubt. With Grant threatening a major movement near Petersburg, and Sherman advancing north toward Virginia and utilizing additional troops just brought from Tennessee under John M. Schofield, the enemy "seem[ed] to have everything their own way," admitted Lee. Because "no man can tell what will be the result," Lee would simply try his best and trust in "a merciful God, who does not always give the battle to the strong. I pray we may not be overwhelmed," he grimly concluded. "I shall . . . endeavor to do my duty, and fight to the last."[1]

Certainly, these were practical, sobering words. Lee had enormous problems, the most severe of which, he suggested, was the need for more men. Various detachments had been made from the Petersburg defenders, and his all-too-attenuated lines were reduced to a skeleton force in several locations. Desertions were so numerous that he had lost fifty-six men from A. P. Hill's corps alone in three days during mid-January. Currently, there were only eight hundred men to guard a line formerly held by two thousand, he somberly reported. Whereas the enemy's strength appeared to continually increase, Lee noted that his army's seemed only to diminish. "All we want to resist them [the enemy] is men," he implored of President Davis.[2]

Jefferson Davis, even at this point, steadfastly refused to concede the possibility of defeat. General Lee, following an interview with Davis, found the president set in his goals and possessed of "a remarkable faith in the possibility of winning our independence."

Davis possessed an unbending resolve, despite his awareness that peace initiatives, foreign intervention, and even prisoner exchanges that might replenish his troops would likely fail. The president's perspective was confirmed by his long-professed policy of fighting to the last man. "The war came," he told a friend, "and now it must go on till the last man of this generation falls in his tracks, and his children seize his musket and fight our battle." On the practical side, the only recourse, he urged his listeners at a public rally in Richmond on February 6, was for the citizens to rush to join the armies. Then there would be great victories on the battlefield, and before the end of June, said Davis, the Yankees would be coming to him seeking peace. "[We are] on the verge of successes," exhorted the president, and they would soon teach the insolent enemy who the masters were.[3]

Although this speech was scoffed at by his critics for being filled with the delusions of a desperate man, Davis's intent was to secure every available person for the Confederacy's fight to the finish. In fact, his commitment to the success of the national cause involved a dramatic change in policy that, to him, had once been unthinkable.[4]

Blacks were now the only untapped source of manpower for the Confederacy's hard-pressed, woefully depleted armies. Many Southerners had long urged that the South's male slaves and free black men should be enrolled in the army. The most formal proposal had been that of Pat Cleburne, which Davis had suppressed at the beginning of 1864.

Whereas Davis had once quashed even mention of Cleburne's initiative, eleven months after that general was discredited for his initiative the president outlined in an address to Congress the beginnings of direct utilization of blacks in the army. Subsequent war pressures and various expressions of support for arming slaves under white officers further encouraged the president. In February 1865 he proposed the enlistment of blacks. "We are reduced to choosing whether the negroes shall fight for or against us," he told a correspondent. For substantial support, Davis had the endorsement of Robert E. Lee, who wrote that this measure was "not only expedient, but necessary." The blacks would make efficient soldiers, Lee predicted, and they should be freed in consideration of their service.[5]

The public emergence of this issue after nearly four years of warfare was symptomatic of the enormous pressures building for military success. It was further proof that the hour of desperation was truly at hand for the Confederacy. After all the haggling and infighting, the controversy over ending slavery was suddenly brought into focus. If blacks were to fight for the South, they had to have the incentive of freedom. The alteration of Southern society was thus under abrupt scrutiny. In reality, the issue represented to the Southern people a choice of priorities—property or independence. As many had foreseen, the continuance of slavery was now at stake.

It was a difficult matter to ponder for many. One veteran Virginia soldier who had carried Stonewall Jackson's battle flag at Cedar Mountain, Lieutenant Bob Isbell, wrote in late February 1865, "I am still oppose[d] to putting negroes into the army, tho I believe they can be made to fight as well if not better than the white [man] does. The whites can [win] if they will fight this war out to a successful termination. But I am afraid too many of them are beginning to show the white feather."[6]

While reactions to enrolling black soldiers were mixed among the Southern populace and army, a good portion, and apparently a majority, favored the use of blacks if necessary to secure Southern independence. The cause was of primary importance, many reasoned, and a Virginian said, "I am for . . . anything or anybody in preference to going back again with the North. If slavery is to be the barrier to our independence, I say let it go to the devil!"[7]

To a plainspoken soldier in the 1st South Carolina Infantry, deciding the issue required only common sense. Private Samuel McAbee noted on February 15, 1865:

I see that Congress is trying to fetch the negroes in the army. . . . I think that two-thirds of the men [in our army] is for it, and if we don't get help we are gone up sure, for they [Yankees] are coming in on every side and half of [our] men won't fight. I tell you this force is very tired of the war, but they will fight if they are pissed. . . . I hope to God that I may never have to fire another gun, but I am sure if the war don't stop, they will make the negro fight. I hate to fight with [alongside] them, but they are not any better . . . [to stay out of the war] than I am.[8]

Another soldier from the Army of Tennessee agreed, regarding the issue of emancipation as secondary to that of Southern freedom. "With me, independence is the paramount question," he asserted. In the 46th Mississippi Infantry, there was a variety of opinion, yet a heightened sense of urgency. This matter was extensively debated among the 46th, and a formal vote was twice taken without a decision. The prospect of fighting alongside blacks in the army caused one soldier to remark that while "it was not right," any resolution must be "for show." The real sentiment, he declared, was for peace, on any terms by any means. The following day the regiment passed a resolution that "the best interests of the country demanded that negroes be placed in the field as soldiers."[9]

Robert Patrick of the 4th Louisiana Infantry expressed the views of many soldiers when he recorded in his diary entry for January 18, 1865:

There are reports floating . . . that we are about to make a proposition to France and England that if they will recognize us . . . we will emancipate the slaves within twenty-five years. . . . For my part, I am in favor of it, and so is every man I have heard speak about it. If we continue to lose ground as we have for the last twelve months, we will soon be defeated, and then slavery will be gone anyway. I think it is better that we should give up slavery and gain our independence. There is no doubt in my opinion that we are gone unless something is done for our welfare, and that very quick.[10]

While some leaders and newspaper editors decried the use of black soldiers and their emancipation, the question had truly evolved to which was more practical—accepting "Yankee subjugation," or mandating a great change within Southern society. The common man seemed to have little remorse in making an expedient adjustment, despite uneasiness about the social implications.

Beyond resorting to enlisting blacks in exchange for their independence loomed the key question of implementation. Did enough time remain to accomplish the organization, training, and employment of a significant number of black soldiers? Overwhelming numbers of Union forces were at the gates of Richmond, while only a remnant of the Army of Tennessee was coming to the Carolinas in a desperate, last-ditch attempt to stop Sherman. Perhaps it was too late for any military measures to be successful. Even Vice President Alexander Stephens decided to take no further part in the government and went home. Stephens was convinced at this point that the Confederacy's cause was hopeless.[11]

The question of black Southern soldiers thus seemed moot to many. Following delays in congressional approval, and disorganization due to the chaos of a crumbling war effort added to the need for requisite action by the states, only a few companies of blacks were organized in Virginia prior to April 1. They failed to see action, and the entire matter, after all the emotion and fury, became a classic example of taking an important measure far too late. The real, ultimate significance of the decision to enlist blacks was in the revised thinking of Southerners. Many Confederates developed a new awareness of how their relations with blacks would be conducted in the future.[12]

Robert E. Lee was insistent. He said "a calamity" was in the offing. Unless his men were fed and forage provided for the cavalry, "dire results" would occur. Lee particularly wanted the government Commissary Department reorganized. "Some of the men [have] been without meat for three days," complained Lee on February 8, 1865, "and all [are] suffering from reduced rations and scant clothing, exposed to battle, cold, hail, and sleet. . . . The physical strength of the men, if their courage survives, must fail under this treatment."[13]

General Lee's pointed criticism of the army's logistics cited a major deficiency that had long existed. The absence of adequate supplies had affected both the performance of his army and its morale. Yet this problem was just the tip of the iceberg. With military matters in a profound state of decline, the urgent need for action in so many areas finally resulted in Lee's emergence as the South's last hope. On February 9, Robert E. Lee assumed command of the military forces of the Confederate States. Together with the new secretary of war, John C. Breckinridge, Lee implemented several key aspects of reform, including appointment of a new commissary general, the assignment of Joseph E. Johnston to command in the Carolinas, and an offer of amnesty for deserters.[14]

Like a sudden breath of fresh air, these changes were largely heralded with enthusiasm by the army, and beneficial results soon became apparent. Bob Isbell of the 2d Virginia Cavalry wrote on February 21, 1865:

I am very glad to hear that the war spirit is reviving throughout the country. It is at a very low ebb in this regiment. But I think it will revive some before the spring campaign opens. I am still as I have always been, for war to the knife, rather than go back into the union under any consideration whatever. I believe that any and every man who has a spark of patriotism will die rather than go back into the union, or see the South overrun by the Yankees. . . . I do not believe as I did some time ago that Virginia will be evacuated. I think it is Genl. R. E. Lee's intention to hold Va. at all hazards.[15]

Like Isbell, other soldiers began reporting better morale and a brighter outlook. Also, an appeal to citizens for help in provisioning and clothing the army had been productive, causing Captain Charles Blackford to write, "Things at the South are brighter. Johnston is collecting a good army, we hope. If we had even a second-class victory it will have a wonderful effect in inspiring our men. Old Virginia, as ever, is giving the keynote to the reaction which is going on."[16]

The staunch Virginia backbone of Lee's army had long been apparent, and even a veteran Georgia captain admired the great resolve of soldiers from the Old Dominion. "I don't think the people of any state in the Confederacy have shown themselves equal to the Virginians," wrote Edgeworth Bird in early 1865. "Their spirit is still unbroken, and their patriotism, under the greatest trials, [is] beyond praise."[17]

As the ultimate Virginian, now the premier leader of all Confederate forces, Robert E. Lee was looked upon as a savior, a person to trust when all else fell apart. "How well it is that we have a commander in whom all of us have such unbounded confidence!" wrote an admiring Virginia lieutenant. "Whatever he does we think it is all right, and whatever he neglects to do, we suppose [it] is for our good."[18]

What was possible for saving the cause of Southern independence rested not so much on the army's heavy numbers as on its fighting spirit—at least that was the premise upon which the soldiers relied. Despite the need for more manpower, Lee tacitly agreed with his men. Because obtaining significant reinforcements or new recruits in the near future was impossible, the existing soldiers' morale and will-power concerned Lee and others the most. In fact, the very crux of the military condition of the country, wrote Robert E. Lee on March 9, involved attitude. "Everything in my opinion has depended and still depends upon the disposition and feelings of the people," he told Secretary of War John C. Breckinridge. "Their representations can best decide how they will bear the difficulties and sufferings of their condition, and how they will respond to the demands. . . ."[19]

Lee knew he could count on the spirit of his men, provided they were reasonably supplied. Yet the support of the general populace played a crucial role in sustaining the war effort. Despite some im-provements in provisions, clothing, and materiel, the advent of fa-vorable weather for campaigning meant that the crucial test would come quickly. Considering the great "peril" of the enemy's over-whelming numbers, said Lee, he needed to be able "to maintain a force adequate to justify a reasonable hope of . . . success."

If the people and soldiers truly believed they might still win, then the effort would be self-perpetuating. Such minor complaints among the troops as arrearages in pay and lack of new clothing would be negated "by military success," predicted Lee. Even the forced aban-donment of the Petersburg lines wouldn't necessarily be fatal, pro-vided the army could be maintained "in an efficient condition."[20]

But the key to all this, Lee well knew, was furthering a viable hope of success among the people and the soldiers alike. The renewal of hope would come only from victory on the battlefield. Thus, prompt and productive military action was needed. In the South's life-or-death crisis Lee had all but mandated his own course of action.[21]

"The army has been quite low spirited under our recent reverses [in Tennessee, Georgia, and the Carolinas]," wrote one of Lee's jun-ior officers in late January 1865, "but I hope a reaction is taking place, and henceforth their spirits will rise. One reason for this is our season of inactivity. None of these complaints would be heard if the army were in motion." The drudgery and hardships of siege warfare had greatly played upon the minds of the men, and they were anxious for relief. "Does it not seem foolish that two nations should sit down and dig, and dig again, and sit down for eight long months in front of each other?" pleaded a Virginian worn out with waiting.[22]

Lee understood their mood, and the dire consequences of inaction as the enemy continued to tighten their stranglehold on the Petersburg lines. Moreover, Sherman was again moving north, and Lee knew that the linkup of Grant and Sherman would force him to abandon the Petersburg defenses, which would result in the fall of Richmond. He initially planned to impede Sherman's progress as much as possible.

In mid-March 1865, Lee told Joe Johnston, who had gathered a force of about twenty thousand men near Raleigh, North Carolina, that the supply route from Raleigh was so important to the Army of Northern Virginia that he would not be able to hold his position at Petersburg if the Raleigh road was interrupted. "Should you be forced back in this direction," continued Lee, "both [of our] armies would certainly starve." Although he acknowledged that "the greatest calamity that [might] befall us is the destruction of our armies," it was apparent that Lee wanted to strike at Sherman should there be "a reasonable probability" of succeeding.[23]

Joe Johnston responded on March 19 by attempting to fall upon one of Sherman's advancing columns and defeat it before the entire Yankee force could unite. Yet the Battle at Bentonville, North Carolina, resulted only in another Rebel failure, with Johnston's forces thereafter being reduced to a reported 13,500 infantry.[24]

Increasingly desperate, Lee planned his own offensive a few days later. Although generally "unwilling to hazard any portion of the troops in an assault upon fortified positions," he seemed now to have little choice. Lee hoped that, by taking the initiative and seizing a somewhat vulnerable position east of Petersburg, he might force Grant to contract his lines. Otherwise, his attack might deceive Grant about the Confederates' real purpose of clearing a way southwest of Petersburg so as to enable the union of Lee's and Johnston's armies.[25]

The predawn attack led by Major General John B. Gordon's corps on March 25 resulted in the capture of Fort Stedman and more than a half mile of the fortified Yankee front line at Hare's Hill. Yet within hours the attackers were driven back into the captured works by heavy fire from an entrenched second line. Such a withering crossfire swept the ground over which the Confederates retreated that nearly two thousand of Gordon's men later surrendered after a Union counterattack was organized. Lee's desperate attempt at victory was costly; he lost about four thousand men in the attack, nearly 10 percent of his effective infantry strength.[26]

The consequences were all too apparent to Lee. "It will be impossible to prevent a junction between Grant and Sherman," he warned Jefferson Davis on March 26. The combined Union armies would outnumber his force by "nearly a hundred thousand," calculated Lee. Thus it was not prudent "that this army should maintain its position" until Sherman's "too near" approach. Lee would therefore make plans for evacuating the Petersburg lines and seek to unite with Joe Johnston by moving west and south.

A few days later, Lee's worst fears were realized when Grant began operations southwest of Petersburg with a view toward cutting off the Confederates' last remaining communications links. The occupation of Dinwiddie Court House by the enemy on March 30 precipitated the Battle of Five Forks, where about twenty thousand infantry led by George Pickett attempted to defeat the Yankees. Instead, on March 31 and April 1, the gray troops were driven back and about five thousand Confederates captured.

Grant's forces were now interposed between major elements of the Confederate army, and Lee worried that the enemy will "close us in between the James and Appomattox Rivers if we remain [in place]."[27]

There was little choice remaining. On Sunday, April 2, Lee informed the government that it was absolutely imperative that the defensive lines be evacuated that night, and that as a consequence Richmond must fall. Notified of Lee's message while at church, Jefferson Davis departed the capital at 11 P.M. via railroad for Danville.[28]

Amid the confusion of looting and rioting, and the eerie conflagration from multiple fires, Richmond was evacuated that night, and on the morning of April 3 the Union army entered the war-torn, smoldering city.

Lee's efforts had been in vain. The army was mortally wounded. They had been too few in the face of too many. Lee had again relied on the valiant spirit of his incomparable army, all the while enduring an enormous burden on his own shoulders. The men had always looked to "Marse Robert" for their deliverance, and he had usually come through for them. Now there was only grim despair amid the ranks. The willpower of the soldiers to continue the war was faltering. Defeat seemed inevitable. For nearly four years, acceptance of defeat in the Army of Northern Virginia had been nil. Following a setback in the Shenandoah Valley in 1864, one of Lee's detached junior officers had reported, "The men are eager to wipe out the shame which they think attaches to a defeat under any circumstances."[29]

But matters had changed. One of Lee's disillusioned North Carolina soldiers wrote to his wife in mid-March 1865, "You don't know how tired I am of this war . . . I have stayed and done my duty for three years as well as any man. . . . How much longer will these wicked people have poor men killed and ruined for life from being wounded? . . . I think that every day this war goes on it is just making a bad matter worse, and every man that is killed is nothing short of murder." To a Georgian detached from Lee's army, the situation in 1865 had turned truly desperate. "Oh, how dark, dark, dark is the future," he complained to his wife. "Hope is all that keeps up one's spirit, . . . [but] there is nothing to make one come to any other conclusion than that all is lost." Legislators and ranking officers might say otherwise, he continued, but the troops were no longer deceived. Some men still "let their head officers do their thinking [for them], . . . but [with] by far the greatest number of those I see . . . it is not so."[30]

Hope had given way to hopelessness, and those at home were deeply affected.

To Mary Chesnut, the final days before Richmond's fall had been filled with a moral inertia. Noting that the newspapers had reported a series of drawn battles involving Lee's and Joe Johnston's forces, Mary recorded her disgust. "Only a few more dead bodies, stiff and stark on an unknown battlefield. . . . A few more men killed. A few more women weeping their eyes out, and nothing whatever decided by it more than we knew before the battle." To another Virginia woman, Mary Cochran, the month of March 1865 had been one of despondency and gloom. "If we give up Richmond, we give up Virginia," she prophesied. "If Virginia is given up, there is nothing worth left fighting for." Even her friends were talking about what they would do "when we are subjugated," and she recoiled in despair.[31]

The failing morale that now prevailed was perhaps best portrayed by a second lieutenant with the 26th Virginia Infantry, who wrote during March to his brother:

If Petersburg and Richmond [are] evacuated, from what I have seen and heard, our cause will be hopeless. It is useless to conceal the truth any longer. Many of the people at home have become so demoralized that they write to their husbands, sons, and brothers that desertion now is not dishonorable. . . . I have just received an order from [General] Wise to carry out on picket tonight a rifle and ten rounds of cartridges to shoot men when they desert. The men seem to think desertion no crime, and hence never shoot a deserter when he goes over—they always shoot, but never hit.[32]

Desertion had become a viable means of ending the agony of a lost cause. Many men were voting on the war with their feet. They were going home despite the consequences to the cause. Although Robert E. Lee might proclaim the strictest punishment for desertion, and even warn that encouraging or advising another soldier to desert would invoke the death penalty, his orders could not stop the mass exodus.[33]

It wasn't from a mistrust of Lee that the men were leaving, but from the realization of their revised priorities. The desertion phenomenon merely reflected a final crushing of the spirits of many of his soldiers. Lee himself admitted that he feared an ultimate progressive breakdown in spirit, for the worst aspect of desertion, he noted, was the "bad effect upon the troops who remain."[34]

The war had taken its toll on Lee's men, and there just wasn't any more latitude for enduring defeat and despair. While dishonor continued to be regarded by many soldiers as a fate worse than death, the majority now found no dishonor in abandoning a hopeless cause.

Robert E. Lee soon began a final, brazen attempt to maintain the cause and save the army in the face of overwhelming odds. On April 3 he ordered a concentration of the army west of Richmond at Amelia Court House, preparatory to marching to Danville for an attempted linkup with Joe Johnston's forces. The remnant of what a few days earlier had been an army of fifty-five thousand men was soon headed west through mud and rain along the Appomattox River line, bleeding men and equipment along every hard-pressed mile.

Robert E. Lee noted in dismay as he watched their painful progress, "The men [being] depressed by fatigue and hunger, many threw away their arms . . ."[35]

As Lee now recognized, this was the beginning of the bitter end.

Chapter Thirty-one

"UNLESS YOU COME HOME, WE MUST DIE"

My dear Edward:
I have always been proud of you, and since your connection with
the Confederate army, I have been prouder of you than ever before. I would not have you do anything wrong for the world. But
before God, Edward, unless you come home, we must die. Last
night, I was aroused by little Eddie's crying. I called and said, 'What
is the matter, Eddie?' and he said, 'Oh, Mamma! I am so hungry.'
And Lucy, Edward, your darling Lucy; she never complains, but she
is growing thinner every day. And before God, Edward, unless you
come home, we must die.

Your Mary[1]

Mr. President:
The apprehension I expressed during the winter, of the moral condition of the Army of Northern Virginia, [has] been realized. The
operations which occurred while the troops were in the entrenchments in front of Richmond and Petersburg were not marked by
the boldness and decision which formerly characterized them. Except in particular instances, they were feeble, and a want of confidence seemed to possess officers and men.

This condition, I think, was produced by the state of feeling in
the country, and the communications received by the men from

their homes, urging their return and the abandonment of the field. . . .

Advantages were gained by him [the enemy] which discouraged the troops, so that on the morning of the 2d April, when our lines between the Appomattox and Hatcher's Run were assaulted, the resistance was not effectual; several points were penetrated and large captures made. At the commencement of the withdrawal of the army from the lines on the night of the 2d, it began to disintegrate, and straggling from the ranks increased. . . .

I have given these details that your excellency might know the state of feeling which existed in the army. . . . From what I have seen and learned, I believe an army cannot be organized or supported in Virginia, and . . . the country east of the Mississippi is morally and physically unable to maintain the contest unaided with any hope of ultimate success. . . . To save useless effusion of blood, I would recommend measures be taken for suspension of hostilities and the restoration of peace.

> Robert E. Lee to Jefferson Davis,
> April 20, 1865[2]

In Lee's mind, continuation of the war had gravitated at the end to a question of the soldiers' low morale. It was heavy irony, for the intense fighting spirit of the Confederate troops had once been perceived as their greatest asset. Many may have wondered, was this new low the inevitable consequence of a lost war, or the failure of the South's belief in its moral superiority? Perhaps the answer lay in the practical reasoning of the defeated gray soldiers and their families.

What had seemed to bond many soldiers together, even after it became apparent that the prospects for Southern independence had vanished, was their devotion to one another. Sharing danger, hardships, and the experiences of army life had endeared the men to each other as a band of brothers. Yet, in sharp contrast to these strong feelings were the sufferings of the men and their awareness of a higher personal responsibility to their families.

In the mind of the soldier, the critical deliberation over continuing on with the war or going home often involved a simple if sometimes subconscious point of reference. Could a man justify sacrificing not only his own well-being but that of his family—perhaps even their survival—for a "common duty" to an all-but-defeated cause? At what point did practicality become foremost? When did the fulcrum tip to the personal side?

What compounded the emotions involved in these often-painful decisions was the difficulty of communications amid the crumbling structure of the Confederate government. Loss of vast amounts of Southern territory had resulted in a breakdown in the delivery of timely news, little word of events elsewhere, and the onerous delay in receiving personal information. Many Confederate newspapers had ceased printing for lack of materials or workmen, or else were under the rigid control of occupation forces. By 1865, a reliance on personal letters, word of mouth, or perhaps even enemy newspapers had become the basis of information for much of the Southern populace.

This breakdown in formal news gathering and dissemination placed a heavy burden on Southern society. Reliable information was at a premium. Delays in mail delivery resulted in news gaps, distortions, and omissions. Rumors and gossip abounded. Often there was little knowledge of what was occurring beyond one's own immediate view. An informed basis for intelligent decision making was generally lacking.

Yet the people and soldiers knew what they saw. And what they saw was disheartening.

By late 1864, much of the South was in ruins. Its farms and plantations had been ravaged, animals and livestock destroyed, and routine maintenance was nil. Moreover, a large number of slaves had run off. Even food sources were in doubt. Yet these hardships only seemed to be signs of a greater ordeal to come. Beyond the dire economic and disastrous living conditions lurked a mounting fear among home-front survivors of further devastation. Sherman's march through Georgia and the Carolinas had demonstrated both the enemy's ruthlessness and the civilian populace's vulnerability. For the folks at home, there was little hope for a better future so long as the war continued.

These difficulties brought into focus the issue of where and to whom one's loyalty was due. Should an individual be faithful to the South as a whole, or to his community and family? The answer, if distasteful to many, was obvious.

The Southern people knew it was the community that formed the practical basis of life, and patriotism had its deepest roots locally. In fact, many of the South's soldiers, while fighting for a national ideal, were more concerned about defense of their homes and values. Thus, when questions of the community's and family's survival reached a critical state, there were obvious implications for the Southern military effort.

So long as there was hope—a viable hope of winning independence—there was justification for the extreme hardships and suffering both at home and in the field. Yet the harsh reality of defeat was now evident in both sectors. The illusions of invincibility from earlier years had been swept away in chaos and disarray, and a fundamental crisis of survival was at hand.

The communications between a soldier and the folks at home, even if meager and infrequent, promulgated an important understanding of one's ultimate responsibilities. Fears that a wife or parents lacked food and other necessities, and that there was no one to help them in a practical sense, were powerful inducements to return home. When the enemy or banditti controlled a family's ability to exist, going home seemed to many the only recourse.

As revealed in letters to gray soldiers, in the spring of 1865 the hour of total desperation was at hand for Southern women, their young, and many aged dependents. The severity of homefront situations was reflected in widespread desertion, which was generally condoned among the ranks as "permanent leave." Although previously many deserters had returned to the army after resolving their personal affairs, under the current circumstances there was so much despair at home that there was little hope for their return. From intuition or just plain common sense, most soldiers knew that it was time to end the war and go home.

Certainly, there were those who chose to leave solely because the war was lost and they saw no profit in further risking their lives. Equally so, there were men who continued to remain until the very last. Perhaps it was a sense of honor and duty, or an obligation to those remaining in the ranks, or the fear of harsh treatment at the hands of the enemy's occupation forces, or even an uncertainty about the extent of continued resistance that caused some to stay on. Amid the army's changing circumstances, a weighing of options—what to do, or what not to do—was constantly on the soldiers' minds. For most, there were dire consequences to consider in taking any action.

In the past, many had been profuse in their complaints, yet enduring in their actions. But as the situation worsened, the mental constraints on leaving had lessened. Personal (or practical) motives began to prevail over conceptual ideals or national patriotism.

Whereas hope had encouraged constancy in carrying out one's military duty, common sense and logic now foretold an end to reasonable hope for success by continued fighting. Southern independence was no longer even remotely likely. Even if an individual was uneducated and prone to let others more qualified make key decisions and provide leadership, it was apparent that such reliance on superiors had failed. The proper course of action was now up to the individual.

As Robert E. Lee had observed, under these circumstances those who did remain in the army generally lacked the bold spirit that had long characterized the Army of Northern Virginia. Perhaps at the most elemental level, a growing fear was bringing the army to its knees—not the fear of fighting, but the fear of wasting their lives in a forlorn effort while those at home needed them more. Four years of grim warfare had instilled wisdom in the Confederate soldier. They didn't need generals or officers to tell them the realities of their existence. The men were the backbone both of the Confederacy and of their families. In fact, they were the only remaining hope of both. If they chose to stay in the army, it was apparent that the war's outcome would not change. Yet the dire plight of their families might be significantly relieved if they left. They were confronted with an ultimate test of their duty.

Under these circumstances, it is remarkable that so many remained in the army until the very end. The final act was played out a week after Richmond's evacuation when Lee's gaunt columns attempted to escape their pursuers along the line of the Appomattox River. After reaching Amelia Court House on April 4, Lee discovered that instead of the provisions he had ordered, only ammunition had been forwarded. His starving ranks were further reduced by defeats at Sayler's Creek, where on April 6 about seven thousand Confederates became casualties, and along the Richmond-to-Danville railroad, where Sheridan cut off Lee's intended line of retreat. Forced to veer westward toward Appomattox Court House, the remnant of Lee's army was brought to bay on April 9 by converging enemy forces that overwhelmed them in front and flank.[3]

Lee was promptly confronted with a final decision. He considered the army's status. Into the early days of April desertions had numbered in the hundreds and then thousands. An observer reflected that Lee's army was "melting like a Scotch mist." Robert E. Lee recognized his imminent defeat; his army was vanishing from beneath his very eyes, and he understood the impetus for such drastic action. The men were needed at home by their desperate families, and he could not sustain the war unless they were willing to stay in the field and fight. Many soldiers had yielded to the mental burden, and Lee knew the consequences. His letters to Jefferson Davis announced the bitter result. To Lee, the South had been lost with the evacuation of Richmond. Although his remaining soldiers were still valiant and courageous, they were fighting without the prospect of winning—the enemy's numbers and resources had ended the practicality of future resistance. If these men were to survive, they had to go home. Their intelligent and discerning commander was unwilling to sacrifice them any longer.[4]

A weary Robert E. Lee wrote to the president on April 12 that he had surrendered the Army of Northern Virginia. On the morning of the 9th, Lee's officers had reported that only 7,892 organized infantry remained under arms. "The enemy was more than five times our numbers," noted Lee. "If we could have forced our way one day longer, it would have been at a great sacrifice of life."[5]

Lee's sense of propriety had prevailed. "I did not see how a surrender could have been avoided," he reflected. "There was no food, and the men were worn out and exhausted. . . . I deemed this course the best under all the circumstances."[6]

Among the men, the emotion of these events was heightened by an overwhelming sense of devastation. Perhaps in some part this feeling came from outrage, and in another, from frustration. Everything had been wrapped up in the war, noted a grieving soldier, and now that it was lost, there was a profound feeling of guilt at having risked so much, for nothing.[7]

"[I feel] a wild spirit of resentment" at giving up, seethed a Mississippi rifleman. "[It] bids me resist, as long as one Southern soldier is left. But this is not the voice of wisdom. Helpless gray hairs, frail women, and innocent children are in the land. They cannot find rest in a soldier's gory grave. We owe to them a duty, for strong arms, broad backs, and stern discipline will be needed. . . ." Continuing the fight was "a useless waste of blood," he asserted, for "we have no armies to fight our victorious foes. Tens of thousands of Confederates are at home."[8]

Another soldier, a long-suffering veteran, recorded on May 14, 1865, following Joe Johnston's surrender, "And the war is over. When I consider all that I have seen and heard, all that I have learned of men and motives, I am constrained to ask myself, what is it all for? I am weary [of] trying to solve the problems that confront us. My heart is sick and sore, and I would . . . shut my eyes to the painful picture. As a people we have failed, [but now] . . . individually we must address ourselves to the material problems of life."[9]

After four years of bloody warfare, what had finally brought the Confederacy to its end in 1865 was not a lost battle. It was mostly unwillingness, a refusal to further endure war's futile ordeal, to fight or persevere in the cause when there was no real hope of winning. The successes and defeats of the past now had little impact, for the final decision had turned on the cutting edge of immediacy. The men had valiantly tried, but the present was foremost as they cast a wary eye toward an uncertain future.

The war for the minds of the people of the South, be they soldiers or civilians, had always been crucial to the final outcome.

Common sense and judgment said that the cost, agony, and consequences of war were no longer justified. This conclusion had been reached by most of the soldiers and people at home well before the bureaucratic machinery called a halt to the fighting through formal surrender.

Although technically the ability to continue to resist, however impotently, still remained, the war had truly ended due to the lack of popular will to continue to fight following military defeat.

The South had lost, not because it lost the will to win, but rather because of the practicalities involving resounding physical defeat. There simply were far too few resources in manpower and logistics, and too much devastation and agony. The occupied and fought-over South was a wasteland, both physically and mentally.

In the end, the South's dire physical status had impinged the most upon continuing the war effort. In the minds of most, it was not so much what minimal gains might be made, but rather what more was to be lost. The dim prospects for the soldiers justified surrender. While there were those who urged continuation of the war on a guerrilla basis—never give up and persevere until death—fortunately, they were a minority. A guerrilla-style warfare promised nothing more than further agony and physical devastation. Irregular warfare, impelled by pride, would not induce the North to yield what they had belatedly gained. The South was once again a part of the nation, not independent.*

---

*In *Why the South Lost the Civil War,* the authors attribute the Confederacy's demise to a loss of will which was largely rooted in a weak nationalism (see p. 439).

Lee's General Order No. 9, issued April 10, 1865, told his soldiers that he had "consented to the result from no distrust in them." Rather, "feeling that valor and devotion could accomplish nothing that would compensate for the loss that must have attended the continuance of the contest," he chose to "avoid the useless sacrifice" of those whose services had so endeared them to their countrymen.

The consciousness of "duty faithfully performed" with "unsurpassed courage and fortitude" would serve as an enduring legacy, said Lee, and prayed that "a merciful God" would extend His blessing and protection.[10]

The final scene at Appomattox Court House had been duly affecting. "On they came, with the old swinging route step and swaying battle flags," noted an observer who stood watching the approaching ranks of gray as they marched forward to surrender on April 12. "In the van [was] the proud Confederate ensign . . . [then] the regimental battle flags . . . following on, crowded so thick, by [such a] thinning out of men, that the whole column seemed crowned with red."

Spontaneously, the commander at the head of the waiting lines of blue soldiers ordered a salute of arms. As the gray ranks began passing, the long lines of Federal troops shifted in succession from "order arms" to "carry arms," the parade-ground marching salute.

Taken momentarily by surprise, Confederate Major General John B. Gordon, his face downcast as he rode ahead, glanced up and saw what was happening. Instantly, he uplifted himself in the saddle, dropped the point of his unsheathed sword to his boot toe, and turning to his men gave the command to carry arms.

Not wishing to confuse the cause with the effect, my views, as encompassed in the text of *Southern Invincibility,* include the following: 1) The South had significantly limited war resources (which after 1863 generally diminished at an escalating rate). 2) The South too often squandered its critical white manpower resources largely by an aggressive, offensive concept of fighting, rather than to utilize the *tactical* defensive to thwart Union campaigns with minimal losses. 3) The loss of many major battles (primarily in the West) led to the loss of large segments of the South, which further restricted access to vital logistical resources. 4) The progressive defeat of Southern arms, abetted by irreplaceable "veteran soldier" losses, led to a general understanding that the South could not militarily defeat Northern war objectives. 5) The depressed civilian and military attitudes that resulted affected the South's willpower to continue the struggle. This led to widespread desertions, or resulted in diminished levels of performance. 6) The collapse of the Confederacy occurred when the further heavy cost of continuing an ineffectual warfare was unjustified due to the negligible prospect of gaining independence.

Honor answered honor.

With "an awed stillness," the Confederate ranks then halted and formed along the opposite side of the road. The gray lines were carefully dressed, bayonets fixed, and arms stacked. Cartridge boxes were removed and set on the ground. Then, with agony on the faces of many, the tattered red battle flags were tenderly folded and placed down.

In the words of the general designated to receive the formal surrender of the Army of Northern Virginia, Joshua Lawrence Chamberlain, "[There stood] before us in proud humiliation . . . the embodiment of manhood; men whom neither toils and sufferings, nor the fact of death, nor disaster, nor hopelessness could bend from their resolve." They were "thin, worn, and famished, but erect, and with eyes looking level into ours," said Chamberlain. It evoked memories that "bound us together as [did] no other bond."

Chamberlain was moved to a profound tribute: "Was not such manhood to be welcomed back into a Union so tested and assured?"

Finally, reflecting on four years of devastation and tragedy, he recorded in gripping words the essence of a new spirit of understanding: "How could we help falling on our knees, all of us together, and praying God to forgive us all!"[11]

Chapter Thirty-two

THE SOUTH SHALL RISE AGAIN

I have cried until no more tears will come, and my heart throbs to bursting night and day," wrote a Richmond wife in the aftermath of the city's evacuation. The past few days had seemed like years, and the anguish of the doomed capital was visible everywhere. Richmond looked like a city from "the Middle Ages, smitten by pestilence," she observed with horror. "The streets were filled with smoke, and flying fire, and were empty of the respectable class of inhabitants, the doors and shutters of every house [being] tightly closed. . . ."[1]

Perhaps it seemed that the stricken city was a cruel metaphor mocking the wretched state of the people of the Confederacy as the war ended in the spring of 1865. Across the South, the misery was profound. A Georgia girl watched as soldiers from Lee's army straggled through their community in May 1865, and she fretted that "the most terrible part of the war is now to come." The Yankee occupation was "closing in upon us," observed Eliza Andrews, even while "our own disbanded armies, ragged, starving, hopeless, reckless, are roaming about without order or leaders, making their way to their far-off homes as best they can. The props that held society up are broken," she fretted. "Everything is in a state of disorganization and tumult. We have no currency, no law save the primitive code that might makes right. We are in a transition state from war to subjugation, and it is far worse than was the transition from peace to war. The suspense and anxiety in which we live are terrible."[2]

Having lost the war, the South now faced a new crisis, and, like Eliza Andrews, dread of life as a conquered people was foremost in the minds of many. "I wonder what they [the Yankees] will do with us, and if all our darkies will leave," wrote an apprehensive Confederate private in April 1865. The more he thought about the consequences of the war, the more depressed he became. "I think we will be a happier people without slaves" was the only optimism he could express.[3]

To a Georgia volunteer, writing in the days before the Army of Northern Virginia's collapse, it was apparent that the Confederacy was being "held together by a thread of sand," and Private John Johnson contemplated the changes ahead. After the war, he predicted they would "be deprived of many of the luxuries, such as being waited on by negroes, riding about in buggies and carriages at any time, and hundreds of other little things." Yet he remained sanguine in spirit. "But our living will be gained by honest and hard toil," Johnson wrote, "and we will learn that the real wants of life are but few compared to what we think they are—[provided] we are but contented with our lot."[4]

Johnson's attitude was reflective of the inner strength that the Southern people would rely upon in coping with their fate. The indomitable spirit of mankind to improvise with worn-out tools and begin anew along the unpredictable path of life would serve as the South's salvation. And, as ever, the will to persevere would count much toward accomplishing the imposing physical tasks ahead. Self-reliance was a Southern tradition, particularly when matters seemed the worst. Thus, in a broad sense, fears of the consequences of subjugation became mental obstacles along the way to a greater society with an important manifest destiny.

Mary Chesnut, a fixture of Richmond society, pondered the war's aftermath and wrote "wearisome thoughts" about how late in life they were to begin anew amid "the laborious, difficult days ahead." Yet, noted Mary, she could still laugh to the point of tears. "With this storm of woe impending, we snatched a moment of reckless gaiety . . . we played cards" and laughed at stories. "I knew the trouble was all out there, but we put it off, kept it out . . . —let it bang at the door as it would."[5]

Humanity's resilient spirit was apparent all across the postwar South, even amid the despair. What had been unthinkable a few years earlier was now a reality, yet beyond failure lay the prospect of a productive civilian life. The future inspired a renewal of hope, of achieving success, not so much by collective endeavor, as by personal perseverance. In fact, for many soldiers the end of the war was a godsend, no matter which side had won. A Georgian of the 19th Volunteer Infantry had little remorse for the war's unfavorable end. "What difference will it make with the poor man which side whips?" he asked. "We are living under a despotic government anyway." Political issues just didn't seem to carry the import of four years ago; a longing for home and family had helped push the war beyond thoughts of patriotism.[6]

"Happiness is not ours until we all meet after the war," a Confederate soldier had prophesied back in 1861. In a fundamental sense he was right. At the end there had been only the overwhelming desire to go home and experience the basic pleasures of peace and family. Being deprived of "everything desirable in life," a Confederate survivor wrote to his wife, "[I] am willing to undergo any danger to see you again." "You won't know me when I get home," another ragged and emaciated soldier informed his wife. "I went to sleep last night and woke up and Charlie [his messmate] had his arms around me. How I wished it was you. One fond embrace from you now would do me more good than anything on earth."[7]

As the men trudged home, the emotions of these gray veterans appeared to be awakening. There were thoughts of beginning again, and of renewing family ties, and somehow providing for the future. The war was too painful to relive, and yet too immediate to forget. The next few years would be a time of soul searching.

Coping with the emotional floodtide of defeat was a trauma beyond the imagination of those who had volunteered in 1861 with such bold spirit and enthusiasm. What had once been a widespread conviction—Southern invincibility—had become only a false premise littering the dark ashes of defeat. "We have failed," announced a Mississippian from the Army of Tennessee in his journal. "It is painful, it is humiliating to write . . . [that] we must give it up, and own that we are whipped." For him, "what might have been" was the most difficult of all to ponder. "Once, it seemed we had the men and means to achieve our independence, but a needless sacrifice of the one, and a prodigal waste of the other, exhausted both in a short time," assessed this former rifleman. "Two hundred thousand of our best men, it is said, have perished, and for what?"[8]

Many former Confederates inclined to "fight to the last man" resisted accepting defeat. En route home from a Yankee prison, an unrepentant Mississippian wrote to his family "not to lament over the past." Instead, he urged that the South "must prepare for the new warfare." This second war he acknowledged, would take place in the political arena, since "the [physical] battle for political freedom [was] over."[9]

Anticipating defeat, a Confederate captain had written to his wife before the war ended, "I do not desire a reconstruction and a hollow truce, a servile place in the family of nations to eat the bread of dependence. . . . I am willing to continue to fight to the last. If we have to succumb, we must do it bravely fighting for our rights, and the remnant must migrate. If the worst comes, we must go over to England or France. . . . Never will I be content to submit to Yankee rule."[10]

Particularly stressful to the surrendered soldiers was the potential for outright humiliation. The "maddening theme" of Yankee domination afflicted one gray veteran to the point of outright torture. "Hundreds, nay thousands, of the northern soldiers will find homes in the South, and make wives of our sisters and daughters," he lamented. "They have fought us bravely, as only brave men can, but their hands are red with southern blood, and it seems that no true southern maid would ever desire to wed one who had helped to subdue her people. But I know that . . . many will be ready to forget it all, and place her affections in the keeping of a stranger, though his hands be reeking with a brother's or a lover's blood."

Later, this veteran could but console himself with an awareness that "there are lessons in it for our own good," and "I seem to realize more and more that God's hand is in it, and that He has ordered it well."[11]

Trust in the Almighty seemed to many soldiers the best recourse in the immediate postwar era, considering the terrible conditions they faced upon resuming their civilian lives. The thought that God would support a deserving individual's efforts, even though He might have allowed the defeat of the Confederacy, consoled many. The survivors knew that if there was despair, there at least was life. Their postwar struggles, moreover, provided a new basis for interpreting wartime experiences.

As time progressed, many former Rebels began to realize that in the fiery cauldron of war they had met the worst of human experiences and prevailed, even if only on a personal level. In that awareness were the meager beginnings of what would lead to a rekindled spirit of Southern pride.

Even in the "terrible times of shipwreck," there had been expressions of pride in embracing the cause of Southern independence. Mrs. Joseph E. Johnston proclaimed in early 1865, "What a glorious struggle our brave people have made for their liberties!" The image of beaten and tattered remnants of Lee's army trudging through their town after Appomattox had one Southern lady in tears. "If they only knew how honorable rags and dirt are now, in our eyes, when endured in the service of our country, they would not be ashamed . . . ," she passionately recorded in her diary. "We had the best fighting material in the world—but it was not properly handled, and our men could only die in their tracks," wrote Mary Chesnut in reflecting on the Confederacy's past glory. Indeed, amid the shadows of military failure, Mary thought that perpetuating memories of Southern valor might provide solace in the trying times ahead.[12]

To many, the outpouring of emotion ultimately served as a catharsis, and furthered the process of coping with a threatening, hostile world. The soldiers had been through so much, and yet there seemed little respite, except in viewing with personal pride what they had experienced. If success often came at great cost, coping well with repeated disaster was far more difficult. The indescribable ordeals of the battlefield and the hardships of army life were finally in the past, but not the grim emotions evoked by the lost war. Coping with the shame of defeat was soon foremost on the minds of many.

The "Lost Cause" mentality engendered in the writings of various Confederate leaders and journalists of the postwar era provided a ready means to justify the War for Southern Independence, and also to obscure its failures. Beginning with the 1866 publication of Edward A. Pollard's book *The Lost Cause*, an explanation of Southern defeat was given in terms of romantic ideals being overcome by superior resources. A Southern culture that epitomized grace, honor, and chivalry had yielded to the heavy numbers and industrial might of a relentless foe, but the righteousness of the South's cause remained inviolate. This argument provided moral reinforcement for the values involved in the War between the States, gave meaning to the sacrifices made, and eased the burden of oppression many experienced in the occupied South.

If perhaps an escape from the reality of losing the war, the Lost Cause concept was intended to help Southerners handle defeat by portraying them as morally superior. Suggestions that Confederates were "better men" than the enemy provided psychological salvation for the beleaguered gray veterans and their families, who now labored to come to terms with defeat, poverty, and social upheaval.

While the arrogance of this mentality was decried in the North, an eventual, if uneasy, accommodation in public perspective enabled the South to keep its head high amid the bitterness of defeat. As such, the recourse to personal pride enabled a certain introspection; of establishing attitudes and beliefs that helped cope with one's existence as a downcast Southerner.

While acrimony remained in the spirits of some, to many former gray soldiers the search within the soul soon seemed most relevant. To know a deep, bittersweet truth about life—its visceral anguish and also the ultimate promise that noncombatants could not fully understand—was in itself of precious value. An indomitable spirit sprang from a veteran's elevated sense of self-worth. Perhaps the former soldiers considered not so much what had or hadn't been accomplished collectively, but rather were proud for having endured and made bold personal efforts. From this pride flowed inner peace and self-respect. These dogged gray veterans had fairly met a supreme challenge. What more could they attempt?

In a large sense, the true purpose of human life—to strive to materially accomplish, or to better understand oneself—has always been pondered. No matter if portrayed in terms of the material or the spiritual, the Civil War resulted in a profound learning experience.

Southern pride in attempting a valiant quest for independence tended to be translated after the war into terms of personal victories. Condensing the ordeal of many into an assertion that the righteous don't always win gave rise to an enduring legend. The saintly status accorded to Robert E. Lee was but one manifestation of the postwar Southern interpretation of the South's superiority.

Indeed, the veneration of Lee assumed religious overtones. This idolatry, even if expanded into myth, served as a metaphor for the

South and her valiant soldiers. The shock of having lost was lessened by embodying values of the highest merit in Lee, the supreme Confederate military leader, who became a Christ-like symbol in the afterglow of the Lost Cause. Lee was more than an icon; he came to represent the South in its tragic but regal postwar existence.

As an intense emotional reflex to the stigma of defeat, the elevation of Lee in the Southern mind was largely enacted by the veterans themselves. Awe of Lee, the military genius and the legend, continued to grow until he was portrayed as a man without defects, a peerless leader held aloft by the South as a paragon of virtue. Whereas other Confederates were sometimes cast down by the reunited nation as flawed and pitiable, or even as traitors and unrepentant Rebels, Lee's demise in 1870 only accentuated his value to the South. By the time of his death, a begrudging yet appreciative Northern populace generally regarded Lee with admiration and respect. Their esteem for Lee in turn, served as a means to a more pervasive understanding of and respect for the defeated Southerners and the enormous price they had paid in "their" war.[13]

In 1866, a graying ex-Confederate officer wrote in his ledger "Conscious of the conquered condition of my country . . . I feel that no history that can now be written will do justice to those who engaged in the late war. . . . [Yet] I feel that there will be a day when this people and this nation will vie with each other in honoring those who are now branded as traitors, and when the North shall unite with the South in keeping green the laurels upon the graves of those who fell in our Cause."[14]

The ideal of immortal and self-sacrificing courage and the expectation that past deeds on the battlefield would be remembered, admired and become a badge of honor for future generations of Americans, gained full credence in the 1880s. "You are in full possession of the heritage purchased by their blood," lectured a Southern college professor. "Shall the purchase price . . . be forgotten, or . . . depreciated?" This heroic image of Southerners would be sharpened and the soldiers made into martyrs in various works of postwar literature. Sam Watkins, formerly a private of the 1st Tennessee Infantry, imagined a "last reveille" in Heaven with comrades who had fallen in the war, and wrote in his memoir, "We shed a tear over their flower-strewn graves. We live after them. We love their memory yet. . . . But when we pass away, . . . a history will then be written in justification and vindication of those brave and noble boys who gave their all in fighting the battles of their homes, their country, and their God.''[15]

Although for some Southerners an emphasis on individual valor in the war was insufficient solace, it was an important part of the healing process. As the years passed, distortion and selective interpretation crept into many accounts. "They never whipped us, Sir, unless they were four to [our] one," announced a grizzled Virginia veteran. "If we had had anything like a fair chance, or less disparity of numbers, we should have won our cause. . . ."[16]

While such banter often involved saving face and glorified the aged participants, beyond superficial boasting lay one important truth. The Southern fighting man had prevailed in an ultimate sense. His virtue was far greater than his failings. The pride of sacrifice inspired a bold spirit in the new South—that of a Southern moral invincibility.

Above all else, the memories of what had once been endured; Confederates could not help but recall the terrible human toll of the war, and the commitment unto death and despair. This continued to mean the most as the years passed. The war's legacy had been indelibly cast when shortly before Appomattox a Confederate lieutenant, contemplating the end, poured forth his emotions:

The soiled and tattered colors borne by our skeleton regiment [are] sacred and dear to the heart of every man. No one would exchange it for a new flag. So it is with us. I go down the lines; I see the marks of shot and shell [on the men], I see where fell my comrades . . . little mounds of dirt, some with headboards, some with none, some with shoes protruding, some with a small pile of bones on one side, showing where a hand was left uncovered; in fact everything near shows desperate fighting. And here I would rather fight it out.[17]

More than forty years later, perspectives had evolved among the once-fierce warriors. "I have had abundant experience that the old feeling of bigotry and bitterness is passing away," wrote former Confederate general Basil Duke in 1909. "[It] has almost passed away on both sides—and 'died in the wool' Yankees and formerly 'unreconstructed' Rebels are alike willing to do each other justice, and begin to regard the heroism of the Civil War with pride, which men regard as a common glory. . . ."[18]

The fight had given way to pride, and pride had yielded to honor. The South would survive, and from the war's ashes the bold, venturesome spirit of her valiant soldiers would rise again in a new birth of wisdom.

Chapter Thirty-three

PERSONAL EPILOGUES

Henry King Burgwyn, Jr.

"Words on a Tombstone"

Anne Devereux kept hoping beyond hope. All of the family was nearly desperate for definitive news of their son in the wake of the Gettysburg bloodletting. On July 13, 1863, Harry Burgwyn's father telegraphed a friend in Richmond, seeking news of his son—had he survived? Rumors were swirling about; several officers earlier thought to be dead or wounded had proved unhurt, and the uncertainty of not knowing was a terrible strain on the family.[1]

The sad news came on July 14 in a telegram from a Richmond friend informing the family that Harry had been shot on July 1 while bearing the 26th North Carolina's flag, and had died two hours later. Soon, in a letter from Harry's close friend Captain J. J. Young, the family learned that he had been buried with tender care beneath a large walnut tree along the Chambersburg Pike near Gettysburg. His personal belongings and a lock of his hair were all that remained, and many of these items had been entrusted along with Harry's two horses to his faithful servant Kincheon, who would carry them home to North Carolina.[2]

The words of consolation,—"the death of one so young, so brave, so accomplished, with every prospect of being at no distant period one of our greatest men, has filled all with sadness and sorrow"— rang hollow. Harry Burgwyn was no more.[3]

There would be no wedding; Anne Devereux was said to be so devastated that she never married and wore mourning for years afterward.

There would be no prosperous life, family, or other accomplishments. The grave in Pennsylvania was a harsh finality. Only the memories of Harry Burgwyn, Jr., remained, but they were not enough. War had ruined everything that mattered in life, even hope.[4]

For the Burgwyn family much of the tragedy endured. Four months following Harry's death his father was stricken and partially paralyzed. He continued to suffer from strokes, but survived until 1877. Bankruptcy, fire at their Thornbury plantation, and failed business ventures left the Burgwyns heavily in debt. The family turned to the North—thankful for Harry's mother's Boston connections—in order to live. Harry's two brothers had survived the war, although William had been wounded and captured. Will eventually became a prosperous banker and entrepreneur in Henderson, North Carolina. The family's survival was greatly due to the efforts of Harry's mother, Anna, who kept her wits about her in times of trial. She later lived in Richmond, remaining there from 1869 until her death in April 1887.[5]

Among the proudest events of Anna Burgwyn's later life was the birth of her first grandchild, a boy, named Henry King Burgwyn Baker, in honor of her beloved Harry. Throughout the remainder of Anna's life, Harry's memory was never far. In her diary for 1886 she wrote of receiving a worsted shawl from Anne Devereux. She then promised, "[I] will always wear it with pleasure, as *she* made it for me." That year on her birthday, October 13, Anna received a framed photograph of Harry in his VMI uniform, and she duly noted in her diary, "Nothing could have pleased me so much." On February 25, 1887, only weeks before Anna died, she recorded that it was the twenty-fourth anniversary "of my last parting with dear Harry."[6]

Twenty years earlier, her dear Harry had at last come home to North Carolina. Removed from the shallow grave near Gettysburg in 1867, he was reburied at Oakwood Cemetery in Raleigh, North Carolina, on June 9, 1867. On Harry's tombstone the family had inscribed Harry's rank, age, and their sentiments about the meaning of it all. "The Lord Gave, and The Lord Hath Taken Away."[7]

The great mystery of life had prevailed, and there was little more to be said. They had only the lingering memories of what he might have become.

Sarah Morgan

"Everybody Cried, but I Would Not"

On New Year's Eve, 1865, Sarah Morgan reflected, as was her custom, on the past year and her concerns for the new. "One year ago . . . I sat shivering over . . . my desk, selfishly rejoicing over the departure of a year that had brought pain and discomfort . . . , and eagerly welcoming the dawning of the new one. . . ." Instead of relief, however, 1864 had brought the death of her brothers George and Gibbes; thus the glaring uncertainty of 1865 caused her to question the future. "How do we know what the coming one has in store for us?" she asked. "What new changes will it bring? Which of us will it take? I am afraid of 1865. . . ."[8]

Sarah Morgan had become a realist, if still spirited in her support for the Confederacy. Her youngest brother, Jimmy, was a naval officer aboard the Confederate cruiser *Georgia*, and had often recounted to her in his letters the ship's successful forays in the North Atlantic. Such was Sarah's despair that she wondered if he, too, might become a victim of this costliest of wars. "Jimmy! Dear Lord, spare us that one! But I have always felt Jimmy must die young, and we have been so cast down that hope seems almost presumption in us . . . God spare him!" she implored.[9]

By April 1865, the end of the Confederacy was in sight, and although Sarah at first pouted that she would "not for an instant believe this [war] could end in our overthrow," she was soon compelled to acknowledge the inevitability of defeat. With news of Lee's surrender, "even the staunchest Southerners were hopeless," admitted Sarah in her diary. Yet her resilient spirit continued to shine. "Everybody cried, but I would not, [being] satisfied that God will save us, even though all should apparently be lost," she announced. Then, when news of Lincoln's assassination reached New Orleans, Sarah was horror-stricken. "Our Confederacy has gone with one crash—the report of the pistol fired at Lincoln," she sighed. Denouncing the act as murder, Sarah wrote forlornly, "Let not his blood be visited on our nation, Lord!"[10]

Uncertainty faced the people of the former Confederacy in mid-1865; but the "subjugation" that all had feared in 1861 was already a reality. Sarah's indignation swelled as wild rumors circulated that "every man above the rank of captain in the [Confederate] army, and above that of lieutenant in the navy, [would] be hanged immediately." Yet her fears were soon mollified. Brother Jimmy had survived the war, and throughout May, as paroled Louisianians from Lee's army arrived in New Orleans, Sarah began to recover her decorum. By June, she could revel in the busy times as friends from olden days poured through the family's doors: "Dozens follow in rapid succession, until the unusual sensation of receiving visitors makes me dizzy." "How I have laughed this week," she recorded in her diary.[11]

Even when the aftermath of war became unpleasant, Sarah kept her resolve. Despite "praying for the [safe] return of those who fought so nobly for us," she had "dreaded their first days at home." Mindful of the "pain it would bring to see [Gibbes's and George's] comrades return without them—to see families reunited, and know that ours never could be again, save in Heaven," Sarah had been apprehensive. Memories of her dead brothers were powerful reminders that they were gone forever and that the war was lost. "It is incomprehensible, this change," Sarah grimly wrote. "Seeing familiar faces on the street is an oddity to which I cannot reconcile myself."[12]

Although acknowledging that "all things are taken from us and become portions and parcels of the dreadful past," Sarah Morgan was not one to dwell on what might have been. "The less I recall . . . sorrow and pain, the better it will be," she prophesied. "My life changes, changes," she acknowledged. "I let it change as God will, feeling He doeth all things well."[13]

Sarah Morgan was a survivor. Even though "a Rebel in heart and soul," she could at last look forward to an existence without the horror of war. Her life, if measured in future tragedies, was a testimonial of Sarah's pluck in surmounting her generation's great ordeal.[14]

Following the war, Sarah Morgan was destined to both happiness and despair during a vivid life that stretched to sixty-seven years until her demise in May 1909. Having left New Orleans in the summer of 1865 with her brother Jimmy for his wedding to Helen Trenholm (the daughter of the former Confederate secretary of the treasury), Sarah would spend much time traveling, prior to living in 1872 at Hampton plantation, in South Carolina, with Jimmy.

Jimmy's wife, Helen, died in childbirth in 1866, and Sarah, her mother, and Gibbes's young son, Howell, remained in South Carolina at Jimmy's residence for several years. While there, Sarah met Francis Warrington Dawson, an English immigrant who had come to America to fight for the Confederacy, and had become editor and part owner of the *Charleston News* (later the *News and Courier*) after the war. In January 1874 Sarah and Frank Dawson were married. Three children were born to the marriage, but the last, a son, died at age five months. The couple shared fifteen years together, until Frank was shot to death in March 1889 by a local doctor during a domestic quarrel. Embittered by the acquittal of her husband's murderer, Sarah was soon embroiled in a financial controversy with his former business partner over settlement of the estate.

By the early 1900s, Sarah was living in Paris with her invalid son Warrington, and was regarded as an accomplished writer, having published various articles in noted publications, including the magazine *Cosmopolitan*. A portion of the final years of her life was devoted to preparing and editing her wartime diary. Although she died before its publication in 1913, *A Confederate Girl's Diary* proved to be a success, and was highly regarded by historians for its candid insight into the "tragic, distant past."

In the back of one of the books in which she kept her wartime diary, Sarah Morgan recorded for posterity thoughts that might well serve as her epitaph: "It is not far to the end now. . . . I shall die here [Paris], far from all I once clung to more than life. So be it! I need no home, no friends, no old associations. The Peace of God supplies all deficiencies."[15]*

---

*The definitive edition of Sarah Morgan's diary was prepared by Charles East, former director of Louisiana State University Press, and was published by the University of Georgia Press in 1991. The softcover edition was published in 1992 by Touchstone/Simon & Schuster, Inc. This book is highly recommended. Sarah Morgan's papers are in the Duke University Library, Durham, North Carolina.

Sandie Pendleton

"Dealing with Adversity"

For Kate Corbin Pendleton, Sandie's widow, the immediate aftermath of the Civil War was measured in terms of survival. After visiting her father and his second family in the fall of 1865, she returned in the spring of 1866 to live with the Pendletons in Lexington, Virginia. Becoming in 1867 a governess for William Preston Johnston, the son of General Albert Sidney Johnston, who had been killed at Shiloh, Kate moved into the Johnston residence in Lexington. Johnston was professor of history and literature at Washington College, and through his contacts she met John Mercer Brooke, a professor at VMI. Brooke, a distinguished naval officer who had converted the U.S.S. *Merrimac* into the Confederate ironclad *Virginia* and invented the Brooke rifle gun, was a widower without children, his young wife having died during the war.

In 1871 Kate and John Brooke were married. They shared thirty-five years together, living in Lexington until his death in 1906. Kate then moved to Washington, D.C., and later New York City, residing with her daughter Rosa and her son-in-law, H. Parker Willis, a distinguished economist and professor at Washington and Lee University. Following Kate's death in November 1919, her body was laid to rest in Lexington Cemetery, near the graves of her second husband, Sandie, little Sandie, and Stonewall Jackson.[16]

Fred Fleet

"Do Not Shrink from the Battle of Life"

By 1865, the war had become that which most men had never imagined. Ensnared in an all-consuming conflict of unknown duration, the weary gray ranks pondered their dire future. There were too few men, scant supplies and resources, and too little hope for change. Yet there seemed to be no practical option but to continue the effort so long as was possible. Young officers like Fred Fleet appeared perhaps the most hopeful and willing to endure. Captain Fleet's belief that Robert E. Lee's ability and the prowess of the Virginia army would lead to success and ultimate Southern victory had been expressed at the beginning of the winter of 1864–1865. "[Ulysses S. Grant] hasn't the [Confederacy's] Western army to fight here" he asserted. Moreover, mindful of the extent of fortifications, trenches, and defensive means constructed around Petersburg by the opposing armies, Fred was convinced that "neither side [would] achieve a complete victory. If the opposing party is whipped ever so badly, they fall back to a perfect network of entrenchments bristling with artillery and almost impregnable to the attacking party . . . ," observed Fleet.[17]

Toward the end of the 1864–65 winter, however, even young lions like Fred Fleet had cause to reappraise their prospects. Fred's concern was rooted in his own increasingly severe ordeal. The cold, freezing weather suffered with few warm clothes, not enough blankets or socks, and even an absence of shoes, gave the army great difficulty. Fred told of how he had to sit up all night in a bomb-proof trench with General Wise, a cold rain dripping down through the logs and so saturating both of them that despite their overcoats they couldn't keep dry or comfortable.[18]

Not only were the soldiers miserable in the mud-choked and filthy trenches, but their unpromising circumstances, and the random violence of siege warfare, had depressed everyone. A few days before Christmas, a soldier Fred knew well had just finished writing a letter to his sister, and having sealed it, stood up in his tent. Suddenly, a stray minie ball ripped through the canvas and struck him in the head, killing him instantly. He came from a large family and had been their sole support, being the only son yet "sound," sadly noted Fred. "Ah!" wrote Fred in despair, "we soon become hardened to such scenes. Scarcely a day passes that someone in the brigade is not killed or wounded. . . ." To Fred, the real tragedy was that death had come to mean so little in the army. War "deadens the sensibilities and destroys the finer feelings of us all," he solemnly reflected. A few men killed "here and there" were not missed, "except in some loving circle at home."[19]

Beyond considering his own death—"I may fall, but there is a glorious and noble consolation to die for one's country, and . . . I never wish to live and see the South subdued"—there was a heightened awareness of where the path of war was leading. Lincoln's re-election in November had insured a continuation of the conflict, and Fred saw little relief ahead. "Oh! how many more years of war and suffering shall we have to endure?" he asked. The new year 1865 seemed ominous and clouded by uncertainty. "No one says '[have] a happy new year,' as we all know there is little happiness [ahead] for a soldier," he had written.[20]

The decline in morale was evident before the stunning final days of the war. "Many are low spirited at the signs of the times, and the weak hearted all over the land are crying peace," he had written in December 1864. Yet, said Fred, "the issue is in the hands of God, and it is our duty to strive against subjugation to the utmost, and never submit, as long as we can possibly hold out."[21]

Although Fred Fleet believed devotedly in Robert E. Lee, his confidence in others under the present circumstances had its limits. The stark reality of the collapsing war effort was all too apparent in the evacuation of the Petersburg lines and the fall of Richmond. Even the words of Fred Fleet's younger sister, Louisa, "The Yankees are coming!" accentuated the despair at home in King and Queen County, Virginia, as the closing scenes began to unfold.[22]

Seventeen-year-old Louisa Fleet poured out her heart in a letter to Fred, expressing her terrible grief about a cause and existence all but lost—if not yet in the minds of some. "Surely, surely, this must be 'the darkest hour' of our night," she agonized in disbelief on hearing of Richmond's fall. "The day[light] can't be very far [away], do you think? . . ."[23]

Giving up hope for success seemed hardest of all, and Louisa continued with insistence, "I think, I almost know, we are right [in our cause], and God will protect the right." Yet, the troublesome new realities and her many doubts remained, creating a terrible conflict in her mind. What her father had recently said about the war having ruined everything seemed harsh: Because of the war there was no corn and fodder for their animals, slavery was all but dead in Virginia with the border being so close and the negroes finding it easy to run away, and their farm fields were being trampled and the crops ruined by neighbors' animals because the fences had been burned by the soldiers. Under the present circumstances, it all seemed only too true, even if a cruel revelation.[24]

Although "Lou" might "not feel conquered one bit, not a single bit," she carefully queried her brother about taking the oath of allegiance to the United States. "[If] we must take the oath or leave our home, sweet home, which would you advise?" she anxiously asked. "Ma" had already said she would take the oath, for where could they go?[25]

By then, it was almost over. Her mother's, and later Louisa's, difficult but inevitable concessions to common sense and practicality were tacit admissions that their war had ended. For the Fleet family, and thousands of others, their efforts had been valiant but fruitless. There was no more Confederacy, only broken dreams, broken bodies, and a hope that somehow matters would improve as the hard-pressed Southern survivors attempted to begin anew.

For the Fleets, however, the devastating pain of the war years was not over. There was still more to suffer. The final days of the war brought yet another sudden, stunning death in their family. The heavy casualties endured at Sayler's Creek, Virginia, caused great despair when word of the "fearful mortality" in the 26th Virginia reached the Fleet home in Green Mount. Fred, it was feared, had perished among the many slain.[26]

Yet, this news was wrong. Fred had survived unscathed. Present at Appomattox when the Army of Northern Virginia was surrendered, he soon came home with the army horse that he had ridden during the final retreat.[27]

When he arrived in mid-April, Fred sadly stood over the grave of his father, Doctor Benjamin Fleet, who had died on March 8 of an acute streptococcus infection (erysipelas) following a fifteen-mile ride in a cold rain to attend to a patient. Fred Fleet could but ponder the fateful words of his father, who only weeks before his death had written of his resolve to confront the new realities of the South: "If slavery is to be the barrier to our independence, I say let it go to the devil! . . . Could we have peace, retaining our lands, I should have no fear of having the best laborers in the world after a time. . . ."[28]

His father's vibrant spirit served as an admonition to rebuild, to persevere, and to carry on no matter what the grueling difficulties. And Fred Fleet took his father's advice to heart. Although discouraged by the family's poor economic circumstances, Fred, with the use of his army horse, planted enough corn to feed his family and that of a former slave, Joshua Gaines, who returned to Green Mount to help, bringing a mule. The large garden planted by Joshua was a godsend: "We all will get along together the best we kin," said Joshua. It was welcome evidence of the freedman's spirited resolve to provide for the Fleet family as well as his own.[29]

Yet mere survival wasn't enough. Fred's mother was determined to see her children educated as she asserted, "at any cost." In the fall of 1865, Fred returned to the University of Virginia, thanks to funds raised largely from the sale of one of the two local ferries that the family owned. Although times remained hard, Mrs. Fleet's insistence that her children finish their education prevailed. Once so discouraged that she wrote, "I never thought I would see the day when I am unable to borrow $200 on 3,000 acres of land," Mrs. Fleet took great pride in her son's graduation in 1867.[30]

Soon Fred was teaching school at a local academy. In 1868 he moved to Missouri, eventually becoming a professor at the University of Missouri, and later organizing a military academy at Mexico, Missouri. He died in 1911, following a distinguished and successful career as an educator and a forty-year marriage that produced eight children.[31]

His devoted mother, Maria Louisa Fleet, ran the Green Mount Home School for Young Ladies from 1878 to 1890, and died from pneumonia in January 1900. When writing to Fred shortly after the war, Mrs. Fleet had told him, "I expect you to be more courageous than to shrink from the battle of life after going through the war as honorably as you did." They were words equally appropriate to her own struggle during a conflict that had cost Americans so severely. Ma Fleet understood the lessons of civil war.[32]

Her last sentiments, "love one another, and help each other all you can," were a message for all.[33]

Epilogue

The Ultimate Flaw

The perception is not always the reality. Rather, it is often only the illusion of such. Reality involves the sum total of all possible knowledge. That the Confederate soldier understood what was in the offing in the spring of 1861 proved to be a gross misperception. By 1865, the spirit of Southern invincibility had given way to an attitude of practical skepticism. The soldier-survivors knew far more than did many of their unfortunate colleagues of a few years earlier, many of whom were dead or maimed.

Indeed, if perceptions of Southern invincibility had been a factor in the resort to war in 1861, by 1865 the premise of the Southern white male's superiority had been clearly demonstrated to be false. If there had been a difference between Northerners and Southerners based upon geographic or cultural ethnicity, it had been shown to be superficial at best. The Southern mind-set at the outset of the Civil War had been defined in emotional terms: courage and the will to win would prevail based upon the South's superiority of lifestyle, heritage, and commitment. Severely underestimated were the factors of technology and resources, which were among the war's most decisive elements. In an emerging era of modern war, with more-lethal weapons and far-reaching communications and transportation capabilities, the primary reliance upon personal prowess was not only outdated and invalid, it was absurd.[1]

Yet the basic problem for the South had been that of underestimating the enemy's will. The idea that in a nationalist war waged against civilized foes, be it short or protracted, the opposing soldiers would prove less brave, less capable, and less committed was erroneous. Beyond the North's overwhelming advantage in numbers and material resources, the basic elements common to mankind, courage and ability, would generally balance on the battlefield, and not define the final outcome.

For centuries, the inherent lessons of war frequently have been obscured and overlooked. In retrospect, the Southern dilemma in 1861 was akin to that which exists in all conflicts. How does one, before it is too late, equate war's awful scourge—the immense anguish, vile inequity, far-reaching devastation, and rampant madness—with both the initial sought-for objectives, and then the random end results? Too often, as in 1861, society's emotions have overshadowed history's lessons. Those who act wisely are both experienced and aware.

Yet one lifetime is but a shallow scratch on the surface of total knowledge, beginning with virtual ignorance, and culminating with a modest degree of knowledge at an advanced age. It should be apparent that there is a greater relevancy beyond one's own understanding and experiences. The collective knowledge gained over time includes an awareness of mankind's tendency to miscalculate.

The basic problem thus has been an enigma: can we act rationally as a nation on the basis of emotion or reason if we as individuals lack awareness of practical realities? Are we doomed to the perpetuation of warfare as an answer to national or international problems because we do not have firsthand knowledge of war's ultimate misery?

The answer is found either in our applied ignorance or wisdom. For the proof of that equation we can examine the efforts of those who have gone before and tried, but often failed. There are many causes worth fighting for, if need be. But any resort to the ultimate commitment of war must be guided by objectivity and practicality, with an understanding that only a nation's truly essential, worthy, and obtainable goals can counterbalance the certain ordeal of armed endeavor. And that the cost to be paid will not exceed any benefits of the end result.

In Southern society's 1861 lurch toward independence there were too many elements of unknown or disproportionate risk. The enemy's "overwhelming numbers and resources," which Robert E. Lee spoke of in 1865 as the basis for surrender, were discounted at the beginning due to the prevailing belief that Southerners were better fighters, and that their will to win would prevail. Yet the nation had remained intact; the parts were not able to defeat the whole. The contest had been more a war of emotion than that of practicality.

Therein lay the South's ultimate flaw—a lack of reason. "Southern invincibility" had been the perception, but not the reality.

It is a lesson for all ages.

Of War, Life, and Love

Southern soldiers, much as warriors of most wars, were willing to risk their lives for a cherished cause. Essentially, the goal of attaining Southern independence was promulgated as of greater value than an individual's life. This was a reasoned attitude, based upon mankind's higher intelligence.

Life itself is traditionally at the pinnacle of our value system—it is our most important possession. Yet the willingness to sacrifice our existence for a higher purpose, if need be, involves an admission that physical life is subordinate to a higher realm. Thus, the mystery of human existence, its purpose and significance in the framework of the universe, is finally defined as a matter of personal perspective and belief.

Most of us acknowledge death as a certainty, to be dealt with in life's litany of experiences, but often with dread or apprehension. Uncertainty and fear of the unknown are a part of these conceptions.

The Confederate soldier was no exception. Yet throughout the letters and diaries of many Southern soldiers are expressions of accepting "God's will" and of the recourse to "a merciful Providence." This belief in the Higher Being had a leavening effect on the psyche, and provided solace to a soldier facing the prospect of imminent death.

Exposure to the real and prevalent danger of a violent death was accepted as a part of the task to be performed—the physical coercion or destruction of the enemy. It was not necessarily with the expectation of dying that one enlisted in the army, but rather with acceptance of a calculated risk that such a price might be paid. This, again, was a reasoned evaluation, and was predicated on the awareness of mankind's mortality; that each individual must die, be it sooner or later.

Although the conditions under which one's demise occurs are sometimes subject to individual control, this is often only to a limited extent. When we drive a car, or fly in an airplane, the risk factor is there, no matter how small. Yet to be a combat-exposed soldier in the Civil War, or any war in history, involved a much-greater-than-normal civil risk. The mental burden thus was pronounced.

In combat circumstances, overcoming the prospect of imminent death involves a tense mental confrontation. To die without establishing one's worth is an ignominious end by conventional reasoning. How much better it is to die in the pursuit of a worthy ideal or for some valid purpose, if necessary. So projects the subconscious mind.

Yet the definition of worthiness in death is always subject to scrutiny. The Southern soldier saw his own sacrifice of life in terms of a greater purpose, the desired end justifying the means. As such, in the practical sense it was an investment in the future—for and because of succeeding generations.

This commitment to others was upheld as a worthy ideal, and it often served as the ideological basis for becoming a soldier. But in the realm of the battlefield, not all decisions were based on ideology. A soldier's thinking amid the awful stress of battle was often more basic. Life-and-death decisions were usually made impulsively. In recent understanding of why a person deliberately causes his death to save another—as when a soldier throws himself over a live grenade to save his buddy, or, in civilian life, a mother jumps in the path of an out-of-control car to save her child—a unique emotional factor is prevalent.

It is the element of love.

Love for one another—to make the total commitment and pay an ultimate price to save another—is perhaps the highest tribute of and to humanity. Amid the deepest tragedy, a higher expression of love reveals a significant human trait. Personal sacrifice in this extreme is but a testimonial of profound love, which is mankind's highest emotion.

Such reasoning, to value another's life more than our own, is an ultimate gift. This giving of one's life is but evidence of a miracle of the human mind; to do what we perceive is right while under dire stress, no matter what the cost. Not that all conform to this standard, but that so many do is cause for further reflection.

Usually, there are covert elements of inconsistency inherent in our accepted behavioral tenets. For example, if love for another is based upon our specific knowledge of that person, is our ignorance (the fact that we don't know the other individual) just cause for violent behavior on the battlefield or elsewhere? In war, a soldier attempts to kill fellow humans to accomplish a nation's political objectives. This, no matter how worthy the cause, is mankind's terrible burden.

The Confederate private who risked his life to drag a wounded comrade from an exposed position on the battlefield was expressing a love for his fellow man—but in the context of being present on the battlefield for the purpose of killing other men, the enemy. This contradiction of behavior was explained in terms of right versus wrong; such being a matter of your side's cause and views (the right) versus the enemy's (the wrong).

The essential question we must ask today in the light of history's rich lessons is, How justified is such rationale, not in our own eyes, but in an all-knowing God's?

Important questions about life, its value and meaning, transcend warfare and impact upon our daily lives throughout the span of time. Currently, they relate to a "mental war" involving the rationale for or against assisted suicide and abortion. Here, essential questions defining the meaning and value of life are prevalent. With what value do we equate our own lives and the lives of others? Is a minimum quality of life as important as life itself? To what extent must we endure suffering? What are the total consequences of bringing an "unwanted" baby into the world? Who controls what we can or can't do to our own bodies—the person or the state?

There are ideological concepts and practical answers on both sides to consider. How we look at these questions in regard to morality or practicality is often a matter of individual perception, based upon which prism we select to look through. Also, the answers are often blurred, reflecting various excruciating and complex circumstances.

Yet, after all, many problems of society may be simpler to resolve than we readily acknowledge.

The fundamental premise we choose to utilize may well involve some basic questions: Do we as humans know absolutely right from wrong? If we do, is this God-given knowledge acquired, or intuitive? Which earthly fate shall we follow? What is the ultimate good?

God gave us a higher intellect, and it is, as always, up to us to use it well.

History tells us where we have been.

Our minds define where we are going.

In Explanation

Any attempt to present the total spectrum of Southern thinking during the Civil War era must necessarily fail. More than a million men served as Confederate soldiers, and 4 million other whites and nearly as many blacks populated the South. It would be impossible, even if the resource materials were extant, to tell what each person was thinking, even part of the time.

This study necessarily is only representative. What it hopes to portray is the mainstream thinking of white Southerners as they experienced the terrible tragedy of civil war. In this sense it is neither complete, nor all encompassing. There are omissions of content and events; for example the entire Trans-Mississippi region is avoided. This is not because of any willful intent to discount or minimize the thoughts and attitudes of those Confederates who fought long and hard in that region (including my great grandfather), but rather a practical decision due to limitations of space, substantial redundancy, and also the peripheral nature of the actions there.

Certain battles such as Shiloh and Gettysburg are analyzed in greater detail than others, simply because of their crucial impact in developing significant attitudes of the gray soldiers and Southern society as a whole.

Some readers may question the inclusion of vignettes about moderately well-known and previously published Southern soldiers or personalities, such as Sandie Pendleton, Harry Burgwyn, and Sarah Morgan. Each has a well-written and comprehensive biography. Yet the intent is not to relate their specific stories so much as to digest individual attitudes amid the framework of the ordeals they experienced. These people were in positions as strategically placed participants to clarify, not only their own thinking, but that of their colleagues and contemporaries as well. Each was articulate, intelligent, and able to vividly convey his or her thoughts in personal journals, letters, or diaries. Their writings provide both a graphic immediacy and clear understanding of how they reasoned and why.

Conversely, the omission of relevant perspectives of blacks as Southerners is related to both their limited influence as decision makers in the white-dominated Old South society, and an absence of sufficient written expressions of attitude (largely due to the denial of formal education).

Throughout the text, relevant Southern thoughts have been focused on, and often analyzed. Many personal stories are intertwined to provide emotional realism and to better define attitudes, but it is the thinking that is the essence. All materials are thus slanted toward the mental side of the Confederate experience.

As for the individuals I have selected to portray or quote in some detail, the basic criterion used was that they be particularly good observers and articulate explainers. Although they were not top leaders, their attitudinal vignettes provide insight as to the real heart and soul of the Southern rebellion. If commanding generals ordered the actions, it was the rank-and-file army backbone that carried out their directives. As the war progressed, implementation often proved to be more significant than conception. The common will to do, or not to do, was crucial.

Moreover, these men quickly acquired the era's equivalent of street smarts as they served and suffered, and their letters home and journals often expressed that they knew intimately, not only about fighting and dying, but about the reasoning involved in war as well. Their extent of willpower represented an awesome potential, or a damning weakness. It remained at the crux of their martial endeavor.

As revealed in the thoughts of various individuals portrayed in these pages, the Southern spirit both flowed with hope and ebbed with despair throughout the war. In substance, the story of "Southern invincibility" is really an object lesson in the attitudes of mankind struggling with an enormous crisis. That we can observe and learn from their expressions as well as experiences would be of importance to those we are studying, were they alive today to so counsel us.

Unfortunately, the limitations of time and cultural evolution insure that we only glimpse rather than truly define their full thought processes. The inability of a common soldier to adequately express his thinking in literary terms had its roots too often in the meager education that many rural volunteers received. Indeed, often it is not from a want of materials that we perceive gaps and omissions, but rather from an absence of articulate expression. This occasionally gives rise to concern about the true beliefs and attitudes of some of the men.

Yet the hard realities ring true in the surviving participants' accounts. And, as always, we must interpret history through the extant written record.

The historian's observations, of course, are subject to debate, and in that sense I would like to clarify my motive in writing about the Southern fighting man's attitudes. Primarily, my intention has been to put into perspective the emotional reality of the war. In the final analysis, physical war depended upon the mental war, and as witnessed by the text, it was the ultimate consideration.

As to the objectivity of my endeavor, I can but express my heartfelt belief that I have tried to accurately portray, with both compassion and understanding as well as critical insight, the attitudes as they truly existed, not as I would have them be. To some, my Northern background will automatically deny me the conviction necessary to write about sensitive Southern moral perspectives. While believing that insight knows no geographic boundary, I would point out that Southern blood is coursing through my veins. My maternal great grandfather fought for the South in Missouri beginning in 1861, and prior to the war his family had emigrated from Culpeper County, Virginia. I value the ideals of our nation, and reflect both admiration for and pride in my forebears' Southern heritage. Yet the fact that I am an American speaks louder than a partisanship for either side.

And finally, I would hope that all understand the merit of that thinking.

WILEY SWORD

Reference Notes

CHAPTER 1

1. Fred Fleet to Benjamin R. Fleet, Nov. 10, 1860, printed in Betsey Fleet and John D. P. Fuller, eds., *Green Mount: A Virginia Plantation Family during the Civil War,* Charlottesville, Va., 1962, 40. [Hereafter cited as *Green Mount.*]
2. Fred Fleet to Pa, Feb. 18, 1861, *Green Mount,* 48.
3. C. B. Fleet to Fred Fleet, Mar. 5, 1861, *Green Mount,* 49–50.
4. Ma and Pa to Fred Fleet, Apr. 29, 1861, Benny's journal, Mar. 29, 1861, *Green Mount,* 50, 53, 58, 61.
5. Fred Fleet to Ma, Aug. 6, 1861; Fred to Pa, Oct. 4, 1861, *Green Mount,* 70, 80–81.
6. Fred Fleet to Benny, Dec. 15, 1861, *Green Mount,* 90.
7. Fred Fleet to Ma, Apr. 15, 1862, author's collection.
8. Fred Fleet to Pa, Apr. 5, 1862, *Green Mount,* 117.

CHAPTER 2

1. William Howard Russell [Fletcher Pratt, ed.], *My Diary North and South,* New York, 1954, 38ff., quoted in James M. McPherson, *Drawn with the Sword,* New York, 1966, 8.
2. James M. McPherson, *Drawn with the Sword: Reflections on the American Civil War,* New York, 1966, 8, 12, 21.
3. Ibid., 3–23; James M. McPherson, *Battle Cry of Freedom: The Civil War*

Era [Oxford History of the United States Series], New York, 1988, 39–41.

4. Bertram Wyatt-Brown, *Southern Honor: Ethics and Behavior in the Old South*, New York, 1982, 29ff.
5. Ibid., 28ff.
6. Ibid.
7. McPherson, *Drawn with the Sword*, 22.
8. Ibid.
9. Mary A. H. Gay, *Life in Dixie during the War*, Atlanta, Ga., 1887, reprint, 1979, 10–11.
10. Wyatt-Brown, *Southern Honor*, 31ff.
11. Ibid., 29ff.
12. Ibid.
13. Ibid., 30ff.
14. Ibid., 34.
15. Ibid., 33.
16. Ibid., 29ff.
17. Ibid., 113.
18. Ibid.
19. Ibid., 14ff.
20. Ibid., 226ff., 281–83.
21. Ibid., 22–28, 34, 59–61.
22. Ibid., 34, 38ff., 42.
23. Ibid., 31–32.

CHAPTER 3

1. C. Vann Woodward, ed., *Mary Chesnut's Civil War*, New Haven, Conn., 1981, 29.
2. Wyatt-Brown, *Southern Honor*, 60.
3. Ibid.
4. Woodward, *Mary Chesnut's Civil War*, li, 29.
5. Woodward, *Mary Chesnut's Civil War*, li, 35ff.; Wyatt-Brown, *Southern Honor*, 14ff.
6. McPherson, *Battle Cry of Freedom*, 37–39.
7. Ibid., 24–25, 28, 88, 195ff.
8. Ibid., 200, 255.
9. Ibid., 33, 39, 86, 92, 100.
10. Ibid., 283–84.
11. McPherson, *Drawn with the Sword*, 22–23, 60.
12. Ibid., 12ff.; Donald E. Reynolds, *Editors Make War: Southern Newspapers in the Secession Crisis*, Nashville, Tenn., 1966, introduction; Wyatt-Brown, *Southern Honor*, 29–32, 402ff.

CHAPTER 4

1. McPherson, *Battle Cry of Freedom*, 234ff.
2. Reynolds, *Editors Make War*, vii–viii, 5.
3. Ibid., 3, 5.
4. Ibid., 5–7.
5. Ibid., 213–14; McPherson, *Battle Cry of Freedom*, 243.
6. Reynolds, *Editors Make War*, 210ff.
7. Ibid., 12ff., 97ff.
8. Ibid., 210ff.; newspaper quotations are as cited, printed in Dwight Lowell Dumond, *Southern Editorials on Secession*, Gloucester, Mass., 1964.
9. Dumond, *Southern Editorials on Secession*.
10. Ibid., 500–502.
11. Ibid.
12. Ibid.
13. Ibid.
14. Ibid.
15. Ibid.
16. Ibid., 498–513.
17. Ibid., 503–9.
18. Ibid., 511–13.

CHAPTER 5

1. T. G. Burwell, letter, Apr. 29, 1861, Olde Soldier Books, Gaithersburg, Md., catalogue 42, item 181, Aug. 1990; O. Anderson, letter, June 18, 1861, Olde Soldier Books, Gaithersburg, Md., catalogue 98, item 202, Nov. 1995.
2. W. H. Sanders [11th Alabama Inf.], letter, July 17, 1861, Olde Soldier Books, Gaithersburg, Md., catalogue 59, item 189, Apr. 1992.
3. Anonymous, "Ten Days in Richmond," *Blackwood's Edinburgh Magazine*, 92, 392–93, printed in Henry Steele Commager, ed., *The Blue and the Gray*, New York, 1950, 65–66.
4. Richard M. McMurry, *Two Great Rebel Armies: An Essay in Confederate Military History*, Chapel Hill, N.C., 1989, 5, 44–45.
5. Ibid., 44–47.
6. Ibid.
7. Pa to Fred Fleet, Nov. 24, 1860, *Green Mount*, 42.
8. McMurry, *Two Great Rebel Armies*, 241ff.; McPherson, *Battle Cry of Freedom*, 197, 255ff., 276.
9. McPherson, *Battle Cry of Freedom*, 278.
10. John Esten Cooke, letter to J. E. B. Stuart, Apr. 4, 1861, Manuscripts Dept., Virginia Historical Society, Richmond, Va.

11. Clifford Dowdey and Louis H. Manarin, eds., *The Wartime Papers of Robert E. Lee,* Boston, 1961, 9–10.
12. Wiley Sword, *Embrace an Angry Wind: The Confederacy's Last Hurrah: Spring Hill, Franklin, and Nashville,* New York, 1992, 75ff.
13. McMurry, *Two Great Rebel Armies,* 93.
14. Ibid., 97ff.
15. Ibid., 98, 104–5.
16. Arney Robinson Childs, ed., *The Private Journal of Henry William Ravenel, 1859–1887,* Columbia, S.C., 1947, 65–67.
17. McMurry, *Two Great Rebel Armies,* 24ff.
18. Ibid.
19. Ibid., 69ff.
20. Ibid., 87ff.
21. Ibid., 47ff.
22. Ibid., 104–5.

CHAPTER 6

1. Woodward, *Mary Chesnut's Civil War.,* 31.
2. Ibid., 69.
3. James I. Robertson, *Soldiers Blue and Gray,* Columbia, S.C., 1988, 5ff.; Joseph Allen Frank and George A. Reeves, *"Seeing the Elephant": Raw Recruits at the Battle of Shiloh,* New York, 1989, 17ff.
4. Robertson, *Soldiers Blue and Gray,* 3ff.
5. Ma to Fred Fleet, May 20, 1861, *Green Mount,* 55.
6. For a general discussion of the psychology of going to war, see Robertson, *Soldiers Blue and Gray;* Reid Mitchell, *Civil War Soldiers,* New York, 1988; Bell Irvin Wiley, *The Common Soldier in the Civil War,* New York, 1952.

CHAPTER 7

1. Nat Dawson to Elodie Todd, 4-27-'61, Nathaniel Henry Rhodes Dawson Papers, Colln. no. 210, Southern Historical Collection, Manuscripts Dept., Wilson Library, Univ. of North Carolina, Chapel Hill, N.C.; photograph of Captain Nat Dawson, 4th Alabama Inf., Alabama Dept. of Archives and History, Montgomery, Ala.
2. Nat to Elodie, 4-27-'61, and biographical data, Dawson Papers, SHC.
3. Nat to Elodie, 6-26-'61, Dawson Papers, SHC; Justin G. Turner and Linda Levitt Turner, *Mary Todd Lincoln: Her Life and Letters,* New York, 1972, 49.
4. Jean H. Baker, *Mary Todd Lincoln: A Biography,* New York, 1987, 3ff., 21–22.

5. Ibid. 25ff.
6. Ibid., 34, 125; Elodie to Nat, 5-22-'61, Dawson Papers, SHC.
7. Baker, *Mary Todd Lincoln,* 222–23.
8. Ibid., 18, 22, 66–67.
9. Turner, *Mary Todd Lincoln: Her Life,* 48–49.
10. Elodie to Nat, 5-26, 27-'61, Dawson Papers, SHC.
11. Elodie to Nat, 7-4-'61, Dawson Papers, SHC.
12. Nat to Elodie, 5-8, 14, 16, 24, 30, '61, Elodie to Nat, 5-9-'61, Dawson Papers, SHC.
13. Elodie to Nat, 5-9-'61, Dawson Papers, SHC.
14. Nat to Elodie, 4-28-'61, 5-7, 11-'61, Dawson Papers, SHC.
15. Nat to Elodie, 5-8, 10, 14, 15-'61, Dawson Papers, SHC.
16. Nat to Elodie, 4-30-'61, Dawson Papers, SHC.
17. Nat to Elodie, 5-19-'61, Dawson Papers, SHC.
18. Nat to Elodie, 5-30-'61, Dawson Papers, SHC.
19. Nat to Elodie, 5-15, 17-'61, Dawson Papers, SHC.
20. Nat to Elodie, 5-16-'61, Elodie to Nat, 5-15-'61, Dawson Papers, SHC.
21. Nat to Elodie, 6-17-'61, Dawson Papers, SHC.
22. Nat to Elodie, 5-14, 19-'61, Dawson Papers, SHC.
23. Nat to Elodie, 5-14, 20, 25, 26-'61, Dawson Papers, SHC.
24. Nat to Elodie, 6-1-'61, Dawson Papers, SHC.
25. Nat to Elodie, 6-6-'61, Dawson Papers, SHC.
26. Nat to Elodie, 6-8-'61, Dawson Papers, SHC.
27. Ibid.
28. Nat to Elodie, 5-28, 29, 30-'61, Dawson Papers, SHC.
29. Nat to Elodie, 5-14, 16-'61, Dawson Papers, SHC.
30. Elodie to Nat, 5-27-'61, Dawson Papers, SHC.
31. Nat to Elodie, 6-17, 19, 23, 26-'61, Dawson Papers, SHC.
32. Nat to Elodie, 5-14-'61, 6-1-'61, Dawson Papers, SHC.
33. Nat to Elodie, 7-11-'61, Dawson Papers, SHC.
34. Nat to Elodie, 6-30-'61, 7-14-'61, Dawson Papers, SHC.
35. Nat to Elodie, 7-14, 16-'61, Dawson Papers, SHC.
36. Elodie to Nat, 5-26-'61, Dawson Papers, SHC.
37. Nat to Elodie, 7-18-'61, Dawson Papers, SHC.
38. Ibid.
39. Nat to Elodie, 5-26-'61, Elodie to Nat, 7-22-'61, Dawson Papers, SHC.
40. Ibid.
41. Ibid.
42. Elodie to Nat, 7-4-'61, Dawson Papers, SHC.
43. Elodie to Nat, 7-23-'61, Dawson Papers, SHC.
44. Nat to Elodie, 7-2-'61, Dawson Papers, SHC.
45. Nat to Elodie, 7-8-'61, Dawson Papers, SHC.
46. Nat to Elodie, 8-15-'61, Dawson Papers, SHC; Gregory Starbuck, "Up Alabamians!" *Military Images Magazine,* vol. 8, no. 1, July–Aug. 1986, 25ff.

47. Starbuck, "Up Alabamians!" *Military Images,* 27–28; Nat to Elodie, 7-21, 25, 16-'61, Dawson Papers, SHC.
48. Nat to Elodie, 7-24-'61, Dawson Papers, SHC.
49. Nat to Elodie, 7-21-'61, 8-29-'61, Dawson Papers, SHC.
50. Nat to Elodie, 8-29-'61, Dawson Papers, SHC.
51. Ibid.
52. Ibid.
53. Ibid.; William F. Fox, *Regimental Losses in the American Civil War 1861–1865,* Albany, N.Y., 1898, 1985 reprint, 560.
54. Nat to Elodie, 7-24, 25-'61, 8-29-'61, Dawson Papers, SHC.
55. Nat to Elodie, 7-21, 24, 25-'61, Dawson Papers, SHC.
56. Nat to Elodie, 7-25-'61, Dawson Papers, SHC.
57. Nat to Elodie, 7-24-'61, Dawson Papers, SHC.
58. Nat to Elodie, 7-25-'61, Dawson Papers, SHC.
59. Nat to Elodie, 7-28-'61, Dawson Papers, SHC.
60. Nat to Elodie, 7-28, 30-'61, Dawson Papers, SHC.
'61. Elodie to Nat, 7-28, 31-'61, Dawson Papers, SHC.
62. Ibid.
63. Nat to Elodie, 7-30-'61, 8-15-'61, Elodie to Nat, 7-31-'61, Dawson Papers, SHC.
64. Nat to Elodie, 8-3-'61, Dawson Papers, SHC.
65. Ibid.
66. Nat to Elodie, 8-4-'61, Dawson Papers, SHC.
67. Nat to Elodie, 7-28, 30-'61, Dawson Papers, SHC.
68. Nat to Elodie, 8-15, 29-'61, Elodie to Nat, 8-24-'61, Dawson Papers, SHC.
69. Nat to Elodie, 8-21-'61, Dawson Papers, SHC.
70. Ibid.
71. Elodie to Nat, 7-31-'61, Nat to Elodie, 8-1-'61, Dawson Papers, SHC.
72. Elodie to Nat, 7-28-'61, Dawson Papers, SHC.
73. Nat to Elodie, 8-15-'61, Dawson Papers, SHC.
74. Elodie to Nat, 8-19-'61, Dawson Papers, SHC.
75. Elodie to Nat, 8-4-'61, Dawson Papers, SHC.
76. Ibid.
77. Nat to Elodie, n.d. [July 1861], Dawson Papers, SHC.

CHAPTER 8

1. George Peddy Cuttino, ed., *Saddle Bag and Spinning Wheel, Being the Civil War Letters of George W. Peddy, M.D., Surgeon 56th Georgia Volunteer Regiment, C.S.A.,* Macon, Ga., 1981, 12–13; Betty Herndon Maury, diary, June 3, 1861, Library of Congress, Washington, D.C., quoted in Bell Irvin Wiley, *Confederate Women,* Westport, Conn., 1975, 141.

2. Mary A. Ward, testimony of, *Report of the Committee of the Senate upon the Relations between Labor and Capital, and Testimony Taken by the Committee,* Washington, D.C., 1885, vol. 4, 331–32, printed in Henry Steele Commager, ed., *The Blue and the Gray,* New York, 1950, 61–63.
3. Woodward, *Mary Chesnut's Civil War,* li, 793.
4. Ibid., li., 31.
5. Ibid., 31, 31n.
6. Ibid.
7. Ibid., 735; Wyatt-Brown, *Southern Honor,* 226ff.
8. Wyatt-Brown, *Southern Honor,* 229, 283.
9. Woodward, *Mary Chesnut's Civil War,* 59, 729.
10. Ibid., li; Wyatt-Brown, *Southern Honor,* 227–29; McPherson, *Battle Cry of Freedom,* 33.

CHAPTER 9

1. Charles East, ed., *Sarah Morgan: The Civil War Diary of a Southern Woman,* Athens, Ga., 1991, 35–36. [Apr. 7, 1862]; The Morgan family papers are at the Duke University Library, Durham, N.C. For ease in reference, citations are given as to the published papers in the Charles East–edited book. The original diary was published in 1913 as *A Confederate Girl's Diary,* and was edited by Warrington Dawson, Sarah Morgan's son.
2. East, *Sarah Morgan,* 40, 65 [May 9, 1862].
3. Ibid., 67 [May 10, 1862].
4. Ibid., 67–68 [May 10, 11, 1862].
5. Ibid.
6. Ibid., 69 [May 11, 1862].
7. Ibid., 68–69 [May 11, 1862].
8. Ibid., 86ff. [May 30, 1862].
9. Ibid., 91–93 [May 30, 31, 1862].
10. Ibid., 98–104 [June 1, 1862].
11. Ibid., 103 [June 1, 1862].
12. Ibid., 95–96 [May 31, 1862].
13. Ibid., 96 [May 31, 1862].
14. Ibid., 96–97 [May 31, 1862].
15. Ibid., 121 [June 16, 1862].
16. Ibid.
17. Ibid., 182, 202 [July 31, Aug. 9, 1862].
18. Ibid., 233 [Aug. 25, 1862].
19. Ibid., 182–83 [July 31]; Wyatt-Brown, *Southern Honor,* 156.
20. East, *Sarah Morgan,* 123ff. [June 16, 1862].
21. Ibid.

22. Ibid.
23. Wyatt-Brown, *Southern Honor,* 155–56.
24. East, *Sarah Morgan,* 64, 140–43n [May 9, June 28, 29, 1862].
25. Ibid., 142 [June 29, 1862].
26. Ibid., 182–83 [July 31, 1862].
27. Ibid., 333ff. [Nov. 12, 1862].
28. Ibid., 482 [Apr. 22, 1863].
29. Ibid., 485ff., 507ff. [Apr., May 1863].
30. Ibid., 490–91 [Apr. 30, 1863]

CHAPTER 10

1. Most of the Burgwyn Family Papers (no. 1687) are at the Southern Historical Collection, Manuscripts Dept., Wilson Library, University of North Carolina, Chapel Hill, N.C. Many letters of Henry King Burgwyn, Jr., and his family are published in Archie K. Davis, *Boy Colonel of the Confederacy: The Life and Times of Henry King Burgwyn, Jr.,* Chapel Hill, N.C., 1985. For ease in reference, citations are given as to the published papers in the Davis book. Davis, *Boy Colonel,* 20, photographs, frontispiece, and 45.
2. Davis, *Boy Colonel,* 32 [Nov. 30, 1856, Apr. 4, 1857].
3. Ibid., 34–35, 39.
4. Ibid., 40.
5. Ibid., 46 [June 3, 1860]; Harry to father, 3-23-'61, SHC.
6. Harry to father, 3-23-'61, SHC.
7. Ibid.
8. Davis, *Boy Colonel,* 58.
9. Ibid., 41ff.
10. Ibid.
11. Harry to father, 1-11-'61, SHC.
12. Henry, Sr., to Harry, 3-8-'61, SHC.
13. Davis, *Boy Colonel,* 72.
14. Ibid., 53 [Dec. 22, 1860].
15. Ibid., 82–83 [war journal, Aug. 1861, 1].
16. Harry to mother, 6-2-'61, SHC.
17. Davis, *Boy Colonel,* 82; George B. Atkins to Harry, May 22, 1861; Joseph B. Starr to Harry, May 22, 1861, SHC.
18. Harry to mother, 6-2-'61, SHC.
19. Davis, *Boy Colonel,* 74, 82–83.
20. Ibid., 99; Harry to father, 1-19-'62, SHC.
21. Davis, *Boy Colonel,* 100 [Feb. 19, 1862].
22. Ibid., 139ff., 194 [war journal, 19].
23. Ibid., 91 [war journal, 1-23-'62]; Harry to father, 2-1-'62.
24. Harry to father, 2-1-'62, SHC.

25. Harry to father, 2-26-'62, SHC.
26. Davis, *Boy Colonel*, 97; Harry to mother, 3-12-'62.
27. Harry to mother, 3-12-'62, SHC.
28. Harry to mother, 3-17-'62, Harry to father, 3-18-'62, SHC.
29. Harry to mother, 3-17-'62, Harry to father, 3-27-'62, SHC.
30. Davis, *Boy Colonel*, 127ff.; Harry to father, 3-20-'62, 4-7-'62, SHC.
31. Harry to father, 3-20-'62, SHC.
32. Ibid.; Davis, *Boy Colonel*, 129.
33. Davis, *Boy Colonel*, 129, 179.

CHAPTER 11

1. Woodward, *Mary Chesnut's Civil War*, 70, 83.
2. Ibid., 83.
3. Ibid.
4. Ibid.
5. William W. Porter, letter, June 12, 1861, courtesy of The Horse Soldier, Gettysburg, Pa. [cat. 21, item L 82]; E. A. Jackson, *Letters of Edgar Allan Jackson*, Sept. 7, 1860 to Apr. 15, 1863, Franklin, Va., 1939, 10.
6. Ibid.
7. Bessie Mell Lane, ed., *Dear Bet: The Carter Letters: 1861–1863*, Clemson, S. C., 1978, 35; W. R. Redding [13th Georgia Inf.], letter, Apr. 13, 1862, W. R. Redding Papers [no. 3348], SHC.
8. Lane, *Dear Bet*, 84; Michael W. Taylor, ed., *The Cry Is War, War, War: The Civil War Correspondence of Lts. Burwell Thomas Cotton and George Job Huntley, 34th Regt. North Carolina Troops*, Dayton, Ohio, 1994, 125.
9. John Johnson [19th Georgia Inf.], letter, Apr. 18, 1862, John Johnson Papers [no. 2398], SHC.
10. Ibid.
11. E. C. Jackson, *Letters*, 5.
12. W. R. Redding [13th Georgia Inf.], letter, Apr. 13, 1862, W. R. Redding Papers [no. 3348], SHC.
13. Ibid.; Taylor, *The Cry Is War*, 65.
14. Taylor, *The Cry Is War*, 76.
15. J. H. Langhorne, letter, Jan. 12, 1862, and G. K. Harlow, letter, January 23, 1862, printed in Robert G. Tanner, *Stonewall in the Valley: Thomas J. "Stonewall" Jackson's Shenandoah Valley Campaign, Spring 1862*, Garden City, N.Y., 1976, 91.
16. Taylor, *The Cry Is War*, 80.
17. See McPherson, *Battle Cry of Freedom*, 429ff.
18. Taylor, *The Cry Is War*, 65.

19. A. H. Mendenhall [1st Texas Inf.], letter, July 8, 1862, Olde Soldier Books, Gaithersburg, Md., catalog 23, item 149, Nov. 1988.
20. Taylor, *The Cry Is War,* 76–77.
21. For example, see John Johnson, letter, Apr. 18, 1862, Johnson Papers, SHC.

CHAPTER 12

1. Elodie to Nat, 9-1-'61, Dawson Papers, SHC.
2. Elodie to Nat, 7-4-'61, Dawson Papers, SHC.
3. Nat to Elodie, 7-11-'61, Dawson Papers, SHC.
4. Elodie to Nat, 7-23-'61, Dawson Papers, SHC.
5. Nat to Elodie, 8-4-'61, 9-24-'61, Dawson Papers, SHC.
6. Nat to Elodie, n.d. [Nov. '61], Dawson Papers, SHC.
7. Nat to Elodie, 1-5-'62, Dawson Papers, SHC.
8. Elodie to Nat, 9-29-'61, 1-5,12-'62, Dawson Papers, SHC.
9. Elodie to Nat, 10-13-'61, Dawson Papers, SHC.
10. Elodie to Nat, 5-22-'61, Dawson Papers, SHC.
11. Elodie to Nat, 8-19-'61, Dawson Papers, SHC.
12. Nat to Elodie, 10-5-'61, Dawson Papers, SHC.
13. Nat to Elodie, 8-18-'61, Dawson Papers, SHC.
14. Nat to Elodie, 8-25-'61, Dawson Papers, SHC.
15. Nat to Elodie, 9-24-'61, Dawson Papers, SHC.
16. Nat to Elodie, 9-2, 8-'61, 10-26-'61, 12-8, 11-'61, Dawson Papers, SHC.
17. Nat to Elodie, 10-3, 5-'61, Dawson Papers, SHC.
18. Nat to Elodie, 9-13-'61, Dawson Papers, SHC.
19. Ibid.
20. Nat to Elodie, 9-8-'61, 11-27-'61, Dawson Papers, SHC.
21. Nat to Elodie, 12-3-'61, 3-20-'62, Dawson Papers, SHC.
22. Nat to Elodie, 12-18-'61, 3-28-'62, Dawson Papers, SHC.
23. Nat to Elodie, 3-28-'62, Dawson Papers, SHC.
24. Nat to Elodie, 9-24-'61, 11-7-'61, Dawson Papers, SHC.
25. Nat to Elodie, 4-4-'62, Dawson Papers, SHC.
26. Nat to Elodie, 12-25-'61, Joel Matthews to Nat, 9-22-'61, Dawson Papers, SHC.
27. Joel Matthews to Nat, 9-22-'61, Nat to Elodie, 1-5-'62, Dawson Papers, SHC.
28. Nat to Elodie, 1-22-'62, Dawson Papers, SHC.
29. Nat to Elodie, 1-8-'62, Elodie to Nat, 4-6-'62, Dawson Papers, SHC.
30. Nat to Elodie, 4-6, 14-'62, Dawson Papers, SHC.
31. Nat to Elodie, 4-14-'62, Dawson Papers, SHC.
32. Nat to Elodie, 4-19-'62, Dawson Papers, SHC.
33. Nat to Elodie, 4-21-'62, Dawson Papers, SHC.
34. Ibid.

35. Elodie to Nat, 7-28-'61, 8-4-'61, 12-27-'61, Dawson Papers, SHC.
36. Elodie to Nat, 4-13-'62, Dawson Papers, SHC.
37. Elodie to Nat, 4-15-'62, Dawson Papers, SHC.
38. Elodie to Nat, 4-15, 16-'62, Dawson Papers, SHC.
39. Ibid.
40. U.S. War Dept., *The War of the Rebellion: A Compilation of the Official Records of the Union and Confederate Armies,* 70 vols., in 128 parts, Washington, D.C., 1880–1901, series 1, vol. 11, part 1, 976, part 2, 635 [hereafter cited as OR].
41. Nat to Elodie, 3-14-'62, Dawson Papers, SHC.
42. Elodie to Nat, 1861–'62, Joel Matthews to Nat, 9-19-'61, Dawson Papers, SHC.
43. Nat to Elodie, 11-21-'61, Dawson Papers, SHC.
44. Nat to Elodie, 11-22-'61, Dawson Papers, SHC.
45. Nat to Elodie, 1-8-'62, Elodie to Nat, 1-5-'62, Dawson Papers, SHC.
46. Nat to Elodie, 1-19-'62, Dawson Papers, SHC.
47. Nat to Elodie, 12-22-'61, Dawson Papers, SHC.
48. Nat to Elodie, 7-14-'61, 12-21-'61, 1-8-'62, Dawson Papers, SHC.
49. Dawson family records, Nat to Elodie, 8-29-'64, Dawson Papers, SHC.
50. Elodie to Nat, 9-4-'64, Dawson Papers, SHC; Baker, *Mary Todd Lincoln,* 222–23.
51. Elodie to Nat, 9-4-'64, Dawson Papers, SHC.
52. Nat to Elodie, 4-13-'62, Dawson Papers, SHC.

CHAPTER 13

1. Clarence C. Buel and Robert U. Johnson, eds., *Battles and Leaders of the Civil War,* 4 vols., New York, 1888, reprint 1956, vol. 1, 645n.
2. Fred Fleet to Ma, June 5, 1862, *Green Mount,* 132.
3. Fred Fleet to Pa, Apr. 5, May 14, 1862, *Green Mount,* 117, 126.
4. Fred Fleet to Benny, Apr. 15, 1862, Fred to Pa, May 14, 1862, *Green Mount,* 122, 126.
5. Fred Fleet to Pa, June 10, 1862, *Green Mount,* 135.
6. Fred Fleet to Pa, July 3, 1862, *Green Mount,* 144–45.
7. Fred Fleet to Ma, June 13, 1862, *Green Mount,* 137.
8. Fred Fleet to Ma, July 5, 1862, *Green Mount,* 146.
9. Ibid.
10. Fred Fleet to Ma, June 13, 1862, *Green Mount,* 137.
11. Ma to Fred Fleet, Aug. 10, 1862, Nov. 23, 1862, *Green Mount,* 158–59, 186.
12. Fred Fleet to Ma, Aug. 13, 1862, *Green Mount,* 160.
13. Fred Fleet to Benny, Mar. 23, 24, 1863, *Green Mount,* 212–13.
14. Ibid.
15. Fred Fleet to Ma, Nov. 14, 1862, *Green Mount,* 181.

16. Ma to Fred Fleet, Oct. 26, 1862, *Green Mount,* 177.
17. Benny Fleet's Journal, Dec. 15, 1861; Ma to Fred Fleet, Feb. 7, 1862; Pa to Fred, Mar. 1, 1862, *Green Mount,* 89, 103, 109.
18. Pa to Fred Fleet, Feb. 8, 1862, *Green Mount,* 104.
19. Ma to Fred Fleet, Feb. 15, 1862; Pa to Fred, Feb. 26, 1862, *Green Mount,* 106, 108.
20. Ibid.
21. Ma to Fred Fleet, Nov. 23, 1862; Pa to Fred, Sept. 1862, *Green Mount,* 166, 186.
22. Ma to Fred Fleet, Sept. 28, 1862, *Green Mount,* 169.
23. Benny's Journal, Dec. 11–14, 1862; Fred to Pa, Apr. 7, 1863; Pa to Fred, Apr. 27, 1863, *Green Mount,* 189, 216, 223.
24. Pa to Fred Fleet, Aug. 4, 1862, *Green Mount,* 157.
25. Fred Fleet to Ma, Oct. 6, 1862, *Green Mount,* 171.
26. Pa to Fred Fleet, June 16, 1863, Fred to Pa, May 12, 1863, June 25, 1863; Fred to Ma, June 4, 1863; *Green Mount,* 228, 236, 242, 247.
27. Fred Fleet to Benny, Mar. 23, 1863; Fred to Ma, June 4, 1863, Benny's Journal, July 1, 1863, *Green Mount,* 212, 237, 248.
28. Fred Fleet to Ma, May 23, 1863, June 21, 1863, *Green Mount,* 231, 244.
29. Fred Fleet to Ma, June 4, 1863, *Green Mount,* 238.

CHAPTER 14

1. William Cash and Lucy Somerville Howorth, eds., *My Dear Nellie: The Civil War Letters of William L. Nugent to Eleanor Smith Nugent,* Jackson, Miss. 1977, letter of May 26, 1862.
2. Larry J. Daniel, *Soldiering in the Army of Tennessee,* Chapel Hill, N.C., 1991, 17.
3. P. W. Watson [45th Alabama Inf.], letter, July 11, 1862, Stones River National Battlefield Park Library, Murfreesboro, Tenn., printed in Daniel, *Soldiering in the Army of Tennessee,* 17.
4. Frank and Reeves, *Seeing the Elephant,* 19.
5. Ibid., 17ff.
6. Joseph B. Lyman [1st Louisiana Cav.], letter, Apr. 1, 1862, Yale University Library, New Haven, Conn.
7. For the furor over Johnston's leadership, see Wiley Sword, *Shiloh: Bloody April,* New York, 1974, reprint by Morningside Bookshop, Dayton, Ohio, 49ff., 72.
8. Frank Schaller [colonel, 22d Mississippi Inf.], letter, Mar. 14, 1862, courtesy of Kathleen Schaller Herty Brown, New York.
9. Charles J. Johnson [surgeon, 11th Louisiana Inf.], letter, Apr. 4, 1862, Dept. of Archives and History, Louisiana State University, Baton Rouge, La.

10. See Sword, *Shiloh: Bloody April*, 223ff.
11. Ibid.
12. Ibid., 257ff.
13. Grady McWhiney, *Braxton Bragg and Confederate Defeat*, vol. 1, New York, 1969, 234ff.
14. See Sword, *Shiloh: Bloody April*, 383ff.
15. Joseph B. Lyman [1st Louisiana Cav.], letter, Apr. 11, 1862, Yale University Library, New Haven, Conn.
16. W. A. Howard [33d Tennessee Inf.], letter, Apr. 10, 1862, Shiloh National Battlefield Park, Shiloh, Tenn.
17. A. H. Mecklin [15th Mississippi Inf.], diary entry, Apr. 6, 1862, Mississippi Dept. of Archives and History, Jackson, Miss.
18. John G. Biel, "The Battle of Shiloh: From the letters and Diary of Joseph Dimmit Thompson," [38th Tennessee Inf.], *Tennessee Historical Quarterly*, vol. 27, no. 3, 267–70.
19. Ibid.; Richard L. Pugh [Washington Artillery], letters, Apr. 8, 11, 13, 1862, Dept. of Archives and History, Louisiana State University, Baton Rouge, La.
20. William J. Hardee, letter to Mrs. Felicia Shover, Apr. 9, 1862, Manuscripts Div., Library of Congress, Washington, D.C.; Braxton Bragg, letter to wife, Apr. 8, 1862, Bragg Papers, Missouri Historical Society, St. Louis, Mo.
21. Thomas Chinn Robertson [4th Louisiana Inf.], letter to mother, Apr. 9, 1862, Dept. of Archives and Manuscripts Louisiana State University, Baton Rouge, La.
22. Charles J. Johnson, letter, 4-11-'62, LSU; B. F. Wilkinson, letter, Apr. 16, 1862, Dept. of Archives and Manuscripts, Louisiana State University, Baton Rouge, La.
23. Biel, "The Battle of Shiloh" [letters of Joseph Dimmit Thompson], THQ, 27-3, 273; C. J. Johnson, 4-20-'62, LSU.
24. C. J. Johnson, 4-15, 20-'62, LSU.
25. Richard L. Pugh, 4-8-'62, LSU; S. R. Latta [13th Tennessee Inf.], letters, Apr. 10, 13, 18, 1862, Dept. of Archives and Manuscripts, Louisiana State University, Baton Rouge, La.
26. C. J. Johnson, 4-9-'62, LSU.
27. Daniel, *Soldiering in the Army of Tennessee*, 20ff.

CHAPTER 15

1. Sandie Pendleton to Nancy, letter, Aug. 16, 1861, William Nelson Pendleton Papers [no. 1466], Southern Historical Collection, Manuscripts Dept., Wilson Library, University of North Carolina, Chapel Hill, N.C. For ease in reference, citations are given where possible

as to a published segment in W. G. Bean's book *Stonewall's Man Sandie Pendleton,* Chapel Hill, N.C., 1959.

2. Sandie to mother, Sept. 23, 1863, Pendleton Papers, SHC, Bean, *Stonewall's Man,* 154.
3. Sandie to mother, Dec. 31, 1862, Pendleton Papers, SHC.
4. Ibid.
5. Sandie to mother, Dec. 31, 1862, Pendleton Papers, SHC.
6. Sandie to mother, Mar. 29, May 28, 1862, Pendleton Papers, SHC, Bean, *Stonewall's Man,* 55, 57, 63.
7. Sandie to mother, June 1, 1862, Pendleton Papers, SHC, Bean, *Stonewall's Man,* 64.
8. Susan Leigh Blackford, *Letters from Lee's Army; or, Memoirs of Life in and out of the Army in Virginia during the War between the States,* New York, 1947, 105.
9. M. O. Young, "History of the First Brigade," 77, Georgia Dept. of Archives and History; J. J. Wilson to father, Sept. 8, 1862, Wilson Papers, Mississippi Dept. of Archives and History, Jackson, Miss., quoted in John J. Hennessy, *Return to Bull Run: The Campaign and Battle of Second Manassas,* New York, 1993, 413, 442.
10. Gary W. Gallagher, ed., *Fighting for the Confederacy: The Personal Recollections of General Edward Porter Alexander,* Chapel Hill, N.C., 1989, 139.
11. Quoted in Stephen W. Sears, *Landscape Turned Red: The Battle of Antietam,* New York, 1983, 345, 801.
12. Sandie to mother, Aug. 8, Sept. 21, 1862, Pendleton Papers, SHC, Bean, *Stonewall's Man,* 78, 81.
13. Sandie to sister, Dec. 5, 1862, Pendleton Papers, SHC, Bean, *Stonewall's Man,* 86.
14. Sandie to mother, Sept. 21, 1862, Pendleton Papers, SHC, Bean, *Stonewall's Man,* 78.
15. OR 1-12-1-380; W. S. H. Baylor to W. N. Pendleton, Aug. 12, 1862, Pendleton Papers, SHC, Bean, *Stonewall's Man,* 66.
16. Sandie to mother, Aug. 8, 1862, Pendleton Papers, SHC, Bean, *Stonewall's Man,* 81.
17. Lizzie Pendleton to W. N. Pendleton, Aug. 11, 1862, Sandie to mother, Aug. 8, 1862, Pendleton Papers, SHC, Bean, *Stonewall's Man,* 74–75.
18. Ibid.
19. Sandie to mother, Dec. 11, 1862, Pendleton Papers, SHC.
20. Sandie to mother, Dec. 14, 1862, Pendleton Papers, SHC.
21. Sandie to sister, Dec. 5, 1862, Pendleton Papers, SHC.
22. Sandie to Mary, Mar. 19, 1863, Pendleton Papers, SHC, Bean, *Stonewall's Man,* 109.
23. Sandie to Kate Corbin, Feb. 26, 1864, Pendleton Papers, SHC, Bean, *Stonewall's Man,* 111.

24. Sandie to mother, Jan. 20, 1863, Pendleton Papers, SHC, Bean, *Stonewall's Man*, 102.
25. Sandie to mother, Dec. 31, 1862, Pendleton Papers, SHC.
26. H. K. Douglas Diary, Dec. 26, 1862, quoted in Bean, *Stonewall's Man*, 64.
27. Sandie to mother, Dec. 31, 1862, Pendleton Papers, SHC.
28. H. K. Douglas Diary, Dec. 26, 1862, quoted in Bean, *Stonewall's Man*, 64.
29. Sandie to mother, Apr. 4, 1863, Pendleton Papers, SHC, Bean, *Stonewall's Man*, 113.
30. James I. Robertson, Jr., *Stonewall Jackson: The Man, The Soldier, The Legend*, New York, 1997, 721.
31. See Robertson, *Stonewall Jackson*, 737ff.
32. Ibid., 755ff.
33. Sandie to Kate, journal, May 3, 1863, Pendleton Papers, SHC.
34. Ibid., June 4, 1863.
35. Clifford Dowdey and Louis H. Manarin, eds., *The Wartime Papers of Robert E. Lee*, Boston, Mass., 1961, 485.
36. Ibid., 484.
37. Ibid., 483.
38. Ibid., 490.
39. Ibid., 488.
40. Ibid., 504–5.
41. Ibid., 507–9.
42. Ibid., 509.
43. Sandie to Kate, journal, June 18, 1863, Pendleton Papers, SHC.
44. Sandie to Kate, journal, June 23, 1863, Pendleton Papers, SHC.

CHAPTER 16

1. Thomas Elder [3d Virginia Inf.], letter to wife, May 8, 1862, Virginia Historical Society, Richmond, Va.
2. Ibid.
3. Gallagher, *Fighting for the Confederacy*, 59.
4. Blackford, *Letters from Lee's Army*, 86.
5. Dowdey and Manarin, *Wartime Papers of R. E. Lee*, 565.
6. See Robertson, *Stonewall Jackson*, 474, 484, 541.
7. Glenn Tucker, "An Appraisal of Robert E. Lee," *Civil War Times, Illustrated*, vol. 4, no. 1, Apr. 1965, 4ff.
8. Blackford, *Letters from Lee's Army*, 115.
9. William C. Oates, *The War between the Union and the Confederacy and Its Lost Opportunities . . . ,* New York, 1905, reprint 1985, 135.
10. McMurry, *Two Great Rebel Armies*, 97ff.

11. Samuel A. Porter [3d North Carolina Inf.], letter, n.d., Olde Soldier Books, catalog 36, item 157, Feb. 1990; E. A. Jackson, *Letters*, 5–6.

12. Taylor, *The Cry Is War*, 76; W. R. Redding [13th Georgia Inf.], letter, n.d., SHC.

13. Joel Walker Perry [3d Georgia Inf.], letter, April 27, 1862, Olde Soldier Books, catalog 51, item 197, June 1991; Thomas Elder [3d Virginia Inf.], letter to wife, May 8, 1862, Virginia Hist. Society, Richmond, Va.

14. Taylor, *The Cry Is War*, 142.

15. Lane, *Dear Bet*, 91.

16. Bean, *Stonewall's Man*, 135.

17. Ibid., 136.

CHAPTER 17

1. Davis, *Boy Colonel*, 185–86.; J. Jones to Harry Burgwyn, Aug. 11, 1862, SHC.

2. Davis, *Boy Colonel*, 186ff.; Harry to mother, 8-23, 24, 27-'62, SHC.

3. Ibid.

4. Ibid.

5. Davis, *Boy Colonel*, 304, 314; Harry to father, 11-1-'62, SHC.

6. Harry to father, 2-19, 26-'62, SHC.

7. Harry to father, 2-26-'62, 5-2-'62, SHC.

8. Harry to father, 4-28-'62, SHC.

9. Harry to father, 2-26-'62, SHC.

10. Harry to father, 3-20-'62, SHC.

11. Harry to father, 5-7-'62; Harry to mother, 5-11-'62, SHC.

12. Harry to mother, 5-11-'62, SHC.

13. Harry to mother, 9-2-'62; Harry to father, 9-9-'62, SHC.

14. Harry to mother, 5-8-'63, SHC.

15. Ibid.

16. Harry to mother, 6-5-'63, SHC.

17. Harry to mother, 5-18, 19-'63; Harry to father, 5-21-'63, SHC.

18. Harry to father, 5-19, 31-'63, SHC.

19. Harry to father, 5-31-'63, SHC.

20. Davis, *Boy Colonel*, 247–48.

21. Harry to mother, 6-15-'63, SHC.

22. Ibid.

23. Harry to mother, 7-14-'62, [journal], SHC.

24. Harry to mother, 7-14-'62, Harry to father, 72-'62, SHC.

25. Ibid.

26. Harry to mother, 7-14-'62, [journal], SHC.

27. Ibid.

28. Ibid.

29. Ibid.
30. Ibid.
31. Harry to father, 7-2-'62; Harry to mother, 7-14-'62, [journal], SHC.
32. Ibid.
33. Harry to father, 7-2-'62, SHC.
34. Ibid.
35. Harry to father, 5-31-'63, SHC.
36. Davis, *Boy Colonel,* 308–15; Harry to mother, 10-14-'62, SHC.
37. Davis, *Boy Colonel,* 308ff.; Lee R. Hadden, "The Deadly Embrace: The Meeting of the Twenty-fourth Regiment of Michigan Infantry and the Twenty-sixth Regiment of North Carolina Troops at McPherson's Woods, Gettysburg, Pennsylvania, July 1, 1863," *The Gettysburg Magazine,* no. 5 [July 1991], 24ff.
38. Davis, *Boy Colonel,* 317ff.; Hadden, "The Deadly Embrace," 26ff.
39. Davis, *Boy Colonel,* 320.
40. Davis, *Boy Colonel,* 327ff.; Hadden, "The Deadly Embrace," 27ff.
41. Davis, *Boy Colonel,* 326; Hadden, "The Deadly Embrace," 24ff.; John W. Bussey and David G. Martin, *Regimental Strengths at Gettysburg,* Baltimore, Md., 1982, 174, 489.
42. Harry to mother, 5-11-'62.
43. Harry to father, 5-14-'63, SHC; Hadden, "The Deadly Embrace," 23ff.
44. Ibid.; Davis, *Boy Colonel,* 328.
45. Davis, *Boy Colonel,* 327–29; Hadden, "The Deadly Embrace," 19ff.
46. Davis, *Boy Colonel,* 329; Hadden, "The Deadly Embrace," 28ff.
47. Ibid.
48. Harry to father, 5-14-'63, SHC.
49. G. P. Collins to H. K. Burgwyn, Sr., 7-3-'63, SHC; Davis, *Boy Colonel,* 329.
50. Davis, *Boy Colonel,* 329–32.
51. Ibid., 333; Hadden, "The Deadly Embrace," 32ff.; Fox, *Regimental Losses,* 439, 569.
52. Hadden, "The Deadly Embrace," 32ff; Fox, *Regimental Losses,* 117, 390, 555–56.
53. Hadden, "The Deadly Embrace," 29ff.; G. P. Collins to H. K. Burgwyn, Sr., 7-3-'63, SHC.
54. Davis, *Boy Colonel,* 334.

CHAPTER 18

1. Quoted in McMurry, *Two Great Rebel Armies,* 104.
2. W. L. Wilson to Dehon family, 6-15-1863, author's collection.
3. Blackford, *Letters from Lee's Army,* 175.

4. Sandie Pendleton to Kate, journal, June 28, 1863, Pendleton Papers, SHC.

5. Ibid.

6. Dowdey, *Wartime Papers of R. E. Lee*, 532, 570; OR 1-27-2-305; Edwin B. Coddington, *The Gettysburg Campaign: A Study in Command*, Dayton, Ohio reprint, 1979, 9.

7. Coddington, *Gettysburg Campaign*, 662, 120.

8. OR 1-27-2-316.

9. OR 1-27-2-308, 318.

10. Dowdey, *Wartime Papers of R. E. Lee*, 547–48.

11. Bean, *Stonewall's Man*, 39; McMurry, *Two Great Rebel Armies*, 30ff.

12. Coddington, *Gettysburg Campaign*, 372ff.

13. OR 1-27-2-319, 320.

14. Coddington, *Gettysburg Campaign*, 454ff.

15. OR 1-27-2-308; McMurry, *Two Great Rebel Armies*, 31; Thomas L. Connelly and Barbara L. Bellows, *God and General Longstreet: The Lost Cause and the Southern Mind*, Baton Rouge, La. 1982, 34ff.

16. Coddington, *Gettysburg Campaign*, 526ff.

17. OR 1-27-2-309.

18. Dowdey, *Wartime Papers of R. E. Lee*, 507–9.

19. OR 1-27-2-298, 308, 317.

20. Ibid.

21. Ibid.

22. Ibid.

23. OR 1-27-2-318; Coddington, *Gettysburg Campaign*, 459.

24. OR 1-27-2-320.

25. Ibid.

26. OR 1-27-2-308, 320, 359.

27. Ibid.

28. Coddington, *Gettysburg Campaign*, 458ff.

29. OR 1-27-2-308, 318.

30. George R. Stewart, *Pickett's Charge: A Microhistory of the Final Attack at Gettysburg, July 3, 1863*, Boston, 1959, 19–22.

31. OR 1-27-2-308, 321.

32. OR 1-27-2-299, 322.

33. David Wyatt Aiken [7th South Carolina Inf.], letter, July 11, 1863, Wyatt Papers, South Caroliniana Library, Columbia, S.C.

34. Taylor, *The Cry Is War*, 148–55.

35. Peter L. Mabry [3d Alabama Inf.], letter of Aug. 7, 1863, The Horse Soldier, catalog 22, item L-06, Cashtown. Pa.

36. Blackford, *Letters from Lee's Army*, 188–90.

37. Sandie Pendleton to Kate, journal, July 7, 16, 1863, Pendleton Papers, SHC.

38. Arthur Crew Inman, ed., *Soldier of the South: General Pickett's War Letters to His Wife*, Boston, 1928, 66–73.

39. Ibid.
40. Spencer G. Welch [13th South Carolina Inf.], letter to wife, Aug. 2, 1863, *A Confederate Surgeon's Letters to His Wife,* New York, 1911.
41. Letter by unidentified soldier named Micah to "Dear Brother," July 3, 1863, the Samuel Richey Collection, Miami University King Library, Oxford, Ohio.
42. Dowdey, *Wartime Papers of R. E. Lee,* 540, 544.
43. Ibid., 589.
44. Ibid., 542.
45. OR 1-27-2-326.
46. Dowdey, *Wartime Papers of R. E. Lee,* 543, 551.
47. Ibid., 561.

CHAPTER 19

1. John Dale [24th Mississippi Inf.], letter, Jan. 5, 1862, Honnoll Family Papers, Emory Univ. Library, Atlanta, Ga.
2. John Dale, letter, Apr. 17, 1862, Honnoll Papers, Emory Univ. Library.
3. John Dale, letter, July 16, 1862, Honnoll Papers, Emory Univ. Library.
4. M. M. C. Fipekin (?), letter Mar. 22, 1862, Honnoll Papers, Emory Univ. Library.
5. John Dale, letter, July 16, 1862, Honnoll Papers, Emory Univ. Library.
6. Hugh L. Honnoll, letters, May 15, 23, 1862, Honnoll Papers, Emory Univ. Library.
7. Ibid.
8. Cash and Howorth, *My Dear Nellie,* letter of May 28, 1862; William B. Honnoll, letter, Dec. 29, 1862, Honnoll Papers, Emory. Univ. Library.
9. Dan L. Kelly, letter, Oct. 31, 1862, Honnoll Papers, Emory Univ. Library.
10. Richard Walpole [15th Mississippi Inf.], letter, Nov. 4, 1862, Bomar Papers [no. 86], Emory Univ. Library.
11. Thomas C. Potter [Battery B, 1st Ohio Lt. Art.], letter, Jan. 12, 1863, author's collection.
12. Quoted in Daniel, *Soldiering in the Army of Tennessee,* 149.
13. William B. Honnoll, letter, May 19, 1863, Honnoll Papers, Emory Univ. Library.
14. See McPherson, *Battle Cry of Freedom,* 546ff.
15. William B. Honnoll, letter, July 17, 1863, Honnoll Papers, Emory. Univ. Library.
16. William D. Kendall [5th Tennessee Inf.], letter, Mar. 1, 1863, Ken-

dall Papers, Henry E. Huntington Library, San Marino, Calif. William B. Honnoll, letter, June 3, 1863, Honnoll Papers, Emory Univ. Library.

17. Dan L. Kelly, letter, Jan. 23, 1863, Honnoll Papers, Emory Univ. Library; Bell Irvin Wiley, ed., *This Infernal War: The Confederate Letters of Sergeant Edwin H. Fay,* Austin, Tex., 1958, letter of May 14, 1862.

18. William B. Honnoll, letter, May 19, Aug. 3, 1863, Dan L. Kelly, letter, Jan. 23, 1863, Honnoll Papers, Emory. Univ. Library. John Dale, letter, Aug. 3, 1863, Honnoll Papers, Emory Univ. Library.

19. John Dale, letter, Aug. 3, 1863, Honnoll Papers, Emory Univ. Library.

20. William P. H. Chambers [46th Mississippi Inf.], journal entries, 1863, Mississippi Dept. of Archives and History, Jackson, Miss.

21. Ibid.
22. Ibid.
23. Ibid.
24. Ibid.
25. Ibid.
26. Ibid.
27. Ibid.
28. Ibid.
29. Ibid.
30. Ibid.
31. Ibid.
32. Ibid.
33. Ibid.

34. Richard Walpole, letter, Jan. 18, 1863, Bomar Papers, Emory Univ. Library.

35. William D. Kendall, letter, July 12, 1863, Kendall Papers, Huntington Library.

36. Dan L. Kelly, letter, July 10, 1863, William P. Andrews letter, August 23, 1863, Honnoll Papers, Emory Univ. Library.

37. William D. Kendall, letter, July 12, 1863, Kendall Papers, Huntington Library.

38. James Hamner [21st Tennessee Cav.], letter, Apr. 11, 1863, West Tennessee Historical Society, Memphis, Tenn.

39. Grady McWhiney, *Braxton Bragg,* vol. 1, 18–22, 234–35

40. Ibid., vol. 1, vi–viii, 346–57.

CHAPTER 20

1. East, *Sarah Morgan,* 517 [July 10, 1863].
2. Ibid., 519 [July 15, 1863].
3. Ibid.

4. Ibid., 580ff. [Nov. 22, 1863].
5. Ibid., 586–87 [Dec. 31, 1863].
6. Ibid., 597 [Feb. 5, 1864].
7. Ibid.
8. Ibid., 599–601 [Mar. 1864].
9. Ibid.
10. Ibid., 604–5.
11. Ibid., 597 [Feb. 11, 1864].
12. Ibid., 602 [Mar. 1864].
13. Ibid., 598 [Mar. 1864].
14. Ibid., 603 [Mar. 1864].
15. Ibid., 603–4 [Apr.–Nov. 1864].

CHAPTER 21

1. Byron R. Abernathy, ed., *Private Elisha Stockwell, Jr., Sees the Civil War*, Norman, Okla., 1958, 8ff.

2. Earl J. Hess, *The Union Soldier in Battle: Enduring the Ordeal of Combat*, Lawrence, Kans., 1997, 110ff.

3. Hugh L. Honnoll, letter, Apr. 29, 1862, Honnoll Papers, Emory Univ. Library.

4. Hess, *Union Soldier in Battle*, 24ff.; Linderman, *Embattled Courage: The Experience of Combat in the American Civil War*, New York, 1987, 135–39.

5. Oscar L. Jackson, *The Colonel's Diary*, Sharon, Pa. 1922, 85–88.

6. Claud E. Fuller, *The Rifled Musket*, Harrisburg, Pa. 1958, 3, 4, 53; Wiley Sword, *Firepower from Abroad: The Conference Enfield and the LeMat Revolver, 1861–1863*, Lincoln, R. I., 1986, 68; Dean S. Thomas, *Ready, Aim, Fire! Small Arms Ammunition in the Battle of Gettysburg*, Biglersville, Pa., 1981, 1–5.

7. Richard A. Baumgartner and Larry M. Strayer, eds., *Echoes of Battle: The Atlanta Campaign*, Huntington, W. Va., 1991, 153.

8. Henry B. McClellan, *The Life and Campaigns of Major General J. E. B. Stuart, Commander of the Cavalry of the Army of Northern Virginia*, Boston, 1885.

8. Roy M. Marcot, *Spencer Repeating Firearms*, Irvine, Calif. 1983; Fuller, *The Rifled Musket*, general references.

9. Ibid.

10. Wiley Sword, " 'Those Damned Michigan Spencers': Colonel Copeland's 5th Michigan Cavalry and Their Spencer Rifles," *Man at Arms Magazine*, no. 5, 1997, 23–37.

11. Ibid.
12. Ibid.
13. Ibid.

14. Spencer Repeating Rifle Co. Catalog, 1866, 16.

15. Sword, *Embrace an Angry Wind*, 331ff.

16. John E. Parsons, *The First Winchester: The Story of the 1866 Repeating Rifle*, New York, 1955, 9ff.

17. Henry A. Potter [4th Michigan Cav.], letter, July 19, 1864, University of Michigan, Bentley Historical Library, Ann Arbor, Mich.

18. Richard McMurry, *John Bell Hood and the War for Southern Independence*, Lexington, Ky., 1982, 183.

CHAPTER 22

1. Arthur J. L. Fremantle, Cold Stream Guards, quoted in Daniel, *Soldiering in the Army of Tennessee*, 20, 32.

2. Ibid., 48.

3. Ibid., 20.

4. Roberson, Elizabeth Whitley, *Weep Not for Me Dear Mother*, Washington, N.C., 1991, 117.

5. John P. Kendall, letter, July 12, 1863, Kendall Papers, Huntington Library; James H. Fraser [50th Alabama Inf.], quoted in Baumgartner and Strayer, *Echoes of Battle—Chattanooga*, 61–63.

6. Peter Cozzens, *This Terrible Sound: The Battle of Chickamauga*, Urbana, Ill., 1992, 6ff.

7. Quoted in Richard A. Baumgartner, *Blue Lightning: Wilder's Mounted Infantry Brigade in the Battle of Chickamauga*, Huntington, W. V., 1997, 144–45.

8. Wiley Sword, *Mountains Touched with Fire: Chattanoooga Besieged, 1863*, New York, 1995, 29ff.

9. Quoted in Baumgartner and Strayer, *Echoes of Battle—Chattanooga*, 85; Roderick Shaw, letter, Oct. 8, 1863, quoted in Daniel, *Soldiering in the Army of Tennessee*, 136; W. R. Montgomery [3d Battn. Georgia SS], letter, Oct. 18, 1863, Chickamauga and Chattanooga National Military Park Library, Ft. Oglethorpe, Ga. Hereinafter cited as Chick-Chatt.

10. Whitley, *Weep Not for Me*, 117.

11. Washington Ives [4th Florida Inf.], letter, Oct. 31, 1863, Chick-Chatt.

12. Sword, *Mountains Touched with Fire*, 19ff.

13. Ibid.

14. Blackford, *Letters from Lee's Army*, 219.

15. Ibid., 211.

16. Washington Ives, letter, Oct. 31, 1863, Chick-Chatt.

17. Sword, *Mountains Touched with Fire*, 106.

18. Andrew Jackson Neal [Marion Lt. Art.], letter, Oct. 1863, Chick-Chatt.

19. Sword, *Mountains Touched with Fire*, 29ff.
20. W. R. Montgomery, letter, Oct. 16, 1863, Chick-Chatt; Blackford, *Letters from Lee's Army*, 219–24.
21. Robert Watson [7th Florida Inf.], journal, Sept.–Oct. 1863, Chick–Chatt.
22. W. R. Montgomery, letter, Oct. 24, 1863, Chick-Chatt; Edwin H. Reynolds [5th Tennessee Inf.], diary entry, Oct. 24, 1863, Chick-Chatt; Washington Ives, letter, Nov. 10, 1863, Chick-Chatt.
23. Lewis L. Poates [63d Tennessee Inf.], letter, Nov. 15, 1863, collection of Lewis L. Poates, Knoxville, Tenn.; G. E Goudelock [2d Arkansas Inf.], letter, Oct. 5, 1863, Chick-Chatt; R. Watson, journal, Oct. 13, 1864, Chick-Chatt.
24. Washington Ives, letter, Nov. 12, 1863, Chick-Chatt.
25. Lewis L. Poates, letter, Nov. 15, 1863, Poates colln.
26. Washington Ives, letter, Nov. 12, 1863, Chick-Chatt.
27. Lewis L. Poates, letter, Nov. 15, 1863, Poates colln.
28. Isaiah Harlan [Texas Inf.], letter, Nov. 15, 1863, Chick-Chatt.
29. OR 1-31-3-700–710.
30. Isaac Miller, letter, Nov. 21, 1863, author's collection; Charles A. Houghton, letter, Nov. 15, 1863, Houghton Papers, U.S. Army Military History Institute, Carlisle Barracks, Pa.
31. OR 1-31-3-716.
32. See Sword, *Mountains Touched with Fire*, 73ff.
33. See Sword, *Mountains Touched with Fire*, 165ff.
34. Sword, *Mountains Touched with Fire*, 86, 188, 272.
35. See Sword, *Mountains Touched with Fire*, 240ff.
36. Sword, *Mountains Touched with Fire*, 321–22.
37. A. J. Neal, letters, Nov. 26, 29, Dec. 6, 1863, Chick-Chatt; Ray Mathis, *In the Land of the Living: Wartime Letters by Confederates from the Chattahoochie Valley of Alabama and Georgia*, Troy, Ala., 1981, 182; Frank Wolfe, "Letter to a Friend: From the Foot of Lookout Mountain," *Civil War Times Illustrated*, vol. 22, no. 4 (June 1983): 44.
38. Sam R. Watkins, *"Co. Aytch": Maury Grays, First Tennessee Regiment; or A Side Show of the Big Show*, Wilmington, N.C., 1987 reprint, 120.
39. *Mobile Daily Register and Advertiser*, Dec. 11, 1863; A. J. Neal, letters of Nov. 26, 29, 1863, Chick-Chatt.
40. A. J. Neal, letters of Nov. 26, 29, 1863, Chick-Chatt.
41. Dunbar Rowland, ed., *Jefferson Davis Constitutionalist: His Letters, Papers, and Speeches*, 6 vols., Jackson, Miss. 1923, vol. 6, 95–96.
42. Sword, *Mountains Touched with Fire*, 320–21.
43. R. Lockwood Tower, ed., *A Carolinian Goes to War: The Civil War Narrative of Arthur Middleton Manigault, Brigadier General, C.S.A.*, Columbia, S.C. 1988, 133–34; Sam R. Watkins, *Co. Aytch*, 118.
44. Sword, *Mountains Touched with Fire*, 352ff.

CHAPTER 23

1. Benjamin Fleet's journal, Dec. 31, 1863, in *Green Mount,* 295.
2. Blackford, *Letters from Lee's Army,* 226.
3. Ibid. 190, 231.
4. Sandie Pendleton to sister (Mary), Apr. 30, 1864, Pendleton Papers, SHC, Bean, *Stonewall's Man,* 198–99; W. R. Redding, letter, Apr. 8, 1864, Redding Papers, SHC.
5. Taylor, *The Cry Is War,* 177; Peter L. Mabry, letter, Feb. 22, 1864, The Horse Soldier, catalog 22, item LO8; Glitch Reilly, letter, n.d. [circa Nov. 1863], Theme Prints, Ltd., catalog, spring 1993, item no. 232.
6. Taylor, *The Cry Is War,* 157.
7. Dan Blain [Rockbridge Artillery], letter, Oct. 20, 1863, Theme Prints, Ltd., catalog, Dec. 1990, item no. 243.
8. Thomas L. Painter, letter, Sept. 2, 1863, Olde Soldier Books, catalog 62, item 219; John Martin, letter, Aug. 1863, Olde Soldier Books, catalog 80, item no. 208.
9. W. Hockaday, letter, Aug. 9, 1863, Olde Soldier Books, catalog no. 78, item 221; John P. Hull, letter, Nov. 22, 1863, Olde Soldier Books, catalog no. 44, item 198.
10. W. R. Redding, letter, Apr. 8, 1864, Redding Papers, SHC.
11. Taylor, *The Cry Is War,* 165–68.
12. Blackford, *Letters from Lee's Army,* 242.
13. Ibid., 246.
14. Taylor, *The Cry Is War,* 178–79.
15. Ibid., 179; Peter L. Mabry, letter, May 25, 1864, The Horse Soldier, catalog 22, item L11; B. B. Hunter, letter, July 21, 1864, Olde Soldier Books, catalog 83, item 214.
16. Blackford, *Letters from Lee's Army,* 246.
17. Joe Shaner, letter to sisters, May 17, 1864, Fredericksburg and Spotsylvania National Military Park, Va.
18. Blackford, *Letters from Lee's Army,* 249; John J. Dillard [26th Georgia Inf.], letter, May 20, 1864, William R. Perkins Library, Duke University, Durham, N.C.
19. Blackford, *Letters from Lee's Army,* 251.
20. John A. Johnson, letters, Dec. 15, 1864, Jan. 3, 1865, Johnson Papers, SHC.
21. Blackford, *Letters from Lee's Army,* 272.
22. John A. Johnson, letter, June 16, 1864, J. Johnson Papers, SHC.
23. Unidentified Confederate letter, Richmond, Va., dated Aug. 31, 1864, Olde Soldier Books catalog 57, item 194; William A. Farley, letter, Sept. 13, 1864, Olde Soldier Books, catalog 60, item 202.
24. Blackford, *Letters from Lee's Army,* 255.

25. Willis F. Jones, letter to mother, Aug. 29, 1864, Jones Papers [no. 354], The Filson Club Historical Society Library, Louisville, Ky.

26. George D. Harmon, ed., "Letters of Luther Rice Mills—A Confederate Soldier," *North Carolina Historical Review*, vol. 4, July 1927, 303–8.

27. Dowdey, *Wartime Papers of R. E. Lee*, 675, 685.

28. Ibid., 700–1.

29. Ibid., 706, 709, 720, 721, 727, 735.

30. Ibid., 825, 868.

31. Ibid., 659, 696.

32. Ibid., 830.

33. Ibid., 842, 847, 881.

34. Ibid., 886.

35. Harmon, "Letters of Luther Rice Mills," 303–8.

36. Dowdey, *Wartime Papers of R. E. Lee*, 870.

CHAPTER 24

1. Howell and Elizabeth Purdue, *Pat Cleburne Confederate General*, Hillsboro, Tex., 1973, 461.

2. Ibid., 458.

3. Ibid., 277–78, 283; Thomas L. Livermore, *Numbers and Losses in the Civil War in America*, Bloomington, Ind., reprint, 1957, of 1900 edition, 45, 48.

4. Purdue, *Pat Cleburne*, 456–57.

5. Ibid., 455–58.

6. Ibid., 458–60.

7. Ibid., 457.

8. Ibid., general reference.

9. Ibid., 269–70.

10. Ibid., 272–73.

11. Ibid.

12. Ibid.

13. See Sword, *Embrace an Angry Wind*, 19ff.

14. See Albert Castel, *Decision in the West: The Atlanta Campaign of 1864*, Lawrence, Kans., 1992, 73ff.; and Sword, *Embrace an Angry Wind*, 25ff., 73.

15. Castel, *Decision in the West*, 29ff.; Sword, *Embrace an Angry Wind*, 25ff.

16. Castel, *Decision in the West*, 32, 77, 100.

17. Ibid., 101–2; John Bell Hood to Bragg, Apr. 13, 1864, Braxton Bragg Papers, 323–24, Western Reserve Historical Society, Cleveland, Ohio.

18. Blackford, *Letters from Lee's Army*, 226.

19. John P. Kendall [5th Tennessee Inf.], letter, Mar. 12, 1864, and William D. Kendall, letter, Apr. 21, 1864, Kendall Papers, Huntington Library, San Marino, Calif.

20. Castel, *Decision in the West,* 198ff.

21. Daniel, *Soldiering in the Army of Tennessee,* 140–43; William D. Kendall, letter, June 24, 1864, Huntington Library, San Marino, Calif.; Watkins, *"Co. Aytch,"* 156.

22. John W. Hill, letter, June 11, 1864, quoted in Daniel, *Soldiering in the Army of Tennessee,* 143.

23. Castel, *Decision in the West,* 328ff.

24. Harold B. Simpson, ed., *The Bugle Softly Blows: The Confederate Diary of Benjamin M. Seaton,* Waco, Tex., 1965, 56.

25. F. Jay Taylor, ed., *Reluctant Rebel: The Secret Diary of Robert Patrick, 1861–1865,* Baton Rouge, La., 1959, 204.

26. Taylor, *Reluctant Rebel,* 192–96.

27. See Sword, *Embrace an Angry Wind,* 28–29.

28. Ibid.

29. See Castel, *Decision in the West,* 344ff.

30. Norman D. Brown, ed., *One of Cleburne's Command: The Civil War Reminiscences and Diary of Captain Samuel T. Foster, Granbury's Texas Brigade, C.S.A.,* Austin, Tex., 1980, 106–7.

31. Ibid.

32. William D. Kendall, letter, July 17, 19, 1864, Kendall Papers, Huntington Library, San Marino, Calif.

33. Elbert D. Willert, July 18, 1864, and J. B. Gracey [51st Tennessee Inf.], quoted in Baumgartner and Strayer, *Echoes of Battle—Atlanta,* 204.

34. William D. Kendall, letter, July 19, 1864, Kendall Papers, Huntington Library, San Marino, Calif.

35. Samuel Kelly, quoted in Daniel, *Soldiering in the Army of Tennessee,* 144.

36. Oliver O. Howard, letter, July 23, 1864, Howard Papers, Bowdoin College Library, Brunswick, Maine.

37. See Sword, *Embrace an Angry Wind,* 32ff.

38. John P. Kendall, letter, Apr. 10, 1864, Kendall Papers, Huntington Library, San Marino, Calif.

39. Andrew J. Neal, letter, May 10, 1864, Chick-Chatt.

40. See McPherson, *Battle Cry of Freedom,* 742ff.

41. See Sword, *Embrace an Angry Wind,* 32, 44, 262.

CHAPTER 25

1. William D. Kendall, letter, July 19, 1864, Kendall Papers, Huntington Library, San Marino, Calif.

2. William E. Bevens [1st Arkansas Inf.] quoted in Baumgartner and Strayer, *Echoes of Battle—Atlanta,* 233.

3. William D. Kendall, letter, July 19, 1864, Kendall Papers, Huntington Library, San Marino, Calif.; Wirt Armistead Cate, ed., *Two Soldiers: The Campaign Diaries of Thomas J. Key, C.S.A., and Robert J. Campbell, U.S.A.,* Chapel Hill, N.C., 1938, 90.

4. Bell I. Wiley, ed., *Four Years on the Firing Line,* Jackson, Tenn., 1963, 209ff.

5. Ibid.

6. C. Irvine Walker, quoted in Baumgartner and Strayer, *Echoes of Battle—Atlanta,* 248.

7. See Livermore, *Numbers and Losses,* 124.

8. John W. Lavender [4th Arkansas Inf.], quoted in Baumgartner and Strayer, *Echoes of Battle—Atlanta,* 264.

9. Wiley, *Four Years on the Firing Line,* 209ff.; William E. Bevens, quoted in Baumgartner and Strayer, *Echoes of Battle—Atlanta,* 233.

10. James A. Connolly, letter of July 31, 1864, quoted in Baumgartner and Strayer, *Echoes of Battle—Atlanta,* 256.

11. Eugene A. McWayne, letter, Aug. 4, 1864, author's collection.

12. Ibid.; James A. Connolly, letter, July 31, 1864, quoted in Baumgartner and Strayer, *Echoes of Battle—Atlanta,* 256.

13. James I. Hall, letter, July 8, 1864, James Iredell Hall Papers [no. 302], Southern Historical Collection, Univ. of North Carolina, Chapel Hill, N.C.

14. Taylor, *Reluctant Rebel,* 199–200.

15. See Purdue, *Pat Cleburne,* and Sword, *Mountains Touched with Fire,* general references.

16. Brown, *One of Cleburne's Command,* 111, 360; OR 1-38-3-730–741.

17. Daniel C. Govan, letter, Dec. 3, 1864, Govan Papers [no. 1000], Southern Historical Collection, Univ. of North Carolina, Chapel Hill, N.C.

18. Blackford, *Letters from Lee's Army,* 223.

19. See Castel, *Decision in the West,* 475ff., 546.

20. Newspapers quoted in ibid.

21. Ibid.

22. Ibid.

23. William B. Honnoll, letter, Aug. 25, 1864, Honnoll Papers, Emory Univ.

24. See Castel, *Decision in the West,* 448ff., 469, 482.

25. Ibid.; also see OR 1-38-5-1006ff.; Baumgartner and Strayer, *Echoes of Battle—Atlanta,* 316ff.

26. Brown, *One of Cleburne's Command,* 125.

27. See Castel, *Decision in the West,* 509ff.; also OR 1-38-5-1006ff.; Baumgartner and Strayer, *Echoes of Battle—Atlanta,* 316ff.

28. OR 1-38-5-1018, 1021; OR 1-39-2-826, 832–37; OR 1-52-2-729–730.

29. OR 1-38-5-909.

30. Castel, *Decision in the West,* 451; OR 1-39-2-836, 893.

31. Van Buren Oldham [9th Tennessee Inf.], diary entry, July 29, 1864, Tennessee State Library and Archives, Nashville, Tenn.

CHAPTER 26

1. Sandie Pendleton to Kate, Kate's journal, July 4, 16, 1863, SHC.

2. Ibid., July 18, 1863.

3. Bean, *Sandie Pendleton,* 157ff.

4. Ibid.

5. Ibid.; Sandie to Kate, Nov. 11, 1863, SHC.

6. Sandie to Kate, Sept. 13, 1863, SHC.

7. Sandie to mother, July 30, 1863, SHC.

8. Bean, *Sandie Pendleton,* 175ff.

9. Sandie to Kate, Nov. 25, 1863, SHC.

10. Sandie to Kate, Nov. 26, 1863, SHC.

11. Sandie to Kate, Dec. 3, 1863, SHC.

12. Bean, *Sandie Pendleton,* 176ff.

13. Bean, *Sandie Pendleton,* 180ff.

14. Ibid.

15. Ibid.

16. Ibid., 181ff.

17. Ibid., 187.

18. Ibid., 190.

19. Ibid., 149–50.

20. Ibid., 151.

21. Ibid., 152.

22. Ibid., 198–99.

23. Ibid.

24. Ibid.

25. Ibid., 200.

26. Ibid., 201.

27. Sandie to mother, June 2, 1864, SHC.

28. Ibid.

29. Bean, *Sandie Pendleton,* 204ff.

30. Ibid., 197, 207.

31. Sandie to sister Nancy, Sept. 16, 1864, SHC.

32. Bean, *Sandie Pendleton,* 209ff.

33. Ibid.; Sue P. Lee to Ned Lee, Oct. 4, 1864, SHC.

34. Bean, *Sandie Pendleton,* 210ff.

35. Ibid., 211; Sue P. Lee to Ned Lee Sept. 25, 1864, SHC.

36. Sue P. Lee to Ned Lee, Oct. 4, 1864, SHC; Bean, *Sandie Pendleton,* 213ff.

37. Bean, *Sandie Pendleton*, 214.
38. Sue P. Lee to Ned Lee, Oct. 4, 1864, SHC; Bean, *Sandie Pendleton*, 214ff.
39. Bean, *Sandie Pendleton*, 215.
40. Ibid., 215ff.
41. Ibid.
42. Sandie to Kate, Apr. 17, 1864, Kate Corbin Brooke Papers, quoted in Bean, *Sandie Pendleton*, 196.
43. Kate to W. N. Pendleton, Feb. 9, 1865, SHC.
44. Anzolette Pendleton to husband, Nov. 6, 1864, SHC.
45. Kate to W. N. Pendleton, Feb. 9, 1865, Bean, *Sandie Pendleton*, 224ff.
46. Ibid.
47. Bean, *Sandie Pendleton*, 227.
48. Ibid., 227–29.
49. Ibid., 229.
50. Kate to father, Sept. 4, 1865 quoted in Bean, *Sandie Pendleton*, 230–31.

CHAPTER 27

1. Ma Fleet to Fred Fleet, Jan. 9, 1863, *Green Mount*, 196.
2. Fred Fleet to Ma, June 13, July 5, 1862, Fred to Pa June 25, 1863, Fred to Lou, Apr. 27, 1864, *Green Mount*, 136, 147, 247, 322.
3. Fred to Ma, Mar. 19, June 21, 1863, *Green Mount*, 210, 244.
4. Fred to Ma, July 16, 1863, C. B. Fleet to Fred, Aug. 8, 1863, *Green Mount*, 251, 258.
5. Ma to Fred, July 26, 1863, C. B. Fleet to Fred, Aug. 20, 1863, *Green Mount*, 255–61.
6. C. B. Fleet to Fred, Aug. 20, 1863, Ma to Fred, July 26, 1863, *Green Mount*, 253, 261.
7. Fred to Pa, Sept. 11, 1863, *Green Mount*, 266.
8. Fred to Ma, Sept. 14, 1863, *Green Mount*, 267.
9. Fred to Pa, Sept. 17, 1863, *Green Mount*, 267–68.
10. Fred to Pa, Oct. 8, Dec. 30, 1863, *Green Mount*, 275, 293ff.
11. Fred to Pa, Dec. 30, 1863, *Green Mount*, 295.
12. Ibid.
13. Fleet, *Green Mount*, 252–60, 295–96.
14. Pa to Fred, Dec. 3, 1863, *Green Mount*, 286.
15. Benny's journal, Dec. 31, 1863, *Green Mount*, 295.
16. Pa to Fred, Dec. 4, 1863, *Green Mount*, 286.
17. Fred to Benny, Mar. 23, 1863, Fred to Ma, July 16, 1863, Ma to Fred, July 26, 1863, *Green Mount*, 212, 251–53, 298.
18. Benny's Journal, Feb. 24, 29, 1864, *Green Mount*, 307–10.
19. Ibid.

20. Fleet, *Green Mount*, 310–12.
21. Ibid., 310–12, 316n.
22. Fred to Pa, Mar. 21, 1864, *Green Mount*, 312–16; Buel and Johnson, *Battles and Leaders*, 4-95, 96.
23. Fred to Pa, Mar. 21, Apr. 11, 1864, *Green Mount*, 316–19.
24. Fred to Ma, Apr. 3, 1864, *Green Mount*, 318–20.
25. Fred to Pa, Apr. 11, 1864, *Green Mount*, 321–22.
26. Fred to Lou, Apr. 27, 1864, *Green Mount*, 322–23.
27. Fred to Pa, May 1, 22, 1864, *Green Mount*, 324–25.
28. Mark Mayo Boatner, III, *The Civil War Dictionary*, New York, 1959, 889–90.
29. Fred to Pa, May 22, 1864, *Green Mount*, 325–27.
30. Ibid.
31. Ibid.
32. Ibid.
33. Fleet, *Green Mount*, 327–32; Fleet, *Green Mount after the War*, 9–10.
34. Ibid.
35. Fleet, *Green Mount*, 327–32.
36. Fleet, *Green Mount*, 330–32; Fleet, *Green Mount after the War*, 10.
37. Fleet, *Green Mount*, 330–32.

CHAPTER 28

1. Marcus B. DeWitt [chaplain, 8th Tennessee Inf.], letters, Aug. 26, Sept. 3, 1864, possession of Ward DeWitt, Jr., Nashville, Tenn.
2. Ibid., Sept. 24, 1864.
3. Daniel, *Soldiering in the Army of Tennessee*, 116–25.
4. Marcus B. DeWitt, letter, Sept. 24, 1864, DeWitt papers; Taylor, *Reluctant Rebel*, 224.
5. Taylor, *Reluctant Rebel*, 224.
6. OR 1-39-2-356, 414ff.; OR 1-38-5-909.
7. Marcus B. DeWitt, letter, Sept. 16, 1864, DeWitt papers.
8. William P. H. Chambers, diary, Sept. 26 1864, Mississippi Dept. Arch. and History; Taylor, *Reluctant Rebel*, 230.
9. See Sword, *Embrace an Angry Wind*, 37, 45–52.
10. Ibid., 45ff.
11. Taylor, *Reluctant Rebel*, 226–28.
12. William P. H. Chambers, diary, Oct. 4, 1864, Mississippi Dept. Arch. and History.
13. See Sword, *Embrace an Angry Wind*, 53ff.; Marcus B. DeWitt, letter, Nov. 12, 1864, DeWitt papers.
14. Taylor, *Reluctant Rebel*, 231.
15. Ibid., 231, 242, 245.
16. See Sword, *Embrace an Angry Wind*, 71ff.; Mrs. D. Giraud Wright

[Louise Wigfall], *A Southern Girl in '61: The Wartime Memories of a Confederate Senator's Daughter,* New York, 1905, 214.

17. See Sword, *Embrace an Angry Wind,* 113ff.
18. Ibid., 177ff.
19. Ibid.
20. Ibid., 267–68.
21. Brown, *One of Cleburne's Command,* 151.
22. W. J. Worsham, *The Old Nineteenth Tennessee Regiment, C.S.A.: June 1861—April 1865,* Knoxville, Tenn., 1902, 339.
23. See Sword, *Embrace an Angry Wind,* 268, 278.
24. Ibid., 342; W. D. Gale, letter, Jan. 29, 1865, Gale-Polk Papers, SHC.
25. See Sword, *Embrace an Angry Wind,* 347–48.
26. Ibid., 376–82.
27. Ibid., 377, 381.
28. Ibid., 377.
29. Ibid., 426.
30. Ibid., 426, 427.
31. William P. H. Chambers, diary, Jan. 1865, Mississippi Dept. Arch. and History.
32. Taylor, *Reluctant Rebel,* 250.
33. William P. H. Chambers, diary, Jan. 1865, Mississippi Dept. Arch. and History.
34. Brown, *One of Cleburne's Command,* 158.
35. William P. H. Chambers, diary, Jan. 1865, Mississippi Dept. Arch. and History.
36. Ibid., Jan. 2, 1865.

CHAPTER 29

1. OR 1-39-3-162.
2. OR 1-39-3-3, 202.
3. OR 1-39-3-222.
4. OR 1-38-2-480.
5. OR 1-39-3-660.
6. OR 1-38-2-418–419.
7. OR 1-39-3-377–378, 659–660; OR 1-44-1-799.
8. OR 1-39-3-660.
9. Gay, *Life in Dixie,* 203.
10. Lee Kennett, *Marching through Georgia: The Story of Soldiers and Civilians during Sherman's Campaign,* New York, 1995, 278, 312.
11. Eliza Frances Andrews, *The War-Time Journal of a Georgia Girl 1864–1865,* Macon, Ga. 1960, 32–33.
12. Elizabeth Wiley Smith, *The History of Hancock County [Georgia],* 2 vols., Washington, Ga., 1974, vol. 1, 61–62.

13. Eugene A. McWayne to family, Dec. 19, 1864, author's collection.
14. Kennett, *Marching through Georgia,* 265–85.
15. Ibid., 275ff.
16. Gay, *Life in Dixie,* 256ff.
17. Andrews, *War-Time Journal,* 31ff.
18. OR 1-44-1-6-66; see Kennett, *Marching through Georgia,* 309ff.
19. John Rozier, ed., *The Granite Farm Letters: The Civil War Correspondence of Edgeworth and Sallie Bird,* Athens, Ga., 1988, 211.
20. Ibid., 215–16.
21. Ibid., 218–19.
22. Ibid., 312, 323; Joseph T. Glatthaar, *The March to the Sea and Beyond: Sherman's Troops in the Savannah and Carolinas Campaigns,* Baton Rouge, La., 1985, 154.
23. Glatthaar, *The March to the Sea,* 79.
24. Ibid., 140ff.
25. Ibid., 128, 153ff.
26. Woodward, *Mary Chesnut's Civil War,* 764.
27. Rozier, *The Granite Farm Letters,* 243.

CHAPTER 30

1. Dowdey, *Wartime Papers of R. E. Lee,* 907.
2. Ibid., 874, 879, 886.
3. William C. Davis, *Jefferson Davis: The Man and His Hour,* New York, 1991, 592–94, 600.
4. Ibid., 597ff.
5. Robert Isbell [2d Virginia Cav.], letter to sister Anna, Feb. 21, 1865, author's collection.
6. Ibid., OR 1-51-2-1229ff; OR 1-52-2-586; OR 4-3-797ff., 1110; Dowdey, *Wartime Papers of R. E. Lee,* 914, 1012–13; Robert F. Durden, ed., *The Gray and the Black: The Confederate Debate on Emancipation,* Baton Rouge, La., 1972, 206.
7. Fleet, *Green Mount,* 356.
8. Samuel McAbee [1st South Carolina Inf.], letter, Feb. 12, 1865, Olde Soldier Books, catalog 55, item 269.
9. Cate, *Two Soldiers,* 181; William P. H. Chambers, diary, Feb. 17, 1865, Mississippi Dept. Arch. and History.
10. Taylor, *Reluctant Rebel,* 250.
11. Davis, *Jefferson Davis—Man and Hour,* 594.
12. See McPherson, *Battle Cry of Freedom,* 833ff.
13. Dowdey, *Wartime Papers of R. E. Lee,* 890–92.
14. Ibid.; Davis, *Jefferson Davis—Man and Hour,* 586ff.
15. Robert Isbell [2d Virginia Cav.], letter to sister Anna, Feb. 21, 1865, author's collection.

16. Blackford, *Letters from Lee's Army,* 279.
17. Rozier, *The Granite Farm Letters,* 232.
18. Fleet, *Green Mount,* 350.
19. Dowdey, *Wartime Papers of R. E. Lee,* 912–13.
20. Ibid.
21. Ibid.
22. Fleet, *Green Mount,* 353, 356.
23. Dowdey, *Wartime Papers of R. E. Lee,* 914–15.
24. Ibid., 916–17.
25. Ibid.
26. Ibid.
27. Ibid., 920ff.
28. Ibid.; Davis, *Jefferson Davis—Man and Hour,* 603ff.
29. Henry Morrison [26th Battn. Virginia Inf.], letter, Sept. 20, 1864, USAMHI, Carlisle Barracks, Pa.
30. J. J. Mendenhall [48th North Carolina Inf.], letter, Mar. 15, 1865, Olde Soldier Books, catalog 20, item 151; John Johnson, letter, Jan. 3, 1865, J. Johnson Papers, SHC.
31. Woodward, *Mary Chesnut's Civil War,* 769; Mary Catherine Noland Cochran, diary entry, Mar. 16, 1865, The Filson Club Library, Louisville, Ky.
32. Harmon, "Letters of Luther Rice Mills," 303ff.
33. Dowdey, *Wartime Papers of R. E. Lee,* 918.
34. Ibid., 910.
35. Ibid., 936.

Chapter 31

1. Ella Lonn, *Desertion during the Civil War,* Lincoln, Nebr. reprint of 1928 edition, 13.
2. Dowdey, *Wartime Papers of R. E. Lee,* 938–39.
3. See OR 1-46 for reports of the Appomattox Campaign.
4. Dowdey, *Wartime Papers of R. E. Lee,* 935ff.
5. Ibid.
6. Ibid.
7. John Johnson, letter, Dec. 15, 1864, J. Johnson Papers, SHC.
8. William P. H. Chambers, diary, Jan. 1865, Mississippi Dept. Arch. and History.
9. Ibid., May 14, 1865.
10. Dowdey, *Wartime Papers of R. E. Lee,* 934.
11. Joshua Lawrence Chamberlain, *The Passing of the Armies: An Account of the Final Campaign of the Army of the Potomac, Based upon Personal Reminiscences of the Fifth Army Corps,* New York, 1915, 248–65.

CHAPTER 32

1. Constance Cary [Mrs. Burton Harrison], *Recollections Grave and Gay,* New York, 1916, 210–19.
2. Andrews, *War-Time Journal,* 181–98.
3. W. Walker, letter, April 12 [1865], Olde Soldier Books, catalog 49, item 184.
4. John Johnson, letter, Jan. 3, 1865, J. Johnson Papers, SHC.
5. Woodward, *Mary Chesnut's Civil War,* 739, 782–83.
6. John Johnson, letter, Jan. 3, 1865, J. Johnson Papers, SHC.
7. James M. Holloway [18th Mississippi Inf.], letter, Dec. 25, 1861, Virginia Historical Society, Richmond, Va.; unidentified Confederate soldier's letter, "Camp near Clinton, Miss., Oct. 28, 1863," Theme Prints catalog, Nov. 1992, item 327; James McCulloch [7th Georgia Inf.], letter to wife, Aug. 8, 1862, Olde Soldier Books, catalog 55, item 257.
8. William P. H. Chambers, diary, Apr. 23, 1865, Mississippi Dept. Arch. and History.
9. John C. Davis [16th Mississippi Inf.], letter, June 11, 1865, Olde Soldier Books, catalog 65, item 192.
10. Cash and Howorth, *My Dear Nellie,* letter of William Nugent [28th Mississippi Cav.], Sept. 7, 1863.
11. William P. H. Chambers, diary, Jan., May 6, 1865, Mississippi Dept. Arch. and History.
12. Wigfall, *A Southern Girl in '61,* 229; Andrews, *War-Time Journal,* 181–98; Woodward, *Mary Chesnut's Civil War,* 724.
13. Connelly and Bellows, *God and General Longstreet,* 73ff.
14. Julia Davis, *Mount Up: A True Story Based on the Reminiscences of Major E. A. H. McDonald of the Confederate Cavalry,* New York, 1967, 191.
15. Watkins, *Co. Aytch,* 245.
16. Quoted in McPherson, *Battle Cry of Freedom,* 855.
17. Harmon, "Letters of Luther Rice Mills," 303ff.
18. Basil Duke to "My Dear Colonel" Jan. 17, 1909, in Olde Soldier Books, Catalog 8, item 54.

CHAPTER 33

1. J. J. Young to H. K. Burgwyn, July 3, 11, 1863, Burgwyn Papers, SHC, Davis, *Boy Colonel,* 336.
2. Ibid.
3. Ibid.
4. Davis, *Boy Colonel,* 247–48.
5. Ibid., 340ff.
6. Ibid., 345–47.

7. Ibid., 347.
8. East, *Sarah Morgan*, 604 [Dec. 31, 1864].
9. Ibid., 581, 603 [Mar. 1865].
10. Ibid., 606–11 [Apr.–May 1865].
11. Ibid.
12. Ibid.
13. Ibid., 605 [Apr. 4, 1865]
14. Ibid., 611 [June 15, 1865].
15. See East, *Sarah Morgan*, preface and introduction.
16. Bean, *Stonewall's Man*, 233–34.
17. Fleet, *Green Mount*, 339, 341.
18. Ibid., 347, 353.
19. Ibid., 348, 351.
20. Ibid., 348, 352.
21. Ibid.
22. Ibid., 350, 353.
23. Ibid., 361, 362.
24. Ibid., 354–61.
25. Ibid., 361–63.
26. Ibid.
27. Ibid.
28. Ibid., 356, 363; Fleet, *Green Mount after the War*, 11, 12.
29. Fleet, *Green Mount after the War*, 12.
30. Ibid., 35; Fleet, *Green Mount*, 364.
31. Fleet, *Green Mount after the War*, 275; Fleet, *Green Mount*, 364.
32. Fleet, *Green Mount after the War*, 27, 262.
33. Ibid., 266.

CHAPTER 34

1. For certain perspectives on Southern superiority, see McPherson, *Battle Cry of Freedom*, 197ff.

Bibliography

ABBREVIATIONS:

Chick-Chatt—Chickamauga and Chattanooga National Military Park Library, Fort Oglethorpe, Ga.
EMORY—Emory University Library, Atlanta, Ga.
FCL—The Filson Club Library, Louisville, Ky.
HEHL—Henry E. Huntington Library, San Marino, Calif.
LSU—Department of Archives and Manuscripts, Louisiana State University Library, Baton Rouge, La.
MDAH—Mississippi Department of Archives and History, Jackson, Miss.
OSB—Olde Soldier Books [catalog number as cited], Gaithersburg, Md.
SHC—Southern Historical Collection, Manuscripts Department, Wilson Library, University of North Carolina, Chapel Hill, N.C.
SHILOH—Shiloh National Military Park Library, Shiloh, Tenn.
USAMHI—United States Army Military History Institute, Carlsile Barracks, Pa.
VHS—Virginia Historical Society, Richmond, Va.
WRHS—Western Reserve Historical Society Library, Cleveland, Ohio.

MANUSCRIPTS:

Aiken, David Wyatt, Papers, letter, July 11, 1863, South Caroliniana Library, University of South Carolina, Columbia, S.C.
Anderson, O., letter, June 18, 1861, OSB, catalog 98, item 202.

Blain, Dan, letter, Oct. 20, 1863, Theme Prints catalog, Bayside, N.Y., Dec. 1990, item 243.

Bragg, Braxton, Papers, letter, Mar. 25, 1862, Apr. 8, 1862, Missouri Historical Society, St. Louis, Mo.

Bragg, Braxton, Papers, Western Reserve Historical Society, Cleveland, Ohio.

Burgwyn Family Papers [no. 1687], SHC.

Burwell, T. G., letter, Apr. 29, 1861, OSB, catalog 42, item 181.

Chambers, William P. H., journal, diary, 1863, 1864, MDAH.

Cochran, Mary Catherine Noland, diary 1863–65, FCL.

Cooke, John Esten, letter to J. E. B. Stuart, Apr. 4, 1861, VHS.

Davis, John C., letter, June 11, 1865, OSB, catalog 60, item 212.

Dawson, Nathaniel Henry Rhodes, Papers [no. 210], SHC.

Deas, Ambrose, letters, Oct. 25 and Nov. 13, 1863, Chick-Chatt.

Dewitt, Marcus Beardon, letter, 1863–65, collection of Ward DeWitt, Jr., Nashville, Tenn.

Dillard, John J., letter, May 20, 1864, William R. Perkins Library, Duke University, Durham, N.C.

Elder, Thomas, letters, 1861–65, VHS.

Farley, William A., letter, Sept. 13, 1864, OSB, catalog 60, item 202.

Field, H., letter, Jan. 5, 1865, OSB, catalog 61, item 198.

Fleet, Fred, letter, Apr. 15, 1862, author's collection.

Gale-Polk Papers [including letters of William Dudley Gale, 1864–65], SHC.

Goudelock, G. E., letter, Oct. 5, 1863, Chick-Chatt.

Govan, Daniel C., Papers [no. 1000], SHC.

Grimes, G. W., letters, 1863–65, collection of Rev. James R. Orr, Connersville, Ind.

Hall, James Iredell, Papers [no. 302], SHC.

Hamner, James, letter, Apr. 11, 1863, West Tennessee Historical Society, Memphis, Tenn.

Hardee, William J., Papers, letters to Mrs. Felicia Shover, Feb.–Apr., 1862, Manuscripts Division, Library of Congress, Washington, D.C.

Hockaday, W., letter, Aug. 9, 1863, OSB, catalog 78, item 221.

Holloway, James M., letters, Nov. 2, 1861, Dec. 25, 1861, VHS.

Honnoll Family Papers, letters, 1861–65, EMORY.

Hooper, John A., letters, 1864, SHC.

Houghton, Charles A., papers, 1863, USAMHI.

Howard, Oliver O., letter of July 23, 1864, Bowdoin College Library, Brunswick, Maine.

Howard, W. A., letter, Apr. 10, 1862, SHILOH.

Hull, John P., letter, Nov. 22, 1863, OSB, catalog 44, item 198.

Hunter, B. B., letter, July 21, 1864, OSB, catalog 83, item 214.

Isbell, Robert [2d Virginia Cav.], letter, Feb. 21, 1865, Wiley Sword collection, Bloomfield Hills, Mich.

Ives, Washington, letters, 1863, Chick-Chatt.

Johnson, Charles James, letters, Apr.–May 1862, LSU.

Johnson, John, Papers [no. 2398], SHC.

Jones, Willis F., letters, 1861–64, FILSON.

Kendall, William D., letters, 1861–65, HEHL.

Latta, S. R., letters, Apr. 1862, LSU.

Lyman, Joseph B., letters, Apr. 1862, Yale University Library, New Haven, Conn.

McAbee, Samuel, letter, Feb. 12, 1865, OSB, catalog 55, item 269.

McCornack, Andrew, letters, 1863–65, Wiley Sword collection, Bloomfield Hills, Mich.

McCulloch, James, letter, Aug. 8, 1863, OSB, catalog 55, item 257.

McWayne, Eugene, letters, 1863–65, Wiley Sword collection, Bloomfield Hills, Mich.

Mabry, Peter, letters, 1863–64, The Horse Soldier, Cashtown, Pa. Catalog 22, items L4 items L4 to L11.

Martin, John, letter, Aug. 1863, OSB, catalog 80, item 208.

Maury, Betty Herndon, diary, 1861, Library of Congress, Manuscripts Division, Washington, D.C.

Mecklin, A. H., diary, 1862, MDAH.

Mendenhall, J. J., letters, Aug. 29, 1864, Mar. 15, 1865, OSB, catalog 20, item 151.

Micah—unidentified letter dated July 3, 1863, Samuel Richey Collection, Miami University Library, Oxford, Ohio.

Miller, Isaac, letter, Nov. 21, 1863, Wiley Sword collection, Bloomfield Hills, Mich.

Montgomery, W. R., letters, Oct. 18, 24, 1863, Chick-Chatt.

Morgan, Sarah, diary, Duke University Library, Durham, S.C.

Morrison, Henry, letter, Sept. 20, 1864, USAMHI.

Murphey, Virgil S., diary, 1864 [no. 534], SHC.

Neal, Andrew Jackson, letters, 1863–64, Chick-Chatt.

Oldham, Van Buren, diary, 1864, Tennessee State Library and Archives, Nashville, Tenn.

Painter, Thomas L., letter, Sept. 2, 1863, OSB, catalog 62, item 219.

Pendleton, William Nelson, Papers [no. 1466], SHC.

Perry, Joel Walker, letter, Apr. 27, 1862, OSB, catalog 51, item 197.

Poates, Lewis L., letter, Nov. 15, 1863, collection of Lewis L. Poates, Knoxville, Tenn.

Porter, Samuel A., letter, n.d., OSB, catalog 36, item 157.

Porter, William Y., letter, June 12, 1861, courtesy The Horse Soldier, Gettysburg, Pa.

Potter, Henry A., letter, 1864, The Bentley Historical Library, University of Michigan, Ann Arbor, Mich.

Pugh, Richard L., letters, Apr. 1862, LSU.

Quintard, Rev. Charles Todd, diary, 1864–65, duPont Library, Dept. of Archives, University of the South, Sewanee, Tenn.

Redding, W. R., Papers [no. 3348], SHC.

Reilly, Glitch, letter, n.d. [circa. Nov. 1863], Theme Prints, Ltd., Bayside, N.Y. catalog, spring 1993, item 232.

Rennolds, Edwin H., Sr., diary, 1863, Chick-Chatt.

Robertson, Thomas Chinn, letter, Apr. 9, 1862, LSU.

Sanders, W. H., letter, July 17, 1861, OSB, catalog 59, item 189.

Schaller, Frank, letters, Mar.–Apr. 1862, courtesy of Kathleen Schaller Herty Brown, New York.

Shaner, Joe, letters, May 17, 1864, Fredericksburg and Spotsylvania National Military Park, Va.

Unidentified Confederate letter, "Camp Near Clinton, Miss. Oct. 28, 1863," Theme Prints, Ltd., Bayside, N.Y. catalog, Nov. 1992, item 327.

Unidentified Confederate letter, "Richmond, Va., Aug. 31, 1864," OSB, catalog 57, item 194.

Walker, W., letter, Apr. 12 [1865], OSB, catalog 49, item 184.

Walpole, Richard, letters, 1862–64, in Bomar Papers, EMORY.

Watson, P. W., letter, to wife, July 11, 1862, Stones River National Battlefield Park Library, Murfreesboro, Tenn.

Watson, Robert, journal, 1863, Chick-Chatt.

Watson, W. J., diary, 1864, Watson Papers [no. 3662], SHC.

Webb, James D., letters, 1861–63, in Walton Family Papers [no. 1437], SHC.

Wilkinson, B. F., letter, Apr. 16, 1862, LSU.

PUBLISHED ARTICLES:

Anonymous, "Ten Days in Richmond," *Blackwood's Edinburgh Magazine,* 92 (1862): 392–93, printed in Henry Steele Commager, ed., *The Blue and the Gray,* New York, 1950, 65–66.

Biel, John G., "The Battle of Shiloh: From the Letters and Diary of Joseph Dimmit Thompson," *Tennessee Historical Quarterly,* 27, no. 3: 250–74.

Hadden, R. Lee, "The Deadly Embrace: The Meeting of the Twenty-fourth Regiment of Michigan Infantry and the Twenty-sixth Regiment of North Carolina Troops at McPherson's Woods, Gettysburg, PA, July 1, 1863," *The Gettysburg Magazine,* no. 5 (July 1991): 19ff.

Harmon, George D., "Letters of Luther Rice Mills—A Confederate Soldier," *North Carolina Historical Review,* 4 (July 1927): 303–8.

McMurry, Richard M., "Confederate Morale in the Atlanta Campaign of 1864," *The Georgia Historical Quarterly,* 44 (1970): 226ff.

Partin, Robert, "A Confederate Sergeant's Report to His Wife during the Bombardment of Fort Pillow," *Tennessee Historical Quarterly,* 15 (1956): 243–52.

Partin, Robert, "A Confederate Sergeant's Report to His Wife during the Campaign from Tullahoma to Dalton," *Tennessee Historical Quarterly,* 12 (1953): 291–308.

Partin, Robert, "An Alabama Confederate Soldier's Report to His Wife," *The Alabama Review,* 3 (Jan. 1950): 22ff.

Partin, Robert, "The Momentous Events of the Civil War As Reported by a Confederate Private-Sergeant," *Tennessee Historical Quarterly,* 18 (1959): 68–86.

Spencer Repeating Rifle Company catalog (1866), Boston, Mass.

Starbuck, Gregory, " 'Up Alabamians!' The 4th Alabama Infantry at Manassas," *Military Images Magazine,* 8, no. 1 (July–Aug. 1986): 25ff.

Sword, Wiley, " 'Those Damned Michigan Spencers,' Colonel Copeland's 5th Michigan Cavalry and Their Spencer Rifles," *Man at Arms Magazine,* Lincoln, R. I. no. 5, 1997: 23–37.

Tucker, Glenn, "An Appraisal of Robert E. Lee," *Civil War Times, Illustrated,* 4, no. 1 (Apr. 1965): 4ff.

Wiley, Bell I., ed., "The Confederate Letters of John W. Hagan" (in two parts), *Georgia Historical Quarterly,* 38 (1954): 170ff. 268ff.

Wolfe, Frank, "Letter to a Friend: From the Foot of Lookout Mountain," *Civil War Times, Illustrated,* 22, no. 4 (June 1983): 44ff.

B O O K S :

Abernathy, Byron R., ed., *Private [Elisha] Stockwell, Jr. Sees the Civil War,* Norman, Okla., 1958.

Andrews, Eliza Frances, *The War-Time Journal of a Georgia Girl 1864–1865,* Macon, Ga., 1960.

Baker, Jean H., *Mary Todd Lincoln: A Biography,* New York, 1987.

Battaile, Andrew Chandler, Arthur W. Bergeron, Thomas Y. Cartwright, Ervin L. Jordan, Richard Rollins, and Rudolph Young, *Black Southerners in Gray: Essays on Afro-Americanism in Confederate Armies,* Murfreesboro, Tenn., 1994.

Baumgartner, Richard A., *Blue Lightning: Wilder's Mounted Infantry Brigade in the Battle of Chickamauga,* Huntington, W.V. 1997.

Baumgartner, Richard A., and Larry M. Strayer, eds. *Echoes of Battle: The Atlanta Campaign,* Huntington, W.V., 1991.

Baumgartner, Richard A., and Larry M. Strayer, eds. *Echoes of Battle: The Struggle for Chattanooga,* Huntington, W.V., 1996.

Bean, W. G., *Stonewall's Man Sandie Pendleton,* Chapel Hill, N.C., 1959.

Beringer, Richard E., Herman Hattaway, Archer Jones, and William N. Still, *Why the South Lost the Civil War,* Athens, Ga., 1986.

Blackford, Susan Leigh, ed., *Letters from Lee's Army; or, Memoirs of Life in and out of the Army in Virginia during the War between the States,* New York, 1947.

Boatner, Mark Mayo, III, *The Civil War Dictionary,* New York, 1959.

Boritt, Gabor S., ed., *War Comes Again: Comparative Vistas on the Civil War and World War II,* New York, 1995.

Brown, Norman D., ed., *One of Cleburne's Command: The Civil War Reminiscences and Diary of Captain Samuel T. Foster, Granbury's Texas Brigade, C.S.A.,* Austin, Tex., 1980.

Buck, Irving, *Cleburne and His Command,* Dayton, Ohio, 1982 reprint of 1908 edition.

Buel, Clarence C., and Robert U. Johnson, eds., *Battles and Leaders of the Civil War,* 4 vols., New York, 1888.

Busey, John W., and David G. Martin, *Regimental Strengths at Gettysburg,* Baltimore, Md., 1982.

Cary, Constance [Mrs. Burton Harrison], *Recollections Grave and Gay,* New York, 1916.

Cash, William, and Lucy Somerville Howorth, eds., *My Dear Nellie: The Civil War Letters of William L. Nugent to Eleanor Smith Nugent,* Jackson, Miss., 1977.

Castel, Albert, *Decision in the West: The Atlanta Campaign of 1864,* Lawrence, Kans., 1992.

Cate, Wirt Armistead, ed., *Two Soldiers: The Campaign Diaries of Thomas J. Key, C.S.A., and Robert J. Campbell, U.S.A.,* Chapel Hill, N.C., 1938.

Chamberlain, Joshua Lawrence, *The Passing of the Armies: An Account of the Final Campaign of the Army of the Potomac, Based upon Personal Reminiscences of the Fifth Army Corps,* New York, 1915.

Childs, Arney Robinson, ed., *The Private Journal of Henry William Ravenel, 1859–1887,* Columbia, S.C., 1947.

Coddington, Edwin B., *The Gettysburg Campaign: A Study in Command,* Dayton, Ohio, 1979 reprint.

Commager, Henry Steele, *The Blue and the Gray: The Story of the Civil War as Told by Participants,* New York, 1950.

Connelly, Thomas Lawrence, *Autumn of Glory: The Army of Tennessee 1862–1865,* Baton Rouge, La., 1971.

Connelly, Thomas Lawrence, and Barbara L. Bellows, *God and General Longstreet: The Lost Cause and the Southern Mind,* Baton Rouge, La., 1982.

Cozzens, Peter, *This Terrible Sound: The Battle of Chickamauga,* Chicago, Ill., 1992.

Crist, Lynda Lasswell, Mary Seaton Dix, Haskell M. Monroe, Jr., James T. McIntosh, and Kenneth H. Williams, eds., *The Papers of Jefferson Davis,* vols. 1–9, Baton Rouge, La., 1971–97.

Crow, Mattie Lou Teague, ed., *The Diary of a Confederate Soldier: John Washington Izner 1834–1928,* Huntsville, Ala., 1977.

Cuttino, George Peddy, ed., *Saddle Bag and Spinning Wheel; Being the Civil*

War Letters of George W. Peddy, M.D., Surgeon 56th Georgia Volunteer Regiment, C.S.A., Macon, Ga., 1981.

Daniel, Larry J., *Soldiering in the Army of Tennessee*, Chapel Hill, N.C., 1991.

Davis, Archie K., *Boy Colonel of the Confederacy: The Life and Times of Henry King Burgwyn, Jr.*, Chapel Hill, N.C., 1985.

Davis, Burke, *Sherman's March*, New York, 1980.

Davis, Julia, *Mount Up: A True Story Based on the Reminiscences of Major E. A. H. McDonald of the Confederate Cavalry*, New York, 1967.

Davis, William C., *Jefferson Davis: The Man and His Hour*, New York, 1991.

Dowdey, Clifford, and Louis H. Manarin, eds., *The Wartime Papers of Robert E. Lee*, Boston, Mass., 1961.

Dumond, Dwight Lowell, ed., *Southern Editorials on Secession*, Gloucester, Mass., 1964.

Durden, Robert F., *The Gray and the Black: The Confederate Debate on Emancipation*, Baton Rouge, La., 1972.

East, Charles, ed., *Sarah Morgan: The Civil War Diary of a Southern Woman*, New York, 1992 reprint.

Faust, Patricia L., ed., *Historical Times Illustrated Encyclopedia of the Civil War*, New York, 1986.

Fleet, Betsey, *Green Mount after the War: The Correspondence of Maria Louisa Wacker Fleet and Her Family 1865–1900*, Charlottesville, Va., 1978.

Fleet, Betsey, and John D. P. Fuller, eds., *Green Mount: A Virginia Plantation Family during the Civil War; Being the Journal of Benjamin Robert Fleet and Letters of His Family*, Charlottesville, Va., 1962.

Foner, Eric, *Reconstruction: America's Unfinished Revolution, 1863–1877*, New York, 1988.

Fox, William F., *Regimental Losses in the American Civil War 1861–1865*, Dayton, Ohio., 1985 reprint of the 1898 edition.

Frank, Joseph Allan, and George Reeves, *"Seeing the Elephant": Raw Recruits at the Battle of Shiloh*, New York, 1989.

Freeman, Douglas Southall, *Lee's Lieutenants: A Study in Command*, 3 vols., New York, 1944.

Freeman, Douglas Southall, *R. E. Lee: A Biography*, 4 vols., New York, 1935.

Fuller, Claud E., *The Rifled Musket*, Harrisburg, Pa., 1958.

Galbraith, Loretta and William, eds., *A Lost Heroine of the Confederacy: The Diaries and Letters of Belle Edmondson*, Jackson, Miss., 1990.

Gallagher, Gary W., *The Confederate War*, Cambridge, Mass., 1997.

Gallagher, Gary W., *Fighting for the Confederacy: The Personal Recollections of General Edward Porter Alexander*, Chapel Hill, N.C., 1989.

Gay, Mary A. H., *Life in Dixie during the War*, Atlanta, Ga., 1887, 1979 reprint.

Glatthaar, Joseph T., *The March to the Sea and Beyond: Sherman's Troops in the Savannah and Carolinas Campaigns*, Baton Rouge, La., 1985.

Hay, Thomas Robson, *Pat Cleburne, Stonewall Jackson of the West,* Dayton, Ohio, 1982 reprint.

Helm, Katherine, *Mary, Wife of Lincoln, by Her Niece,* Chicago, Ill., 1983 reprint.

Hennessy, John J., *Return to Bull Run: The Campaign and Battle of Second Manassas,* New York, 1993.

Hess, Earl J., *The Union Soldier in Battle: Enduring the Ordeal of Combat,* Lawrence, Kans., 1997.

Hitchcock, Henry, *Marching with Sherman: Passages from the Letters and Campaign Diaries of Henry Hitchcock, Nov. 1864–May 1865,* edited by M. A. DeWolfe Howe. Lincoln, Nebr., 1995 reprint of 1927 edition.

Inman, Arthur Crew, ed., *Soldier of the South: General Pickett's War Letters to His Wife,* Boston, Mass., 1928.

Jackson, Edgar Allan, *Letters of Edgar Allan Jackson, Sept. 7, 1860–April 15, 1865,* Franklin, Va., 1939.

Jackson, Oscar L., *The Colonel's Diary,* Sharon, Pa., 1922.

Jones, John B., *A Rebel War Clerk's Diary,* 2 vols., Philadelphia, Pa., 1966 reprint.

Kennett, Lee, *Marching through Georgia: The Story of Soldiers and Civilians during Sherman's Campaign,* New York, 1995.

Lane, Bessie Mell, ed., *Dear Bet, The Carter Letters: 1861–1863: The Letters of Lieutenant Sidney Carter, Co. A., 14th Regiment South Carolina Volunteers, Gregg's-McCowan's Brigade, C.S.A., to Ellen Timmons Carter,* Clemson, S.C., 1978.

Linderman, Gerald F., *Embattled Courage: The Experience of Combat in the American Civil War,* New York, 1987.

Livermore, Thomas L., *Numbers and Losses in the Civil War in America 1861–1865,* Birmingham, Ind., 1957 reprint of 1900 edition.

Lonn, Ella, *Desertion during the Civil War,* Lincoln, Nebr., 1998, reprint of 1928 edition.

McClellan, Henry B., *The Life and Campaigns of Major General J. E. B. Stuart, Commander of the Cavalry of the Army of Northern Virginia,* Boston, Mass., 1885.

McMurry, Richard M., *John Bell Hood and the War for Southern Independence,* Lexington, Ky., 1982.

McMurry, Richard M., *Two Great Rebel Armies: An Essay in Confederate Military History,* Chapel Hill, N.C., 1989.

McPherson, James M., *Battle Cry of Freedom: The Civil War Era* [The Oxford History of the United States], New York, 1988.

McPherson, James M., *Drawn with the Sword: Reflections on the American Civil War,* New York, 1996.

McWhiney, Grady, *Braxton Bragg and Confederate Defeat,* vol. 1, New York, 1969.

McWhiney, Grady, and Perry D. Jamieson, *Attack and Die: Civil War Military Tactics and the Southern Heritage,* University, Ala., 1982.

Marcot, Roy, *Spencer Repeating Firearms*, Irvine, Calif., 1983.

Mathis, Ray, *In the Land of the Living: Wartime Letters by Confederates from the Chattahoochie Valley of Alabama and Georgia*, Troy, Ala., 1981.

Matter, William D., *If It Takes All Summer: The Battle of Spotsylvania*, Chapel Hill, N.C., 1988.

Mitchell, Reid, *Civil War Soldiers: Their Expectations and Their Experiences*, New York, 1988.

Mitchell, Reid, *The Vacant Chair: The Northern Soldier Leaves Home*, New York, 1993.

Oates, William C., *The War between the Union and the Confederacy and Its Lost Opportunities, with a History of the 15th Alabama Regiment, and the Forty-eight Battles in Which It Was Engaged*, Dayton, Ohio, 1985 reprint of 1905 edition.

Myers, David G., *Psychology*, New York, 1995.

Nolan, Alan T., *Lee Considered: General Robert E. Lee and Civil War History*, Chapel Hill, N.C., 1991.

Paludan, Philip Shaw, *"A People's Contest": The Union and Civil War 1861–1865*, Lawrence, Kans., 1996.

Parsons, John E., *The First Winchester: The Story of the 1866 Repeating Rifle*, New York, 1955.

Pollard, Edward A., *The Lost Cause*, New York, 1866.

Purdue, Howell and Elizabeth, *Pat Cleburne Confederate General*, Hillsboro, Tex., 1973.

Reynolds, Donald E., *Editors Make War: Southern Newspapers in the Secession Crisis*, Nashville, Tenn., 1970.

Roberson, Elizabeth Whitley, *Weep Not for Me Dear Mother* [Letters of Eli P. Landers, 16th Georgia Inf.], Washington, N.C., 1991.

Robertson, James I., *Soldiers Blue and Gray*, Columbia, S.C., 1988.

Robertson, James I., *Stonewall Jackson: The Man, the Soldier, the Legend*, New York, 1997.

Roller, David C., and Robert W. Twyman, eds., *The Encyclopedia of Southern History*, Baton Rouge, La., 1979.

Rollins, Richard, *Pickett's Charge: Eyewitness Accounts*, Redondo Beach, Calif., 1994.

Rowland, Dunbar, ed., *Jefferson Davis Constitutionalist: His Letters, Papers, and Speeches*, 6 vols., Jackson, Miss., 1923.

Rozier, John, ed., *The Granite Farm Letters: The Civil War Correspondence of Edgeworth and Sallie Bird*, Athens, Ga., 1988.

Russell, William Howard, *My Diary North and South*, edited by Fletcher Pratt. New York, 1954.

Sears, Stephen W., *Landscape Turned Red: The Battle of Antietam*, New York, 1983.

Simpson, Harold B., ed., *The Bugle Softly Blows: The Confederate Diary of Benjamin M. Seaton*, Waco, Tex., 1965.

Smith, Elizabeth Wiley, *The History of Hancock County [Georgia]*, 2 vols., Washington, Ga., 1974.

Stewart, George R., *Pickett's Charge: A Microhistory of the Final Attack at Gettysburg, July 3, 1863*, Boston, 1959.

Strode, Hudson, ed., *Jefferson Davis: Private Letters 1823–1889*, New York, 1966.

Sword, Wiley, *Embrace an Angry Wind: The Confederacy's Last Hurrah, Spring Hill, Franklin, and Nashville*, New York, 1992.

Sword, Wiley, *Firepower from Abroad: The Confederate Enfield and the LeMat Revolver, 1861–1863*, Lincoln, R.I., 1986.

Sword, Wiley, *Mountains Touched with Fire: Chattanooga Besieged, 1863*, New York, 1995.

Sword, Wiley, *Shiloh: Bloody April*, New York, 1974.

Tappert, Annette, ed., *The Brothers' War: Civil War Letters to Their Loved Ones from the Blue and Gray*, New York, 1988.

Taylor, F. Jay, ed., *Reluctant Rebel: The Secret Diary of Robert Patrick 1861–1865*, Baton Rouge, La., 1959.

Taylor, Michael W., *The Cry Is War, War, War: The Civil War Correspondence of Lieutenants Thomas Cotton and George Job Huntley, 34th Regiment North Carolina Troops, Pender-Scales Brigade of the Light Division, Stonewall Jackson's and A. P. Hill's Corps, Army of Northern Virginia, C.S.A.*, Dayton, Ohio, 1994.

Thomas, Dean S., *Ready, Aim, Fire! Small Arms Ammunition in the Battle of Gettysburg*, Biglersville, Pa., 1981.

Tower, R. Lockwood, ed., *A Carolinian Goes to War: The Civil War Narrative of Arthur Middleton Manigault, Brigadier General, C.S.A.*, Columbia, S.C., 1988.

Turner, Justin G. and Linda, *Mary Todd Lincoln: Her Life and Letters*, New York, 1972.

U.S. Government, *Report of the Committee of the Senate upon the Relations between Labor and Capital, and Testimony Taken by the Committee*, Washington, D.C., 1885.

U.S. War Department, *The War of the Rebellion: A Compilation of the Official Records of the Union and Confederate Armies*, 70 vols. In 128 parts. Washington, D.C., 1880–1901.

Watkins, Sam R., *"Co. Aytch": A Side Show of the Big Show*, New York, 1962.

Welch, Spencer Glasgow, *A Confederate Surgeon's Letters to His Wife*, New York, 1911.

Wigfall, Louise [Mrs. D. Giraud], *A Southern Girl in '61: The War-Time Memories of a Confederate Senator's Daughter*, New York, 1905.

Wiley, Bell Irvin, *The Common Soldier in the Civil War*, New York, 1952.

Wiley, Bell Irvin, *Confederate Women*, Westport, Conn., 1975.

Wiley, Bell Irvin, *Four Years on the Firing Line [Letters of Colonel James C. Nisbet, 66th Georgia Vol. Inf., 26th Georgia Battn.]*, Jackson, Tenn., 1963.

Wiley, Bell Irvin, *This Infernal War: The Confederate Letters of Sergeant Edwin H. Fay,* Austin, Tex., 1958.

Woodward, C. Vann, ed., *Mary Chesnut's Civil War,* New Haven, Conn., 1981.

Woodworth, Stephen E., *Davis and Lee at War,* Lawrence, Kans., 1995.

Worsham, W. J., *The Old Nineteenth Tennessee Regiment, C.S.A., June 1861– April 1865,* Knoxville, Tenn., 1902.

Wyatt-Brown, Bertram, *Southern Honor: Ethics and Behavior in the Old South,* New York, 1982.

Index